Management and Marketing for Improved Competitiveness and Performance in the Healthcare Sector

José Duarte Santos
Polytechnic Institute of Gaya, Portugal

Inês Veiga Pereira
ISCAP, Polytechnic Institute of Porto, Portugal

A volume in the Advances in Marketing, Customer Relationship Management, and E-Services (AMCRMES) Book Series

IGI Global
PUBLISHER of TIMELY KNOWLEDGE

Published in the United States of America by
IGI Global
Business Science Reference (an imprint of IGI Global)
701 E. Chocolate Avenue
Hershey PA, USA 17033
Tel: 717-533-8845
Fax: 717-533-8661
E-mail: cust@igi-global.com
Web site: http://www.igi-global.com

Library of Congress Cataloging-in-Publication Data

Names: Santos, Jose Duarte, 1966- editor. | Pereira, Ines Veiga, 1977- editor.
Title: Management and marketing for improved competitiveness and performance in the healthcare sector / Jose Duarte Santos, and Ines Veiga Pereira, editors.
Description: Hershey : Business Science Reference, 2021. | Includes bibliographical references and index. | Summary: "This book provides knowledge and skills to allow readers with the ability to apply management and marketing techniques on strategic, tactical and operational aspects of organizations with emphasis on the healthcare industry presenting strategies on topics such as operations management, quality management, human resources, brand management, digital marketing, content marketing, customer experience"-- Provided by publisher.
Identifiers: LCCN 2021012378 (print) | LCCN 2021012379 (ebook) | ISBN 9781799872634 (hardcover) | ISBN 9781799872665 (paperback) | ISBN 9781799872641 (ebook)
Subjects: LCSH: Health services administration. | Medical care--Marketing. | Medical care--Quality control.
Classification: LCC RA971 .M34234 2021 (print) | LCC RA971 (ebook) | DDC 362.1068/8--dc23
LC record available at https://lccn.loc.gov/2021012378
LC ebook record available at https://lccn.loc.gov/2021012379

This book is published in the IGI Global book series Advances in Marketing, Customer Relationship Management, and E-Services (AMCRMES) (ISSN: 2327-5502; eISSN: 2327-5529)

British Cataloguing in Publication Data
A Cataloguing in Publication record for this book is available from the British Library.

All work contributed to this book is new, previously-unpublished material.
The views expressed in this book are those of the authors, but not necessarily of the publisher.

For electronic access to this publication, please contact: eresources@igi-global.com.

Advances in Marketing, Customer Relationship Management, and E-Services (AMCRMES) Book Series

ISSN:2327-5502
EISSN:2327-5529

Editor-in-Chief: Eldon Y. Li National Chengchi University, Taiwan & California Polytechnic State University, USA

MISSION

Business processes, services, and communications are important factors in the management of good customer relationship, which is the foundation of any well organized business. Technology continues to play a vital role in the organization and automation of business processes for marketing, sales, and customer service. These features aid in the attraction of new clients and maintaining existing relationships.

The Advances in Marketing, Customer Relationship Management, and E-Services (AMCRMES) Book Series

addresses success factors for customer relationship management, marketing, and electronic services and its performance outcomes. This collection of reference source covers aspects of consumer behavior and marketing business strategies aiming towards researchers, scholars, and practitioners in the fields of marketing management.

COVERAGE

- Web Mining and Marketing
- Customer Relationship Management
- Ethical Considerations in E-Marketing
- Mobile Services
- Social Networking and Marketing
- Telemarketing
- Cases on Electronic Services
- Mobile CRM
- E-Service Innovation
- Cases on CRM Implementation

IGI Global is currently accepting manuscripts for publication within this series. To submit a proposal for a volume in this series, please contact our Acquisition Editors at Acquisitions@igi-global.com or visit: http://www.igi-global.com/publish/.

The Advances in Marketing, Customer Relationship Management, and E-Services (AMCRMES) Book Series (ISSN 2327-5502) is published by IGI Global, 701 E. Chocolate Avenue, Hershey, PA 17033-1240, USA, www.igi-global.com. This series is composed of titles available for purchase individually; each title is edited to be contextually exclusive from any other title within the series. For pricing and ordering information please visit http://www.igi-global.com/book-series/advances-marketing-customer-relationship-management/37150. Postmaster: Send all address changes to above address.

Titles in this Series

For a list of additional titles in this series, please visit:
www.igi-global.com/book-series/advances-marketing-customer-relationship-management/37150

Handbook of Research on IoT, Digital Transformation, and the Future of Global Marketing
Hatem El-Gohary (College of Business and Economics, Qatar University, Qatar) David Edwards (Birmingham City University, UK) and Mohamed Slim Ben Mimoun (Qatar University, Qatar)
Business Science Reference • © 2021 • 425pp • H/C (ISBN: 9781799871927) • US $295.00

Advanced Digital Marketing Strategies in a Data-Driven Era
Jose Ramon Saura (Rey Juan Carlos University, Spain)
Business Science Reference • © 2021 • 342pp • H/C (ISBN: 9781799880035) • US $225.00

Blockchain Technology and Applications for Digital Marketing
Rohit Bansal (Department of Management Studies, Vaish College of Engineering, India) Pacha Malyadri (ICSSR, Center for Economic and Social Studies, India) Amandeep Singh (Chitkara Business School, Chitkara University, Punjab, India) and Asif Pervez (Jamia Millia Islamia University, India)
Business Science Reference • © 2021 • 329pp • H/C (ISBN: 9781799880813) • US $225.00

Big Data Analytics for Improved Accuracy, Efficiency, and Decision Making in Digital Marketing
Amandeep Singh (Chitkara Business School, Chitkara University, Punjab, India)
Business Science Reference • © 2021 • 310pp • H/C (ISBN: 9781799872313) • US $215.00

Handbook of Research on Future Policies and Strategies for Nation Branding
Victoria Pistikou (Democritus University of Thrace, Greece) Andreas Masouras (Neapolis University, Cyprus) and Marcos Komodromos (University of Nicosia, Cyprus)
Business Science Reference • © 2021 • 383pp • H/C (ISBN: 9781799875338) • US $295.00

Developing Successful Global Strategies for Marketing Luxury Brands
Fabrizio Mosca (University of Turin, Italy) Cecilia Casalegno (University of Turin, Italy) and Rosalia Gallo (Universitat Autònoma de Barcelona, Spain)
Business Science Reference • © 2021 • 351pp • H/C (ISBN: 9781799858829) • US $225.00

For an entire list of titles in this series, please visit:
www.igi-global.com/book-series/advances-marketing-customer-relationship-management/37150

IGI Global
PUBLISHER of TIMELY KNOWLEDGE

701 East Chocolate Avenue, Hershey, PA 17033, USA
Tel: 717-533-8845 x100 • Fax: 717-533-8661
E-Mail: cust@igi-global.com • www.igi-global.com

Editorial Advisory Board

Table of Contents

Detailed Table of Contents

This study identifies the criteria underlying the buying decision-making process of medical devices in reproductive medicine. This research had three main objectives. The first one was to translate the criteria mentioned by the decision-makers into theoretical constructs, while the second objective was intended to establish the relationship between the constructs, creating a conceptual model of buying decision-making for medical devices in reproductive medicine. The third objective was to identify suitable business and marketing strategies for such a decision-making process. Four constructs were evaluated in the pre-purchase phase, namely the brand, the product's performance, the training associated with the product, and the price. In the post-purchase phase, decision-makers evaluated the following constructs: service provided by the company, the relationship with the salesperson, and loyalty. Regarding marketing strategies, market-orientation strategy, relationship-marketing strategy, and brand-equity strategy were identified as possible strategies.

There is currently a wide-ranging debate on whether it is ethical for pharmaceutical companies to profit and obtain large economic benefits by patenting and controlling the sale of essential medicines that can save thousands of lives, or, on the contrary, whether these medicines should be considered social products and offered at low prices so that anyone, in any country in the world, regardless of their purchasing power, can have access to them. This debate has intensified since health was considered a fundamental human right by the World Health Organization (WHO) and was expressly included in the Sustainable Development Goals (SDGs) adopted by the United Nations (specifically, in Goal 3: "Health and Well-Being"). Consequently, the overall objective of this chapter is to reflect on these questions: Should economic interests prevail over social ones in the case of essential life-saving medicines? Should the fundamental right to health prevail over the right granted by a patent? How far should corporate social responsibility (CSR) go in the pharmaceutical industry?

This chapter examined the organizations of a university dealing with healthcare and clinical activities operating in an extremely complex network connection. In the framework of qualitative research, with the help of a series of interviews, the authors researched in which networks the university's healthcare organization and organizational units participate, and how participation in these networks influences the value creation implemented in each field. By what means can the organization handle the contradictions and conflicts that arise along the inter-organizational relations embedded in the networks. Interviews were conducted with institution leaders, business leaders, and care workers. Based on the research results, network complexity results in three types of conflicts in healthcare institutions: conflicts related to organizational management, conflicts arising in organizational processes, and personal conflicts.

Healthcare services, in particular, are one of the areas in which Lean can be applied and benefits can be reached through it. In order to analyze the suitability of Lean

and hotel discounts, employment maintenance aids, cultural events, etc., disseminating hope. The bad policymakers want the opposite and restrict family's circumstances and socialization. And finally, COVID-19 is blamed for all inefficiencies in the public health system, even those before the epidemic. This chapter explores why COVID-19 is innocent and not entirely responsible for health inefficiencies. The authors explore the main health concerns, analyzing earlier articles with recent documents before and during COVID-19.

In this chapter, the authors are looking for the answer to how novel coronavirus disease (COVID-19) has influenced health communication in online platforms. The aim was to investigate with a newer qualitative research method (netnography) how the scenes of communication have been changed during the COVID-19 crisis. The content of some popular online public forums was analyzed that came up during the outbreak in Hungary. The participant opinions and attitudes regarding health communication of COVID-19 crisis management were observed. The community acceptance of two measures were investigated: necessity of wearing a mask and the mandatory evacuation of hospital beds. These topics divided the opinion of the citizens. In spite of the efficient COVID-19 outbreak management, there were very extreme and different opinions (skepticism, indignation, accusation, acceptance) in the online community about the accuracy and reliability of health communication. The results may support the future improvement of health crisis management.

This study aims to analyse the colours associated with Portuguese healthcare units and medical centres—namely the colour of their logo, through environmental colour mapping—and understand if the colour management choices match the desired perception of a healthcare unit and identify new colour combinations that can serve as a differentiation factor and simultaneously get the desired interpretation of the brand. The logos of 24 healthcare centres were randomly selected. The images were collected through the SNS web page dedicated to each facility and were later processed in Adobe Photoshop CC. The colours of each logo were catalogued and sorted according to their hue. It was observed that the majority of the colours used corresponded to blues and greens, which was to be expected considering their symbolism: stability, calm, relaxation, and serenity. Lastly, four new colour schemes were created, which, in addition to being differentiated from the previously identified schemes, are evocative of desirable characteristics for a brand associated with a healthcare unit.

Electronic social networks have expanded communication possibilities. This chapter aims to present how such platforms allow the formation of virtual communities to support and exchange information and the inclusion of people with ASD (autism spectrum disorders) by comparing brand virtual communities from two countries, five from Brazil and one from the USA. Among interpretative methods, netnography and manual content analysis considering posts on each community were performed. Also, tweets about Autism Awareness Day were analyzed. As a result, it was possible to see that virtual communities' contribution allows dialogue among autists' relatives, releasing their suffering and sharing acceptable practices. Among contributions, this study helps to know the differences among various virtual communities and content in terms of viralization in health marketing.

In health, as in any other industry, technology adoption, if used appropriately, is an important asset and a success factor for a company. Nowadays, it is no longer feasible to talk about health without addressing the role of technology. In this context, the present study aims to understand the impact and role of technologies in a hospital context (e.g., Hospital de Braga) and in the relationship management from an internal perspective (internal marketing). Based on a qualitative approach, the research also aims to analyze how internal communication is made between employees and between employees and managers in the Hospital of Braga. Semi-structured interviews were conducted with five employees of the health institution, and a focus group with eight employees as well (four nurses, one computer technician, one administrative, one operational assistant, and a technical/administrative assistant). The results show that this technology is successful, but there are still some points to point out. The results also provide some discontent regarding internal marketing.

This study aimed to identify quantitative and qualitative KPIs for the implementation of apps and use of digital data in healthcare management. To this end, a systematic review of the literature was undertaken to analyze relevant scientific articles downloaded from reputed scientific databases (Scopus, PubMed, PsyINFO, ScienceDirect, and WOS). The databases were searched using the following keywords: "Big Data," "Artificial Intelligence," "Mobile Technologies," "APP," "Disease," "Geolocation," and "Health." Subsequently, 25 qualitative and quantitative KPI values, as rating, product quality, or unique users, were identified for the successful preparation and management of healthcare based on apps and the use of digital data.

Given the crucial need to bridge the mental health service divide, the author examines the emerging trends in digital well-being management by focusing on the mobile health market. Using a bottom-up perspective and leveraging literature from positive technology and generalized unsafety theory of stress, the author conceptualizes how positive technology as a mobile health solution can help end users to respond effectively to different kinds of stressors during a crisis. It is further argued that the use of positive technology can positively reverse the automatic route to mental ill health that is plausible in the absence of safety perceptions. The chapter offers a theory-driven conceptualization of digital coping through positive technology. By showing how a simple, scalable, and sustainable positive technology design can cater to different user segments, the author urges policymakers, entrepreneurs, and healthcare service providers to participate in the design, propagation, adoption, and diffusion of such holistic positive technologies for fostering societal resilience.

Preface

The health cluster is becoming increasingly important in society, and its development is crucial to increase longevity and quality of life of human beings.

Scientific research and development are the base of this industry growth. Despite that, there are different areas where companies operate, playing different roles, developing different activities, which are important for the cluster's value chain. The diversity of existing companies, in size, with domestic, international or global presence, distributed by production and/or services, provides a diversity of examples in the area of management, marketing and the incorporation of technology.

In healthcare, for the average citizen, the sector's evaluation depends largely on the level of satisfaction he or she obtains when requiring support from medical professionals. However, this is the tip of the iceberg as the various operators that intervene in the cluster need to be increasingly optimized and customer-oriented, given that there is increasing pressure for a timely response and the customer is better informed, more demanding and active in sharing experiences. On the other hand, we cannot forget that the iceberg sails in a sea - government - which conditions its movement. Political options and decisions affect the whole of society. In healthcare, where there tends to be a need for state investment, if resources are poorly or not applied conditions the present and the evolution of society in a more pressing way.

To be able to answer to changes in consumer behavior and the diversity of variables that act on the organization, management and marketing must be dynamic and act organically. Despite in healthcare this ability to react is important for the well-being of human beings and for the society to exist in harmony, for a modern organization operating in this sector it is not enough. It's necessary to act proactively, in advance, trying to discover trends and also anticipate threats. Although it's not easy and despite some alerts and some events in the past (such as the bird flu), almost all organizations were caught by surprise with the pandemic crisis that started in 2020.

Due to COVID-19, the sector has never been under as much pressure as it is today. This pressure has motivated organizations to reinvent themselves, which have driven management and marketing to become more active. Thus, there is a need to incorporate in organizations a stronger culture of management and marketing orientation that allows companies to define their course, optimize their resources, communicate with their stakeholders in a more efficient and effective way, making the customer more present throughout the organization.

This book, *Management and Marketing for Improved Competitiveness and Performance in the Healthcare Sector*, is intended to contribute to a stronger internalization of concepts inherent to management and marketing by institutions operating in the healthcare cluster. So, this book is ideal for management and marketing academics, their students (undergraduate/graduate programs), researchers, managers, advertisers, healthcare organizations, hospital boards, pharmaceutical representatives, and marketers who need to optimize the potential of management, marketing and technology applied in the healthcare industry.

The order of the book's 12 chapters are aligned with the book's title. Thus, first are presented chapters that fall under the management perspective, followed by chapters with emphasis on marketing, and finally chapters that introduce the theme of technology, which tends to be associated with one of the first two themes.

In the first chapter, "The Buying Decision-Making Process in the Selection of Device Suppliers in Reproductive Medicine: A Preliminary Mode," a conceptual model applied to the decision making process in the selection of device suppliers is presented and marketing strategies - market-orientation strategy, relationship-marketing strategy, and brand-equity strategy - are identified to leverage the variables present in the various stages of the process, namely, the pre-purchase, purchase, and post-purchase phases.

Business ethics is an eternal and always up-to-date theme. In healthcare, the exorbitant profits in certain companies tend to keep alive the debate about the ethically correct amount to charge for medical care. How to maintain a balance between economic and social interests? How to boost corporate social responsibility in the pharmaceutical industry? Two questions on which Chapter 2, entitled "Economic Profit vs. Social Benefit: An Approach to the Pharmaceutical Industry," seeks to answer.

The next chapter, "Conflicts of Network Embeddedness in Healthcare Organizations," seeks to analyze the conflicts in organizations that operate in the health care area, namely conflicts related to organizational management, conflicts that arise during organizational processes and affect the implementation of organizational processes and the boundaries of their value creating ability, and personal conflicts that arise on an individual level during the performance of each action.

"The Implementation of Lean in Emergency Hospital Screening During the COVID-19 Pandemic" chapter presents a study, developed in a Hospital during the pandemic of COVID-19. This study focuses on the implementation of the Lean methodology on the urgencies department and how it contributed to the improvement of patient care, having also facilitated the realignment of processes in order to be able to identify more quickly the disease suspects and to segregate users more efficiently.

The impact of employee emotions on the functioning of organizations is a topic of concern in resource management. Chapter 5, "Use of Emotional Intelligence in Human Resource Management in Healthcare Organizations for Competitive Advantage: A Systematic Literature Review," assumes its relevance by making an exhaustive analysis between 1960 and 2020 of what has been published. Further, the authors propose a new conceptual framework for marketing of emotional intelligence in the healthcare sector.

The chapter "The Good, the Bad, and the Ugly: Don't Blame COVID-19 for Health System Inefficiencies" seeks to highlight concerns, namely inefficiencies in healthcare area, from the perspective of patients and organizations. Thus, different stakeholders are identified, the supply of goods and services, tax revenues, distribution of resources, how value improvement, demand and technology are characterized.

COVID-19 has changed consumer needs, transformed consumer behavior, and forced organizations to adapt their marketing, including the way they communicate, the format, and the message itself. "Health Communication During the COVID-19 Pandemic in Hungary" analyzes the content of some popular online public forums in Hungary on the topics of wearing masks and the evacuation of hospital beds for the purpose of hospital care for coronavirus patients.

"Colour Theory in Healthcare Corporate Identity" is the title of Chapter 8, which seeks, through the analysis of 24 healthcare center logos, to analyze the implications of colors in healthcare units logos and its impact on brand associations. Choosing a logo is not an easy task, it is not an operational decision, it is an element that contributes to the corporate identity. If in services, the logo can contribute to tangibilization, in healthcare it also has the important role to convey trust.

Chapter 9, "How Social Media Contribute to Autists' Wellbeing: A Netnographic Analysis of Virtual Communities Content," aims to present how such platforms allow the formation of virtual communities to support and exchange information and the inclusion of people with ASD (autism spectrum disorders) by comparing brand virtual communities. It was possible to see that virtual communities' contribution allows dialogue amongst autists' relatives, releasing their suffering and sharing acceptable practices.

In health, as in any other industry, technology adoption, if used appropriately, is an important asset and a success factor for a company. Nowadays, it is no longer feasible to talk about health without addressing the role of technology. In this context, the chapter "The Role of Technologies in Relationship Management and Internal Marketing: An Approach in the Health Sector" aims to understand the impact and role of technologies in a hospital context and in the relationship management from an internal perspective (internal marketing).

Mobile applications are part of our daily life, existing for almost every purpose, namely in healthcare. In Chapter 11, "KPIs for Mobile Apps and Digital Data Management in Healthcare," through the analysis of relevant scientific articles, 25 qualitative and quantitative KPI values, such as rating, product quality, or unique users, were identified. These KPIs should be taken into consideration for the successful preparation and management of healthcare based on apps and the use of digital data.

The last chapter, "Positive Technology: A Growing Market With a Potential to Rebuild a Resilient Society During and After COVID-19 Crisis," analyzes the emerging trends in digital well-being management by focusing on mobile health market. It offers a conceptual model that has attempted to propose interesting new connections to the psychological notions of stress and coping during pandemic. Further, it analyses how positive technology can help in building coping self-efficacy and resilience in society.

Chapter 1
The Buying Decision-Making Process in the Selection of Device Suppliers in Reproductive Medicine:
A Preliminary Model

Paulo Botelho Pires
https://orcid.org/0000-0003-3786-6783
Porto Business School, Portugal

António Correia Barros
Politécnico do Porto, Portugal

Filipe Taveira Santos
Faculdade de Economia, Universidade do Porto, Portugal

ABSTRACT

This study identifies the criteria underlying the buying decision-making process of medical devices in reproductive medicine. This research had three main objectives. The first one was to translate the criteria mentioned by the decision-makers into theoretical constructs, while the second objective was intended to establish the relationship between the constructs, creating a conceptual model of buying decision-making for medical devices in reproductive medicine. The third objective was to identify suitable business and marketing strategies for such a decision-making process. Four constructs were evaluated in the pre-purchase phase, namely the brand, the product's performance, the training associated with the product, and the price. In the post-purchase phase, decision-makers evaluated the following constructs: service provided by the company, the relationship with the salesperson, and loyalty. Regarding marketing strategies, market-orientation strategy, relationship-marketing strategy, and brand-equity strategy were identified as possible strategies.

DOI: 10.4018/978-1-7998-7263-4.ch001

INTRODUCTION

The degree of competitiveness in the health industry is characterized by increasing intensity, with globalization also taking place, being made up of companies with different sizes and strategies. Even in small market segments that are apparently unattractive, with low growth rates, companies try to gain market share and remain profitable. Therefore, it is crucial to know what strategies companies in the health industry should adopt, bearing in mind the decision criteria underlying the purchasing process by health service providers, specifically public hospitals, and clinics. Reproductive medicine or medically assisted procreation uses a set of therapeutics and laboratory techniques, resorting to medical devices, reagents, and equipment.

Questions about the role of the brand, the importance of price, technical specifications, or performance that probably will influence the buying decision-making process are relevant. Surely, in some cases obtaining information regarding how the buying decision-making process takes place and proceed with the right adjustment to it will mean survival in the market. Therefore, the research question is about how the decision-makers choose the suppliers of medically assisted reproduction devices.

This research was developed in a sequence of phases, in which, first, a review of the bibliography will be carried out that includes the relevant themes for the objectives, including the literature review on the types of strategies, the review on consumer behavior models, and decision making in B2B. Subsequently, a qualitative methodology will be used to collect data from decision-makers who are responsible for the buying decision-making process in public hospitals and private clinics. The data collection method will consist of semi-structured interviews, which after analysis will produce the preliminary constructs and the relationship between them. The objective of the investigation is therefore to obtain a preliminary model of the buying decision-making process of medical devices, reagents, and equipment in medically assisted reproduction.

LITERATURE REVIEW

Business and Marketing Strategies

According to Hunt (2010, p. 359) "R-A theory (Resource-Advantage) is an evolutionary, process theory of competition that is interdisciplinary … has affinities with numerous other theories and research traditions, including evolutionary economics, Austrian economics, the historical tradition, heterogeneous demand theory, differential advantage theory, industrial-organization economics, the resource-based tradition, the competence-based". Hunt and Morgan (1997) claim that R-A theory is a general theory of marketing being the closest thing to a general theory of marketing provided by Alderson (1957). The R-A theory has been the subject of profound developments by numerous authors (Hunt, 2010, 2015, 2017a, 2017b; Hunt & Lambe, 2000; Hunt & Madhavaram, 2020; Hunt & Morgan, 1995, 1997; Hunt &Wooliscroft, 2012) and states the following central premises. To achieve competitive advantage and, thereby, superior financial performance through business strategy theories, companies should adopt one of four alternatives: 1) industry-based strategy; 2) resource-based strategy; 3) competence-based strategy; 4) knowledge-based strategy. As for the industry-based strategy, companies must (1) choose industries and/or modify their structures, (2) then select one of three generic strategies (cost leadership, differentiation, and or focus), and (3) manage well the activities in their value chains. For resource-based strategy, companies must (1) seek resources that are valuable, rare, imperfectly mobile, inimitable and no substitutable. For competence-based strategy, companies must (1) identify, seek, develop, reinforce, maintain, and leverage distinctive competencies. For knowledge-based strategy, companies must (1) systematically accumulate a storehouse of knowledge, and (2) systematically use that knowledge to guide innovation. As important as the business strategy is the marketing strategy, which overlaps with the first one and proposes the existence of four marketing strategies (Hunt, 2010): 1) market-segmentation strategy; 2) market-orientation strategy; 3) relationship marketing strategy; 4) brand-equity strategy. To achieve superior and sustainable competitive advantage through market-segmentation strategy companies must (Hunt & Arnett, 2004): (1) identify segments of the industry and (2) target specific segments, and (3) develop a marketing mix for each targeted market segment. For market-orientation strategy companies must (Kohli & Jaworski, 1990; Narver & Slater, 1990): (1) steadily gather information on customers and competitors and (2) use that information to formulate a strategy. For relationship marketing, strategy companies must (Berry, 1983; Berry, 2002): create, develop, and cultivate a portfolio of relationships that are efficient and effective. For Aaker (2004) and Keller (2013), brand-equity strategy provides a primary source of competitive advantage, and therefore, the underlying theory of brand-equity strategy states to accomplish competitive advantage companies have to acquire, build, develop, and leverage an effectiveness-enhancing portfolio of brands.

Brand and the Decision Process in B2B

The literature has emphasized the importance of the brand in the buying decision-making process in B2B (business-to-business) markets and the literature displays different theories about this subject. The more influential perspective claims that organizational buyers handle their increasing buying risk by pursuing decision strategies centered on the evaluation of objective criteria, information search being the key method for risk minimization; this perspective is in complete opposition to the brand-driven perspective, stating that B2B buyers have resort to empirical cues in contexts of high-risk purchase situations (Brown et al., 2011). However, it is now well established from a variety of studies, that purchasing managers are prone to consider more rational and objective aspects (Gomes et al., 2014). When B2B brands are the base of research, their tangible characteristics and features are mostly studied (Veloutsou & Taylor, 2012). The leading perspective on B2B buying behavior suggests that purchasers tend to rely on objective criteria when making choice decisions and therefore the influence of subjective factors, in particular brands, decreases the risk of selecting the wrong alternative (Brown et al., 2011). Similarly, brands provide a base to minimize risk and they also provide signals that allow the simplification of the buying decision-making process in low-risk situations, when there is no need to perform a systematic search (Brown et al., 2011). Risk increases the significance of impressions and emotions related to the cooperation with another company as a whole during the selection process and corporate brand image is particularly valuable when buyers need to identify new collaborations, where the brand's primary task is to appeal to interest and offer trust (Blombäck & Axelsson, 2007). These authors also argue that the purpose of corporate brand image is not to be related to emotions or irrational behavior, most of the times associated with spontaneous or unplanned purchases based on feelings or opinions, without weighting the characteristics, features, and benefits of the product, but rather to set the impressions about the company as a proxy for quality.

One relevant finding states that branding does not have the same importance to all B2B buyers or in all situations, because buying and context needs are related to the relevance given to brand popularity (Gomes et al., 2014). Furthermore, previous research on consumer markets revealed that brand relevance usually is guided by three purposes: image benefits, information cost, and risk reductions (Backhaus et al., 2011). Additionally, it was established that brand attributes (specifically brand reputation, brand popularity, and frequency of prior purchases to the same supplier) are relevant in B2B even when the decision-making process is rational (Gomes et al., 2014). The concept of reputation is also interesting which is considered as important as functional or utilitarian attributes because it improves corporate credibility (Gomes et al., 2014). Brand relevance in B2B markets depends largely on risk and information cost-reducing effects and, consequently, companies must allocate their investments to their brands, specifically to actions that help to decrease risk and information search costs for decision-makers (Backhaus et al., 2011). Distinct purchase circumstances and decision-maker traits have an impact on brand relevance, specifically, brand reputation, prior purchases, and brand awareness (Gomes et al., 2016). Two dimensions of corporate reputation have been recognized as remarkably essential in establishing positive or negative brand associations and they are corporate ability and financial position (Lambkin & Muzellec, 2010).

Closely related to the central topic of this research is the study of Veloutsou and Taylor (2012). The authors state that the brand as a person can be used for the conceptualization of B2B brands since brand personality characteristics and brand nationality have been identified as characteristics of the brands. They argue that brands are described as possessing human personality traits by buyers and the nationality of the brands is an evaluation criterion in the decision-making process. Accordingly, Wang et al. (2010) stress the role played by the brand promise in B2B customer relationships, declaring that it can increase customer satisfaction, improve corporate image, maintain and attract more customers.

Previous investigations suggest that B2B brands influence organizational buying decisions, but their relative importance is limited comparing with other factors such as logistics, pricing, and service (Zablah et al., 2010). The authors suggest that the decision-making process is compressed in a hierarchy of effects, composed by the sequence of beliefs, attitudes, intentions, and behaviors, which are associated respectively with constructs such as brand consciousness, brand preference, brand sensitivity, and brand importance.

The mainstream of B2B brand investigation still embraces a slim and biased perspective and there are five broad areas (benefits of B2B brands, relevance of B2B brands in the decision-making process, B2B brand architecture, B2B brands as communication enablers, and relationship builders and B2B brand equity) that require a more methodical and scientific examination to further comprehend how to make use of brands in B2B markets (Leek & Christodoulides, 2011). But still, several questions require an explanation between the function of the B2B brand and the buyer-seller relationship (Leek & Christodoulides, 2011). One should note that there are relatively few studies about the selection of equipment and device suppliers in medically assisted procreation. Nevertheless, the allocation of brand investments must bear in mind the relevance of brands to the purchase decision process (Backhaus et al., 2011).

Product Characteristics and Performance and the Decision Process in B2B

A large and growing body of literature has investigated the importance of product characteristics, features, and benefits and the literature has emphasized that these factors are crucial in B2B decision-making. Al-Kwifi et al. (2014) confirmed that product features are the most prominent reason underlying brand switching and that product features are crucial for medical companies who want to sustain their competitive advantage. Besides, it is very important to point out the set of reasons that affect the decision-maker switch to another brand is unique for each segment in the same industry.

Product characteristics or features and their performance are the most important criteria in gaining a sustainable competitive advantage (Zablah et al., 2010) and some products characteristics or features turn out to be appealing if they provide a higher performance such that it differentiates them from other offers (Brown et al., 2011) Therefore, to understand customers' needs or involve customers in new products development is an important strategic decision that improves new product performance and, accordingly, managers should recognize how institutional environments or market research should relate to the companies' strategic choices (Wang et al., 2019).

Training and the Decision Process in B2B

Some activities in the healthcare industry, although essential, have been continuously neglected by researchers such as employee and customer training, tracking, and visibility (Dixit et al., 2019b). Training is a set of activities directly related to the acquisition of knowledge, skills, and attitudes targeted for immediate or short-term application (Nicod & Llosa, 2018). Dixit et al. (2019b) clearly state that employee and customer training make a significant impact on the performance of healthcare services and products and provide higher levels of motivation and performance to accomplish the operations effectively, improving health and lowering healthcare costs. In healthcare services and products, the lack of knowledge, skills, and motivation may set an undesirable effect on service quality and costs (Burton, 2002; Dixit et al., 2019a). Nicod and Llosa (2018) argue that the training given to customers as a performance tool should be adapted according to the strategy of the company because its impact on productivity is remarkable.

Price and the Decision Process in B2B

Price has been an integral component of the marketing mix since only pricing creates revenue (Kienzler & Kowalkowski, 2017). These authors state that developing a suitable pricing strategy is crucial and very complex because it depends on a variety of factors, such as the environment, company objectives, customer characteristics, competitors, and the pricing situation, thus distinct pricing strategies echo these exigencies, such as price skimming, penetration pricing, price bundling, price promotion, and complementary pricing. Although pricing is the most important driver of profits, managers overlook this important factor because they have assumptions, namely pricing myths that are (Hinterhuber, 2016): costs are the foundation for price setting; small price alterations have a modest impact on profits; customers are extremely price-sensitive; products are hard to differentiate; a high market share conducts to high profits; managing price involves adjusting prices.

Henke et al. (2008) state that a company can apply price reduction pressure while maintaining a trusting working relationship with the pressured suppliers. On the opposite side are those companies that adopt a relational pricing strategy (Argouslidis & Indounas, 2010). Corporate brand image can also be a determinant of price premium, and it can be conceptualized in six dimensions, namely brand familiarity, product solution, service, distribution, relationship, and company associations (Persson, 2010). However, one should note that even if low price is usually important for a company selection as a supplier, quality-sensitive buyers are prone to choose companies with higher prices to prevent quality degradation. However, despite the importance of supplier reputation on choice, decision-makers are not prepared to pay a premium price to companies with a quality reputation (Biong, 2013). Töytäri et al. (2015) contribute to the discussion stating that value-based pricing in industrial buyer-seller relationships is feasible, and many companies are adopting this strategy. Another contribution is made by Johnston and Mora Cortez (2018), who propose the blend of the unit and the value-based pricing as a new approach for pricing strategy.

Carricano et al. (2014) showed that environmental determinants influence pricing strategy, explaining that the structure of pricing determinants is a five dimensions construct, namely market-based, value-based, position-based, competition-based, and production-based. The authors state that companies may have pricing flexibility strategies based on environmental determinants. They also refer that managers use very straightforward techniques and practices to set their prices. Hinterhuber (2015) claims that there are several violations of rational choice which customers make in their decisions about purchase prices: price-quality effect, irrelevant attributes, framing, price–precision effect, 9-endings, sale signs, discount presentation format, color, centimes and type size, denominator neglect, unit effect, deal obsession, paying more and being happy about it, justifications for discounts, price partitioning, scarcity effect, preference reversals, decoy effect, compromise effect, anchoring, advertised reference prices, and deliberate overpricing. Iyer et al. (2015) add that price can also be seen from a behavioral perspective, and several issues can arise, such as interpretation, cognitive biases, and heuristics. Kienzler (2018) adds a few more, in particular perceived lack of control, herding, fixed-pie bias, ambiguity aversion, and egocentric fairness bias. Monroe et al. (2015) have also examined the price behavioral perspective, analyzing five price concepts: reference price, price thresholds, acceptable price range, price as an indicator of quality, and the price-perceived value model. Saab and Botelho (2020) sustain that price influences functional risk perception and that price still appears to be salient to the final selection of who gets a particular contract (Blombäck & Axelsson, 2007).

Salespersons and the Decision Process in B2B

A product has certain features, an associated brand, a certain price and may have a salesforce training need. But, to sell it you need a vehicle, a way to present it and consummate the sale. Often it is the salesperson who plays this role and who interacts with buyers through meetings or visits, calls, or e-mails.

Jayakody and Sanjeewani (2006) found that the idealized influence behavior of salespersons influences positively customer trust, which when are combined with individualized consideration of salespersons affects customer commitment. Palmatier et al. (2007) go further claiming that salesperson relationships have a major effect on financial outcomes and when the salesperson performs the main function, relationship quality with the salesperson has a meaningful, straightforward effect on financial outcomes. In the same line of thought salesperson's marketing relationship activities can create a buyers' trust in the salesperson, which in turn leads to higher sales performance, a higher share of wallet, and lower buyer propensity to switch (Palmatier et al., 2008). The same was found by Singh and Koshy (2011), who proved that salespersons' customer orientation has an impact on value creation and relationship development with customers. Another key aspect is loyalty-building and Wang et al. (2015) showed that in some circumstances, salespersons can contribute to building strong customer loyalty.

Service and the Decision Process in B2B

A controversial issue remains open and the question is to know if customer service influences B2B buying decision-making. As stated by Wouters (2004), in B2B, to make use of customer service as a competitive advantage, it is appropriate to recognize the conditions for customer service indispensability. The truth is that customer service or service quality in a B2B environment is a complex and multifaceted subject, and both the customer and the seller may have different perceptions of what constitutes service quality or customer service (Zolkiewski et al., 2007). The relation between sales and customer service was analyzed by Claro and Ramos (2018), who concluded that the number of ties with customer service results in superior sales outcomes.

Loyalty and the Decision Process in B2B

Customer loyalty is the attachment or commitment to a product, service, brand, or organization and it is generally evaluated by the recommendation of these items to other customers or by the number of products or services purchased from the same seller (Lam et al., 2004). These authors claim that customer loyalty mediates customer value and customer satisfaction. However, Chumpitaz Caceres and

Paparoidamis (2007) have a different perspective, stating that loyalty is an outcome of the relationship quality (including commitment and trust constructs), which in turn is the result of functional and technical quality. Rauyruen and Miller (2007) follow the concept but argue that attitudinal loyalty is the result of relationship quality, and this construct is composed of service quality, commitment, trust, and satisfaction. Čater and Čater (2010) deepen even further, sustaining that product quality impacts commitment, relationship quality (cooperation and trust) also impact commitment, and commitment, in turn, influences attitudinal and behavioral loyalty. Liu et al. (2011) contributed with new insights, affirming that relationship quality consists of two constructs, namely satisfaction and trust. They proposed that loyalty is influenced by satisfaction, trust, and switch barriers.

METHODOLOGY

Research Propositions and Model Development

Based on the literature previously presented eight research propositions were developed and they are:

1. **Research Proposition One:** The brand is an influencing factor in the purchase decision of reproductive medicine devices.
2. **Research Proposition Two:** The greater the performance of the product, the greater the probability of purchasing reproductive medicine devices.
3. **Research Proposition Three:** More customers' training increases the likelihood of purchase of reproductive medicine devices.
4. **Research Proposition Four:** The price decisively influences the purchasing process and decision of reproductive medicine devices.
5. **Research Proposition Five:** Service quality associated with the product influences future product purchase decisions of reproductive medicine devices.
6. **Research Proposition Six:** The salesperson has a key role in the future buying process of reproductive medicine devices.
7. **Research Proposition Seven:** Loyalty influences the consumers' future purchasing decisions of reproductive medicine devices.
8. **Research Proposition Eight:** Market-orientation strategy, relationship-marketing strategy, and brand-equity strategy are viable marketing strategies.

The research propositions and the literature previously presented, are intended to develop a preliminary model that conceptualizes the buying decision-making process in the reproductive medicine or medically assisted procreation market. For this purpose, it is proposed to verify that the brand, product characteristics, and performance, training, and price constructs are used as selection criteria. Knowing that the purchase process is recurrent, it is assumed that the salesperson, services, and loyalty constructs influence new decision-making processes. The model is illustrated in Figure 1.

Figure 1. Buying decision-making model in reproductive medicine devices
Source: Authors

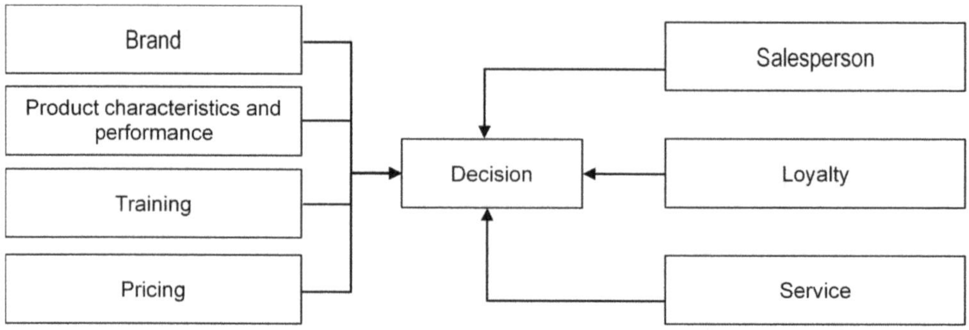

The following bibliographic list describes the constructs' composition and the authors that sustain that construct:

- **Brand:** (1) Risk (Brown et al., 2011); (Blombäck & Axelsson, 2007); (Backhaus et al., 2011). (2) Trust (Blombäck & Axelsson, 2007). (3) Quality (Blombäck & Axelsson, 2007). (4) Reputation (Gomes et al., 2014); (Gomes et al., 2016); (Lambkin & Muzellec, 2010).
- **Product characteristics and performance:** (1) gaining a sustainable competitive advantage (Al-Kwifi et al., 2014); (Zablah et al., 2010). (2) differentiates them from other offers (Brown et al., 2011).
- **Training:** (1) impact on the execution (Dixit et al., 2019b). (2) higher levels of motivation and performance (Dixit et al., 2019b). (3) effect on service quality and costs (Burton, 2002; Dixit et al., 2019a). (4) impact on productivity (Nicod & Llosa, 2018).
- **Price:** (1) pricing is the most important driver of profits (Hinterhuber, 2016); (Saab & Botelho, 2020). (2) low price is usually (Biong, 2013). (3) value-based pricing is feasible (Töytäri et al., 2015). (4) environmental determinants (Carricano et al., 2014).
- **Salesperson:** (1) customer trust (Jayakody & Sanjeewani, 2006) (Palmatier et al., 2007); (Palmatier et al., 2008); (Singh & Koshy, 2011). (2) value and

financial outcomes (Palmatier et al., 2007); (Palmatier et al., 2008); (Singh & Koshy, 2011).

- **Service:** (1) service quality (Zolkiewski et al., 2007).
- **Loyalty:** (1) relationship quality produces loyalty (Chumpitaz Caceres & Paparoidamis, 2007); (Rauyruen & Miller, 2007); (Čater & Čater, 2010); (Liu et al., 2011).

RESEARCH METHOD

The objective of this research is to evaluate if the buying decision-making process of devices in reproductive medicine can be conceptualized by the model illustrated in figure 1. Qualitative research allows studying a business phenomenon, in market contexts, by perceiving and understanding it through the players who participate in those contexts and have the ability to influence that business phenomenon. To ensure that the aim of qualitative research is accomplished it is necessary to apply data collection methods in order to allow researchers to get the full understanding of the business phenomenon being investigated. Therefore, empirical research was designed as a qualitative study, resorting to structured interviews, specifically, interviews with experts, which is a particular way of conducting semi-structured interviews (Flick, U., 2009). "Interviews are one of the most commonly recognized forms of qualitative research method" (Mason, j., (2018, p. 63); qualitative research is suitable to discover people's reasonings or judgments about events or situations in which they participated (idem); the data we want is not "feasibly available in any other form" (p.66), which makes qualitative interviews the most adequate choice (idem); interviews will be "read" literally, interpretatively and reflexively; "an interpretive reading will involve you in constructing or documenting a version of what you think the data mean or represent, or what you think you can infer from them" while "a reflexive reading will locate you as part of the data you have generated" (idem, p.149); interviews will be tape-recorded, to understand how people articulate their ideas, not only the substance of what is said, like Mason, j. (2018) recommend.

According to Saunders, Lewis & Tornhill (2009), after transcribing the interviews, a new document will be created with the main topics summarizing the original information which can be divided by categories or in this case by dimensions.

This study is exploratory in nature and was performed in Portugal.

Healthcare providers select, buy or use a range of products for medical procedures in reproductive medicine. There are approximately twenty-seven reproductive medicine centers in Portugal operating in public hospitals or private clinics. It is intended to study individual buying behaviors and how they influence the decision of organizations. The interviewees were health care services technicians or those people responsible for services or clinics who are in fact the decision-makers in the purchase decision process. Seven face-to-face interviews with audio recordings were carried out. Five interviewees work in the public sector (one of them also works in a private clinic) and two interviewees in the private sector. All have more than 10 years of experience in this subspecialty. Respondents were female aged between 35 and 50 years. Six interviews were performed at the interviewee's workplace and one interview, for the interviewee´s convenience, was conducted elsewhere. Subsequently, the interviews were fully transcribed and analyzed.

To evaluate the research proposals, a questionnaire was developed which served as a guide for the interviews. This questionnaire consists of a set of open questions, allowing the interviewee to expound his/her point of view. The following table includes the referred questions and the corresponding research constructs and propositions.

RESULTS AND DISCUSSION

This section analyzes the data obtained from face-to-face interviews to examine if the research propositions are confirmed or not. Proposition one claims that the brand is decisive in the purchase decision process. The results were consistent for all the questions (1, 3, 4, and 5) and therefore one can say that brand construct influences the buying process of reproductive medicine devices.

A brand with a strong presence in the market, revealing high quality and encompassing innovative products was valued by all the interviewees and strongly contributes to the purchase decision.

The product characteristics and performance construct were intended to assess the influence of product characteristics and performance on the purchase decision process. After analyzing answers to question number 9, it was found that it is very similar to question number 10 and therefore could be removed. The answers to the other questions (6-11) permit to conclude that research proposition two is validated.

An extended portfolio also contributes to the purchase decision. Products that fulfill their core function and that achieve results, which in this field means generating successful pregnancies, are considered as having high performance. These products are under huge scrutiny. Confidence in the product is created by perceived quality and the achievement of good results.

The training construct was meant for discovering whether the training provided by the company to users of its products and services increases the likelihood of purchase, thus positively influencing the purchase decision process. Questions 12, 13, and 14 are relevant to the model but question number 15 provided inconclusive results. One can state that the construct is part of the model, although it requires further future research.

Table 1. Questions and the related research constructs and propositions

Question	Construct	Research Proposition
1. Refer to the importance ascribed to brands in the decision to purchase reproductive medicine products. 2. What influence do the brand characteristics have on the purchase of reproductive medicine products? What are these characteristics? Which are the most important? 3. How does the size of the product range (offered by the supplier) relate to the decision to purchase reproductive medicine products? 4. What is the relationship between the safety conveyed by the brand and the decision to purchase reproductive medicine products? 5. What is the relationship between the perception of differentiation conveyed by the brand and the decision to purchase the products?	BRAND	ONE EIGHT
6. What does it mean to you "the product fulfills its function"? 7. In what way is quality important to you? How important is quality to you? 8. What type of information do you collect about the product? 9. Concerning product performance, what do you value more? 10. What is most important to you in the product? What are the most important features to you? 11. Is it relevant to you that the product purchased is compatible with other products? How relevant is to you the compatibility between the product to be purchased and other products possessed by the company?	PRODUCT	TWO EIGHT
12. Why is training important to you? 13. When buying products and services, do you attach importance to the training you receive? 14. What aspects more are relevant in the education offered by companies? 15. Do you value more the training given at your workplace or outside? Why?	TRAINING	THREE
16. To what extent is the price important to you? 17. How does the price relate to the competition? 18. What other factors associated with price are important to you? 19. Do you think the price is somehow related to quality?	PRICE	FOUR
20. Concerning the service, how important is it? 21. Which service features are important to you? 22. Of the factors that you consider important, which is the most important? 23. Before buying the product, what kind of information do you try to gather about the quality of the service?	SERVICE	FIVE
24. In the purchase process, how do you rate the way the seller provides all the necessary information? 25. Which seller features do you attach more importance to? 26. How do you think the seller should relate to you? 27. What support should be given by the seller? 28. What kind of commercial activity would you prefer the company to undertake?	SALESPERSON	SIX EIGHT
29. What factors lead to repeated purchases from the same seller? 30. To what extent do you value a company treated differently due to its frequent customer status? 31. How should the company reward you for being a frequent customer?	LOYALTY	SEVEN EIGHT

Source: Authors

Training activities are highly valued as they allow professionals in this field to be updated. Companies actively promote training by sponsoring workshops where professionals can exchange opinions and experiences. Training either directly or indirectly through congresses attendance has been provided mainly by companies. This is important since public hospitals do not have the budgets to do so, and private clinics have limited financial resources.

Moving forward to the price construct, questions number 16, 18, and 19 provided results showing that all the answers were consistent, and consequently, these questions are relevant to the construct. As for question number 17, the answers were inconclusive, and it should be removed from the model. Therefore, price is important in the buying decision-making process.

As for the "price" dimension, respondents working in public hospitals strongly value this factor due to budget limitations and specific rules imposed on the public sector. On the other hand, respondents in the private sector assign less importance to price as a determining factor in the purchase decision, quality assuming a more relevant role.

As for the service construct, it was intended to analyze whether the quality of service associated with the product influences customer loyalty and future purchase decisions. Questions number 20, 21, and 23 provided coherent results and it was identified a redundancy in question 22 so it can be excluded. In sum, one can say that service plays a role in the purchase decision process.

Concerning the "service" dimension, the most valued aspects are the ordering process, the delivery time, and the technical assistance. The speed was highlighted by several of the interviewees as being a positive feature, closely related to the brand.

The salesperson construct intended to analyze whether the salesperson is a key factor in the purchasing process. All the questions provided pertinent findings to the model. Hence, the salesperson is the link between buyers and suppliers, and he/she must have several skills and be close to his/her customers. One can conclude that this construct is part of the proposed model, i.e., salespersons influence the buying decision-making process.

The study clearly shows that salespeople still play a crucial role in the decision-making process. The salesperson must establish close and professional long-term relationships with the customers. Availability and empathy are important characteristics to achieve such a goal, by adopting the customer-centric strategy mentioned in the literature review. As for the technical component, the interviewees value the relationship they maintain with the seller allowing the salesperson to give advice and even to support decisions. Besides, the salesperson acts as a bridge to other departments of the company. Due to the tight regulation existing in health, a sale is still closely linked to the interaction with the seller.

Finally, the loyalty construct was meant to analyze its influence on the purchase decision process and its repetition. Interviewees' answers prove that is necessary for the model, i.e., it influences the existing buying decision-making process, since coherent results were obtained in all the answers of the interviewees.

"Loyalty" to a brand and a good relationship with it and the company leads to a more automatic decision-making process, the final choice being assigned to a previously selected company. The need for differentiated treatment of loyal customers was highly valued by interviewees. Loyal customers are satisfied customers, and so they can be employed as a reference to other customers. This can be beneficial for both parties because it helps the seller to close the deal and simultaneously gives greater confidence to the buyer. Trust, in turn, helps to create bonds with the supplier company and thus to increase loyalty. Among the various sources of information used by decision-makers, word of mouth from their peers certainly is an important one. Strong brands usually have strong products.

After conducting the content analysis of data gathered, one can conclude that the model is empirically validated in its different dimensions, describing the buying decision process in the business-to-business market, specifically in the medically assisted reproduction sector.

CONCLUSION

Going back to the objectives defined at the beginning of this research, it is now feasible to sum up the outcomes, recalling that in the introduction we mentioned that the project was intended to achieve three main aims. The first one was to identify the theoretical constructs that influence the buying decision-making process, the second one was to describe the relationship between the constructs, and the third one was to propose the business and marketing strategies suitable for the buying decision-making process for medical devices, reagents, and equipment in reproductive medicine.

The main findings are relevant, and the implications are substantial. This research provides the first systematic identification of the determinants of the buying decision-making process for medical devices, reagents, and equipment in reproductive medicine. The research revealed seven such determinants, namely: the brand, the product characteristics and performance, the training, the price, the salespersons, the service, and the loyalty. Four of these are pre-purchase constructs, specifically, the brand, the product characteristics and performance, the training, and the price. The three remaining constructs are part of the post-purchase phase, namely the salespersons, the service, and the loyalty. Such findings lead to the conclusion that the four determinants that are part of the pre-purchase phase are the criteria that influence the buying decision process in the first purchase, while in repeated purchases processes, the three determinants of the post-purchase phase also influence the buying decision-making process. Therefore, the proposed model represents a contribution effort to lay the relationships between the constructs of the buying decision-making process and proves unequivocally the fulfillment of the second objective. Regarding business and marketing strategies, the results achieved are mixed. Concerning business strategies, it was not possible to identify which strategy is most suitable for companies in this market. As for marketing strategies, and based on the A-R theory, it was identified that brand-equity, market-orientation, and relationship marketing strategies are preferred by decision-makers.

The most relevant contribution of this investigation is the opening of a promising research line, presenting a preliminary model and its constructs, conceptualizing the buying decision-making process in medical devices, reagents, and equipment in medically assisted reproduction. This is undoubtedly a contribution to the theory. Also worth mentioning is the suggestion of the most appropriate marketing strategies for this kind of market. This result has managerial implications because it provides managers with guidance on which strategy or strategies are most appropriate or to be followed, being supported by the perspective of buyers and decision-makers, in other words, it is an outside-in strategic perspective instead of an inside-out strategic perspective.

REFERENCES

Aaker, D. A. (1996). *Building strong brands*. Free Press.

Aaker, D. A. (2004). *Brand portfolio strategy: creating relevance, differentiation, energy, leverage, and clarity*. Free Press.

Aaker, D. A. (2011). *Brand relevance: making competitors irrelevant* (1st ed.). Jossey-Bass.

Aaker, D. A., & Biel, A. L. (1993). *Brand equity &advertising: advertising's role in building strong brands*. Lawrence Erlbaum Associates.

Aaker, D. A., & Joachimsthaler, E. (2000). *Brand leadership*. Free Press.

Aaker, D. A., & Keller, K. L. (1990). *Consumer evaluations of brand extensions*. Marketing Science Institute.

Al-Kwifi, S., Ahmed, Z. U., & Yammout, D. (2014). Brand switching of high-technology capital products: How product features dictate the switching decision. *Journal of Product and Brand Management*, *23*(4-5), 322–332. doi:10.1108/JPBM-12-2013-0473

Alderson, W. (1957). *Marketing behavior and executive action; a functionalist approach to marketing theory*. R. D. Irwin.

Argouslidis, P. C., & Indounas, K. (2010). Exploring the role of relationship pricing in industrial export settings: Empirical evidence from the UK. *Industrial Marketing Management, 39*(3), 460–472. doi:10.1016/j.indmarman.2009.09.001

Backhaus, K., Steiner, M., & Lügger, K. (2011). To invest, or not to invest, in brands? Drivers of brand relevance in B2B markets. *Industrial Marketing Management, 40*(7), 1082–1092. doi:10.1016/j.indmarman.2011.09.002

Berry, L. L. (1983). Relationship marketing. *Emerging Perspectives on Services Marketing, 66*(3), 33-47.

Berry, L. L. (2002). Relationship Marketing of Services Perspectives from 1983 and 2000. *Journal of Relationship Marketing, 1*(1), 59–77. doi:10.1300/J366v01n01_05

Biong, H. (2013). Choice of subcontractor in markets with asymmetric information: Reputation and price effects. *Journal of Business and Industrial Marketing, 28*(1), 60–71. doi:10.1108/08858621311285723

Blombäck, A., & Axelsson, B. (2007). The role of corporate brand image in the selection of new subcontractors. *Journal of Business and Industrial Marketing, 22*(6), 418–430. doi:10.1108/08858620710780181

Brown, B. P., Zablah, A. R., Bellenger, D. N., & Johnston, W. J. (2011). When do B2B brands influence the decision making of organizational buyers? An examination of the relationship between purchase risk and brand sensitivity. *International Journal of Research in Marketing, 28*(3), 194–204. doi:10.1016/j.ijresmar.2011.03.004

Burton, D. (2002). Consumer education and service quality: Conceptual issues and practical implications. *Journal of Services Marketing, 16*(2), 125–142. doi:10.1108/08876040210422673

Carricano, M. (2014). Pricing myopia: Do leading companies capture the full value of their pricing strategies? *Management Decision, 52*(1), 159–178. doi:10.1108/MD-03-2013-0184

Čater, T., & Čater, B. (2010). Product and relationship quality influence on customer commitment and loyalty in B2B manufacturing relationships. *Industrial Marketing Management, 39*(8), 1321–1333. doi:10.1016/j.indmarman.2010.02.006

Chumpitaz Caceres, R., & Paparoidamis, N. G. (2007). Service quality, relationship satisfaction, trust, commitment and business-to-business loyalty. *European Journal of Marketing, 41*(7/8), 836–867. doi:10.1108/03090560710752429

Claro, D. P., & Ramos, C. (2018). Sales intrafirm networks and the performance impact of sales cross-functional collaboration with marketing and customer service. *Journal of Personal Selling & Sales Management, 38*(2), 172–190. doi:10.1080/08853134.2018.1437353

Dixit, A., Routroy, S., & Dubey, S. K. (2019a). Analysis of government-supported health-care supply chain enablers: A case study. *Journal of Global Operations and Strategic Sourcing, 13*(1), 1–16. doi:10.1108/JGOSS-02-2019-0011

Dixit, A., Routroy, S., & Dubey, S. K. (2019b). A systematic literature review of healthcare supply chain and implications of future research. *International Journal of Pharmaceutical and Healthcare Marketing, 13*(4), 405–435. doi:10.1108/IJPHM-05-2018-0028

Flick, U. (2009). *An introduction to qualitative research* (4th ed.). Sage Publications.

Gomes, M., Fernandes, T., & Brandão, A. (2014). The Role of Branding in a B2B Purchasing Context. *4th Conference of the International Network of Business and Management Journals.*

Gomes, M., Fernandes, T., & Brandão, A. (2016). Determinants of brand relevance in a B2B service purchasing context. *Journal of Business and Industrial Marketing, 31*(2), 193–204. doi:10.1108/JBIM-08-2014-0151

Henke, J. W. Jr, Parameswaran, R., & Mohan Pisharodi, R. (2008). Manufacturer price reduction pressure and supplier relations. *Journal of Business and Industrial Marketing, 23*(5), 287–300. doi:10.1108/08858620810881566

Hinterhuber, A. (2015). Violations of rational choice principles in pricing decisions. *Industrial Marketing Management, 47*, 65–74. doi:10.1016/j.indmarman.2015.02.006

Hinterhuber, A. (2016). The six pricing myths that kill profits. *Business Horizons, 59*(1), 71–83. doi:10.1016/j.bushor.2015.09.002

Hunt, S. D. (2010). *Marketing theory: foundations, controversy, strategy, resource-advantage theory*. M.E. Sharpe.

Hunt, S. D. (2015). The theoretical foundations of strategic marketing and marketing strategy: Foundational premises, R-A theory, three fundamental strategies, and societal welfare. *AMS Review, 5*(3-4), 61–77. doi:10.100713162-015-0069-5

Hunt, S. D. (2017a). Advancing marketing strategy in the marketing discipline and beyond: From promise, to neglect, to prominence, to fragment (to promise?). *Journal of Marketing Management, 34*(1-2), 16–51. doi:10.1080/0267257X.2017.1326973

Hunt, S. D. (2017b). The prospects for marketing strategy and the marketing discipline in Era V: Is the prognosis promising or problematic? *Journal of Marketing Management, 34*(1-2), 86–95. doi:10.1080/0267257X.2017.1401381

Hunt, S. D., & Arnett, D. B. (2004). Market Segmentation Strategy, Competitive Advantage, and Public Policy: Grounding Segmentation Strategy in Resource-Advantage Theory. *Australasian Marketing Journal, 12*(1), 7–25. doi:10.1016/S1441-3582(04)70083-X

Hunt, S. D., & Lambe, C. J. (2000). Marketing's contribution to business strategy: Market orientation, relationship marketing and resource-advantage theory. *International Journal of Management Reviews, 2*(1), 17–43. doi:10.1111/1468-2370.00029

Hunt, S. D., & Madhavaram, S. (2020). Adaptive marketing capabilities, dynamic capabilities, and renewal competences: The "outside vs. inside" and "static vs. dynamic" controversies in strategy. *Industrial Marketing Management, 89*, 129–139. doi:10.1016/j.indmarman.2019.07.004

Hunt, S. D., & Morgan, R. M. (1995). The Comparative Advantage Theory of Competition. *Journal of Marketing, 59*(2), 1–15. doi:10.1177/002224299505900201

Hunt, S. D., & Morgan, R. M. (1997). Resource-Advantage Theory: A Snake Swallowing Its Tail or a General Theory of Competition? *Journal of Marketing, 61*(4), 74–82. doi:10.1177/002224299706100406

Hunt, S. D., & Wooliscroft, B. (2012). The evolution of resource-advantage theory. *Journal of Historical Research in Marketing, 4*(1), 7–29. doi:10.1108/17557501211195046

Iyer, G. R., Hong Xiao, S., Sharma, A., & Nicholson, M. (2015). Behavioral issues in price setting in business-to-business marketing: A framework for analysis. *Industrial Marketing Management, 47*, 6–16. doi:10.1016/j.indmarman.2015.02.001

Jayakody, J. A. S. K., & Sanjeewani, W. M. A. (2006). The impact of salesperson transformational leadership behavior on customer relationship marketing behavior. *International Journal of Bank Marketing, 24*(7), 461–474. doi:10.1108/02652320610712085

Johnston, W. J., & Mora Cortez, R. (2018). Unit pricing and its implications for B2B marketing research. *Industrial Marketing Management, 69*, 32–39. doi:10.1016/j.indmarman.2018.01.026

Keller, K. L. (1998). *Strategic brand management: Building, measuring and managing brand equity*. Prentice Hall.

Keller, K. L. (2013). *Strategic brand management: Building, measuring, and managing brand equity* (4th ed.). Pearson.

Keller, K. L., Apéria, T., & Georgson, M. (2008). *Strategic brand management: a European perspective*. Prentice Hall Financial Times.

Keller, K. L., Apéria, T., & Georgson, M. (2012). *Strategic brand management: a European perspective* (2nd ed.). Financial Times/Prentice Hall.

Kienzler, M. (2018). Value-based pricing and cognitive biases: An overview for business markets. *Industrial Marketing Management, 68*, 86–94. doi:10.1016/j.indmarman.2017.09.028

Kienzler, M., & Kowalkowski, C. (2017). Pricing strategy: A review of 22 years of marketing research. *Journal of Business Research, 78*, 101–110. doi:10.1016/j.jbusres.2017.05.005

Kohli, A. K., & Jaworski, B. J. (1990). Market orientation: The construct, research propositions and managerial implications. *Journal of Marketing, 54*(2), 1–18. doi:10.1177/002224299005400201

Lam, S. Y., Shankar, V., Erramilli, M. K., & Murthy, B. (2004). Customer value, satisfaction, loyalty, and switching costs: An illustration from a business-to-business service context. *Journal of the Academy of Marketing Science, 32*(3), 293–311. doi:10.1177/0092070304263330

Lambkin, M. C., & Muzellec, L. (2010). Leveraging brand equity in business-to-business mergers and acquisitions. *Industrial Marketing Management, 39*(8), 1234–1239. doi:10.1016/j.indmarman.2010.02.020

Leek, S., & Christodoulides, G. (2011). A literature review and future agenda for B2B branding: Challenges of branding in a B2B context. *Industrial Marketing Management, 40*(6), 830–837. doi:10.1016/j.indmarman.2011.06.006

Liu, C.-T., Guo, Y. M., & Lee, C.-H. (2011). The effects of relationship quality and switching barriers on customer loyalty. *International Journal of Information Management, 31*(1), 71–79. doi:10.1016/j.ijinfomgt.2010.05.008

Mason, J. (2018). *Qualitative researching* (3rd ed.). SAGE.

Monroe, K. B., Rikala, V.-M., & Somervuori, O. (2015). Examining the application of behavioral price research in business-to-business markets. *Industrial Marketing Management, 47*, 17–25. doi:10.1016/j.indmarman.2015.02.002

Narver, J. C., & Slater, S. F. (1990). The effect of a market orientation on business profitability. *Journal of Marketing*, *54*(4), 20–35. doi:10.1177/002224299005400403

Nicod, L., & Llosa, S. (2018). How should customers be trained in their role as coproducers? The influence of training and its characteristics on the benefits of coproduction. *Recherche et Applications en Marketing*, *33*(4), 46–73. doi:10.1177/2051570718783151

Palmatier, R. W., Scheer, L. K., Evans, K. R., & Arnold, T. J. (2008). Achieving relationship marketing effectiveness in business-to-business exchanges. *Journal of the Academy of Marketing Science*, *36*(2), 174–190. doi:10.100711747-007-0078-5

Palmatier, R. W., Scheer, L. K., Houston, M. B., Evans, K. R., & Gopalakrishna, S. (2007). Use of relationship marketing programs in building customer–salesperson and customer–firm relationships: Differential influences on financial outcomes. *International Journal of Research in Marketing*, *24*(3), 210–223. doi:10.1016/j.ijresmar.2006.12.006

Persson, N. (2010). An exploratory investigation of the elements of B2B brand image and its relationship to price premium. *Industrial Marketing Management*, *39*(8), 1269–1277. doi:10.1016/j.indmarman.2010.02.024

Rauyruen, P., & Miller, K. E. (2007). Relationship quality as a predictor of B2B customer loyalty. *Journal of Business Research*, *60*(1), 21–31. doi:10.1016/j.jbusres.2005.11.006

Saab, A. B., & Botelho, D. (2020). Are organizational buyers rational? Using price heuristics in functional risk judgment. *Industrial Marketing Management*, *85*, 141–151. doi:10.1016/j.indmarman.2019.10.001

Saunders, M. N. K., Lewis, P., & Thornhill, A. (2009). *Research methods for business students* (5th ed.). Financial Times/Prentice Hall.

Singh, R., & Koshy, A. (2011). Does salesperson's customer orientation create value in B2B relationships? Empirical evidence from India. *Industrial Marketing Management*, *40*(1), 78–85. doi:10.1016/j.indmarman.2010.09.012

Töytäri, P., Rajala, R., & Alejandro, T. B. (2015). Organizational and institutional barriers to value-based pricing in industrial relationships. *Industrial Marketing Management*, *47*, 53–64. doi:10.1016/j.indmarman.2015.02.005

Veloutsou, C., & Taylor, C. S. (2012). The role of the brand as a person in business-to-business brands. *Industrial Marketing Management*, *41*(6), 898–907. doi:10.1016/j.indmarman.2012.02.004

Wang, B. L., Tian, H. Y., & Chen, X. L. (2010). The study on customer relationship management of B2B enterprise based on the brand promise of customer perception. *2010 International Conference on E-Product E-Service and E-Entertainment*. 10.1109/ICEEE.2010.5660795

Wang, G., Wang, X., Long, Y., Hou, W. C., & Ching, L. A. (2015). Buyer Loyalty in Business Markets: Can the Firm and Salesperson Get What They Truly Desire? *Journal of Business-To-Business Marketing*, *22*(3), 197–210. doi:10.1080/1051712X.2015.1081018

Wang, L., Jin, J. L., & Zhou, K. Z. (2019). Institutional forces and customer participation in new product development: A Yin-Yang perspective. *Industrial Marketing Management*, *82*, 188–198. doi:10.1016/j.indmarman.2019.01.015

Wouters, J. P. M. (2004). Customer service strategy options: A multiple case study in a B2B setting. *Industrial Marketing Management*, *33*(7), 583–592. doi:10.1016/j.indmarman.2003.12.003

Zablah, A. R., Brown, B. P., & Donthu, N. (2010). The relative importance of brands in modified rebuy purchase situations. *International Journal of Research in Marketing*, *27*(3), 248–260. doi:10.1016/j.ijresmar.2010.02.005

Zolkiewski, J., Tyler, K., Lewis, B., Yuan, F., & Yuan, J. (2007). An assessment of customer service in business-to-business relationships. *Journal of Services Marketing*, *21*(5), 313–325. doi:10.1108/08876040710773624

ADDITIONAL READING

Ansermet, F. (2019). Défis contemporains éthiques et cliniques des biotechnologies de la procréation, du genre et de la prédiction. *Neuropsychiatrie de l'Enfance et de l'Adolescence*, *67*(4), 189–193. doi:10.1016/j.neurenf.2019.03.005

Belaisch-Allart, J., & Buxeraud, J. (2017). Assistance médicale à la procréation, techniques et protocoles. *Actualites Pharmaceutiques*, *56*(570), 29–36. doi:10.1016/j.actpha.2017.09.007

Gaumont-Prat, H. (2014). La réflexion du Comité consultatif national d'éthique sur la procréation médicalement assistée. *Médecine & Droit*, *2014*(125), 29–33. doi:10.1016/j.meddro.2013.10.006

Panagiotopoulou, N. (2013). Ethics on procreation: Does everyone have the right to found a family? *Clinical Ethics*, *8*(2-3), 44–46. doi:10.1177/1477750913486243

KEY TERMS AND DEFINITIONS

Brand: Noun of a product which can be distinguished by a brand name or by a design; the trademarked of a product; the personality and visual identity given to a name.

Loyalty: Repeatedly buying the same brand or using the same shop, company, or brand; commitment to continue buying from a company based on the benefits received from it.

Price: Cash which must be given to buy something; the value of a product or a service; price is one of the components of the value placed on what is exchanged between a provider and a customer.

Product: An object or something which is made or fabricated; tangible, physical entities that increase people's or organizations utility; a product can be an idea, a service, a good, an organization, information, an event, a place, or a combination of these.

Salesperson: A person who sells goods or services to members of the public or to retailers or other intermediaries on behalf of a company; performs sales activities, service to customers activities and information providing activities.

Satisfaction: A good feeling of happiness and contentment; how pleased customers are with a company products, services, and capabilities.

Service: Benefits which are sold to customers or clients; generic characteristics of services differentiate them from products, such as: intangibility, inseparability, heterogeneity, and perishability.

Training: Set of specific knowledge that is taught or acquired; teaching or learning a certain action or practice.

Chapter 2
Economic Profit vs. Social Benefit:
An Approach to the Pharmaceutical Industry

M. Mercedes Galán-Ladero
University of Extremadura, Spain

M. Ángeles Galán-Ladero
Hospital Universitario Virgen de Valme, Andalusian Health Service, Spain

ABSTRACT

There is currently a wide-ranging debate on whether it is ethical for pharmaceutical companies to profit and obtain large economic benefits by patenting and controlling the sale of essential medicines that can save thousands of lives, or, on the contrary, whether these medicines should be considered social products and offered at low prices so that anyone, in any country in the world, regardless of their purchasing power, can have access to them. This debate has intensified since health was considered a fundamental human right by the World Health Organization (WHO) and was expressly included in the Sustainable Development Goals (SDGs) adopted by the United Nations (specifically, in Goal 3: "Health and Well-Being"). Consequently, the overall objective of this chapter is to reflect on these questions: Should economic interests prevail over social ones in the case of essential life-saving medicines? Should the fundamental right to health prevail over the right granted by a patent? How far should corporate social responsibility (CSR) go in the pharmaceutical industry?

DOI: 10.4018/978-1-7998-7263-4.ch002

INTRODUCTION

There is currently a wide-ranging debate on whether it is ethical, for pharmaceutical companies, to profit and obtain large economic benefits by patenting and controlling the sale of essential medicines that can save thousands of lives; or, on the contrary, these medicines should be considered social products and offered at low prices so that anyone, in any country in the world, regardless of their purchasing power, can have access to them.

This debate has intensified since health was considered a fundamental Human Right by the World Health Organization (WHO) and was expressly included in the Sustainable Development Goals (SDGs) adopted by the United Nations (specifically, in Goal 3 - "*Health and Well-being*").

On the one hand, it must be recognized that pharmaceutical companies invest large amounts of money in research and development (R&D), in an environment of great uncertainty. For months, and even years, they invest in research, but nothing guarantees that they will finally find an optimal new drug, and before any other company. The patent is a stimulus for these companies, because it protects them from possible "copies" and allows them to recover this investment, guaranteeing them a monopoly on their product for a certain period of time.

Thus, for example, there was a race against time to find a vaccine against COVID-19 in 2020. Pharmaceutical companies spared no effort, investing enormous resources to be the first to obtain the long-awaited vaccine, so wanted worldwide.

As companies, their objectives are to be profitable, to offer more value to their shareholders, to reinforce their corporate image, as well as to consolidate their position in international markets by offering a unique, essential, or even "revolutionary" product to deal with a certain disease.

However, on the other hand, ethics comes into play. Focusing only on the economic benefit provided by a patent, by setting a price that maximizes profits for the company that takes advantage of its monopoly situation (thus controlling the supply of that product on the market), can make that price too high in some developing countries, where the majority of the population does not have sufficient purchasing power to have access to drugs. Thus, diseases that could be treated and cured with these drugs continue to ravage the populations of these countries.

In this sense, some non-governmental organizations (NGOs) demand low prices for certain drugs that could save many lives, and they consider that these drugs should be declared social products. But this would imply that pharmaceutical companies should then receive public and/or private funds on a continuous and regulated basis, so that their existence would last over time and, even if lower economic profits, or even losses, were generated, these private companies would not be affected by this (as they would then cease to be attractive to their investors). Only in this way would social benefit prevail and the desired SDG 3 ("*Good Health and Well-Being: ensuring healthy lives and promoting well-being at all ages*") could be achieved.

An example of this has been observed with the COVID-19 vaccines. The financial effort made had not been known before. Due to the emergency situation, governments have urgently tried to find a solution to the COVID-19 pandemic by investing €7.2 billion in different projects, while non-profit organizations (NPOs) have contributed €1.6 billion, and private investment from companies has been €2.8 billion (Hooker & Palumbo, 2020).

Thus, most of the investment to finance the different vaccine projects has come from governments, while private companies have been more reluctant. The reason for this is that, in previous health emergencies, vaccine projects were not very cost-effective (only one or two doses were administered). Thus, only diseases that remain over time, such as influenza, could be profitable for companies (Hooker & Palumbo, 2020).

Also supranational organizations, such as the European Commission, "in order to reduce the risks of pharmaceutical companies, and accelerate and increase the production of vaccines, financed part of the initial costs incurred by vaccine producers under the Emergency Support Instrument (this financing was considered as a payment on account of the vaccines that the Member States would actually buy). In addition, it provided additional support through loans from the European Investment Bank" (European Commission, 2020).

However, in the face of so much external funding, the debate has also arisen in this case: Should pharmaceutical companies cover only costs, as AstraZeneca (US$4 per dose) and Johnson & Johnson have announced, or should they make a profit, as Moderna (US$37 per dose)?

Also the US announcement to support the temporary suspension of patents on COVID-19 vaccines[1] (on May 5, 2021), to boost the production and distribution of vaccines worldwide (Borger, 2021), and which should subsequently be approved by the World Trade Organization - WTO, caused the shares of US pharmaceutical companies to fall sharply (that day, Moderna's share value fell by 10%, while Novavax fell by 9% and BioNTech, by 6% - Pardo & Rios, 2021). The announcement was quickly welcomed by the World Health Organization - WHO, and emerging countries, as well as by numerous humanitarian aid organizations; on the contrary, it was not to the liking of the pharmaceutical industry.

In any case, the temporary suspension of patents against COVID-19 is a highly controversial measure because, although in theory the waiver of intellectual property rights would allow developing countries to manufacture their own vaccines, it could also act as a disincentive to the development of new vaccines, it could also discourage drug research against COVID-19, and would not lead to rapid immunization of countries such as India, which at that time (May, 2021) were suffering a dramatic situation due to the pandemic (Pardo & Rios, 2021), with alarming rates of infections (Woodward, 2021).

Consequently, the general objective of this chapter is to reflect on these questions: Should economic interests prevail over social interests, in the case of essential drugs that can save lives? Should the fundamental right to health prevail over the right granted by a patent? How far should Corporate Social Responsibility (CSR) go in the pharmaceutical industry? And the specific objectives would be the following:

1. To describe the current situation regarding patents and drug control, which affects access to medicines and provokes debate between "right to health" vs. "right to patent".
2. To analyze the role of the main actors in this situation: pharmaceutical industry, governments, and NGOs:
    a. To study the scope of CSR in the pharmaceutical industry and the ethical issues that arise in this sector.
    b. To find out how Governments can intervene to guarantee access to essential medicines.
    c. To learn how NGOs are pushing to ensure universal access to essential drugs.
3. To reflect on which interests (economic vs. social) should prevail in the case of essential medicines that can save many lives.
4. To analyze the case of the NGO "Doctors Without Borders" ("Médecins Sans Frontières" - MSF) and its *Access Campaign* (and, specifically, its campaign to reduce the price of bedaquiline).

The methodology used in this paper has been the search for secondary information on the issue of drug prices and the analysis of the MSF case, also based on secondary sources (MSF's official website, and published academic articles on this subject). The result has been a reflection on the ethical debate created by the price of medicines.

ACCESS TO MEDICINES: RIGHT TO HEALTH VS. RIGHT TO PATENT

Medicines are essential to seek the maximum degree of health, and they have an impact on the quality of life of the population (Spinelli, 2015). However, access to medicines is sometimes very difficult, if not impossible, especially in developing countries, where it has become one of the main public health problems (Spinelli, 2015).

Access to medicines is determined by the following conditions (Caro, 2020; Spinelli, 2015; URMED, 2015; WHO, 2021):

- **Opportunity:** The medicine should be in due time and form to act correctly in the evolution of the disease.
- **Quality:** The drug should meet minimum quality standards, approved by the health authorities. Its characteristics (composition, stability, etc.) must be maintained over time (until its expiration date), in all units manufactured. The quality assurance system must ensure their *safety*. That is, the therapeutic benefits obtained with the application of the doses supplied outweigh the possible risk of their use (adverse effects, contraindications, etc.).
- **Quantity:** There must be a sufficient number of units of the drug to supply the demand (*drug availability*).
- **Efficacy / Effectiveness:** The drug should achieve the desired effects (to cure a certain disease). Both terms measure the ability of an individual, in a defined population, to benefit from a particular drug that solves a health problem:
    - Determined under ideal conditions of performance (*efficacy*) – it is usually established experimentally and has universal validity.
    - Under real conditions (*effectiveness*) - not universally applicable.

It is not possible to measure the effectiveness of a drug without first measuring its efficacy.

- **Efficiency:** The drug should reach the desired objective (to cure a certain disease) with the least amount of resources required (e.g. lowest monetary and non-monetary cost).
- **Cost:** The price of the drug must allow it to be obtained without affecting the users' living conditions. Cost is often the main limit or barrier to access to medicines in developing countries. The high price of patent-protected medicines "has become an almost insurmountable barrier for citizens of developing countries to access essential, new, and quality medicines" (Ortega, 2016).
- **The level of information:** It must be adequate and understandable for users, updated, accurate, and unbiased.

Difficulties in accessing medicines have led to a broad legal debate on the right to health versus right to patent:

- Right to health

Health is considered a "fundamental right of every human being" (Spinelli, 2015: 83) and "universal access to quality medical care and essential medicines should be promoted" (according to the Universal Declaration on Bioethics and Human Rights; in Spinelli, 2015: 83).

Medicines are essential products for health. They have a "direct link with individual and social well-being through their influence on health" (Spinelli, 2015, p. 84), and have an impact on people's quality of life. For this reason, "universal access to safe, effective, quality, and affordable medicines and vaccines is one of the goals of the SDGs, and the objective is to achieve universal health coverage" (OHCHR, 2015).

But not in all countries do people have the same opportunity to access medicines. According to the WHO, in 2015 only two-thirds of the population in developing countries had any access to essential medicines. In other words, more than 2 billion people do not have access to essential medicines for reasons such as (OHCHR, 2015): patents, lack of funding, weak or non-existent health systems, poverty, inequality, or discrimination, among others.

However, access to medicines is an issue related to public health, social justice, and international obligations in matters of human rights (OHCHR, 2015), so they should be affordable, acceptable, accessible, of quality, and available.

- Right to patent

A patent is defined as "a title granted by the State that gives its holder the right to temporarily prevent others from manufacturing, selling, or commercially using the protected invention" (OEPM, 2020); that is, "it is an exclusive right for the economic exploitation of an invention" (Spinelli, 2015, p. 87). Patents protect industrial property and, in the case of the pharmaceutical sector, "stimulate research and development of new treatments that improve the quality of life" (Spinelli, 2015, p. 83).

In this way, patents establish exploitation monopolies - for 20 years[2], from the date of their presentation (OEPM, 2020, p. 3) -, which affect the price of the product and prevent competition. After that time, the invention is in the public domain and anyone can use it freely (OEPM, 2020, p. 4).

Patents must be registered in all countries where they want to be commercialized (OEPM, 2020: 18). In those countries where the invention is not protected, it is considered to be in the public domain, and anyone can freely exploit it (OEPM, 2020, p. 18).

In the case of the pharmaceutical industry, during the period of validity of a patent, the holder company enjoys the exclusive right to "manufacture the drug, market it, license it, import it, and export it" (Spinelli, 2015, p. 85). This situation can cause difficulties in access to certain drugs, especially in developing countries.

An additional problem arises with the so-called "evergreening" of a patent, "a tactic used by pharmaceutical companies to extend their drug monopolies beyond the standard 20-year period, by registering a new form, presentation or use, which does not provide therapeutic improvements" (MSF, 2019). These patents, also called "secondary patents", "satellite patents", or even "perennial or imperishable patents", "do not describe a new molecule or chemical product, but a new presentation of the drug, tablets, or drops, or a new dosage" and, when they manage to be registered, although they do not increase the effectiveness of these drugs, "they block or delay competition in the markets" (Spinelli, 2015, p. 85).

The result of this debate between which right should prevail, whether the right to health, or the right to patent, has been that "the right of access to medicines is necessarily placed in a higher legal sphere than the patent right, since the legal good protected is a higher good (life, health) than the property right that the patent holder has over a specific invention" (Ortega, 2016, p. 30).

THE PHARMACEUTICAL INDUSTRY. ITS CORPORATE SOCIAL RESPONSIBILITY

The pharmaceutical industry, made up of drug research, production, and marketing oligopolies, is characterized by (Spinelli, 2015, pp. 82-87):

- High innovation costs: high R&D costs and the need for multiple clinical trials.
- The need for highly qualified professionals.
- Recovery of investment in a limited period of time: pharmaceutical companies have a limited period to recover R&D&I expenses, including the cost of compounds that did not reach their aim, and before other companies start producing the same drug or discover new uses. Also the costs of advertising and sales promotion to reinforce their brands.
- Demand is inelastic: price variations do not affect demand (especially when there are no substitute treatments or drugs, or pharmaceutical companies control supply – their production and marketing).
- Regulations on the production, use and innovation of drugs are mainly governed by the standards established by the World Trade Organization (WTO) and not by the World Health Organization (WHO), which implies that drugs are considered a market good and not a social good.

The pharmaceutical sector, "by its very essence and main activity related to health, influences the quality of life of society" (SINC, 2009). Hence, CSR is (or should be) a fundamental part of the business strategy in pharmaceutical companies. Thus, some examples of CSR actions for pharmaceutical companies include (Langa, 2020):

- To promote healthy habits and attitudes that help prevent the development of diseases.
- To develop programs that promote the inclusion of people diagnosed with a particular disease.
- To train social-health professionals (by organizing conferences, workshops, training classrooms, etc.).
- To promote sustainability (reducing polluting emissions, promoting the implementation of renewable energies, constructing intelligent buildings, etc.), improving resource management, and reducing environmental impact.
- To develop new drugs or research streams (creating training centers, scholarships for social and health professionals to develop projects that benefit health).
- To raise awareness: to give visibility to people suffering from diseases and destigmatize pathologies.
- To humanize: to create play areas for children in hospitals.
- Etc.

However, despite this type of initiatives, the criticism of the pharmaceutical sector has been, and still is, very important. One of them particularly focuses on the price of drugs, especially those that are essential for health and which, due to their high price, are a luxury for millions of people, being out of their reach.

Pharmaceutical companies "are co-responsible, with the States, for guaranteeing and satisfying the right to health, making medicines accessible, affordable, in the shortest possible time and in sufficient quantity; however, they have no legal obligation to ensure compliance with the human right to medicines" (Ortega, 2016, p. 28). But if they really assume their CSR, they should do so.

Thus, companies such as Glaxo Smith Kline (GSK), have opted to register patents and obtain full protection of their inventions only in developed countries, adopting alternative formulas in countries with development problems (Ortega, 2016, p. 31). Gilead has also chosen to establish differentiated prices for drugs depending on the countries for which they are intended (offering a lower price in developing countries). However, there is still a long way to go.

THE ROLE OF STATES

States are responsible for protecting and implementing the right to health of their population, so "they should allocate the necessary public resources available for the procurement of essential medicines" (Ortega, 2016, p. 27). Consequently, States should implement policies that ensure the availability of and access to medicines (Spinelli, 2015, p. 83), creating efficient systems for their supply and distribution (WHO, 2021).

In some cases, the intervention of the States is proposed as the only way to generate competition in developing countries and thus, obtain generic drugs that allow a reduction in price, but maintaining "the same active principle, concentration, route of administration, and use" (Spinelli, 2015: 88). However, in many developing countries, there is little capacity and/or effort to acquire medicines (Ortega, 2016, p. 25)[3].

The problem of access to medicines could be solved with (Ortega, 2015, pp. 30-32):

- *Compulsory licenses to manufacture or import patented drugs*: they are an important public policy instrument that allows a State to obtain the supply of a specific drug at a lower price than that established by a patent holder or its licensee. It can be used to guarantee the supply of medicines and/or to limit excessive corporate profits. However, in practice, it is rarely applied, because it is a complex and time-consuming process.
- *Generic drugs* (based on licenses voluntarily surrendered by the patent-holding companies).
- *Donations of drugs made by NGOs, by patent-holding companies, or by the International Drug Purchase Mechanism.*
- *Parallel imports*: imports of products traded in other markets at lower prices.
- *Differentiated pricing system*: this would require the involvement of both pharmaceutical companies and States. Thus, for example (Ortega, 2016, p. 36):
- States should strengthen customs controls to prevent possible commercial diversion of drugs at reduced prices destined for developing countries.
- There should also be greater involvement of developed States in favor of technology transfer.
- And there should be greater harmonization of patent rules on a global scale, to create a scenario of greater legal certainty for innovative companies.

NGOs

Some NGOs propose guaranteeing universal accessibility to essential medicines (Spinelli, 2015, p. 83), because medicines are useless if the sick cannot receive them (*"medicines shouldn't be a luxury*" - MSF, 2020 -, drugs should be available to all) – Figure 1.

Figure 1. "Medicines shouldn't be a luxury"
Source: MSF, 2020

Thus, for example, in the European Union, Medicus Mundi has opposed the patent on Gilead's sofosvubir, a new drug for the treatment of viral hepatitis caused by HCV, to the European Patent Office. The rejection of the patent in one State "would open the way to the production of this medicine in the territory of the State in question at a low price and to its commercialization in any country in the world where the patent does not exist" (Ortega, 2016, p. 34).

Doctors Without Borders (MSF) has also questioned the price of medicines for several decades, and has demanded affordable access to life-saving drugs, fighting to prioritize people's health and transparency in R&D over the economic benefits of pharmaceutical companies.

In this regard, MSF's criticisms of the pharmaceutical industry have focused, above all, on (MSF, 2019):

1. *R&D costs:* MSF considers them exaggerated (according to its estimates, medicines cost 10 times less than what pharmaceutical companies indicate, so MSF believes that they include expenses that are not related to R&D&I).
2. *The price of medicines:* MSF denounces that pharmaceutical companies take advantage of research done by public and university laboratories, financed with public funds and taxes paid by citizens, and receive tax credits and financial incentives to reduce their R&D investment risk. But then, they privatize and patent the resulting drugs, marketing them under monopoly conditions. In the end, they charge high prices to both governments and citizens - the taxpayers.
3. *More development than research and innovation:* MSF also points out that pharmaceutical companies focus more on developing drugs similar to previous ones, duplicating treatments, rather than investing in discovering real therapeutic breakthroughs[4].
4. *Maintaining patents to prolong monopolies:* MSF denounces the common strategy of pharmaceutical companies to apply for additional patents on small changes made to existing drugs, prolonging their monopoly on specific treatments, and blocking affordable generic drugs.
5. *High profits:* MSF points out that, although the large pharmaceutical companies claim they need high profits in order to invest in R&D&I, they spend more on marketing, sales, and share buybacks to increase their stock market value.
6. *They threaten developing countries if they go against their interests:* MSF denounces that large pharmaceuticals pressure and take oppressive legal action against developing countries when they prioritize people's health over corporate interests; and they have also tried to influence international trade rules to benefit themselves.

Although in May 2019 the WHO World Assembly passed the resolution for "Improving the transparency of the markets for medicines, vaccines, and other health-related technologies"[5], thus taking a firm and positive first step towards some more affordable medicines for all (MSF, 2019), MSF believes that it is not enough, that the resolution passed lacks strong rules and actions to ensure transparency in key areas. Therefore, there is also a need to know (MSF, 2019):

1. The mark-ups charged by pharmaceutical corporations.
2. The actual costs of production and costs of clinical trials.

3. The percentages of investment by pharmaceutical companies.
4. The percentage of that investment that they cover with public aid, scholarships and subsidies, taxpayer grants, and non-profit initiatives.

Figure 2. MSF global campaign urging Johnson & Johnson to reduce the price of bedaquiline
Source: MSF, 2019

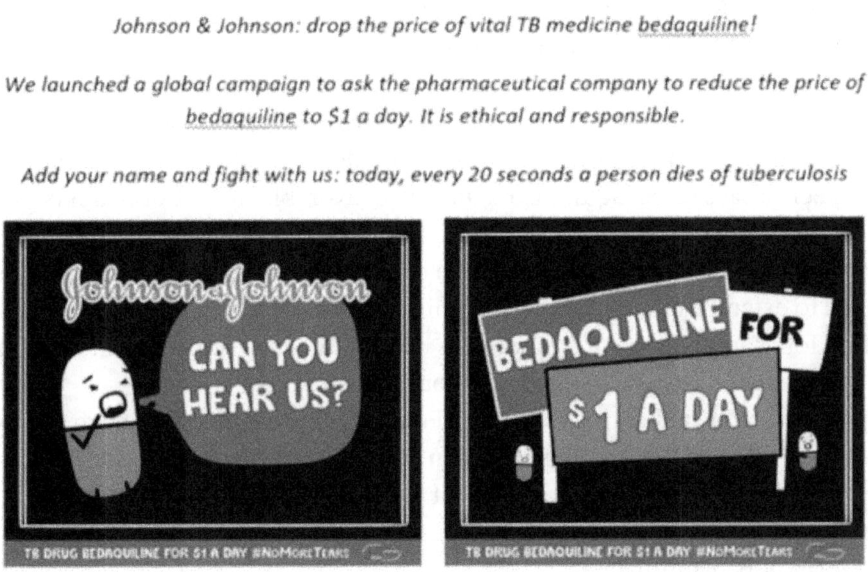

According to MSF (2019), as long as there is no transparency, fair negotiations will not be possible and, therefore, neither will there be fair and affordable prices.

The following is an analysis of MSF's *Access Campaign*, which focuses on the need to lower the price of essential medicines that can save thousands of lives (and, specifically, its 2019 campaign to reduce the price of bedaquiline, a new drug for the treatment of multidrug-resistant tuberculosis).

DOCTORS WITHOUT BORDERS (MSF) CAMPAIGN TO REDUCE THE PRICE OF BEDAQUILINE

Doctors Without Borders (MSF) is one of the leading international NGOs working in the medical and humanitarian field. It is currently the largest non-governmental provider of tuberculosis (TB) treatment in the world (MSF, 2020).

This NGO has been dedicated to TB care for three decades (MSF, 2020). And, since bedaquiline came onto the market in 2012, it has urged Johnson & Johnson, the pharmaceutical company that owns the patent on this drug, to lower its price. But on October 9, 2019, MSF launched a global campaign (Figure 2) to request Johnson & Johnson to allow the disposal of bedaquiline, as well as a reduction in its price.

Bedaquiline is a new drug in the fight against multidrug-resistant tuberculosis. In 2018, it was recommended by the World Health Organization (WHO) as a central part of an all-oral treatment for multidrug-resistant tuberculosis[6].

According to MSF (2019), bedaquiline is a safer drug than traditional medicines and improves cure rates for multidrug-resistant tuberculosis, so it could save thousands of lives, in addition to reducing the suffering of the sick. A 2019 study conducted by MSF and its collaborators in 17 countries revealed that people treated with the newest oral drugs for multidrug-resistant tuberculosis achieved 77.6% success rate. In the specific case of bedaquiline, results were favorable in 72% of patients treated with this drug (MSF, 2020).

But the patent on this drug is protected until 2023, although Johnson & Johnson intended to extend its monopoly on the saline form of bedaquiline (if it were finally granted, Johnson & Johnson's monopoly on bedaquiline would be extended until 2027, delaying the entry of generics by four more years).

Therefore, MSF had also supported, in February 2019, the action of two surviving TB activists who tried to challenge Johnson & Johnson's patent at the Bombay Patent Office (India), as they did not consider it fair that this company had a monopoly on this key drug in the TB treatment and, in addition, intended to extend it on the saline form of bedaquiline.

With this campaign, MSF wanted to give visibility and intensify its pressure so that essential medicines, in this case bedaquiline, with a high price that is an insurmountable barrier for many countries, are marketed in a cheap and accessible way to reach all patients with this disease (there are millions of TB patients around the world).

Anti-TB activists, volunteers and members of civil society joined the protests organized in front of Johnson & Johnson offices in the United States, South Africa, Brazil, Belgium, and Spain, to demand that the pharmaceutical company make the drug available to patients for a maximum of US$ 1 A day. They also protested in front of the New York Stock Exchange. Until then, MSF estimated that 80% of patients who needed it could not access it (MSF, 2019). In total, 120,707 people joined this campaign and signed the demand for Johnson & Johnson to lower the price (MSF, 2020).

In July 2020, J&J announced a price reduction to $400 for 6 months of bedaquiline treatment for South Africa and countries purchasing the drug through the Global Drug Facility (the World Drug Service). That is, at 1.5 dollars per day.

Figure 3. MSF global campaign
Source: MSF, 2020

However, MSF believes that the development of this drug is not so expensive[7] and that this decrease is not enough to make the drug affordable in all countries (as bedaquiline is only one of multiple drugs needed in a TB treatment regimen). Therefore, it continues to demand and maintain its initial request for a maximum price of US$1 per day.

In addition, this request to Johnson & Johnson is also based on the fact that the development of bedaquiline was not carried out by this pharmaceutical company alone, but rather benefited from considerable public investment in different countries (including grants from the US government and various financial incentives) and donations from non-profit and philanthropic institutions, for R&D. Much of the fundamental work to substantiate the drug use and demonstrate its therapeutic value, the evidence of its potential to improve cure rates with fewer side effects, was the result of a collective effort by the global community working on and researching TB (organizations such as MSF also contributed to drug research) - MSF (2020). However, only Johnson & Johnson holds the patent for the drug in many countries and has the exclusive right to determine in which countries the drug will be sold. Therefore, MSF (2019) affirms that "Johnson & Johnson should not charge high prices for this drug anywhere, and should provide access to more people ... Johnson

& Johnson should not be the sole decision-maker regarding who has access to the medicine ... " – Figure 3.

And as in the face of the current COVID-19 pandemic the WHO has advised countries to treat people affected by multidrug-resistant tuberculosis with all-oral regimens (including bedaquiline) so that they are safe at home and do not have to travel to medical centers for injections, the issue of the price of this drug is back in the spotlight.

At this time, MSF continues to work to (MSF, 2020):

- Overcome the patent barriers to this drug and ensure the entry of multiple producers as a long-term solution for access to an affordable bedaquiline.
- Urge the Indian Government to revoke the patent and encourage its TB drug manufacturers to supply bedaquiline for its national TB program by granting a 'compulsory license', as multi-resistant TB is a public health emergency.

MSF proposes that "this can be an effective way to eventually overcome patent barriers to access vital healthcare products. Likewise, other countries could follow in their wake and use the high price as a basis for issuing compulsory licenses as well" (MSF, 2020).

In short, the exorbitant prices of some essential medicines threaten the sustainability of health systems and place severe constraints on patients' access to treatment (MSF, 2020). For this reason, this NGO proposes that governments seek a different model than the current one (based on a monopoly regime) for medicines, which (MSF, 2020):

- Develop more tailored processes to support the researchers' work.
- Cultivate fair collaborations with private organizations for real needs-oriented R&D&I and provide effective medicines at sustainable and affordable prices for health systems.
- Set a price (for medicines) that reflects the collective effort (public and private funding included).
- Review the current "incentives" that exist for the pharmaceutical industry, which condition and motivate its participation in R&D&I.
- Apply mechanisms based on an antitrust system, to support and finance R&D&I adapted to people's real needs.

With the COVID-19 pandemic, MSF has updated its *Access Campaign*, calling for "lives over profit", and "No Patents, No Monopolies in a Pandemic" – Figure 4.

Figure 4. "Lives over Profit"
Source: MSF, 2021

CONCLUSION

The main conclusions or final reflections of this work would be the following:

- The right to health is a fundamental right, and should prevail over the right to patent, at least in the case of essential drugs. For this reason, these drugs should be declared social products and access to them should be universal. In other words, social interests should prevail over purely economic ones if the United Nations Sustainable Development Goal 3 (*Health and Well-being*) is really wanted to be achieved, and the fundamental human right to health is respected.
- The fight against certain diseases (including multidrug-resistant tuberculosis) requires the collaboration and joint effort of the entire world community: international organizations, the pharmaceutical industry, governments, universities and research institutes, non-profit organizations (Foundations, NGOs, etc.).
- Pharmaceutical companies are businesses and, therefore, they are for-profit organizations. However, due to the peculiarities of the products they market (medicines that save lives), they should integrate social responsibility into their core business strategy. In addition, they should work closely with governments to preserve the population's health and quality of life.

- Government authorities should become more involved, improving the existing specific regulation for drug patents and their control, as well as creating efficient health systems so that all citizens can access and be covered by them.
- International organizations, led by WHO, should continue to insist on prioritizing international health coverage, collaborating and advising Member States to develop efficient and sustainable national health systems and policies; facilitating access to effective, safe, affordable technologies and drugs; promoting and maintaining access to prevention, treatment and care of certain diseases, as well as reducing vaccine-preventable diseases.
- NGOs must remain vigilant, informing, raising awareness, and reminding that the right to health and life should take precedence over any purely economic interest, in any country in the world, developed or not. Their role is therefore essential in trying to achieve SDG 3.
- Universities and Research Institutes must also assume their social responsibility and take care of their commitment to society through the transfer of knowledge, contributing to sustainable development, and improving people's quality of life.

Ultimately, only with close collaboration between all stakeholders will it be possible to achieve SDG 3 and, as stated by MSF (2020), "*medicines shouldn't be a luxury*".

REFERENCES

Borger, J. (2021). US declares support for patent waiver on COVID-19 vaccines. *The Guardian*. https://www.theguardian.com/world/2021/may/05/us-declares-support-for-patent-waiver-on-covid-19-vaccines

Caro, F. C. (2020). *La calidad del medicamento*. Revista Panacea. http://www.revistapanacea.com/la-calidad-del-medicamento/

Carrasco, L. (2020). *¿Quién ha financiado las vacunas contra la covid?* VozPopuli Sanitatem, 16/12/2020. https://www.vozpopuli.com/sanidad/financiacion-vacunas-covid-pfizer-moderna-oxford_0_1419758359.html

European Commission. (2020). *Official Website*. https://ec.europa.eu

Galán-Ladero, M. M., & Galán-Ladero, M. Á. (2020). La Responsabilidad Social Corporativa (RSC) de las Empresas Farmacéuticas: Beneficio Económico vs. Beneficio Social. *II Congreso AIMPN-LATAM – II Congreso Latinoamericano de Marketing Social.*

Hooker, L., & Palumbo, D. (2020). Cuánto dinero pueden ganar realmente las farmacéuticas con la vacuna contra la covid-19. *BBC News Mundo*. https://www.bbc.com

Langa, C. (2020). *Ejemplos de acciones de RSC para empresas farmacéuticas*. https://www.cicerocomunicacion.es/rsc-empresas-farmaceuticas/

Médicos Sin Fronteras. (2019). *Tuberculosis: reducir el precio de la bedaquilina salvaría miles de vidas y reduciría el inmenso sufrimiento de los enfermos*. https://www.msf.es/actualidad/sudafrica/tuberculosis-reducir-precio-la-bedaquilina-salvaria-miles-vidas-y-reduciria

Médicos Sin Fronteras. (2020). *Official Website*. https://www.msf.es

Médicos Sin Fronteras. (2021). *Lives over Profit*. https://www.msf.es

Oficina del Alto Comisionado para los Derechos Humanos - OHCHR. Naciones Unidas (2015). *Acceso a los medicamentos en el contexto del derecho a la salud*. https://www.ohchr.org

Oficina Española de Patentes y Marcas - OEPM. (2020). *Cuestiones básicas acerca de Patentes y Modelos de Utilidad*. https://www.oepm.es

Ortega-Gómez, M. (2016). El derecho de acceso a los medicamentos y el derecho de patente en países en desarrollo. *Revista de Bioetica y Derecho*, *37*, 23–36.

Pardo, P., & Ríos, B. (2021). EE.UU. apoya suspender las patentes contra el COVID-19 y las acciones de las farmacéuticas se desploman. *El Mundo*. https://www.elmundo.es/economia/2021/05/06/609333cffc6c83a5378b464d.html

SINC. (2009). *La responsabilidad social de la industria farmacéutica no es reconocida por la sociedad, según un estudio*. https://www.agenciasinc.es/Noticias/La-responsabilidad-social-de-la-industria-farmaceutica-no-es-reconocida-por-la-sociedad-segun-un-estudio

Soto-Vázquez, R., Parra-Cervantes, P., & Juárez-López, R. (2015). ¿Qué sabe usted acerca de propiedad intelectual farmacéutica? *Revista Mexicana de Ciencias Farmacéuticas*, *46*(1), 77–79.

Spinelli, S. L. (2015). Acceso a los medicamentos: Las patentes y los medicamentos genéricos. Las consecuencias de considerar al medicamento como un bien de mercado y no social. *Revista de Bioetica y Derecho*, *34*, 81–89.

United Nations. (2021). *Sustainable Development Goals*. https://sdgs.un.org/es/goals

URMED. (2015). *Eficacia y efectividad de un fármaco*. https://urmed.wordpress.com/2015/09/27/eficacia-y-efectividad-de-un-farmaco/

Woodward, A. (2021). US announces support for patent waiver on Covid vaccines. *Independent*. https://www.independent.co.uk/news/world/americas/us-politics/biden-covid-vaccine-patent-waiver-b1842731.html

World Health Organization. (2021). *Official Website*. https://www.who.int

KEY TERMS AND DEFINITIONS

Bedaquiline: A drug used to treat people with multidrug-resistant tuberculosis. It has been recommended by the WHO to treat this disease.

Essential Medicine (or Essential Drug): Key product for the cure of a specific disease. It can save thousands of lives. According to WHO, a drug is considered essential when it meets the priority health care needs of the population. Consequently, an essential medicine is selected because of its public health relevance, evidence on its efficacy and safety, and its comparative cost-effectiveness.

MSF (Médecins Sans Frontières – Doctors Without Borders): A recognized and leading international non-profit organization that works in the medical and humanitarian field.

Patent: A right granted by the State to the inventor of a new product, thus protecting industrial property. The registration of a patent allows its holder to create a temporary monopoly situation for the commercialization of this product, in exchange for the disclosure of the invention.

Pharmaceutical Industry: Sector of economic activity made up of companies engaged in the research, manufacture, and marketing of products that can prevent, treat, and cure diseases, thus improving people's quality of life.

SDGs – Sustainable Development Goals: Objectives adopted by the United Nations to give continuity to the development agenda arising from the Millennium Development Goals. They are 17 goals, applicable to all countries (developed, developing, and underdeveloped).

WHO – World Health Organization: International organization within the United Nations focused on the management of health prevention, promotion, and intervention policies at a global level. Its commitment is to "achieve better health for everyone, everywhere".

ENDNOTES

1 India and South Africa had been backing a waiver proposal since October 2020, with the support of a hundred emerging economies, and humanitarian aid organizations (Woodward, 2021). But, at the same time, wealthy countries had been blocking the debate on this issue at the WTO's Trade-Related Aspects of Intellectual Property Rights (Trips) council (Borger, 2021). At the time of closing this case study (May 6, 2021), the European Union and Switzerland were still resisting to a patent waiver. And G7 called for "greater funding for a UN-administered distribution scheme, Covax, and for voluntary licensing and technology transfer agreement" (Borger, 2021).

2 However, in Spain, in the case of patents for pharmaceutical products, Complementary Protection Certificates can be applied for. These extend, for a maximum period of 5 years, the protection conferred to the products sold once the patents have expired. (OEPM, 2020: 4).

3 However, in relative terms, "pharmaceutical products represent between 15% and 30% of healthcare spending in countries with economies in transition, and between 25% and 66% in developing countries" (WHO, 2020).

4 According to MSF, two thirds of the new drugs coming onto the market are no better than the existing ones (they are similar, they do not represent a real therapeutic advance).

5 However, countries such as Germany, Hungary, and the United Kingdom formally disassociated themselves from the adopted resolution, and others such as the United States and Japan did not accept the previous draft, which had to be modified (deleting the most controversial points). The previous draft addressed four areas in which transparency was necessary and urgent (MSF, 2019): R&D&I, the cost of clinical trials, the duration of drug patents, and the real prices at which they are sold. The resolution passed was the result of the historic mobilization of governments around the world, which demanded "*improved transparency in the markets for medicines, vaccines, and other health-related technologies*" (MSF, 2019). This is a positive first step towards correcting the imbalance of power that currently exists during negotiations between buyers and sellers of medicines. Thanks to this resolution, governments will have the information they need to negotiate fairly and responsibly for the medicines they need to fight for the health of their citizens (MSF, 2019).

6 The oldest and longest-lasting standard treatment for multidrug-resistant tuberculosis used by many countries to date, required patients to take up to 20 pills a day (up to 14,000 pills over the course of nearly two years), and endure up to eight months of painful daily injections (MSF, 2020). Side effects were severe (e.g. psychosis, persistent nausea, and even hearing loss) - MSF (2020).

7 MSF refers to a study conducted by researchers at the University of Liverpool (UK), which showed that bedaquiline could be produced and sold at a profit for as little as US$0.25 per day, if at least 108,000 courses of treatment were sold per year.

Chapter 3
Conflicts of Network Embeddedness in Healthcare Organizations

Márton Vilmányi
University of Szeged, Hungary

Hetesi Erzsébet
University of Szeged, Hungary

Margit Tarjányi
University of Szeged, Hungary

ABSTRACT

This chapter examined the organizations of a university dealing with healthcare and clinical activities operating in an extremely complex network connection. In the framework of qualitative research, with the help of a series of interviews, the authors researched in which networks the university's healthcare organization and organizational units participate, and how participation in these networks influences the value creation implemented in each field. By what means can the organization handle the contradictions and conflicts that arise along the inter-organizational relations embedded in the networks. Interviews were conducted with institution leaders, business leaders, and care workers. Based on the research results, network complexity results in three types of conflicts in healthcare institutions: conflicts related to organizational management, conflicts arising in organizational processes, and personal conflicts.

DOI: 10.4018/978-1-7998-7263-4.ch003

INTRODUCTION

According to the representatives of embeddedness, economic processes are linked to specific social and institutional conditions. For organizations in complex network relationships, the various aspects of social integration pose challenges in which the correct interpretation of decisions, activities and processes creates uncertainties and the resulting sources of error result in conflicts.

In the study, the researchers examine how certain aspects of embeddedness affect conflicts during operation and what patterns can be identified in a special field of organizations operating in complex network relationships, in relation to health and clinical units with university backgrounds.

In the first part of the study, we briefly review the literature background of embeddedness, then conduct qualitative (in-depth) research and present the researchers' results.

THE THEORETICAL BACKGROUND OF THE TOPIC

Health Care as a Complex Network

Organizations are embedded in extremely heterogeneous networks. These networks provide resources, opportunities, and inter-organizational ties (through which resources and opportunities become available); in addition, they provide a position that makes it possible to exploit resources and opportunities (Uzzi, 1996). The extent and multiplexity of inter-organizational relationships determine the value creation, identity, and performance of organizations (Shipilov et al., 2014). This phenomenon is not only observed in business organizations, but also in such non-business areas with complex networks as healthcare (Provan & Sebastian, 1998).

Berry et al. (2004) distinguishes four types of networks in the public sector. Social networks, which describe interpersonal relationships, policy networks which focus on forming and shaping public policies, public management networks which include actors involved in the micro-implementation of a given service and their relationships. Finally, governance networks, which are aimed at coordinating the activities of actors involved in public services. The types and forms of each network are well captured, but their objectives and rules are different. An actor is not only a member of one type of network, but, where appropriate, it is a member of all the networks, which means that this actor in its operation forces the conflicting and parallel management of different logics and rules.

Healthcare-operated markets in themselves constitute a connectivity market, where the functions of the institutions require a multifaceted use of individual units and resources (Launberg, 2011; Wagrell, 2011), however, medical institutions with a university background have a multiplied network embeddedness in addition to the above. They organize their activities and allocate their resources along a number of functions (production, development, use) (Launberg, 2011). Of course, the appearance of individual functions or a combinations of these functions may have a different character in each clinical organizations but along the lines of each function, these organizations operate under the expectations and constraints of countless networks, which forces complex network management (Chakraborty & Dobrzykowski, 2013). Chakraborty and Dobrzykowski (2013) understand the characteristics that go towards this complexity, based on the concept of complexity, according to which complexity (as a complexity) is subjective, its meaning and value formed and changed according to the purpose of the system considered. In their work, they capture five characteristics to characterize the complexity of clinical networks: (1) the number of subsystems, such as the number of networks in which organizations are embedded in the operation; (2) the existence of reciprocal relations between the participants of each network; (3) the volume and frequency of interactions between the clinical organization and the members of the related networks; (4) the quality and nature of the relationships and (5) level of discrimination between actors. This multiple embeddedness results in a number of conflicts among participants.

Social Embeddedness of the Economy - Conceptual Background of Embeddedness

The social embeddedness of organizations is the result of many conflicts, and the nature of conflicts and their management also depend on the context in which they arise, and the social embeddedness of organizations in this sector is decisive. Mapping the complex world of clinical networking networks within universities should not be without touching on the economic sociological issue of social inclusion. The cognitive, cultural, structural and political aspects of the social integration of organizational actions (Dacin et al., 1999; Zukin & DiMaggio, 1990) show an increased presence in the health sector.

The cognitive dimension of social integration draws attention to the fact that there is no perfect rationality, no full information, rational economic decisions are also influenced by mental processes (Tversky & Kahneman, 1991). Decision uncertainties can be found in almost all areas of health care, i.e. rational decisions cannot be made in all situations (Sackett et al., 1996). What factors are present and why are they present in the action decisions of health actors, what motivating factors should be taken into account?

The networked functioning of health care raises several ethical dilemmas. The health network must ensure equal and adequate care for all. It should be maximum effective and minimally harmful and least detrimental to the patient's autonomy. When these ethical standards are viewed from the point of view of three main coordination mechanisms, government, the market and civil society, different stakeholders (by their very nature) approach them differently. The role of government is to ensure that the allocation of resources for health care is equal and fair. At the same time, members of health networks must face economic realities. The role of market mechanisms is to ensure that services are economically sustainable. Finally, health care must not only be equal, fair and sustainable, but also value-based. The latter is provided by the civil society. In short, "government makes health networks fair, the market makes them sustainable and civil society shapes them into value-based" (Raus, 2018, p. 5.). If the balance between the coordination mechanisms is overturned, it will lead to ethical risk and conflict between actors (Raus et al., 2018).

The cultural embeddedness of economic actions is the impact of social values (norms) that shape economic goals and strategies. According to socioeconomics, the two main sources of human action are self-interest and morality: people follow two unrepentable "usefulnesses" and their values and emotions play a role in the choice of their goals and means (Etzioni, 1988). Social values, norms and customs orient people in how they should behave, what is free and what is not in a particular society. The examination of the cultural integration of health is an important issue because there is a greater need for social control here, and if the "homo sociologicus" behaviour does not prevail, the fundamental purpose of healing, the very activity of healing as a basic human need, may be overshadowed (Antal, 2018).

According to structural embeddedness, personal networking influences economic actions and institutions (Granovetter, 1992). Social relations lead to social capital and have an impact on market processes, economic decisions and actions. The health system can be conceivably a system of exchange in a regulated network. In this system, networks operating under different rules and objectives are interconnected, where the relationship between (or within) organizations for the implementation of an activity is always influenced by a third party. In this context, third parties appear as rules or mechanisms laid down or followed by a network of other types (e.g. funders, market participants, operators of other activities). Embeddedness in this context means that the exchange is always influenced by other relationships (Gulati, 1998). Mutually influencing interests encourage stakeholders to seem to follow common interests, but in reality they are solely self-interested. The realization of the activities of each actor is in this way the result of a conflicting process, ultimately influenced by the functioning and dynamics of the whole system. Unique connections in this convoluted network are intertwined and embedded in the environment through the aspects of trust, judgment and discretion (Uzzi, 1996; Yang et al., 2012).

Perhaps it does not require any particular explanation that one of the defining aspects of the social integration of the economy is the political and legal environment in which the organizations and members of a given society are "forced" to make their decisions. The political-legal structure of society, the relations of power, the behavior and values of political actors have a direct impact on the economy. The following dimensions can be seized: power relations, a system of political relations, a legal environment, a legal system, an agreed system of collective bargaining, actors in the state and the political domain. Health organizations operate embedded in a growing network of stakeholders that influence, strengthen or extinguish each other's activities. Individuals, groups or organizations with a contractual, ethical, financial and/or political interest in the decisions or activities of a particular health organization may be considered to be interested in this context. Health organizations therefore face the effects on the organization of the changing and often conflicting interests and objectives of individual stakeholders in their activities (Savage et al., 1997).

The Conflicting Nature of Health Care Networks

Because of their multiple embeddedness, organizations that are wedged into complex networks operate in a rather conflicting way. In a general sense, conflict can be seen as an interactive process that is manifested in incompatibility, disagreement, or dissonance within a social entity or between them (Rahim, 2002). Conflicts can generally arise between subjects for a number of reasons: interests, preferences, a mutually exclusive use of resources, values, forms of behavior, or as a result of colliding interdependent performances (Rahim, 2002).

The best-known segregation of conflicts causes Christopher W. Moore (1996) to separate five types of conflict:

1. **Relationship conflict:** The root causes may be the existence of stereotypes and prejudices in the world of human relationships, as well as communication disorders or negative mechanisms that provoke tension.
2. **Value conflict:** In connection with some kind of life situation, it is due to decision or choice between actors. The source of this is the different values and life perception of individuals, contrast of identities of individuals, which may arise from different external factors such as family background, education, social affiliation, political resolution or other reasons.
3. **Structural conflict:** The most typical feature of such disagreements at organizational and community levels, which mainly generates unequal power, distribution, control conditions, and any other physical and environmental factors that obstruct effective cooperation.
4. **Information Conflict:** Will occur when incorrect information for the parties is available or the information is interpreted differently by actors. In such cases,

that adequate clarification of the information itself can solve the established disagreement.

5. **Interest conflict:** The ostensible or actual conflict of interest between the actors will be placed on the surface and cause conflict. The apparent conflict of interest means that the parties believe that their interests are in contrast to each other, while in the case of actual conflicts of interest, these interests are known to both parties.

According to their effect, it can be distinguished constructive (builder, positive, value creator) and destructive (destroyer, negative) conflicts. In the constructive conflicts, the parties agree on core values and the outcome of their competition will be beneficial for both parties and this process helps to move the actors and to facilitate the harmony between them. The conflict can be considered destructively if due to the behavior of the parties, the willingness to consensus decreases cyclically and the tension between the actors is gradually increasing. At this point, the participants feel that they can only get out of that particular situation at a loss, thereby some damage (Morton et al., 2006).

Conflicts may occur at different levels of human relationships. Based on this, there are intrapersonal conflicts, where the individual is contradicted by its own needs and desires. Interpersonal conflicts are between persons, then arise when the views, desires and needs of at least two or more persons face each other.

In the case of conflicts within the organization, conflicts arise at the individual or group levels, but the conflict of interest itself is primarily relevant to organizational operation. If the opposites are established between the leaders or representatives of the organization, they are considered as conflicts within an organization. Finally, global and international conflicts are examined in the case of different states, peoples and ethnic groups, which are usually related to some social system or religious ideology (Morton et al., 2006).

Thomas-Killman (2018) conflict management model examines the individual's behavior according to two basic dimensions (cooperativeness and assertiveness), as to what kind of behavior will be chosen during a discussion situation. (1) Competitive strategy is assertive and uncooperative—the individual places its own intention to focus on the use of violent tools. (2) Accommodating Strategy is unassertive and cooperative—the complete opposite of competing. An individual waive the validation of their own interests and desires from consideration, fear or constraints, thereby adapting to its partner. (3) Avoiding strategy: is assertive and uncooperative— a commonly used method used by an individual to analyze the situation, qualifying a relationship and to assess chances. (4) Compromise-looking strategy: Search for a satisfactory solution for both parties. It is often used for equal parties, time and opportunities to search for more efficient solutions and have a networking role. (5)

Problem-solving strategy: The parties strive for a solution in which interests and needs of both sides can prevail.

The type and nature of conflicts that arise in clinical organizations are widely researched areas, and it is generally accepted that several levels of these conflicts can be identified. Personal, interpersonal, intragroup and intergroup levels can be differentiated (Rahim, 1985), while some research also add an inter-professional perspective (Mills, 2002), and others include the level of work organization, a clinical or patient care level (Bochatay et al., 2017). Inter-organizational conflict is also frequently identified (Csupor et al. 2017). Researchers provide a number of reasons to explain clinical conflicts that arise between the actors at each level and all of those reasons are linked to complex embeddedness, (Mills, 2002; Bochatay et al., 2017; Csupor et al., 2017; Patton, 2014):

- Personal reasons that come from a lack of respect for and acceptance of each other, or arise from a lack of relationship between the actors;
- Work organization problems that come from not having clear-cut duty boundaries regarding a position, there are different approaches to work methods and techniques relating to professional and other duties, and from overload;
- Resource shortages that come from the need to concurrently use scarcely available resources;
- Cultural differences that come from the differences in values, ethics, religion, gender, and the perception of roles;
- Managerial problems that come from the uncertainty that arises from an unclear allocation of entitlements related to power and authority and unsettled professional and organizational roles within the organization and between levels of an organization; and
- Gaps in sharing information and communication.

There is a general agreement in the literature on the causes of direct conflicts that arise between health care actors/groups, as well as on the means to implement conflict management. At the same time, the varieties of the sources of conflicts that arise in clinical organizations with a university background is an unexplored (or at least not explicitly published) area.

RESEARCH QUESTIONS AND RESEARCH METHOD

In the study, the researchers summarize one of the sub-problems, partial results and experiences of a wider study over several years. In this study, we look for answers to the research problem: *In the case of units (clinics, hospitals) operating as part of universities, what kind of organizational conflicts does complex network embeddedness create?*

During this research, the research unit was reported by a Hungarian university and the highest-level care clinics. In order to answer the research problem, the following questions have been detailed:

1. What is the role of social embeddedness in the operational relationships of healthcare organizations?
2. What kind of conflicts arise as a result of the co-existence of multiple networks?
3. What is the nature of the conflicts, are there specific characteristics resulting from network embeddedness?

With regard to the nature of the research, exploratory and semi-structured interviews were implemented. The basic population of the research was reported by leaders related to the university's (health) units. During the collection of data collection, it was intended that the properties of the examined phenomena could be revealed to all the perspectives of the management of the organization undertaken (academic higher management, chief finance officer, professional and support unit management). In order to be able to answer the research questions, personal interviews have been conducted with four groups:

1. **The senior leadership of the institution:** Actors who carry out/or used to carry out the duties of the institution's rector or the dean's duties in a relevant health care faculty. As regards this group, the researchers asked the Rector, Vice - Rectors and the Deans and the Deputy-Deans.
2. **Senior financial managers of the institution:** People who carry out/or used to carry out the duties of the financial director general of the institution or acting as financial director general in a partner institution. The researchers interviewed the director general of economics and the economic director and management of the hospital.
3. **The heads of professional units in the institution:** People who carry out/or used to carry out certain managerial duties in clinics/departments that provide health care. Interviewees were clinic guides and department managers.
4. **The heads of the institution's support unit:** People who carry out/or used to carry out managerial duties in certain organizational units that are responsible for maintaining support processes needed in the management of a health care institution. In this circle, we asked about the development of the healthcare organization, the organizational coordination of professional tasks and the manager of the operation of the healthcare organization.

There were a total of 10 discussions. An interview took between 1-3 hours. The interviews were recorded between 1 September 2018 and 30 June 2019.

During the analysis of the interviews, we rely on the starting point of Grounded Theory as a result of the nature of the analysis (Glaser &Strauss, 1967). On this basis, prior categories or frames haven't been created. In the first step, the research participants identified the units (sentences) of the transcripts (independently) which expressed a conflict between actors or suggested. Then we consolidated the database of conflict identification descriptions and encoded the answers received by identifying keywords, categories and patterns. These categories were defined on the basis of the content of categories units. Depending on the relationship between each category, higher categories were formed. These have facilitated the review of each category and the organization of test results. As the last step in the analysis, researchers finalized the conformity of the definitions along the original content test. The process of analysis was interactive with feedback between each phase and continuously shaping the results of the analysis.

RESEARCH RESULTS

Existing networks that are diverse, and in nature and purpose may even be significantly varied, create an extremely wide field of conflicts in the health-care-providing university, the subject of this study. Based on how these conflicts are perceived and managed, these have been classified into three key groups:

1. First, there are conflicts related to organizational management. These arise during organizational governance and the implementation of organizational development. Looking at these conflicts, the study has demonstrated that the network impact of each network extinguishes the value creation of the networks (strategic conflict), that inter-organizational conflicts (conflicts of power) arise when, with various success, each network enforces its interests on the different levels of the organization and, finally, that there are financing conflicts because capacities are cross-financed.
2. Second, conflicts that arise during organizational processes and affect the implementation of organizational processes and the boundaries of their value creating ability. From these conflicts the following ones have clearly been captured: conflicts for resources that reflect on the competition each network has within an organization, conceptual conflicts that describe the various regulatory and operational settings of each network, and professional conflicts that arise from the tension that exists between the discrete job portfolios of

each unit and the necessity to cooperate because of the complexity of value creation.

3. Third, personal conflicts that arise on an individual level during the performance of each action. From these conflicts, the participants highlighted that there is a moral conflict (cultural conflict): tension between the pragmatic expectations of organizational management and the humanitarian values that exist in the ethical system of health care work; that, as a result inter-organizational relations there are conditions that generate conflict linked to organizational and personal accountability relating to the performance of duties (conflict of accountability); and that there is conflict between income and professional success that is to be achieved through the performance of duties (career conflict).

We put those conflicts into the first group that *have arisen during the implementation of organizational management.*

The first of those conflicts are conflicts of a strategic nature. Conflicts of a strategic nature manifest themselves primarily in conflicts related to development. The reason for that is that the diverse value creation of those networks that exist within an organization's relationship system require (partly) diverse and competing development needs. Depending on the extent a clinical unit is embedded in a certain network, each unit is interested in investing in different resources, different function-related and operational competencies. Furthermore, the area and dimension of strategic investments often become a source of conflict even within one clinical organizational unit.

In the field of organizational management, the researchers have identified the range of power conflicts as the next conflict type. Conflicts of power occur when the expectations of individual networks are to be met and arise from enforcing interests in the course of influencing a method of operation. These are customary regulatory conflicts which arise from prioritizing the various types of action (treatment, other service, basic research, pre-clinical research, clinical research, intellectual property sales, etc.), their superior-subordinate relationships and how judgments of performance on these activities are weighted.

In the field of organizational management, we have identified financing conflicts as the third conflict type. Organizations and organizational units that are engaged in clinical activities have dissimilar financing portfolios - because of their network embeddedness - and, consequently, particular activities are managed with different weight. As a result of that, the various clinical and healthcare organizations/units form different judgements on what value creation really is, and what the method and framework of value creation are; this inevitably generates conflicts.

Table 1. Conflicts linked to organizational management

Form of perceived conflict	Examples to demonstrate
Strategic conflict	"...It is impossible to carry out rapid learning and development in a field because every action belongs to many networks, thus, meaningfully and in a value-creating way, these can only be altered over a long period of time. Consequently, learning and development are the same as making changes in micro-level relationships, which is time consuming."
Conflict of power	"...conflict between functions is frequent... who has what to do and who does what... and who has the authority to do it..."
Financing conflicts	"I've heard several times: take the patient from us because the financing is not worth for us, we have a lot of people waiting for a spot, but not so much with you..."

Source: Authors

In the second group, the researchers put those conflicts that *arise in organizational processes*. This category refers to conflicts that affect the performance of operational processes with clinical task and, in the long run, - probably - lead to strategic conflict in one form or another. Resource conflicts were identified as a typical manifestation of such conflicts. The value creation of numerous networks competes simultaneously for the use of the same resource/capacity. For example, that is the case with the running time of clinical equipment which time is to be spent on patient care, clinical research, or contracted research; and there is a similar conflict in how workforce working time is shared/can be shared.

In a similar fashion, a source of conflict that influences the implementation of organizational processes is the range of conceptual conflicts. Value creation that is performed for the various types of network requires various focal points, consequently, the differently weighted action-portfolios in healthcare and clinical organizations/organizational units lead to different perceptions. As a result of that, in the various networks the same action is performed according to different rules and different perceived outcome criteria. Because of that, through the various perspectives, the same fact is perceived differently. All that may lead to conflicts during organizational interactions.

The third form of conflict range that arises from organizational processes is, as a range of professional conflicts have been identified, Again, the background of this is the dissimilar network embeddedness of each organization/organizational unit. Organizations/organizational units that have different (weighted) action-portfolios because of their dissimilar network embeddedness, lay emphasis on different areas of the same series of action, which this leads to different outcomes and outcome conflicts. Unlike with conceptual conflicts when the judgement of the same results leads to conflicts, in this case, the source of the conflict is that actions performed with the same goal lead to different outcomes.

Table 2. Conflicts linked to organizational processes

Form of perceived conflict	Examples to demonstrate
Conflict of resources	"...the same capacity serves a wide range of activities, a network is behind each one waiting for the outcome, every network pays for fulfilment..."
Conceptual conflict	"...in some cases, keeping 40 people healthy has no value, but saving 1 person is a worldwide success..."
Professional conflict	"Many people complete the clinical research, but cannot offer an alternative to the side effects, and then they close the experiment... that is unethical..."

Source: Authors

Finally, as the last group of conflicts, the researchers have identified *conflicts of a personal nature*. Under conflicts of a personal nature, we understand those conflicts and frustrations that arise in individuals, influence their attitudes towards other individuals, their action and ultimately lead to one of the process conflicts. A typical manifestation of personal conflicts is cultural conflicts. Cultural conflicts are value system conflicts that arise from tensions that exist between the expectations of a given organization (its management) and the networks that hold expectations regarding a certain action, or action that serve various networks. Examples include the sometimes tense relationship between the value systems of cost-effectiveness and life-saving, the not irreconcilable contrast between a learning approach, that is typical of research, and the zero-error approach demanded by patient care, or working in a rigid, disciplined and hierarchical way, as it is demanded when saving lives, and in an atmosphere where, as it is required for learning, it is necessary to face mistakes openly.

As the second type of personal conflict, the conflicts of accountability have been identified. Conflict of accountability arises from the mixture of organizational functioning, administration and the individual accountability when performing health care duties. The background of this conflict is that the perception of the boundary of accountability between the organization and the individual is unclear, and this affects, and sometimes limits, the individual completion of tasks during the performance of duties.

Finally, as conflicts of personal nature, we have identified career conflicts. Career conflicts are generated because, as expected by the participants, the completion of tasks linked to each network create various opportunities for income and professional success. A clinical organization/unit with a particular embeddedness is interested in specializing its resources (including its available workforce) for that particular network. For the participants, that fact is partly an opportunity and partly a limitation as specialization also leads to interdependence in other areas. This duality (maximizing professional success via specializations and capitalizing on that through interdependence) affects what attitudes individuals have toward each other as well as how work is carried out in the processes.

Table 3. Conflicts of a personal nature

Form of perceived conflict	Examples to demonstrate
Cultural conflict	"...the culture rejects mistakes because these are harmful, but in this way meaningful quality assurance cannot be carried out..."
Conflict of accountability	"...according to the regulations, accountability always lies with the person who does something, even if the equipment he has obtained is faulty..."
Career conflict	"...a strict force of interdependence, which is also the cultural organizing principle; on the other hand, nothing is to be done that would profoundly threaten that problems are still solved together in the future..."

Source: Authors

A distinguished outcome of this study is that the senior participants of organizational management and those who represent a managerial position in the professional units of health care institutions primarily perceived those conflicts that are related to organizational management and organizational processes, while senior financial managers and support unit managers perceived the characteristics of conflicts in all three categories.

As a summary of the results of our analysis, based on the answers we will try to explain the causes of the conflicts detected and the social integration complexity of these consequences in in Table 4.

The situation summarized in table no. 4, which describes the superior categories of their nature, suggests the possibility of structured management of the conflicts. By examining the same conflicts through the glasses of embeddedness, we came to a very different result by creating the superior categories along their result, the result of which is reflected in Figure 1.

Resource and strategic conflicts in organizational management are directly influenced by the regulatory environment of health care. Capacity control, government development plans, the form and nature of funding cause tensions between clinics and even between universities with clinics. On the other hand, the social and economic relationships developed/created along the lines of the activities of individual clinics have a significant impact on the power, funding and resource conflicts between

Table 4. Summary of detected conflict fields

Area of conflict detected	Form of perceived conflict	Explanation of perceived form of conflict
Conflicts related to governance	Strategic conflict	The networks in the organization's relationship system has (in part) different value creation approaches that set competing development goals.
	Power conflicts	Organizational conflicts of interest arising from the advocacy of networks in the organization's relationships at different levels and areas of the organization.
	Funding conflicts	For some activities, the logic and extent of value creation and capacity financing separate from one another.
Conflicts in organizational processes	Resource conflict	Multiple networks compete for the same resource/capacity at the same time.
	Attitude conflict	The same activity is carried out in different networks under different rules and different result criteria.
	Professional conflicts	Organizational units with different activity portfolios that are based on different network embeddedness focus on different professional activities.
Personal conflicts	Cultural conflicts	The tension between the expectations of governance and operation and the (in part) different values of health care.
	Conflicts of responsibility	The mixing of individual responsibilities for organizational management, operation and health care.
	Career conflicts	The tasks associated with each network bear different incomes and different opportunities for professional success.

Source: Authors

clinics as well as on the career conflicts that certain individuals experience. The informal network of contacts influences the resources that can be obtained and the position in the power structures influences the possibilities for advocacy. At the same time, participation in a variety of hierarchy requires the parallel enforcement of a variety of norms and values, the success of which influences the development of power or career conflicts as well as the forced taking on of professional, mindset or even cultural conflicts. All of this cannot be related from the ethical, moral and self-interested behavior of the individual, which also plays a role in the development of professional, mindset, cultural and at certain cases even responsibility conflicts.

On the basis of Figure 1, we concluded that, although the conflicts and tensions identified in the institutional units are perceived at the level of network embeddedness, the reasons for their incurrence cannot be traced back only to participation in the organizational network, but rather to the consequences of the complex socio-economic integration of the sector. The explanations for the conflicts show that these contradictions cannot be addressed solely by management routines because they have different origins.

Figure 1. Source of detected conflict fields by source of their embeddedness
Source: Authors

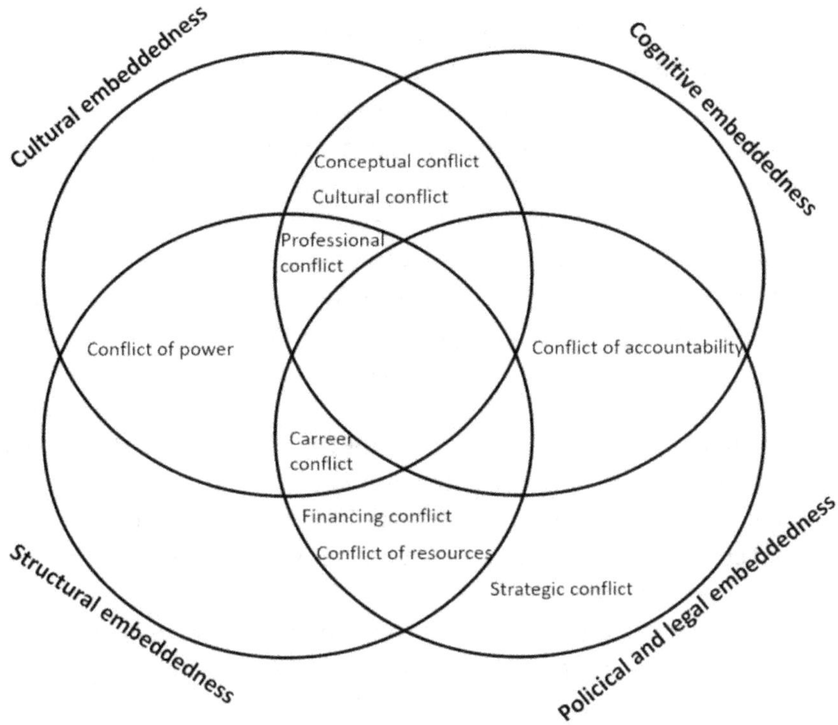

CONCLUSION

As a result of the in-depth interview survey, the researchers have concluded that network complexity in the functioning of health care institutions results in three types of conflicts that are constantly present. On the one hand, *conflicts related to governance appear* in the implementation of organizational governance and organizational development. On the other hand, there are conflicts in *organizational processes that affect the operation and efficiency of organizational processes.* Thirdly, *personal conflicts* that occur at the individual level in the course of their individual activities. The research results are also in line with those obtained in previous researches. It should be noted, however, that we have identified *strategic, liability and career conflicts* as new types of conflicts, which have not yet been identified, all of which are directly related to the operational characteristics of the complex network.

The results of the qualitative research point to the specific appearance and heterogeneity of conflicts arising from the complex embeddedness of health care institutions, which exist but often not mentioned. After identifying and categorizing conflicts, when we tried to find explanations and reasons for tension, it has been found that they could not necessarily be attributed to the participation in certain networks. We have come to the conclusion that conflicts in health units are poorly understandable or manageable from a single perspective, they require a broad interpretation of embeddedness. *Political-legal, cultural, structural and cognitive embeddedness together*, in interaction with each other, are significant factors in the emergence of tensions and contradictions, so their management cannot be implemented without taking all of them into account.

Summarizing the results, the management of the factors causing tensions in an organization or between organizations due to the complex social embeddedness of healthcare is system-wide task. Their elimination is impossible, as we cannot lift the economy out of the social environment. Embeddedness will still have an effect on the operation of the organization. However, what this social embeddedness is like, what the social environment is like, can be changed. A cultural, structural, political legal environment that generates constructive conflicts would probably be more beneficial to all actors.

Instead of destructive conflict, when competition takes place between unequal parties (structurally one party has no chance against the other), when there is little agreement on the rules to follow, and the parties have less confidence in each other's adherence to the rules, a different conflict situation effort should be made to make these conflicts constructive. A conflict can be very beneficial. A constructive conflict situation precludes stagnation of the social system, promotes change, frees up energies, and encourages experimentation and better selection of action alternatives. It would be desirable to have an environment that makes power and other relationships transparent, that clarifies issues, develops problem-solving skills, and increases efficiency. This endeavor is a system-wide task, only a very long process can result in a change in the circumstances. It's a painful process where many people's interests can be damaged on the fly in short term, but in the long run, all actors can win. In such an environment, it would make sense to re-conduct an inter-organizational collaborative research, as presented in this study.

The limitation of the study is, on the one hand, that the researchers examined a single clinical organization with a university background, and on the other hand, this research is based only on the applied methodology type. From a methodological point of view, the following can be highlighted: low number of interviews, lack of validity and reliability requirements. However, the current results provide a good starting point for both managing complex network operations and understanding the network operations of health management. The interpretation of the results presented in this study can be seen as thought-provoking, sharing experiences from a case rather than as an exact result, and the authors' approach is experimental in nature.

REFERENCES

Antal, Z. L. (2018). *A gyógyítás társadalmi beágyazottsága*. Argumentum Kiadó.

Berry, F. S., Brower, R. S., Choi, S. O., Goa, W. X., Jang, H. S., Kwon, M., & Word, J. (2004). Three Traditions of Network Research: What the Public Management Research Agenda Can Learn from Other Research Communities. *Public Administration Review*, *64*(5), 539–552. doi:10.1111/j.1540-6210.2004.00402.x

Bochatay, N., Bajwa, N. M., Cullati, S., Muller-Juge, V., Blondon, K. S., Perron, N. J., Maitre, F., Chopard, P., Kim, S., Savoldelli, G. L., Hudelson, P., & Nendaz, M. R. (2017). A Multilevel Analysis of Professional Conflicts in Helath Care Teams: Insight for Future Training. *Academic Medicine*, *92*(11S), S84–S92. doi:10.1097/ACM.0000000000001912 PMID:29065028

Chakraborty, S., & Dobrzykowski, D. D. (2013). Supply Chain Practices for Complexity in Healthcare: A Service-Dominant Logic View. *The IUP Journal of Supply Chain Management*, *10*(3), 53–75. doi:10.1016/S2212-5671(14)00233-0

Csupor, É., Kuna, Á., Pintér, J. N., Kaló, Z., & Csabai, M. (2017). Konfliktustípusok és konfliktus kezelés magyar egészségügyi dolgozók körében [Conflict types and conflict management among Hungarian healthcare workers]. *Orvosi Hetilap*. doi:10.1556/650.2017.30736

Dacin, M. T., Ventresca, M. J., & Beal, B. D. (1999). The Embeddedness of Organizations: Dialogue & Directions. *Journal of Management*, *25*(3), 317–356. doi:10.1177/014920639902500304

Deutsch, M., Coleman, P. T., & Marcus, E. C. (Eds.). (2006). *The Handbook of Conflict Resolution: Theory and Practice* (2nd ed.). Wiley Publishing.

Etzioni, A. (1988). *The Moral Dimension*. The Free Press. doi:10.1002/hrm.3930270407

Glaser, B. G., & Strauss, A. L. (1967). *The Discovery of Grounded Theory: Strategies for Qualitative Research*. Aldine.

Gulati, R. (1998). Alliances and Networks. *Strategic Management Journal*, *19*(1), 293–317. doi:10.1002/(SICI)1097-0266(199804)19:4<293::AID-SMJ982>3.0.CO;2-M

Launberg, A. (2011). Commercializing Academic Research Results: When a University wants to Further Innovation. *27th IMP-Conference*. https://www.impgroup.org/uploads/papers/7652.pdf

Mills, M. E. C. (2002). Conflict in Health Care Organisations. *Journal of Health Care Law & Policy*. Advance online publication. doi:10.1080/08998280.2001.11927749 PMID:15017948

Moore, C. W. (2006). *The Mediation Process: Practical Strategies for Resolving Conflict*. Jossey-Bass.

Patton, C. (2014). Conflict in healthcare: A Literature Review. *The Internet Journal of Healthcare Administration*, *9*(1), 1–11.

Provan, K. G., & Sebastian, J. G. (1998). Networks within Networks: Service Overlap, Organizational Cliques, and Network Effectiveness. *Academy of Management Journal*, *41*(4), 453–463. doi:10.5465/257084

Rahim, M. A. (1985). A Strategy for Managing Conflict in Complex Organisations. *Human Relations*, *38*(1), 81–89. doi:10.1177/001872678503800105

Rahim, M. A. (2002). Toward a Theory of Managing Organisation Conflict. *International Journal of Conflict Management*, *13*(3), 206–235. doi:10.1108/eb022874

Raus, K., Mortier, E., & Eeckloo, K. (2018). Organizing Health Care Networks: Balancing Markets, Government and Civil Society. *International Journal of Integrated Care*, *18*(3), 6. doi:10.5334/ijic.3960 PMID:30093844

Sackett, D. L., Rosenberg, W. M., Gray, J. A., Haynes, R. B., & Richardson, W. S. (1996). Evidence based medicine: What it is and what it isn't? *BMJ (Clinical Research Ed.)*, *312*(7023), 71–72. doi:10.1136/bmj.312.7023.71 PMID:8555924

Savage, G. T., Taylor, R. L., Rotarius, T. M., & Buesseler, J. A. (1997). Governance of Integrated Delivery Systems/Networks: A Stakeholder Approach. *Health Care Management Review*, *22*(1), 7–20. doi:10.1097/00004010-199724000-00002 PMID:9058084

Shipilov, A., Gulati, R., Kilduff, M., Li, S., & Tsai, W. (2014). Relational Pluralism within and between Organisations. *Academy of Management Journal*, *57*(2), 449–459. doi:10.5465/amj.2013.1145

Thomas, K. W., & Kilmann, R. H. (2017). *Conflict Mode Instrument*. Profile and Interpretive Report. https://eu.themyersbriggs.com/-/media/Files/PDFs/Reports-in-English/TKI/TKI-Profile-and-Interpretive-Report-US-English-Pat-Sample.pdf

Tversky, A., & Kahneman, D. (1991). Ítéletalkotás bizonytalanság mellett: heurisztikák és torzítások. In Z. Pápai & P. Nagy (Eds.), *Döntéselméleti szöveggyűjtemény* (pp. 77–93). Aula.

Uzzi, B. (1996). The Sources and Consequences of Embeddedness for the Economic Performance of Organisations: The Network Effect. *American Sociological Review*, *61*(4), 674–698. doi:10.2307/2096399

Vecchio, R. P. (2000). Negative Emotion in the Workplace: Employee Jealousy and Envy. *International Journal of Stress Management*, *7*(3), 161–179. . doi:10.1023/A:1009592430712

Wagrell, S. (2011). Achieving Innovation in Healthcare: The Public Quasi-Market Paradox. *27th IMP-Conference*. https://www.impgroup.org/uploads/papers/7793.pdf

Yang, W. H., Hu, J. S., & Chou, Y. Y. (2010). Analysis of Network Type Exchange in Health Care System: A Stakeholder Approach. *Journal of Medical Systems*, *36*(3), 1569–1581. doi:10.100710916-010-9618-5 PMID:21046205

Zukin, S. P., & DiMaggio. (Eds.). (1990). *Structures of Capital. The Social Organization of the Economy.* Cambridge University Press.

KEY TERMS AND DEFINITIONS

Complex Network: The networks provide resources, opportunities, and inter-organizational ties (through which resources and opportunities become available); in addition, they provide a position that makes it possible to exploit resources and opportunities. The extent and multiplexity of inter-organizational relationships determine the value creation, identity, and performance of organizations.

Conflicts in Networks: Conflict can be seen as an interactive process that manifests itself in conflict of interest, disagreement or dissonance within or between actors. Conflicts can arise for a variety of reasons: interests, preferences, mutually exclusive use of resources, values, behaviours, or as a result of conflicting, interdependent performances.

Intra-Organisational Conflicts: Conflicts that arise at the individual and group levels in relation to the functioning of the organisation. These can be intrapersonal conflicts, where individuals' own needs and desires conflict, or interpersonal conflicts, where conflicts arise between the views, desires and needs of at least two or more individuals.

Levels of Conflict Within the Organisation: Organisational governance conflicts, which are related to organisation government and development, process conflicts, which concern the implementation of processes and the value creation, and finally personal conflicts, which can be moral or career conflicts.

Social Embeddedness: The integration mechanisms of the economy are linked to specific social and institutional conditions. The cognitive, cultural, structural and political aspects of the social embeddedness of economic actions have an impact on the functioning of health care organisations.

Chapter 4
The Implementation of Lean in Emergency Hospital Screening During the COVID-19 Pandemic

Inês Veiga Pereira
https://orcid.org/0000-0002-7906-612X
ISCAP, Polytechnic of Porto, Portugal

Patricia Oliveira Faria
Faculty of Economics, University of Porto, Portugal

Amélia Maria Pinto da Cunha Brandão
https://orcid.org/0000-0003-2751-7272
Faculty of Economics, University of Porto, Portugal

ABSTRACT

Healthcare services, in particular, are one of the areas in which Lean can be applied and benefits can be reached through it. In order to analyze the suitability of Lean implementation in healthcare units, this research focused on a case study, namely in Hospital of Santo António emergency area, in the city of Porto, Portugal. The study was conducted in the year 2020, during the pandemic of COVID-19, which forced the change of screening processes. This research analyses and compares the new and previous sorting model and discusses if Lean methodology was applied. It was concluded, through data collected in the interview to the leading nurse, that despite de fact she is not familiar with the Lean concept and methodology, as process simplification and time reduction were taken into account, the new process can be considered Lean. The flow charts that reflect both the sorting structure used in the urgencies before and after were developed. Hospital culture, lack of communication before the new process implementation, and the facilities were some of the identified barriers.

DOI: 10.4018/978-1-7998-7263-4.ch004

INTRODUCTION

In an increasingly globalized world, companies seek the best use of their operational capacity with a focus on optimizing results and maximizing profits. Thus, the use of methods and tools to improve the design of processes is essential for the best use of their workforce. To guarantee the effectiveness of processes and flows, process mapping and redesign are important project tools.

The process and routine management of large companies is of fundamental importance to ensure targets and the correct allocation of existing resources (Chopra & Meindl, 2011). From this perspective, it becomes relevant the management of internal services offered to meet the needs of other internal areas, with the expected quality standard and adding value for all those involved in these operations.

Lean is a management tool widely used in process management to define activities, tasks and workflows. Research on management of health services has been increasing and the latent need for improvement of managerial processes in the healthcare area led to the adaptation of *lean* methodology to healthcare (D'Andreamatteo et al., 2015). As with any managerial change, changes in routines and protocols may generate fear and little adherence of the collaborators to the new realigned workflow routines. Difficulties in understanding and adapting to the new management, problems in the adherence and cooperation of leaders to the new strategic management may be major barriers to the effective implementation of lean healthcare (Sim & Rogers, 2009).

In the context of the worldwide pandemic COVID-19, which began in 2020, hospital management has taken on new aspects in the management of emergency procedures: How can infected service users be more easily identified and the contact between service users with suspected COVID-19 and service users without symptoms be reduced?

Taking into consideration the realignment of emergency triage processes, in the scenario of the COVID-19 pandemic, the importance of using *lean* methodology in the hospital environment has increased. This research is directly oriented towards the internal workflow, which affects employees and their satisfaction with the project and the success of the triage process.

PROCESS MANAGEMENT

Process management consists of measuring, designing and aligning activities. Its importance occurs when we need to visualize in a clear and cohesive way the activities of an organization. A process is a sequence of activities with a specific objective (Campos, 2014). When organized as a set, in a structured way, they create a pre-established work routine guiding employees to perform their tasks correctly and on time to meet the expectations of internal and external customers of the organization, which are part of the strategic planning (Rebouças, 2007).

Focusing on improving service delivery, the management of processes and flows in companies has been a great tool for achieving excellence in customer service. Understanding what processes are and visualizing them as components of a chain leads to improvement of the performed tasks (Chopra & Meindl, 2011). Failures in the interaction between workflows and developed activities or unstructured processes may compromise the entire organization generating an unsatisfactory result. Processes are parallel activities with a common purpose and poor management can affect the entire work chain (Chopra & Meindl, 2011).

In the context of services, due to their immateriality and intangibility, it becomes more difficult to measure the quality of the deliveries (della Volpi & Paulino, 2018). The proximity of the final consumer and his participation during the service production process brings a different perspective from manufacturing, due to the close contact to the need to strengthen the training and the standardization of processes (Fitzsimmons & Fitzsimmons, 2014). The management of processes in the context of services requires greater attention as to their execution, consumption and response time, which are immediate and where any failure becomes evident very easily. Such situations may lead to a breach of reliability in the relationship, which is not re-established in a short period of time.

Lean Management

Lean is a management process technique based on the Toyota Production System (TPS), it leads to improved communication and greater homogeneity in value chain, connects stakeholders more effectively and consequently reflects in the effectiveness of the operation (Womack & Jones, 2015). The lean approach compacts tasks, reduces deadline and increases the quality in the deliveries, the reasoning of integration proposes the best union of links in the value chain in a way that clarifies the function and importance of each of its components, so that the workflow is pulled towards the final customer (Womack & Jones, 2015). Originally focused on manufacturing, the Japanese technique was developed to improve the manufacturing production process and has been widely used to organize business processes.

More than a change in management procedures lean is also a sociocultural practice that needs involvement and recognition of its actors to work efficiently. According to Sim and Rogers (2009), lean should be considered more than a set of mechanistic tools and techniques and the human dimensions of motivation, empowerment and respect for people are very important. The study states that there is direct link between leadership relationships and employee involvement in lean implementation, employees who do not feel valued as an asset of the company tend not to contribute to the improvement process. "Lean means changing and working with a different mindset. If training only involves new techniques and metrics, workers who fear for their jobs tend to lose motivation for these programs" (Sim & Rogers, 2009, p. 46). In contrast, Bortolotti et al. (2015) attribute the success of lean implementation with soft practices of process management and a direct relationship with organizational culture, i.e., lean practices were more successful when there was concern with employee training and human development.

Lean proposes that cultural changes happen in a positive way. Leaving the comfort zone in search for better results can be challenging for employees, so that they feel included it is important that they can express their opinions and make suggestions for new process designs. Consultation with operations, enriches the processes, carrying them with the vision of those who perform them. for the success of the project. Understanding of the new scenario should occur at all hierarchical levels, from management to the operation, for the project success (da Silva Xavier et al., 2016).

Taking advantage of the vision proposed by the intelligent management of processes, the techniques of task control are adaptable in various areas where the importance of quality and continuous improvement in provided services are identified. The health sector is no different, in search of the best practices in the hospital area, the management of health services has become essential for good service delivery and quality assurance of healthcare with better use of available resources.

Hospital Process Management

The improvement of hospital processes reflects a global need in which, users of medical services, due to competition, become increasingly demanding in the quality. Therefore, it is important to research the best way to provide health services, whether addressing the customer regarding specific issues of care and quality or improving internal processes in which will be directly impacted in the end (Gonzalez, 2019). Hospital process management is quite delicate and can be divided into three major pillars: medical, commercial and nursing areas (Huhs et al., 2019). Total quality systems have been increasingly used as a competitiveness tool by means of a globalized economy (Sim & Rogers, 2009), the search for activity standardization metrics has become increasingly common in the hospital environment, with the goal of operational excellence (de Regge et al., 2019).

Lean Healthcare

The lean methodology is increasingly used in the healthcare chain, either by better dividing operations and workflow or for better use of time and resources in the hospital environment (Lindsay et al., 2020). Lean healthcare was developed with the intention of providing better care and increasing quality to the customer. The tool proposes a culture change in the hospital environment that allows waste reduction, connecting the workflow from end to end in a more compact and effective way. So, lean healthcare methodology involves guiding internal and external workflows directed to continuous improvement (Graban, 2016).

In this context, lean can be a good management tool because it contributes to improving the value chain, processes and workflow with a focus on excellence in delivery (Graban, 2016). However, although promising, the results of lean in healthcare cannot yet be defined entirely as positive (D'Andreamatteo et al., 2015). There are still gaps, barriers and difficulties to be explored academically, mainly because of the costs involved and all organizational change management. Currently there is pressure for change and innovation in the hospital environment, new business management concepts have been implemented in the health area to update management models in search of survival, standardization, commercial adjustments and in Information Technology are examples of sectors to be improved within health services (Borchers & Evans, 2011). In the discussion on the current challenges for health management, the article highlights the importance of patient empowerment to ensure the efficiency and effectiveness of health service delivery.

COVID-19 has led to the change of several processes. Iswanto (2021) analyzed the impact of Lean implementation on hospital profitability in the case of a pharmacy. The inventory purchase in the pharmaceutical unit dramatically decreased after implementation, both during the pandemic and the new normal. Further, the hospital deficit decreased after implementation before and during the pandemic, although at lower levels. However, during the new normal, the deficit increased by 29%, indicating a diminished effect of lean six sigma (LSS) on the hospital profits. When LSS topics that directly relate to COVID-19 are considered, four thematic areas were identified: tools, applications, benefits and challenges (Hundal et al., 2021). According to this research, personal safety is the primary subject, followed by supporting dimensions of process redesign, and telemedicine.

Changes made in workflows and routines cause positive and negative impacts regarding the reception of employees to the new processes. Not always the change is made in a clear and comfortable way so that the employees feel prepared to perform the new tasks, thus the care in the implementation of Lean processes is vital.

RESEARCH AIM AND OBJECTIVES

The present study aims to analyze the triage process at a Central Hospital and compare the process before and after COVID-19 pandemic, analyzing if the Lean methodology was used for setting the triage processes.

Faced with a pandemic that took on global proportions in a few months, healthcare processes had to be realigned and rethought in order to better fulfil their role in identifying and assisting users more quickly and try to reduce the spread of the virus. The new patient triage processes are focused on the fast identification of infected patients and shorter response times. It is important that the behavior of hospitals follows the needs of their patients, adjusting to meet them. Mapping processes and identifying chances of improvement is fundamental for the smooth running of operations and gains in quality, delivering the service properly increases the chances of winning over the consumer. It is considerable that with the concern for continuous improvement in health care systems, the barriers to the implementation of process management are investigated about the relationship of the teams' collaborators with the new system of processes. Therefore, other objectives of this research are to understand the barriers for lean process implementation and the culture and leadership characteristics which may facilitate lean process implementation.

RESEARCH METHODOLOGY

Since the research was developed in a health care unit in order to assess processes, the qualitative approach was chosen as the methodology for the chapter, which seeks to understand the real conditions of the participant, collect representativeness of opinions and perspectives of the interviewees in addition to enrich knowledge sources (Yin, 2015). To investigate the prepositions presented the case study strategy was used. Because it is a research that focuses on a specific organizational process, the case study is a tool, which uses qualitative analysis with open questions, the case study is an effective tool in collecting data and complementing the information (Pádua, 2007). The interview conducted to the nurse responsible for the triage sector of COVID was composed of open questions. The Bizagi software was used to draw all process maps.

The present research took place at the emergency sector of Santo António Hospital, one of the main hospitals in the emergency rooms of COVID in the city of Porto. An exploratory case study analysis was determined for understanding the triage processes before and after the COVID pandemic.

The investigation process was carried out with process mapping and interview for a better understanding of the routine activities developed by the Hospital's triage.

DATA ANALYSIS AND RESULTS

Context of the Research

In March 2020, Portugal entered a state of emergency due to the COVID -19 pandemic. Not only were there drastic changes in day-to-day life, but also in management processes. This time, changes in the hospital process chains went beyond improvement and use of available resources. The goal was to develop an effective way to contingency the contamination and provide adequate support, as soon as possible for the users was needed. In view of our chosen sample, the Santo António Hospital, due to its strong relevance in the context of treatment of COVID in the country, a special ward was created for COVID-19 suspects, there were also changes in the patient triage processes, with the aim of reducing the risk of infection and providing better care. Thus, the administrative processes were changed, initiating a series of new procedures that were analysed in this research.

Implementation

This study aimed to investigate the change to the triage process at the Hospital de Santo António do Porto and analyse whether the new process follows a lean methodology. The interview with the head of nurses of COVID at the Santo António Hospital, Nurse Ana Diniz, aimed at clarifying the procedures, identifying the processes as *lean,* and identifying the barriers to implementation. Table 1 summarizes the Mapping Interview Guide and identifies the research focal points where information about the process was required.

Considering Yin's model, an interview script was used Huhs et al. (2019) that was previously tested in Swiss and Austrian hospitals in order to measure barriers and *lean* workflows in healthcare. The script divides the questions into categories in order to question the tasks in clearer and more concise ways.

RESULTS AND DISCUSSION

In order to answer the main research question, data collection was done through a telephone interview with Ana Diniz, the nurse in charge; this interview aimed at mapping processes and identifying if the workflow was Lean. Question Q1 of the script seeks to understand the workflow and changes in the screening process, in addition to identifying the interviewee this question measures the changes in the processes in a way that facilitates the understanding of activities performed. In

Table 1. Mapping interview script

Area	Question
Introductory question	Q1 - Please explain briefly what work you are currently doing and what are the main areas of focus? How was screening done before and after the implementation of Lean management.
Implementation	Q2 - What does the term Lean mean to you?
	Q3 - Why do you think a hospital usually decides to implement Lean management?
	Q4 - Is the Lean philosophy anchored in the hospital where you work and what are its objectives?
	Q5 - How has the implementation of Lean management been anchored structurally and in the corporate culture?
Leadership	Q6 - What kind of leadership do you think hospitals need to successfully implement the Lean management approach into the organisational culture?
	Q7 - Can you name the main critical success factors for implementation?
Processes	Q8 - What obstacles and challenges can you cite when implementing Lean management?

Source: Adapted from Huhs et al., 2019

order to better understand the data, some parts of the interview are transcript, to clarify the results.

Q1 - Please explain briefly what work you are currently doing and what are the main areas of focus? How was screening done before and after the implementation of *Lean* management.

I am responsible for the area dedicated to COVID at St. Anthony's hospital. That department was set up exclusively to separate users with suspected Covid-19 from users without the symptoms.

Previous Screening Process

The Santo António Hospital uses Manchester Triage system, in which the user, after registering in the administrative sector, is forwarded to triage where he answers some questions to a triage nurse, who inputs the answers into the system and forwards him/her directly to the medical specialist. The MTs has been the national triage method in the UK and the republic of Ireland for more than a decade and, since 2001, in Portugal too (Mackway-Jones et al., 2006).

Developed by the Manchester Triage Group, which comprised doctors and nurses from different EDs in Manchester (Mackway-Jones et al., 2006) it has five categories, each with a colour and level (Table 2) and is presented in an easy-to-follow flow chart.

Table 2. Manchester Triage system

Level	Status	Colour	Time to assessment
1	Immediate	Red	0 minutes
2	Very urgent	Orange	10 minutes
3	Urgent	Yellow	60 minutes
4	Standard	Green	120 minutes
5	Non-urgent	Blue	240 minutes

Source: Mackway-Jones et al., 2006

The Manchester Triage system automatically calculates the severity of the user and separates him/her with coloured wristbands where each colour represents the level of severity and predicts waiting time. The programme has around 40 flowcharts, thus analysing previously and their clinical picture and determining their level of urgency. With the aid of the Bizagi software, the process map illustrated in Figure 1 was created.

Figure 1. Triage before Covid 19 pandemic
Source: Authors

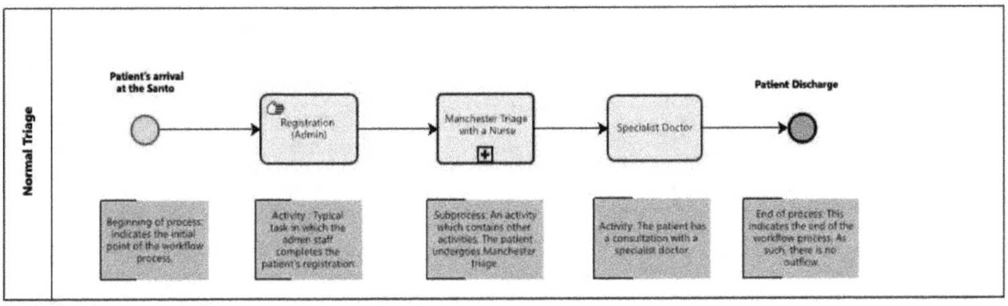

Post COVID-19 Pandemic Screening

Considering the pandemic scenario installed with the COVID-19 crisis, a realignment of processes was necessary in order to be able to identify more quickly the disease suspects and to segregate users more efficiently. Thus, after the registration of the user in the administrative sector, at the first point of contact the user answers questions in which symptoms of COVID could be identified, that is, triage begins in the administrative sector, shortening the workflow and optimising the identification process of the disease suspects.

Afterwards, the patient is directed to the triage sector where he/she goes through the Manchester triage and, in case of suspicion of COVID-19, is directed to the COVID ward; with the new flow, the waiting time of the patient in triage was limited to 30 minutes. After the Manchester triage, if the patient is identified as suspected of COVID, he/she will still be evaluated again to be forwarded to one of the groups, respiratory patients, those with some respiratory difficulty, which makes the clinical picture more aggravated, in a ward with 11 vacancies, and non-respiratory patients who will continue their usual routine. The map of processes below in figure 2 illustrates how the new workflow is performed.

Figure 2. Triage after Covid 19 pandemic
Source: Authors

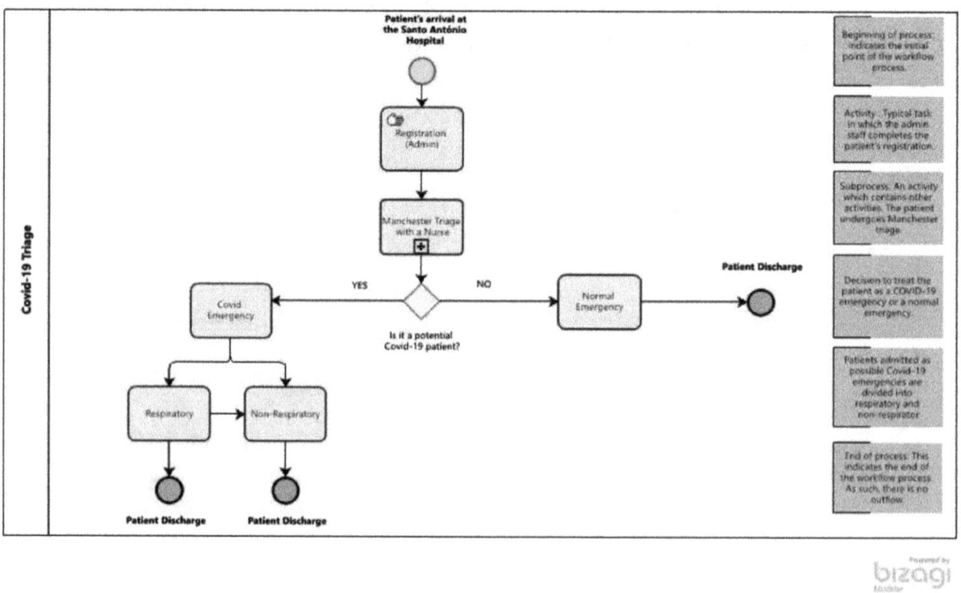

The new process developed can be considered Lean due to its fluidity and shortening of activities, in addition to the pre-screening performed with users at the beginning of the process, aspects that are the basis of the Lean system can be identified, such as the best use of available resources. In this case the registration team, shortening of workflows and activity redesign, these features aimed at Lean Healthcare streamline the screening process and improve outcomes, "increased efficiency of hospital clinical care through the application of Lean Healthcare has been identified as a powerful strategy to reduce costs and improve outcomes" (Tlapa et al., 2020, p. 26).

The question Q2 proposes that the interviewee identifies whether the new implemented processes can be identified as Lean or not, in her opinion. The question intends to give the interviewee a framework on the central theme of the research. In order to familiarize the interviewee with process nomenclature, a brief explanation about the term Lean was given.

Q2: What does the term Lean means to you?

I am not familiar with terminology, however, dealing in process reduction and continuous improvement for employees regarding the effectiveness of procedures, I believe the processes can be considered Lean.

The approach of the research regarding the scope of implementation in the survey is composed of the following 3 questions Q3, Q4 and Q5. These will assess the obstacles encountered when the new process was implemented, and the difficulties encountered. Question Q3 asks the interviewee about the need to update processes, that is, why processes and activities were remodelled. The main cause of the remodelling of the triage processes of the Santo António Hospital, within the scope of the COVID pandemic, was to stop the spread of the virus, the change in triage processes was made to protect the health of patients and professionals, thus reducing the movement between units.

Question Q4 inquires the interviewee regarding the implementation of the lean philosophy in the hospital culture as a whole and whether the objectives were perceived. According to the interviewee, the team objectives were well-defined. The main the objectives of the implementation of the philosophy in the COVID situation was to reduce contact between users, reduce waiting times, and classify users as quickly and efficiently as possible. They were all accomplished.

The last question about the implementation variable, Q5, aims to investigate the implementation of the organisational culture, how the changes were received by the workforce, and how they adapted to the changes in routines. According to the interviewee, the implementation of the new processes was quite confusing at first, professionals were only informed about the changes after the processes had been changed. There was no training, only information about PPEs, which generated a lot of fear to employees.

Following, question Q6 addresses leadership and its impact on the implementation process. What factors would be of utmost importance for a successful lean implementation with a good degree of acceptance in the organizational culture and how leadership should be performed in a lean implementation? In the interviewee's opinion, for success to be guaranteed, the leadership should listen more to the employees who are in the field, more organization is needed in new processes implementation, procedures should be standardized. The changes should be implemented according to the suggestions of the employees who are directly involved in the processes. The leadership lacked a more practical approach.

On the advantages identified by the change in the process's routine questions Q7 and Q8 directly address the critical factors for the success of the implementation and the obstacles encountered in changing the processes. Regarding the success of the implementation the interviewee states that the success of the operation during the pandemic was primarily due to the collaboration of the team, their willpower and the rigor in following the proposed schemes. Further, the collaboration of other sectors such as the administrative ones which helped in the screening processes. The organization and the entire body of collaborators focused on the same objective, and ready to face the challenge. About the difficulties encountered, the interviewer identified the facilities and emotional management as the main problems.

The physical space was a major obstacle, because at certain times there were no more vacancies in the COVID sector, the separate space for these users was not enough. The biggest challenge was emotional management, despite having all the psychological support provided by the hospital, staying strong and away from the family, in addition to the many hours of work followed for the greater good.

CONCLUSION

This work investigated the change in the triage process at the Santo António Hospital brought about by the pandemic due to COVID-19.

Through a telephone interview with the head of nursing at Hospital de Santo António, where we performed the process mapping and defined the management structure as Lean. At this stage, we concluded that the newly implemented processes could be considered lean and that the process change aimed at reducing waiting times and patient exposure.

The lack of communication and practical perspective from the leaders was the main problem identified concerning leadership characteristics, and the leading nurse considers that nurses' (who are in contact with the patients) opinion, should be taken into consideration. Despite not being familiar with Lean process and methodology, the objectives were clear, and the processes were followed. The lack of training and clarity made implementation harder and processes a little confuse in the beginning. Team effort helped solving the problems and adapting to the new processes.

This research contributes to health area managers, regarding the observation of processes and the design and mapping of hospital processes. The research suggests the continuous improvement of internal processes and the investigation of their barriers, for example questioning other nurses, and also proposes more care to be observed in the implementation of new management processes.

REFERENCES

Borchers, U., & Evans, M. (2011). Das "nutzerorientierte" Krankenhaus–Chance und Herausforderung für die Gesundheitswirtschaft. *Zeitschrift Fuer Evidenz. Fortbildung Und Qualitaet Im Gesundheitswesen*, *105*(8), 616–623. doi:10.1016/j.zefq.2011.07.019

Bortolotti, T., Boscari, S., & Danese, P. (2015). Successful lean implementation: Organizational culture and soft lean practices. *International Journal of Production Economics*, *160*, 182–201. doi:10.1016/j.ijpe.2014.10.013

Campos, A. L. N. (2014). *Modelagem de Processos com BPMN* (2nd ed.). Brasport.

Chopra, S., & Meindl, P. (2011). *Gestão da cadeia de suprimentos: estratégia, planejamento e operações*. Pearson.

D'Andreamatteo, A., Ianni, L., Lega, F., & Sargiacomo, M. (2015). Lean in healthcare: A comprehensive review. *Health Policy (Amsterdam)*, *119*(9), 1197–1209. doi:10.1016/j.healthpol.2015.02.002 PMID:25737260

da Silva Xavier, C. M., da Silva Xavier, L. F., Xavier, A. C., & da Rocha Paranhos, R. P. (2016). *Gerenciamento de Projetos de Mapeamento e Redesenho de Processos: uma adaptação da metodologia*. Basic Methodware. Brasport.

de Pádua, E. M. M. (2007). *Metodologia da Pesquisa* (13th ed.). Papirus Editora.

de Regge, M., Gemmel, P., & Meijboom, B. (2019). How operations matters in healthcare standardization. *International Journal of Operations & Production Management*, *39*(9/10), 1144–1165. doi:10.1108/IJOPM-03-2019-0227

della Volpi, Y., & Paulino, S. R. (2018). The sustainability of services: Considerations on the materiality of accommodation services from the concept of life cycle thinking. *Journal of Cleaner Production*, *192*, 327–334. doi:10.1016/j.jclepro.2018.04.166

Fitzsimmons, J. A., & Fitzsimmons, M. J. (2014). *Administração de Serviços-: Operações, Estratégia e Tecnologia da Informação*. Amgh Editora.

Gonzalez, M. E. (2019). Improving customer satisfaction of a healthcare facility: Reading the customers' needs. *Benchmarking*, *26*(3), 854–870. doi:10.1108/BIJ-01-2017-0007

Graban, M. (2016). *Lean hospitals: improving quality, patient safety, and employee engagement*. CRC Press. doi:10.1201/b11740

Huhs, E., Gliebe, W., & Sendlhofer, G. (2019). Qualitative Analyse zu Lean Management im Gesundheitswesen: Sichtweisen österreichischer und Schweizer Experten. *Zeitschrift für Evidenz, Fortbildung und Qualität im Gesundheitswesen*, *143*, 8–14. doi:10.1016/j.zefq.2019.05.003 PMID:31153810

Hundal, G. S., Thiyagarajan, S., Alduraibi, M., Laux, C. M., Furterer, S. L., Cudney, E. A., & Antony, J. (2021). Lean Six Sigma as an organizational resilience mechanism in health care during the era of COVID-19. *International Journal of Lean Six Sigma*. doi:10.1108/IJLSS-11-2020-0204

Iswanto, A. H. (2021). Impact of lean six sigma at pharmacy unit on hospital profitability before and during Covid-19 pandemic. *International Journal of Lean Six Sigma*. doi:10.1108/IJLSS-10-2020-0182

Lindsay, C. F., Kumar, M., & Juleff, L. (2020). Operationalising lean in healthcare: The impact of professionalism. *Production Planning and Control*, *31*(8), 629–643. doi:10.1080/09537287.2019.1668577

Mackway-Jones, K., Marsden, J., & Windle, J. (2006). *Emergency triage*. Wiley Online Library.

Rebouças, D. (2007). *Administração de processos: conceitos, metodologias e práticas* (2nd ed.). Atlas.

Sim, K. L., & Rogers, J. W. (2009). Implementing lean production systems: Barriers to change. *Management Research News*, *32*(1), 37–49. doi:10.1108/01409170910922014

Tlapa, D., Zepeda-Lugo, C. A., Tortorella, G. L., Baez-Lopez, Y. A., Limon-Romero, J., Alvarado-Iniesta, A., & Rodriguez-Borbon, M. I. (2020). Effects of lean healthcare on patient flow: A systematic review. *Value in Health*, *23*(2), 260–273. doi:10.1016/j.jval.2019.11.002 PMID:32113632

Womack, J. P., & Jones, D. T. (2015). *Lean solutions: how companies and customers can create value and wealth together*. Simon and Schuster.

Yin, R. K. (2015). *Qualitative research from start to finish*. Guilford Publications.

KEY TERMS AND DEFINITIONS

COVID-19: A global pandemic or coronavirus disease 2019, which is caused by SARS-CoV-2 (severe acute respiratory syndrome coronavirus 2).

Bizagi Software: Process mapping software used by organizations to create and document business processes to gain a better understanding of each step and identify process improvement opportunities to increase organizational efficiency.

Lean: A management process which focuses on improving communication and all the value chain, by compacting tasks in order to reduce deadlines and improve quality.

Lean Healthcare: The process of analyzing and guiding internal and external workflows to continuous improvement, in healthcare units such as hospitals, clinics and pharmacies.

Manchester Triage System: A system developed by the Manchester Triage Group, to automatically calculates the severity of the user and separates him/her with colored wristbands where each color represents the level of severity and predicts waiting time.

Chapter 5
Use of Emotional Intelligence in Human Resource Management in Healthcare Organizations for Competitive Advantage:
A Systematic Literature Review

Deeba Hasan
Indian Institute of Technology, Madras, India

T. J. Kamalanabhan
Indian Institute of Technology, Madras, India

ABSTRACT

Recent years have seen escalating interest in the impact of emotions within organizations. However, research on the role of emotional intelligence specifically in the domain of human resource management in healthcare organizations has been ignored. This chapter compiles a comprehensive, systematic review of literature on the impacts of emotional intelligence in the healthcare sector spanning a period from 1960 to 2020. The authors aim to explore and raise pertinent questions about the impacts of emotional intelligence on healthcare outcomes, job stress, emotional labor, and linkages of emotional intelligence with a competitive advantage for healthcare organizations. A major contribution of this work is the proposal of a novel conceptual framework for the marketing of emotional intelligence in the healthcare sector. Literature gaps, relationships among works, and current trends are discussed.

DOI: 10.4018/978-1-7998-7263-4.ch005

INTRODUCTION

Since its popularization around three decades back, the concept of Emotional Intelligence (EI) has largely taken the management world by storm. Its value-addition in organizations has been greatly eulogized with claimed benefits ranging from manager competence and employee well-being to enhanced organizational performance (Grossman, 2000). It is surprising then, that the claimed benefits have neither managed to sway more Healthcare (HC) managers into incorporating it within their organizations, nor into making more efforts towards understanding it as a concept (Gilmartin & Aunno, 2007). Healthcare Organizations (HCO) are by nature, steeped in complexity. Critical decisions need to be taken on an evolving basis; interpersonal communication is crucial; the margin for errors is low and there is no room for fatigue and emotional exhaustion. The need for emotional labor only adds to challenges that are faced by HC personnel (Erickson & Grove, 2008). Another noteworthy change that has occurred with time is that patients' have become more aware and demanding of their rights as '*consumers*' (Copperman et al., 2012). Not surprisingly then, extant healthcare literature is rich in studies that document the increasing stress levels in personnel and its resultant consequences like burnout, negative attitudes, inappropriate behavior and inharmonious relationships (Magnavita, 2014). However, research exploring the benefits of applying EI to counteract the professional challenges is scarce. Nonetheless, among the studies that do broach this topic, there is a near unanimous agreement that EI significantly impacts HC outcomes like improving the quality of caregiving, reducing medical errors, and improving patients' perceptions of doctors' attitudes (Newton, et al., 2016; Rosenstein, 2015). It boosts trust-building and loyalty in the doctor-patient relationship (Nightingale, et al., 2018). It stands to reason that these will result in greater patient-compliances and revisits. Logically, far more attention should have been paid to EI by the HC sector than has been seen hitherto. The motivation behind this study stems from the fact that despite mounting empirical evidence of the benefits of EI application in organizations, the HC sector has still not been adequately studied in this regard (Gilmartin & Aunno, 2007). Further, there has been a skewed representation of HC-related stress in existing literature. The numerous deleterious consequences of stress have been extensively reported but the psychological resources that can overcome these consequences have hardly been discussed. In the current scenario, it appears as if the problem has been paid far more attention as compared to the efforts being made towards finding solutions. This linear representation of medical stress is at odds with various theoretical frameworks that challenge a unidimensional depiction of stress and highlight the role of "*individual resources and appraisals*" that determine personal and professional outcomes. Some popular theories are: the job-demands-resource theory (Bakker & Demerouti, 2007), Lazarus' transactional theory of stress (Lazarus & Folkman, 1984), job-demand-control-support theory (Karasek & Theorell, 1990), challenge-hindrance stressor theory (Cavanaugh et al., 2000), Holahan and Moos's (1987) coping theory, holistic stress theory (Simmons & Nelson, 2007), Hobfall's (1989) conservation of resources theory, and Fredrickson's(1998) broaden-and-build-theory (1998).The commonality in all these theories is the emphasis placed on the power of personal resources in dealing with stressors. Stressors themselves are neutral. They can be either advantageous or disadvantageous. This is where emotional intelligence comes into play. Emotional intelligence is the capacity to be aware of one's own as well as others' emotions, manage one's emotions and interpersonal relationships (Salovey& Mayer, 1990). This is a powerful psychological resource that helps individuals overcome professional stressors (Newton et al., 2016). The key operating mechanism through which this occurs is through positive emotion regulation engendered by EI (Szczygiel & Mikolajczak, 2017). In the face of unavoidable job-stressors, it is still possible that employees maintain emotional equilibrium by drawing upon inner psychological resources and deliberately enhancing positive emotions and downplaying negative ones (Gross, 1998). Meta-analyses confirm a positive correlation between EI and intentional modulation of positive emotions (savoring) and suppression of the frequency of negative emotions (dampening) (Quoidbach et al., 2010). In the HC sector, however, the lack of comprehensive studies makes it difficult to reach indubitable conclusions. The purpose of this work is to review and highlight the potential benefits of incorporating EI skills-both from the Human Resource Management (HRM) perspective as well as healthcare-outcomes' perspective and offer ways in which the EI concept can be disseminated more widely within organizations. The authors assert that such work is essential because stress is inherent to the nature of the HC profession and this cannot be changed. It would be better to devote energies towards finding ways in which employees can build personal resources to combat stress "*as a resistance armamentarium*" (Hobfall, 2002, p. 312). EI can be one such powerful personal resource. With EI training, personnel can learn to appraise their jobs better, regulate their emotions and enhance their subjective well-being. For managers, it can be a boon in managing employees with the desired empathy and sensitivity. For HCOs as a whole, it can result in greater patient visits, a strengthened workforce and become a competitive advantage. Seeing the multifarious benefits, there is a need to include EI competencies in current HC practices.

The study contributes to existing literature in a number of ways. Firstly, drawing mainly from the challenge-hindrance stressor theory (Cavanaugh et al, 2000), this work extends it to the HC sector. It posits that medical stressors can be perceived as challenges to be overcome rather than considering them as stumbling blocks. Viewed this way, their detrimental effects on personnel may be diminished. Secondly, it positions emotional intelligence as a personal resource that can combat professional challenges. This argument gains ground from theoretical models like the job-demands-resource model (Bakker & Demerouti, 2007), Hobfall's (1989) conservation of resources model, job-demand-control-support model (Karasek & Theorell, 1990), and the holistic stress model (Simmons & Nelson, 2007). Concurrence with multiple popular models strengthen the authors' arguments. Thirdly, the authors develop a conceptual frameworkon marketing of EI to and by HCOs, thus increasing the practical implications of this work. It is the authors' belief that EI can be marketed successfully in the HC sector as a skill that can lead to greater organizational performances, and thus become a competitive advantage. The study reveals the beneficial impacts of EI on patient outcomes, emotional labor, and employee management. It also reveals pertinent gaps in literature and makes provision for addressing them.

The specific objectives of this work have been to answer the following fundamental questions: Do emotions and emotional intelligence affect healthcare outcomes? If so, what are the evidence-based outcomes that are impacted by EI abilities? Is there an emotional dimension to human resource management within the healthcare sector? Can it be used to improve HR practices? Has any attempt been made to market the EI concept within the healthcare sector? If so, how successful has this been?

BACKGROUND

Recent years have seen a burgeoning of interest in the impact of emotions within organizations. Research in this field, however, has been impeded by the fleeting nature of emotions and the lack of an integrated multilevel model (Ashkanasy, 2003). The term '*emotional intelligence*' is not a very old one. It was defined by Salovey and Mayer in 1990 as the ability to be aware of one's own as well as others' emotions in managing their interpersonal relationships. Although this review centres primarily on current developments in the field, relevant past literature has also been included as building blocks for the current work and to indicate where the concept of EI is historically situated. Before proceeding further with any study on EI, one needs to define emotion. Previous researchers have defined it as "*a sequence that unfolds chronologically*" (Ekman, 1992). Emotional experience is understood as the psychological and physiological sense of being affected emotionally by an event (Frijda, 1986).

The HC sector has been inadequately represented in the study of emotions. This is because, until very recently, emotional display within the formal hospital setup was considered unprofessional. It was believed that the best way to deal with emotions is to not have any (Kerasidou& Horn, 2016). However, emotional dimensions permeate the entire gamut of human behavior and cannot be wished away (Ashforth

& Humphrey, 1995). Damasio (1994) argued that the dualist separation of emotions from rationality as proposed by the great philosopher Descartes is an error. This error is now famously known as *'Descarte's error'*. Now it is accepted that the experience of work is saturated with emotions. Therefore, the study of any facet of HC, while ignoring its emotional aspects is a fallacy. An individual's emotions are followed by ramifications in cognition, behavior, and attitudes. These not only manifest externally in facial expressions and body language, but also have intense in-depth manifestations on motivation, interpersonal skills, empathy, and in immersing oneself in one's profession proactively (Roether et al, 2009). In a number of ways, an individual's job performance in the organization is largely dependent on the individual's talent at emotional-expression and emotional-management (Ashkanasy, 2003). In HC, it is even necessary at times to display one emotion, while feeling another emotion concurrently (Kinman & Leggeter, 2016).

It is thus extremely important for administrators to understand employees' emotional dynamics that are communicated by verbal and non-verbal cues and the role played by empathy and awareness in the context of organizational outcomes. Emotional understanding among co-workers is an essential social process in group formation and team work. Understanding this can guide administrators in forming sensitive, empathetic relationships with their employees. HC literature abounds with studies on the deleterious consequences of job-stress (Bilal, 2017). What has been ignored however, is that stress itself need not be harmful. The cognitive theory of emotions claims that it is the cognition of a stimulus, and not the stimulus itself that determines the kind of response elicited (Lazarus, 1991). Emotion-management skills can contain and channelize stress in a positive direction (Szczygiel & Mikolajczak, 2017). The point of greatest interest for an organizational administrator is the understanding that within the emotional process, there are recognizable emotion-regulation stages, which, if practiced continually, can become automated (Gross, 1998). The emotion-regulation stage is distinct for each individual and is subject to individual disparities and group norms (Mesquita & Frijda, 2011). Therefore, EI is an '*agent provocateur*' for energizing HC. Meaningful emotional exchanges are essential for professionalism and group cohesion and the role of the leader in displaying, regulating, and managing these emotions is central (Birks & Watt, 2007). Hence, the emotional paradigm of HC and its management is largely under-stated, yet vital, considering that these are the places where human health and life are regulated.

METHOD OF CONDUCTING THE SYSTEMATIC LITERATURE REVIEW

The aim of this academic review was to investigate the current status of the integration of EI within the HC sector. The authors undertook this by means of a systematic review and conceptual analysis of academic literature that specifically included the constructs of emotional intelligence, healthcare, nursing, and human resource management. The search was conducted in three stages.

1. **First Stage - Electronic Databases**

Google Scholar and the electronic databases for health sciences and health administration (PubMed, Medline), management (Elsevier, Academy of Management, Harvard Business School Publishing, Taylor & Francis, Wiley Online Journal, Sage, Emerald Insight, Springer), and psychology (PsycNet) were scanned prior to conducting more detailed searches. Keywords used in the literature searches included: Emotional Intelligence, Healthcare and Human Resource Management. The number of records identified after removal of duplicates at this stage were 207.

2. **Second Stage - Partial Screening Criteria:**

   a. Inclusion Criteria:
      i. Temporal Criteria: Articles/books published during the time period1960-2020 were selected for forming the body of this work. However, older studies were included only if they were classical works that served as the foundation of the EI construct and demonstrated its historical standing;
      ii. Contextual Criteria: Articles that pertained to the role of EI in the healthcare sector; articles that were in English; and articles that were relevant to the research questions were included. Papers were selected based on titles and publishers.
   b. Exclusion Criteria:
      i. Opinion-driven reports (editorials, commentaries, and letters);
      ii. Older articles, unless they served to build the foundation of the paper; and
      iii. Articles that were not in English were excluded.

Due to the dearth of published literature pertaining specifically to EI in HC management, literature on the impact of EI in nurses, and other professions were included. 149 articles, journal papers and books were reviewed at this stage and 58 were removed after reading abstracts. Further, 64 of the 149 articles were removed after quality assessment.

3. Third Stage - Final Selection

In this stage, full texts of 85 articles were read, and 66 articles that met all the inclusion criteria were finally selected.

Figure 1 highlights the flow chart depicting the method of conducting the systematic literature review in accordance with PRISMA (Preferred Reporting Items for Systematic Reviews and Meta-Analyses) guidelines (Moher et al., 2009).

Figure 1. Flow diagram of conducting the systematic literature review
Source: Moher, Liberati, Tetzlaff & Altman, 2009

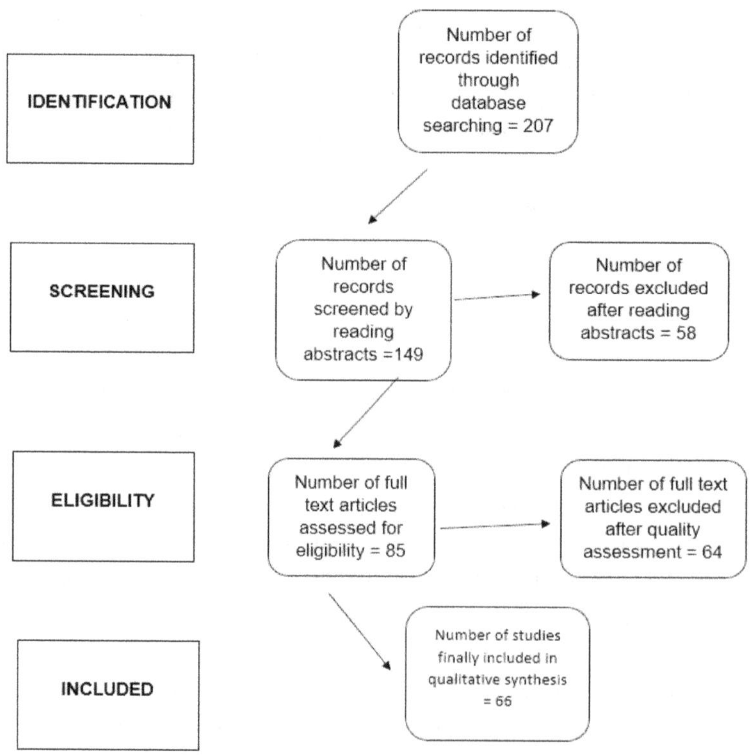

Figure 2 highlights the distribution of selected articles by journals.

Figure 3 highlights the distribution of selected articles by the type of research method used.

Figure 2. Distribution of selected articles by journals

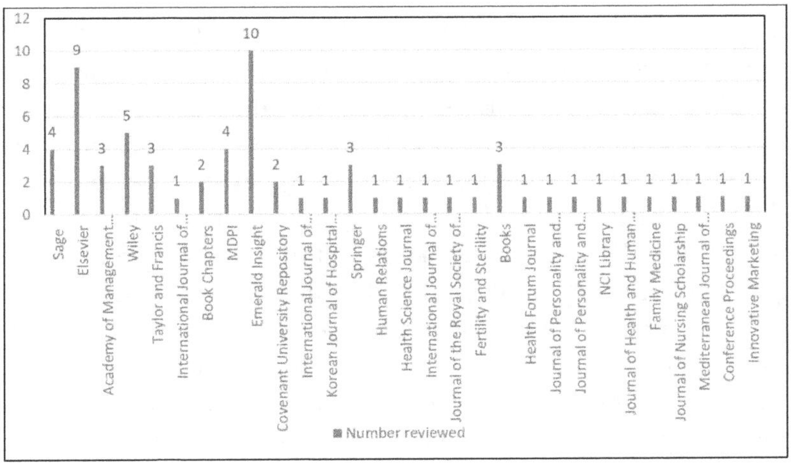

Figure 3. Distribution of selected articles by the type of research method used
Source: Authors

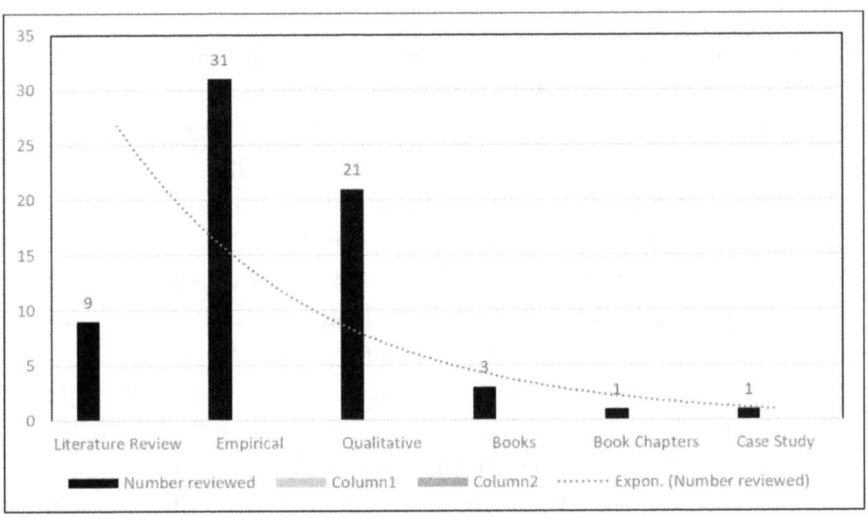

MAIN FOCUS OF THE CHAPTER: SYNTHESIS AND SUMMARY OF EVIDENCE

Classical Models

There are three classical models of EI namely: the ability-model, the trait-model and the mixed-model. The ability model focuses on the individual's ability to process emotional information and use it to navigate the social environment (Mayer & Salovey, 1997; Salovey & Mayer, 1990). In the ability model, EI is treated as a measure of standard intelligence that grows with age, experiences and training. The test for ability EI is based on one's ability to perform set tasks that involve correct or incorrect answers. The trait model posits that EI is a self-perceived, personality related aptitude (Petrides & Furnham, 2003). Lying in between these two ends is the Boyatzis-Goleman mixed model (Boyatzis et al., 2000) which is a broad model of EI comprising of personality traits as well as abilities. The trait and mixed models are measured by self-reports and hence are susceptible to social desirability bias and feigning. They have also shown a lack of discriminant validity (Brackett et al., 2006). Therefore, for the purposes of this review, the ability model will be focussed on since this model best represents EI as a measurable, standard intelligence and also maintains that EI abilities can be developed. According to the founders of the EI construct (Mayer& Salovey, 1997), whenever there is a discourse about EI, the central theme of the discourse should be the opportunity for individual development. The ability model is in concurrence with this perspective.

Another model of importance as far as the focus of this work is concerned is the four-cornerstone model of emotional intelligence proposed by Cooper and Sawaf in 1998. This model is particularly suited for the present work because it directly links EI with competitive advantage for an organization. The model sharply shifts the focus from theoretical musings to practical applications of EI within organizations. The four EI-capacities or cornerstones put forward in this regard are emotional-literacy, emotional-depth, emotional-fitness, and emotional-alchemy. The capacities have four components each, leading to a total of sixteen components namely- emotional- honesty, emotional-energy, emotional-feedback, practical intuition, authentic presence, trust radius, constructive discontent, resilience, commitment, unique potential, applied integrity, and influence without authority. The model stresses that EI generates emotional drive, inner guidance, self-discipline, creativity, and self-efficacy in the workforce which are the competencies that lead to organizational success and give competitive advantages. The model has been validated by multiple academic and organizational studies (Kewalramani et al., 2015).

ANSWERS TO RESEARCH QUESTIONS

The following section discusses the specific questions that the authors attempted to answer through the review of literature.

RQ1: Do Emotions and Emotional Intelligence Play a Part in Healthcare Outcomes?

In order to answer this question, the authors reviewed empirical studies, qualitative studies, integrative review papers and books. Converging evidence was found that EI affects clinical judgement, caregiving and decision-making skills. EI was found to elicit compassion, conscientiousness, altruism and courtesy in practitioners. Contrarily, one study reported that doctors in UK are perceived by patients to be uncaring. This was associated with low EI levels of doctors. Stress and burnout were prevalent amongst caregivers and EI had a mitigating effect on both. High EI had significant associations with better patient care and patient outcomes. It was also associated with team work, motivation, and interestingly, decreased healthcare expenditure. Thus, it can be concluded that emotions and EI do indeed affect multiple aspects of caregiving.

Table 1 is a brief tabulation of the papers that had literature apropos to answering RQ1.

Figure 4 shows the distribution of articles by type of study for RQ1.

Figure 5 shows the distribution of articles by type of journal for RQ1.

RQ2: What is the Role that 'Emotional Labor' Plays in the Healthcare Scenario- Is it a Good Thing to Feel One Emotion Whilst Portraying Another?

Emotional labor is a part and parcel of providing HC services. Sometimes it is essential to hide from the patient the real emotions that arise in the care-provider during the course of treatment. Be that as it may, hiding distressing emotions and feigning a calm persona takes its toll on caregivers. Implicit power differences contribute to this, but EI can mitigate the end fatigue significantly. Interestingly, surface acting is associated with greater fatigue as compared to deep acting. EI is positively associated with efficiency and negatively associated with turnover and burnout consequent to emotional labor. From a HRM perspective, if employers build an emotional rapport with employees, it will help them while dealing with the exhaustion following emotional labor.

Table 2 is a brief tabulation of the papers that had literature apropos to answering RQ2.

Table 1. Distribution of articles by number of papers, study type, percentage of articles by study type, range of years of publication and primary findings for RQ1

Characteristics of Papers Containing Apropos Literature	Primary Findings
Number of papers with pertinent literature for RQI = 20 Percentage of distribution of articles by study type • Empirical = 60% • Qualitative = 25% • Literature review = 10% • Book = 5% Range of years of publication = 1968-2019 References • Ashforth & Humphrey (1995) • Ashkanasy (2003) • Birks & Watt (2007) • Cooper (1997) • Copperman et al. (2012) • Damasio (1994) • Foster et al. (2018) • Flippo (1968) • Goleman (2000) • Grossman (2000) • Jamshed & Majeed (2019) • Liu et al. (2018) • Magnavita (2014) • Malik et al. (2019) • Mikolajczak & Bellegem (2017) • Mumby & Putnam (1997) • Newton et al. (2016) • Psilopanagioti et al. (2012) • Rosenstein (2015) • Smith et al. (2009)	• Emotions are a vital element at the workplace and should be normalized. • EI is associated with courtesy, altruism, virtuousness, logical thinking, decision-making, student learning, and employee-retention. • EI is an essential competency in HC. Suggestions provided for training and assessment. • EI is associated with caring behavior. Doctors in UK criticised for lacking caring attitude. • Burnout is a psycho-social behavior which decreases with EI. • Increase in EI results in decrease in HC expenditure. • Emotionally intelligent people indulge in consistent emotion-regulation. • EI has potential in clinical psychology. • Theorists should desist from separating emotionality and rationality. Hidden assumptions behind such views should be unearthed. • Positive correlation seen between manager's EQ and key profit areas of organization.

Source: Authors

Figure 6 shows the distribution of articles by type of study for RQ2.

Figure 7 shows distribution of articles by type of journal for RQ2.

RQ3: What are the Emotional Dimensions of Human Resource Management in Healthcare?

HRM in HC is a highly demanding area that needs careful navigation and expertise. Employees work under constant stress and experience intense and conflicting emotions in the face of overwhelming demands. The emotional state of an employee can affect their interpretation of their circumstances and resultant responses; hence they need to be handled with sensitivity and care. EI skills of managers can help

Figure 4. Distribution of selected articles by type of study for RQ1
Source: Authors

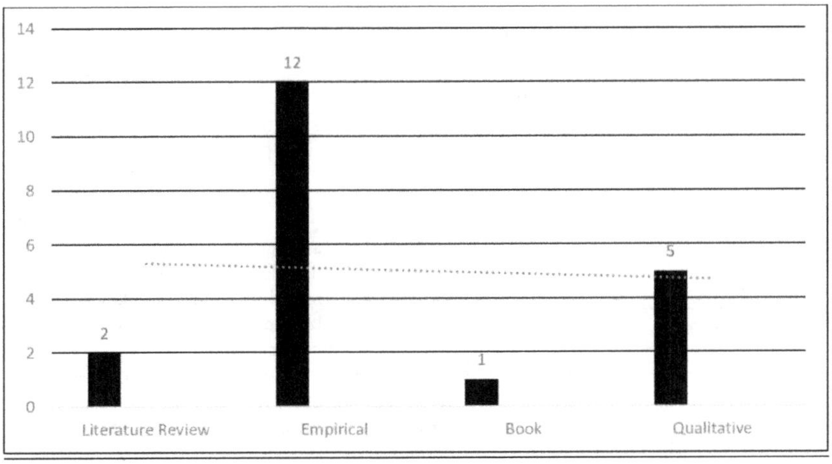

to facilitate employees' performances and guide them carefully. Studies reveal that administrators' EI plays a vital role in HRM in the HC sector.

Significant positive associations have been found between emotional skills of managers and employees' organizational commitment. EI leads to knowledge-

Figure 5. Distribution of selected articles by journals for RQ1
Source: Authors

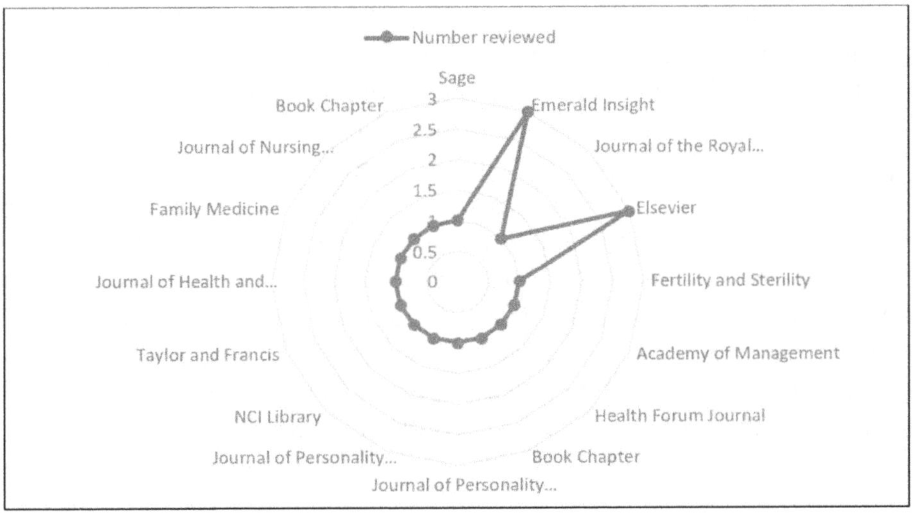

Table 2. Distribution of articles by number of papers, study type, percentage of articles by study type, range of years of publication and primary findings for RQ2

Characteristics of Papers Containing Apropos Literature	Primary Findings
Number of papers with pertinent literature for RQ2 = 14	• HC workers face intense, contradictory, and turbulent emotions. They build routines as a defence against their anxieties, resulting in emotional labor. There are personal, organizational, gendered, and socio-cultural influences in emotional labor. • Emotional labor leads to high fatigue which EI is capable of mitigating. • EI can be enhanced through self-practices and formal training. • Job-satisfaction is positively associated with EI. • EI is positively associated with quality of care, work-life balance, reduction of errors, productivity, and patient outcomes. • EI moderates the effects of burnout and stress and promotes wellbeing in jobs demanding emotional labor.
Percentage of distribution of articles by study type • Literature Review= 21.4% • Empirical= 50% • Qualitative= 21.4% • Case Study=7.14%	
Range of years of publication = 1960-2019	
References • Clarke (2006) • Erickson & Grove (2008) • Feather (2009) • Joung &Kim (2006) • Kerasidou& Horn (2014) • Liu et al. (2011) • Malik et al. (2019) • Menzies (1960) • Meyer et al. (2004) • Psilopanagioti et al. (2012) • Riley & Weiss (2016) • Smith et al. (2009) • Trivellas (2013) • Walsh (2009)	

Source: Authors

sharing that result in team bonding and enhanced performances. It also facilitates gender inclusiveness and diversity management. Managers who are familiar with the emotion-sequential process can guide employees in recognizing their emotion-regulation stages. This can be transformational for emotion-management in the workplace. What is most exciting perhaps, is that emotion-regulation can become an automatic process with practice (Gross, 1998). This is brought about by new neural synapses forming in the brain over time (Goleman, 1995). Thus, it can be stated that the HC environment is a dynamic one and EI of managers can help them immensely to negotiate HR demands and circumvent professional pitfalls. Table 3 is a brief tabulation of the papers that had literature apropos to answering RQ3.

Figure 8 shows distribution of articles by type of study for RQ3.

Figure 9 shows distribution of articles by type of journal for RQ3.

Figure 6. Distribution of selected articles by type of study for RQ2
Source: Authors

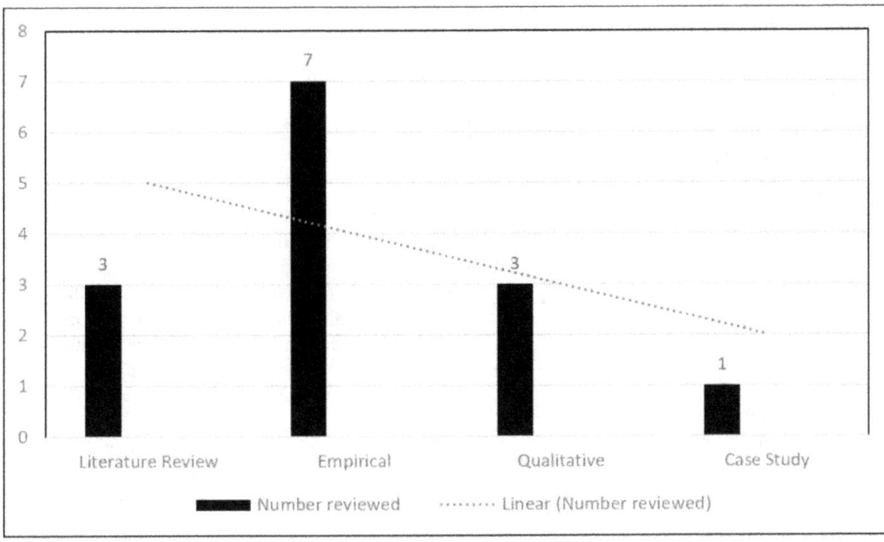

Figure 7. Distribution of selected articles by journals for RQ2
Source: Authors

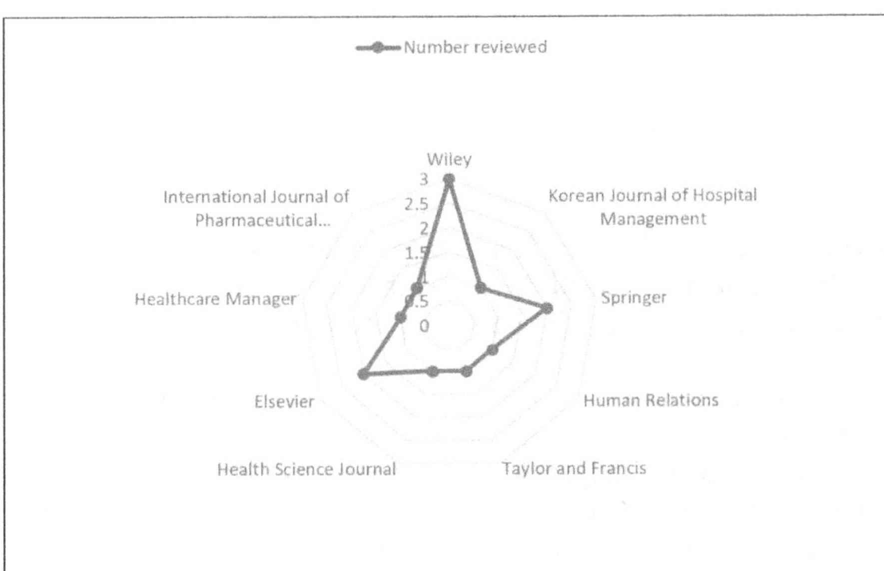

Table 3. Distribution of articles by number of papers, study type, percentage of articles by study type, range of years of publication and primary findings for RQ3

<table>
<tr><th>Characteristics of Papers Containing Apropos Literature</th><th>Primary Findings</th></tr>
<tr><td>Number of papers with pertinent literature for RQ3 = 20</td><td rowspan="4">• Emotions are an important part of rational decision making in organizations.
• Communication skills and emotional intelligence are two crucial skills needed by health care managers.
• Significant correlation seen between EI and organizational commitment, conflict management, coping, CSR, patient satisfaction, knowledge sharing, and team-bonding.
• Inclusiveness and diversity management is a challenge in HCOs which can be addressed by EI.
• EI can be incorporated in key profit areas of organizations.
• EI can be useful in recruitment, selection, and training of managers.
• Very few HCOs recognize that EI skills are required for organizational success.
• EI can be learnt and developed.
• Research in HC is lacking in the areas of developing leadership theories in the context of EI. More research is required to substantiate EI's claims in HC sector.</td></tr>
<tr><td>Percentage of distribution of articles by study type
• Empirical = 45%
• Qualitative = 35%
• Literature review =10%
• Book Chapter= 5%
• Book =5%</td></tr>
<tr><td>Range of years of publication = 1995-2020</td></tr>
<tr><td>References
• Ashforth & Humphrey (1995)
• Basogul & Ozgur (2016)
• Bilal (2017)
• Christiansen et al. (2010)
• Clarke (2006)
• Eriguc & Kose (2013)
• Feather (2009)
• Fernandez et al. (2012)
• Freshman & Rubino (2002)
• Gilmartin & Aunno (2007)
• Goleman (2000)
• Humphreys et al. (2005)
• Langhorn (2004)
• Meyer et al. (2004)
• Oyewunmi (2015)
• Oyewunmi et al. (2018)
• Pradhan & Jena (2018)
• Rao (2006)
• Ward et al. (2018)
• Weiszbrod (2020)</td></tr>
</table>

Source: Authors

RQ4: Has Emotional Intelligence been Marketed as a Soft Skill in the Healthcare Industry, and if so, how Successful has the Practice Been?

The review has revealed an interesting finding. The authors could not find a single study pertaining to EI being marketed as a soft-skill in the HC industry. This is surprising given the strong linkages of EI with competitive advantage for organizations (Cooper & Sawaf, 1998). HCOs can potentially benefit greatly from EI application in areas like recruitment and selection, training and deployment, team selection and decision-making. Apathy towards promotion and marketing of such a salient skill in HC is a major gap that needs to be addressed. Towards this end, the authors propose a novel, conceptual framework for the marketing of EI in the HC sector. This is discussed in detail in the solutions and recommendations section.

Figure 8. Distribution of selected articles by type of study for RQ3
Source: Authors

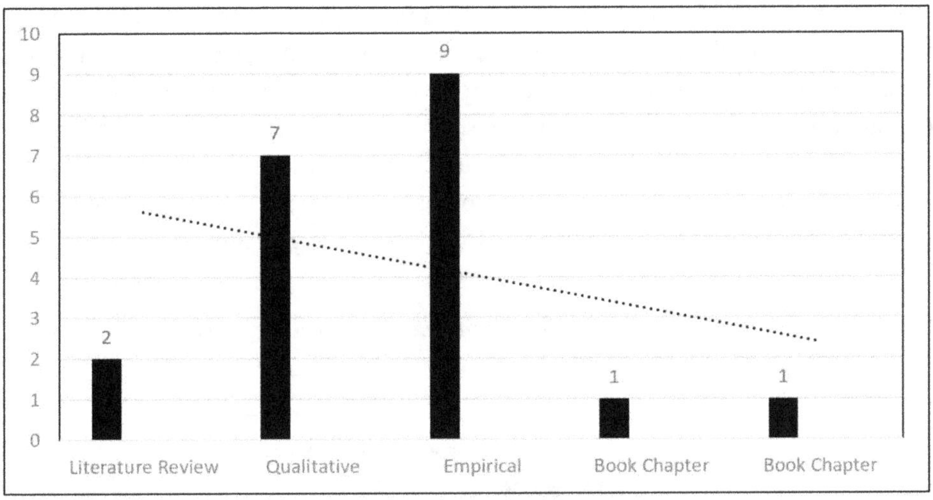

Figure 9. Distribution of selected articles by journals for RQ3
Source: Authors

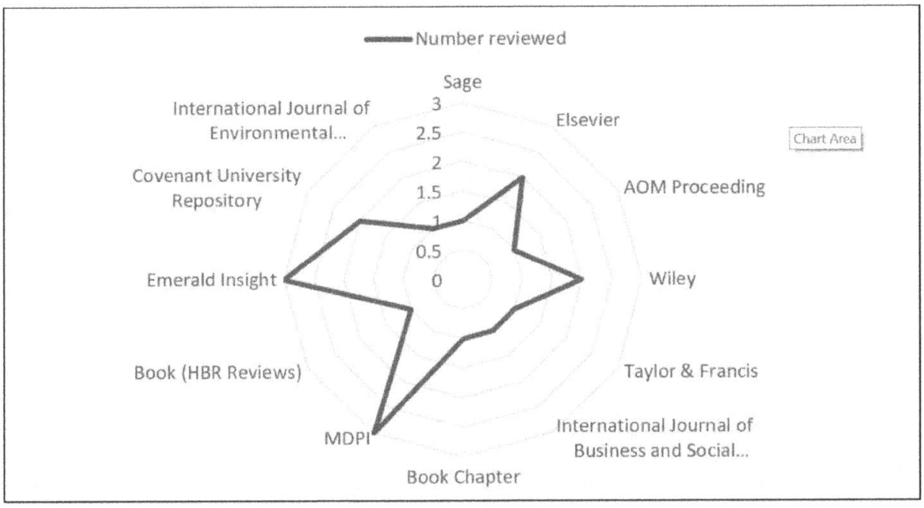

SOLUTIONS AND RECOMMENDATIONS

A key contribution of this work is that, drawing from an analysis of the present findings, current trends in research and consultations with subject-matter experts, the authors proposed a conceptual framework for the marketing of EI in the HC sector. In order to enhance the model's practical relevance, it subsumes a dual perspective-that of marketing EI to HC organizations as well as marketing of EI by HC organizations- both of which may lead to gaining a competitive advantage. Seven domains are identified as being particularly relevant for EI marketing in HC and ten approaches for marketing are proposed. The framework unveils literature gaps, suggests related literature and proposes methodologies that can be undertaken by researchers to advance this field of study. This framework can be utilized by scholars for future research as well as by practitioners for pragmatic usage. Figure 10 highlights the conceptual framework for EI marketing in the HC sector.

Figure 10. Conceptual framework for EI marketing within the HC sector
Source: Authors

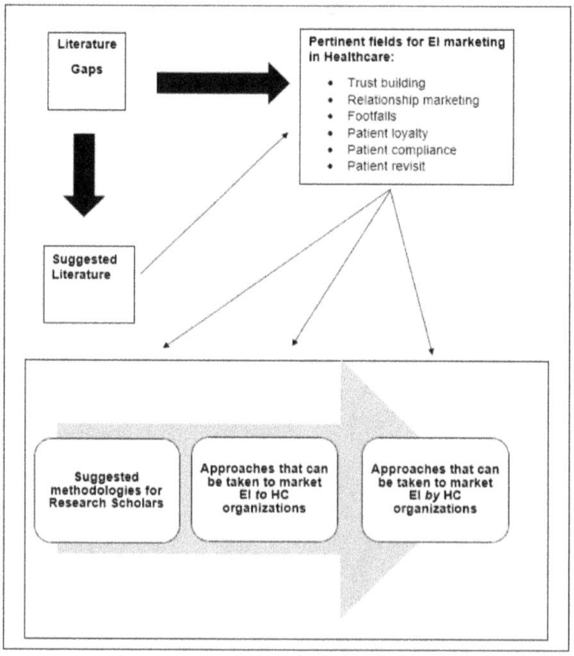

The first and foremost approach towards marketing lies in increasing the awareness levels about the concept being marketed. Only when an organization becomes willing to adopt a concept or practice, can other approaches become successful. In line with this, hiring experts for holding talks on EI and clarifying any doubts that personnel might have, would be helpful. These should be followed by training programs for personnel to incorporate these practices in key areas of the organization. The various approaches that can be taken towards EI marketing in the HC sector are discussed in the following section.

Approaches That Can Be Taken to Market EI to HC Organizations

Digital Content Streaming

Once personnel have been introduced to the concept, targeted digital content can convincingly demonstrate how EI leads to organizational effectiveness. The primary advantage of digital streaming is that content can be customized for organizations. One way in which personnel can be assisted in determining their emotional quotient is through the use of embedded quizzes. Interactive sessions may provide further instructions on ways to increase the score. A particularly effective approach in marketing is providing proof of the value of the concept being marketed (Purcarea, 2019). For this, testimonials can be streamed from organizations where EI practices have already been successfully implemented. Repetitive streaming of targeted content can serve as an implicit and highly functional reminder for employees to adopt EI-appropriate changes at the behavioral level. The authors stress that it is important that this approach is employed only after the staff has been familiarized with the EI concept. Constant stimulating reminders about a familiar information subliminally shapes long-term decisions (Ruch et al., 2016).

Social Media

Employing social media services is one of the most popular approaches in contemporary marketing. The main advantage with using social media platforms lies in their wide outreach that can be leveraged to build awareness about unfamiliar concepts. For EI marketing, especially in the HC sector, where it has erstwhile been relegated, social media platforms would serve as the ideal vehicles for directly approaching the target population and communicating with them to proffer convincing arguments for EI incorporation. Engaging in ongoing exchanges with one's target population rather than focusing on unitary transactions is essential for the marketing success (Prentice, 2019). Social media outlets and influencers serve this purpose by creating ongoing, relevant conversations around EI and disseminating it through their social following.

Media houses can also create personalized marketing strategies to showcase to HCOs how EI delivers competitive advantage.

Digital Noticeboards

Digital noticeboards are a relatively newer means of advertising that are not very widely used presently. Findings from this review, however, indicate that they will become an increasingly important means of communication in the future. Interactive content is likely to play an especially prominent role in engaging the attention of the customers. The level of customer engagement depends to a large extent on organizational culture and employees' perceived autonomy (Fortin et al., 2014). These findings can be utilized to formulate marketing strategies that encourage customer engagement and boost organizational support. Digital noticeboards with interactive content that propagate EI should be increasingly included in an HCOs marketing strategy. Used in an appropriate environment, digital noticeboards have the potential to be a highly effective and yet affordable means of marketing EI.

Scrupulously Selected Partners

One of the most convincing marketing techniques for evincing trust in potential customers is collaborating with reliable brands. When marketing a nascent concept like EI in HC, it is essential that credibility is fostered in the form of verifiable parameters like having partners whose trustworthiness has been well-established. Ensuring a strategic fit in partnerships goes a long way towards demonstrating sincerity and integrity to an admittedly sceptical client and convincing them to change their outlook towards caregiving practices (Kim & Lee, 2016). One way of improving '*strategic expediency*' in the face of insufficient knowledge about potential partners is to choose reputable partners (Bierly & Gallagher, 2007).

Approaches That Can Be Taken to Market EI by HC Organizations

HCOs that utilize EI practices can promote the resultant benefits to the community to showcase their progressive approach and commitment to quality-caregiving. In a dynamic sector like HC, fast-paced and demonstrable changes are needed to sustain patient interest. Application and marketing of EI is a potent means of demonstrating an HCOs commitment to patient welfare and organizational performance, which results in increased footfalls and patient revisits.

Interactive Website With Image Galleries, Testimonials, and Online Reviews

An HCOs website is essentially its digital representative. It is a repository of information that the patient wants, at the same time, it can effectively serve as the organization's central promotional tool. As a medium of communication, it should be interactive and easily navigable. Image galleries showcasing '*emotionally intelligent*' staff sensitively dealing with patients demonstrate the organization's commitment towards patient welfare. Testimonials from satisfied patients and online reviews can help to advance the HCOs cause cogently.

Free Health Check-Ups and Outreach Clinics

In order to showcase a humanistic face of the organization HCOs can conduct free health check-ups and establish outreach clinics. Such exercises not only help in impression management of the organization, they also accord potential patients a first-hand experience of an EI-trained staff's behavior. Directly experiencing a service should result in a far greater conversion rate and footfalls than is to be expected by disconnected or digital promotions.

Niche Marketing

A deliberate marketing strategy that can be effectively taken up by HCOs to promote EI-specific practices is niche marketing. The niche group is a group that the HCO either specializes in or wishes to promote. Niche marketing requires careful consideration at any time, and when propagating an ephemeral concept like EI, various internal and external factors like revenue generation and interdependencies among departments and groups need to be considered (Purcarea, 2019). Identifying the right niche that warrants special marketing efforts is most important (Kidwell et al., 2011). Once this is established, the HCO can showcase emotionally intelligent practices to the chosen group to its advantage. The proven benefits of addressing a niche sector are lesser competition, a greater conversion rate, and enhanced customer loyalty (Dalgic & Leeuw, 1994).

Internal Marketing

One significant area that should not be overlooked in any marketing strategy is internal marketing. Especially in HC, where the service delivery system is directly dependent on employees, any marketing strategy that neglects employee needs and employee satisfaction is bound to fail. Indeed, internal marketing by an organization, by virtue of applying the EI capacities of empathy and relationship-management, straightaway delivers a competitive advantage through employee satisfaction (Huang et al., 2019). Internal marketing helps in patient retention, word-of-mouth-publicity, and converting inquiries into appointments. Most importantly, it creates a sense of familiarity and comfort amongst both patients and staff (Piercy & Morgan, 1991). Some scholars have advocated considering patients of HCOs as its internal customers. Since patients are a part of the delivery system (Purcarea, 2019) and contribute to it by providing time and effort, the same principles of segmentation and customer targeting should be applied to them as the employees (Kim & Lee, 2016). Whichever way it is implemented, it is clear that EI training and application is essential to an HCOs internal marketing success (Mintz & Currim, 2013).

Table 4 details the conceptual framework for EI marketing within the HC sector. It highlights the literature gaps, related literature, suggested methodologies for research, and approaches that can be taken to market EI to HCOs and by HCOs.

The above framework forms the central recommendation of this review. Interestingly, this study has revealed a finding that affects the way HCOs need to devise marketing tactics for the different segments. EEG brain analyses of a wide range of individuals reveal that people react differently to different marketing messages depending on their EI (Ciorciari et al, 2019). High EI groups have people-focused cognition and prefer related messages whereas low EI groups prefer object-focused messages.

Whatever the level of EI, there are certain generalized short-term and long-term measures that can be adopted to effectively train, develop, and edify workforces in the EI discipline. In the short-term, training modules and inclusion of an EI component in promotions would be an effective, expedited measure. Long-term measures require changes at the policy-level to incorporate EI principles in employee selection, diversity management, gender inclusiveness, and to provide greater latitude for employees. These would ensure that there would be a strengthened workforce and a more productive work-environment. Figure 11 shows distribution of articles by type of study for RQ4.

Figure 12 shows distribution of articles by type of journal for RQ4.

DISCUSSION

The goal of this paper was to visit the '*emotional landscape*' of the HC sector and analyze published literature in this context. Specifically, this work attempted to highlight the impacts of EI on clinical outcomes, emotional labor, and HRM. It also attempted to find out the efforts made, if any, to market EI in the HC sector. The review has confirmed that emotionally intelligent leadership is both an art

Table 4. Conceptual framework for EI marketing in healthcare for RQ4

Literature Gap	Suggested Methodologies for Research Scholars	Related Literature	Pertinent Fields for EI Marketing in HC	Approaches That Can Be Taken to Market EI To HC Organizations	Approaches That Can Be Taken to Market EI By HC Organizations for Competitive Advantage
Marketing of EI as a soft skill within the healthcare industry.	Field Study	• Balamohan et al. (2015) • Bierly & Gallagher (2007) • Ciorciary et al. (2019) • Dalgic & Leeuw (1994) • Fortin et al. (2014) • Hashem (2010) • Heffernan et al. (2018) • Huang et al. (2019) • Kidwell et al. (2011) • Lassk & Shepherd (2013) • Mintz & Currim (2013) • Nwokah & Ahiauzu (2009) • Piercy & Morgan (1991) • Prentice (2019) • Prentice (2020) • Purcarea (2019)	Trust building	Digital content streaming	'Human'-centric advertising
	Experimental interventions		Relationship Marketing	Social media	Image galleries showcasing 'emotionally-intelligent' staff
	Survey design				
Marketing of EI by/ to healthcare organizations for competitive advantage.	Internet survey		Patient loyalty	Digital noticeboards	Free health check-ups/camps to show humanistic face of the organization
	Electroencephalography analysis of the brain with EI psychometrics		Footfalls	Scrupulously selected partners	Marketing for niche group of clienteles.
			Patient compliance		Internal marketing
			Patient revisit		
			Advertising		

Source: Authors

and a science. Emotions do indeed affect almost every aspect of caregiving, be it decision-making, patient care, turnover, interpersonal communications, or leadership competence. It is surprising that there are only a few HCOs that recognize the benefits of EI incorporation (Grossman, 2000). The health industry now recognizes that the current managerial performance needs major improvements (Clarke, 2006) and EI can provide the much-needed competitive advantage.

Areas of Emphasis

HC literature has conventionally concentrated on job-stress and its deleterious consequences. There are ample studies pertaining to burnout, perceived-stress, turnover, and decreased motivation and job-satisfaction. Another area of concentration is the nursing sector where most studies have focussed their attention because of the inordinate amounts of stress faced by this group. Menzies (1960) stressed that nurses operate in a whirlpool of emotions ranging from joy, gratitude, respect, to resentment, and contempt. However, the authors argue that this emotional jostling is not limited to nurses. Rather, it is applicable to the entire spectrum of HC personnel as all of them function in the same milieu of unforgiving expectations and demands.

Figure 11. Distribution of selected articles by type of study for RQ4
Source: Authors

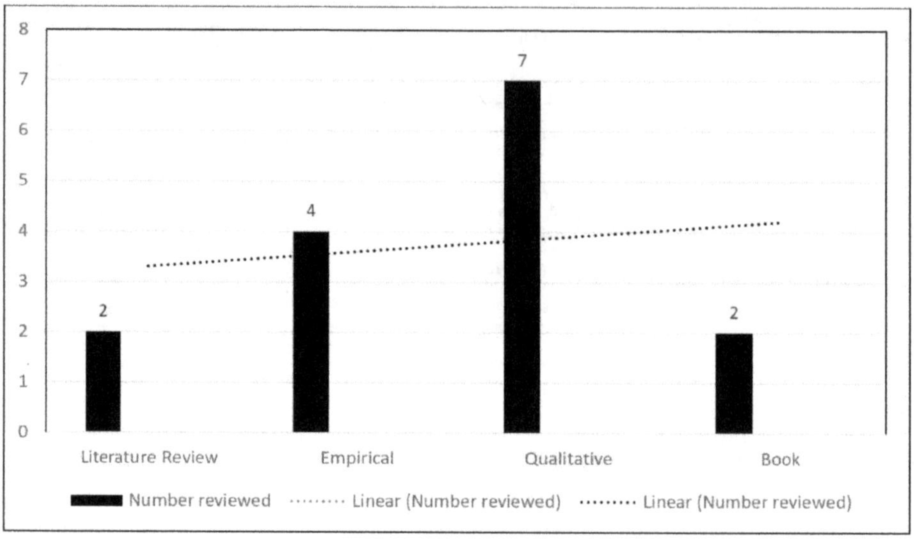

Figure 12. Distribution of selected articles by journals for RQ4
Source: Authors

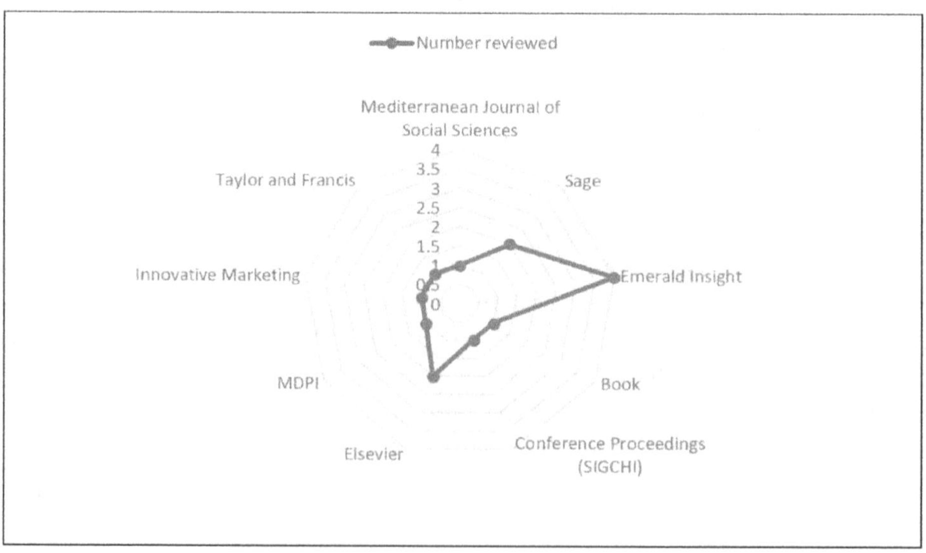

Gaps Identified

EI as a concept has not been exhaustively explored in the HC domain. Despite current research increasingly acknowledging the significance of emotions, there is a critical dearth of studies on personnel apart from nurses. Studies exploring the administrators' points-of-view are especially scarce. This work has revealed an interesting slant in EI research in the HC domain. Most studies have been accomplished in the West and cater predominantly to the Western population's perspectives and issues. Replicating the same in non-Western nations with socio-culturally diverse populations will help to generalize the findings and strengthen the construct.

Relationship Among Different Works

The majority of published literature on EI concurs that it is a skill that leads to better work productivity, job-satisfaction and decreased stress levels. Researchers are now more aware of the significance of emotions and their finely meshed connections to diverse organizational phenomenon (Mesquita & Frijda, 2011). There is some debate around the different models of EI, but the ability model has exhibited the maximum reliability and discriminant validity (Mayer & Salovey, 1997).

Major Trends

Distinct From IQ

The major trend in EI now is to study it as an entity that is distinct from IQ. Psychologists believe that conventional measures of intelligence in use today are unidimensional and incapable of comprehending the full range of a human's mental dimensions. Researchers agree that EI is a set of competencies that can be learned unlike IQ, where learning tapers off after 19-20 years of age. It is also possible for highly qualified individuals to have low EI and vice versa (Goleman, 1995).

Use in Assessment Tests

Following the recognition of EI's impact on work performance, there is an increasing usage of EI in assessment tests used during recruitment and hiring. The most important development in the domain of health administration is the stress being laid on competency assessment for new HC managers (Christiansen et al., 2010).

FUTURE RESEARCH DIRECTIONS

The study of EI in HC is still nascent, and while the current work provides intriguing glimpses into how EI affects a broad range of life skills, further research is needed before its role in organizational life can be completely understood. The findings reveal that most studies have focussed on the nursing sector and have been carried out in the West. Future research could focus on studying the non-nursing staff like administrators and paramedics. An interesting avenue for research would be establishing the impacts of EI-marketing on organizational outcomes. This study discusses linkages between EI and competitive advantages via cognitive and behavioral changes engendered at the individual level, like increased self-discipline and motivation. However, there can be boundary conditions involved in this relationship. It would be interesting to explore the effect of moderators at the team and organizational level that could render the influence of EI on organizational performance or competitive advantage more or less pronounced. Another interesting avenue of research could be exploring the dynamic nature of the processes in the proposed model between EI and organizational performance. It seems likely that EI and organizational performance will mutually influence each other over time (possibly through divergent mechanisms). Studying the reciprocity in the model might be a substantive advancement. Current trends point towards rapid digitalization of HC practices which might lead to personal-professional boundaries becoming increasingly permeable. It will be interesting to understand the influence of individual coping mechanisms on digitally-connected behavior and the extent to which they shape responses to work-life balance and technostress in the future. The proponents of EI (Salovey& Mayer,1990) opine that the EI field is still evolving and there is a lot left to learn about it. More comprehensive studies and a commensurable analysis of a diverse HC population would enrich the quality of EI research.

CONCLUSION

In summarizing what has been discussed so far, the authors conclude that EI has established itself as a fundamental life skill when it comes to dealing with people and coping with stressors. Returning to the questions raised in the beginning of this study, EI has proven to play a vital role in HC outcomes and HR managerial performances. EI skills equip managers with perceptiveness and sensitivity in dealing with employees. In employees, it engenders positive emotional appraisals that mitigate stress outcomes. It enriches the quality of care and reduces fatigue consequent to emotional labor. Thus, EI leads to competitive advantage for HCOs by effectuating cognitive and behavioral changes at the individual level that lead to organizational success. A novel conceptual framework is proposed by the authors for the marketing of EI in the HC sector. The authors hope that the guidelines offered lead to practical applications in organizations. It is also hoped that the insights on management and marketing gleaned from this study will pave way for further research on EI, elucidating how emotions affect human judgment and relational skills. This might have far-reaching outcomes for practicable management of emotional cues by both the leader and the '*led*', and might prove invaluable in building organizations that are not only profitable, but also function as spaces where the work-force might rediscover the passion that had led them into the profession of care giving.

REFERENCES

Ashforth, B. E., & Humphrey, R. H. (1995). Emotion in the workplace: Reappraisal. *Human Relations, 48*(2), 97–125. doi:10.1177/001872679504800201

Ashkanasy, N. M. (2003). Emotions in organizations: A multilevel perspective. *Research in Multi-Level Issues, 2*, 9-54.

Bakker, A. B., & Demerouti, E. (2007). The job demands-resources model: State of the art. *Journal of Managerial Psychology, 22*(3), 309–328. doi:10.1108/02683940710733115

Balamohan, P., Tech, M., & Gomathi, S. (2015). Emotional intelligence–It's importance and relationship with individual performance, team-effectiveness, leadership and marketing effectiveness. *Mediterranean Journal of Social Sciences, 6*(1), 120.

Başoğul, C., & Özgür, G. (2016). Role of emotional intelligence in conflict management strategies of nurses. *Asian Nursing Research, 10*(3), 228–233. doi:10.1016/j.anr.2016.07.002 PMID:27692253

Bierly, P. E. III, & Gallagher, S. (2007). Explaining alliance partner selection: Fit, trust and strategic expediency. *Long Range Planning, 40*(2), 134–153. doi:10.1016/j.lrp.2007.03.001

Bilal, A. (2017). The Role of Emotional Dissonance and Emotional Intelligence on Job-Stress, Burnout, and Well-being. In Academy of Management Proceedings (Vol. 2017, No. 1, p. 12770). Briarcliff Manor, NY: Academy of Management.

Birks, Y. F., & Watt, I. S. (2007). Emotional intelligence and patient-centred care. *Journal of the Royal Society of Medicine, 100*(8), 368–374. doi:10.1177/014107680710000813 PMID:17682030

Boyatzis, R. E., Goleman, D., & Rhee, K. (2000). Clustering competence in emotional intelligence: Insights from the Emotional Competence Inventory (ECI). Handbook of Emotional Intelligence, 99(6), 343-362.

Brackett, M. A., Rivers, S. E., Shiffman, S., Lerner, N., & Salovey, P. (2006). Relating emotional abilities to social functioning: A comparison of self-report and performance measures of emotional intelligence. *Journal of Personality and Social Psychology, 91*(4), 780–795. doi:10.1037/0022-3514.91.4.780 PMID:17014299

Cavanaugh, M. A., Boswell, W. R., Roehling, M. V., & Boudreau, J. W. (2000). An empirical examination of self-reported work stress among US managers. *The Journal of Applied Psychology, 85*(1), 65–74. doi:10.1037/0021-9010.85.1.65 PMID:10740957

Christiansen, N. D., Janovics, J. E., & Siers, B. P. (2010). Emotional Intelligence in Selection Contexts: Measurement method, criterion-related validity, and vulnerability to response distortion. *International Journal of Selection and Assessment, 18*(1), 87–101. doi:10.1111/j.1468-2389.2010.00491.x

Ciorciari, J., Pfeifer, J., & Gountas, J. (2019). An EEG study on emotional intelligence and advertising message effectiveness. *Behavioral Sciences (Basel, Switzerland), 9*(8), 88. doi:10.3390/bs9080088 PMID:31443219

Clarke, N. (2006). Developing emotional intelligence through workplace learning: Findings from a case study in healthcare. *Human Resource Development International, 9*(4), 447–465. doi:10.1080/13678860601032585

Cooper, R. K. (1997). Applying emotional intelligence in the workplace. *Training & Development, 51*(12), 31–39.

Cooper, R. K., & Sawaf, A. (1998). *Executive EQ: Emotional intelligence in leadership and organizations*. Penguin.

Copperman, K., Lee, J., Barritt, J., Gruber, R., Gutmann, J., Arredondo, F., & Copperman, A. B. (2012). A Multi-Center Analysis of Emotional Intelligence (EI) in Infertility Practices: A Comprehensive Self-Assessment. *Fertility and Sterility, 97*(3), S15. doi:10.1016/j.fertnstert.2012.01.032

Dalgic, T., & Leeuw, M. (1994). Niche Marketing Revisited: Concept, Applications and Some European Cases. *European Journal of Marketing, 28*(4), 39–55. doi:10.1108/03090569410061178

Damasio, A. R. (1994). *Descartes' error: Emotion, rationality and the human brain*. Putnam.

Ekman, P. (1992). Facial expressions of emotion: An old controversy and new findings. *Philosophical Transactions of the Royal Society of London. Series B, Biological Sciences*, *335*(1273), 63–69. doi:10.1098/rstb.1992.0008 PMID:1348139

Erickson, R. J., & Grove, W. J. (2008). Emotional labor and health care. *Sociology Compass*, *2*(2), 704–733. doi:10.1111/j.1751-9020.2007.00084.x

Erigüç, G., & Köse, S. D. (2013). Evaluation of emotional intelligence and communication skills of health care manager candidates: A structural equation modeling. *International Journal of Business and Social Science*, *4*(13), 115–123.

Feather, R. (2009). Emotional intelligence in relation to nursing leadership: Does it matter? *Journal of Nursing Management*, *17*(3), 376–382. doi:10.1111/j.1365-2834.2008.00931.x PMID:21456323

Fernandez, C. S., Peterson, H. B., Holmstrőm, S. W., & Connolly, A. (2012). Developing emotional intelligence for healthcare leaders. In A. Di Fabio (Ed.), *Emotional intelligence–New perspectives and applications* (pp. 239–260). InTech., doi:10.5772/31940

Flippo, E. B. (1968). Integrative schemes in management theory. *Academy of Management Journal*, *11*(1), 91–98.

Fortin, C., Neustaedter, C., & Hennessy, K. (2014). Posting for community and culture: Considerations for the design of interactive digital bulletin boards. In *Proceedings of the SIGCHI Conference on Human Factors in Computing Systems*. Association for Computing Machinery. 10.1145/2556288.2556970

Foster, K., Fethney, J., Kozlowski, D., Fois, R., Reza, F., & McCloughen, A. (2018). Emotional intelligence and perceived stress of Australian pre-registration healthcare students: A multi-disciplinary cross-sectional study. *Nurse Education Today*, *66*, 51–56. doi:10.1016/j.nedt.2018.04.001 PMID:29665505

Fredrickson, B. L. (1998). What good are positive emotions? *Review of General Psychology*, *2*(3), 300–319. doi:10.1037/1089-2680.2.3.300 PMID:21850154

Freshman, B., & Rubino, L. (2002). Emotional intelligence: A core competency for health care administrators. *The Health Care Manager*, *20*(4), 1–9. doi:10.1097/00126450-200206000-00002 PMID:12083173

Frijda, N. H. (1986). Studies in emotion and social interaction. The emotions. Cambridge University Press.

Gilmartin, M. J., & D'Aunno, T. A. (2007). 8 Leadership research in healthcare: A review and roadmap. *The Academy of Management Annals*, *1*(1), 387–438. doi:10.5465/078559813

Goleman, D. (1995). *Emotional Intelligence*. Bantam Books, Inc.

Goleman, D. (2000). Leadership that gets results. *Harvard Business Review*, *78*(2), 4–17.

Gross, J. J. (1998). Antecedent-and response-focused emotion regulation: Divergent consequences for experience, expression, and physiology. *Journal of Personality and Social Psychology*, *74*(1), 224–237. doi:10.1037/0022-3514.74.1.224 PMID:9457784

Grossman, R. J. (2000, September). Emotions at work. *Health Forum Journal*, *43*(5), 18–22. PMID:11066984

Hashem, T. N. (2010). Impact of Managers' Emotional Intelligence on Marketing Creativity in Jordan Commercial Banks. *Innovative Marketing*, *6*(3), 78–86.

Heffernan, T., O'Neill, G., Travaglione, T., & Droulers, M. (2008). Relationship marketing: The impact of emotional intelligence and trust on bank performance. *International Journal of Bank Marketing*, *26*(3), 183–199. doi:10.1108/02652320810864652

Hobfoll, S. E. (1989). Conservation of resources: A new attempt at conceptualizing stress. *The American Psychologist*, *44*(3), 513–524. doi:10.1037/0003-066X.44.3.513 PMID:2648906

Hobfoll, S. E. (2002). Social and psychological resources and adaptation. *Review of General Psychology*, *6*(4), 307–324. doi:10.1037/1089-2680.6.4.307

Holahan, C. J., & Moos, R. H. (1987). Personal and contextual determinants of coping strategies. *Journal of Personality and Social Psychology*, *52*(5), 946–955. doi:10.1037/0022-3514.52.5.946 PMID:3585703

Huang, Y. T., Rundle-Thiele, S., & Chen, Y. H. (2019). Extending understanding of the internal marketing practice and employee satisfaction relationship: A budget Chinese airline empirical examination. *Journal of Vacation Marketing*, *25*(1), 88–98. doi:10.1177/1356766718757270

Humphreys, J., Brunsen, B., & Davis, D. (2005). Emotional structure and commitment: Implications for health care management. *Journal of Health Organization and Management*, *19*(2), 120–129. doi:10.1108/14777260510600040 PMID:16119051

Jamshed, S., & Majeed, N. (2019). Relationship between team culture and team performance through lens of knowledge sharing and team emotional intelligence. *Journal of Knowledge Management, 23*(1), 90–109. doi:10.1108/JKM-04-2018-0265

Joung, M. S., & Kim, K. J. (2006). A study on the effect of emotional labor and leader's emotional intelligence on job satisfaction and organizational commitment for nurses. *Korea Journal of Hospital Management, 11*(4), 1–18.

Karasek, R., & Theorell, R. (1990). *Healthy work: Stress, productivity, and the reconstruction of working life*. Basic Books.

Kerasidou, A., & Horn, R. (2016). Making space for empathy: Supporting doctors in the emotional labour of clinical care. *BMC Medical Ethics, 17*(1), 1–5. doi:10.118612910-016-0091-7 PMID:26818248

Kewalramani, S., Agrawal, M., & Rastogi, M. R. (2015). Models of emotional intelligence: Similarities and discrepancies. *Indian Journal of Positive Psychology, 6*(2), 178–181.

Kidwell, B., Hardesty, D. M., Murtha, B. R., & Sheng, S. (2011). Emotional intelligence in marketing exchanges. *Journal of Marketing, 75*(1), 78–95. doi:10.1509/jm.75.1.78

Kim, B., & Lee, J. (2016). Relationships between personal traits, emotional intelligence, internal marketing, service management, and customer orientation in Korean outpatient department nurses. *Asian Nursing Research, 10*(1), 18–24. doi:10.1016/j.anr.2015.10.005 PMID:27021830

Kinman, G., & Leggetter, S. (2016). Emotional labour and wellbeing: What protects nurses? *Health Care, 4*(4), 89. PMID:27916880

Langhorn, S. (2004). How emotional intelligence can improve management performance. *International Journal of Contemporary Hospitality Management, 16*(4), 220–230. doi:10.1108/09596110410537379

Lassk, F. G., & Shepherd, C. D. (2013). Exploring the relationship between emotional intelligence and salesperson creativity. *Journal of Personal Selling & Sales Management, 33*(1), 25–37. doi:10.2753/PSS0885-3134330103

Lazarus, R. S. (1991). Progress on a cognitive-motivational-relational theory of emotion. *The American Psychologist, 46*(8), 819–834. doi:10.1037/0003-066X.46.8.819 PMID:1928936

Lazarus, R. S., & Folkman, S. (1984). *Stress, appraisal, and coping*. Springer.

Liu, L., Xu, P., Zhou, K., Xue, J., & Wu, H. (2018). Mediating role of emotional labor in the association between emotional intelligence and fatigue among Chinese doctors: A cross-sectional study. *BMC Public Health, 18*(1), 881. doi:10.118612889-018-5817-7 PMID:30012126

Magnavita, N. (2014). Workplace violence and occupational stress in healthcare workers: A chicken-and-egg situation—results of a 6-year follow-up study. *Journal of Nursing Scholarship, 46*(5), 366–376. doi:10.1111/jnu.12088 PMID:24754800

Malik, M., Haider, Z., & Hussain, A. (2019). Perceived emotional intelligence, work life balance and job satisfaction among healthcare professionals in Pakistan. *International Journal of Pharmaceutical Research & Allied Sciences, 8*(2), 80–86.

Mayer, J. D., & Salovey, P. (1997). What is emotional intelligence? In P. Salovey & D. Sluyter (Eds.), *Emotional Development and Emotional Intelligence: Implications for Educators* (pp. 3–31). Basic Books.

Menzies, I. E. (1960). A case-study in the functioning of social systems as a defence against anxiety: A report on a study of the nursing service of a general hospital. *Human Relations, 13*(2), 95–121. doi:10.1177/001872676001300201

Mesquita, B., & Frijda, N. H. (2011). An emotion perspective on emotion regulation. *Cognition and Emotion, 25*(5), 782–784. doi:10.1080/02699931.2011.586824 PMID:21824020

Meyer, B. B., Fletcher, T. B., & Parker, S. J. (2004). Enhancing emotional intelligence in the health care environment: An exploratory study. *The Health Care Manager, 23*(3), 225–234. doi:10.1097/00126450-200407000-00006 PMID:15457840

Mikolajczak, M., & Van Bellegem, S. (2017). Increasing emotional intelligence to decrease healthcare expenditures: How profitable would it be? *Personality and Individual Differences, 116*, 343–347. doi:10.1016/j.paid.2017.05.014

Mintz, O., & Currim, I. S. (2013). What drives managerial use of marketing and financial metrics and does metric use affect performance of marketing-mix activities? *Journal of Marketing, 77*(2), 17–40. doi:10.1509/jm.11.0463

Moher, D., Liberati, A., Tetzlaff, J., & Altman, D. G.Prisma Group. (2009). Preferred reporting items for systematic reviews and meta-analyses: The PRISMA statement. *PLoS Medicine, 6*(7), e1000097. doi:10.1371/journal.pmed.1000097 PMID:19621072

Mumby, D. K., & Putnam, L. L. (1992). The Politics of Emotion: A Feminist Reading of Bounded Rationality. *Academy of Management Review*, *17*(3), 465–486. doi:10.5465/amr.1992.4281983

Newton, C., Teo, S. T., Pick, D., Ho, M., & Thomas, D. (2016). Emotional intelligence as a buffer of occupational stress. *Personnel Review*, *4*(5), 1010–1028. doi:10.1108/PR-11-2014-0271

Nightingale, S., Spiby, H., Sheen, K., & Slade, P. (2018). The impact of emotional intelligence in health care professionals on caring behaviour towards patients in clinical and long-term care settings: Findings from an integrative review. *International Journal of Nursing Studies*, *80*, 106–117. doi:10.1016/j.ijnurstu.2018.01.006 PMID:29407344

Nwokah, N. G., & Ahiauzu, A. I. (2009). Emotional intelligence and marketing effectiveness. *Marketing Intelligence & Planning*, *27*(7), 864–881. doi:10.1108/02634500911000199

Oyewunmi, A. E. (2018). Normalizing Difference: Emotional intelligence and diversity management competence in healthcare managers. *Intangible Capital*, *14*(3), 429–444. doi:10.3926/ic.1050

Oyewunmi, A. E., Oyewunmi, O. A., & Oludayo, O. O. (2015). Leaders' emotional intelligence and employees' performance: A case in Nigeria's public healthcare sector. *International Journal of Human Resource Studies*, *5*(3), 23–37. doi:10.5296/ijhrs.v5i3.7854

Petrides, K. V., & Furnham, A. (2003). Trait emotional intelligence: Behavioural validation in two studies of emotion recognition and reactivity to mood induction. *European Journal of Personality*, *17*(1), 39–57. doi:10.1002/per.466

Piercy, N., & Morgan, N. (1991). Internal marketing—The missing half of the marketing programme. *Long Range Planning*, *24*(2), 82–93. doi:10.1016/0024-6301(91)90083-Z

Pradhan, S., & Jena, L. K. (2018). Emotional intelligence as a moderator in abusive supervision-intention to quit relationship among Indian healthcare professionals. *Asia-Pacific Journal of Business Administration*, *10*(1), 1–20. doi:10.1108/APJBA-09-2017-0089

Prentice, C. (2019). Emotional intelligence and internal marketing. In *Emotional intelligence and marketing* (pp. 85-111). World Scientific Publishing Co. Pte. Ltd. https://econpapers.repec.org/RePEc:wsi:wschap:9789811203558_0005

Prentice, C. (2020). Enhancing the tourist experience with emotional intelligence. *Tourism Review*, *75*(5), 733–744. doi:10.1108/TR-06-2019-0254

Psilopanagioti, A., Anagnostopoulos, F., Mourtou, E., & Niakas, D. (2012). Emotional intelligence, emotional labor, and job satisfaction among physicians in Greece. *BMC Health Services Research*, *12*(1), 1–12. doi:10.1186/1472-6963-12-463 PMID:23244390

Purcarea, E. V. L. (2019). The impact of marketing strategies in healthcare systems. *Journal of Medicine and Life*, *12*(2), 93–96. PMID:31406509

Quoidbach, J., Berry, E. V., Hansenne, M., & Mikolajczak, M. (2010). Positive emotion regulation and well-being: Comparing the impact of eight savoring and dampening strategies. *Personality and Individual Differences*, *49*(5), 368–373. doi:10.1016/j.paid.2010.03.048

Rao, P. R. (2006). Emotional intelligence: The Sine Qua Non for a clinical leadership toolbox. *Journal of Communication Disorders*, *39*(4), 310–319. doi:10.1016/j.jcomdis.2006.02.006 PMID:16563422

Riley, R., & Weiss, M. C. (2016). A qualitative thematic review: Emotional labour in healthcare settings. *Journal of Advanced Nursing*, *72*(1), 6–17. doi:10.1111/jan.12738 PMID:26212890

Roether, C. L., Omlor, L., & Giese, M. A. (2009). Features in the recognition of emotions from dynamic bodily expression. In *Dynamics of visual motion processing* (pp. 313–340). Springer. doi:10.1007/978-1-4419-0781-3_14

Rosenstein, A. H. (2015). Emotional Intelligence: A Critical Tool to Understand and Improve Behaviours That Impact Patient Care. *Journal of Psychology & Clinical Psychiatry*, *2*(1), 1–4. doi:10.15406/jpcpy.2015.02.00066

Ruch, S., Züst, M. A., & Henke, K. (2016). Subliminal messages exert long-term effects on decision-making. *Neuroscience of Consciousness*, *2016*(1). Advance online publication. doi:10.1093/nc/niw013 PMID:30386634

Salovey, P., & Mayer, J. D. (1990). Emotional intelligence. *Imagination, Cognition and Personality*, *9*(3), 185–211. doi:10.2190/DUGG-P24E-52WK-6CDG

Simmons, B. L., & Nelson, D. L. (2007). Eustress at work: Extending the holistic stress model. In D. L. Nelson & C. L. Cooper (Eds.), *Positive organizational behavior* (pp. 40–53). SAGE. doi:10.4135/9781446212752.n4

Smith, K. B., Profetto-McGrath, J., & Cummings, G. G. (2009). Emotional intelligence and nursing: An integrative literature review. *International Journal of Nursing Studies*, *46*(12), 1624–1636. doi:10.1016/j.ijnurstu.2009.05.024 PMID:19596323

Szczygieł, D., & Mikolajczak, M. (2017). Why are people high in emotional intelligence happier? They make the most of their positive emotions. *Personality and Individual Differences*, *117*, 177–181. doi:10.1016/j.paid.2017.05.051

Trivellas, P., Gerogiannis, V., & Svarna, S. (2013). Exploring workplace implications of Emotional Intelligence (WLEIS) in hospitals: Job satisfaction and turnover Intentions. *Procedia: Social and Behavioral Sciences*, *73*, 701–709. doi:10.1016/j.sbspro.2013.02.108

Walsh, E. (2009). The emotional labor of nurses working in her Majesty's (HM) prison service. *Journal of Forensic Nursing*, *5*(3), 143–152. doi:10.1111/j.1939-3938.2009.01047.x PMID:19702741

Ward, M. E., De Brún, A., Beirne, D., Conway, C., Cunningham, U., English, A., Fitzsimons, J., Furlong, E., Kane, Y., Kelly, A., McDonnell, S., McGinley, S., Monaghan, B., Myler, A., Nolan, E., O'Donovan, R., O'Shea, M., Shuhaiber, A., & McAuliffe, E. (2018). Using co-design to develop a collective leadership intervention for healthcare teams to improve safety culture. *International Journal of Environmental Research and Public Health*, *15*(6), 1182. doi:10.3390/ijerph15061182 PMID:29874883

Weiszbrod, T. (2020). Health care leader competencies and the relevance of emotional intelligence. *The Health Care Manager*, *39*(4), 190–196. doi:10.1097/HCM.0000000000000307 PMID:33079771

KEY TERMS AND DEFINITIONS

Emotion Regulation: The ways in which individuals' can alter their experience of an emotion by using various strategies, namely: situation-selection, situation-modification, attentional-deployment and response-modulation (Gross, 1998). By these strategies, individuals change the intensity or valence of specific emotions.

Emotional Dimensions of Human Resource Management: The specific and practicable ways in which EI can be applied to HRM in HCOs is what this term focusses on. The practical ways in which managers' emotional skills facilitate employee performance or employees' emotional skills enhance organizational-outcomes is what this term implies. It should be noted that this definition should not be confused by the dimensional models of emotions wherein authors attempt to categorize emotions discretely along two- or three-dimensions of valence or arousal. This definition is specifically aimed at the applied end of EI within HRM.

Emotional Labor: The term broadly refers to portraying one emotion while concurrently experiencing another. Healthcare employees are at times required to down-play or induce certain emotions pertinent to caregiving so that patients feel safe. There are two variants of emotional labor- *'surface acting'* is the method by which employees merely alter their physical countenance to convey safety, whereas in *'deep acting'* caregivers actually change their emotions to impart dependability and security to patients.

Healthcare Outcomes: This review approaches healthcare outcomes in the form of measurable results like employee burnout, job-satisfaction, emotion-regulation by employees, team-performances, patient-satisfaction, gender diversity, and profitability in organizations.

Models of Emotional Intelligence: Emotional intelligence has been studied from the perspectives of trait, ability, or a mixed model. The ability model focuses on one's ability to use emotional information as a standardized intelligence. The trait model is of the view that EI is an inbuilt, personality related aptitude. The mixed model comprises of multiple constructs of personality traits and developable abilities. For the purposes of this review, the ability model is the most relevant one since it argues that EI abilities can be honed and developed with adequate training and practice.

Personal Resources: According to the job-demands-resource model, there are two determinants of a work-environment: job demands and personal resources. Job-demands require efforts, whereas personal resources are those physical, social, psychological, or organizational aspects that help employees in reducing efforts and tackling job-demands. Personal resources also help employees' growth and development. Here, EI is treated as a powerful personal resource that mitigates job-stress.

Systematic Literature Review: It is a synthesized, comprehensive review of published literature in a systematic manner. It is generally accepted to be one of the best ways to provide a thorough overview of a relevant field and identify research gaps. It is usually carried out in order to explore answers to relevant research questions based on an analysis of literature. The findings are synthesized qualitatively or quantitatively.

Chapter 6
The Good, the Bad, and the Ugly:
Don't Blame COVID-19 for Health System Inefficiencies

Oscar Bernardes
Porto Accounting and Business School, Polytechnic Institute of Porto, Portugal

Vanessa Amorim
Porto Accounting and Business School, Polytechnic Institute of Porto, Portugal

Berto Usman
https://orcid.org/0000-0003-0210-3858
Faculty of Economics and Business, University of Bengkulu, Indonesia

ABSTRACT

The good policymakers are creating marketing stimulus to social economy, restaurant and hotel discounts, employment maintenance aids, cultural events, etc., disseminating hope. The bad policymakers want the opposite and restrict family's circumstances and socialization. And finally, COVID-19 is blamed for all inefficiencies in the public health system, even those before the epidemic. This chapter explores why COVID-19 is innocent and not entirely responsible for health inefficiencies. The authors explore the main health concerns, analyzing earlier articles with recent documents before and during COVID-19.

DOI: 10.4018/978-1-7998-7263-4.ch006

INTRODUCTION

According to new OECD - Organization for Economic Co-operation and Development forecasts, health expenditure will outpace GDP - gross domestic product growth over the next 15 years in almost every OECD country. The health expenditure per capita will expand at an average annual rate of 2.7% across the OECD, and it will reach 10.2% of GDP by 2030, up from 8.8% in 2018, a percentage more or less unchanged since 2013 (Lorenzoni et al., 2019). The outlook is aligned with past developments. In recent decades, healthcare expenditures have grown very significantly in most OECD countries, from 3.9% of GDP in 1960 (Oxley, 1994) to 8.8% according to the last, 2019, health at a glance OECD Indicators.

Sustainability is not a new issue. Some national health systems (NHS) have stated this concern since their foundation principles, e.g., United Kingdom (UK) NHS, proclaim the commitment to running the most effective, reasonable, and sustainable use of finite resources (NHS, 2020) on the 6th principle of 7. Sustainability presents itself as an accounting problem, where health system revenue is insufficient to meet health system obligations.

The articulation of supply and demand in the health field does not obey the same rules as the general economy. In this sector, there are signs of a lack of elasticity in demand, and the demand is insufficient, which is made clear by the long waiting lists. The supply induces the demand because prices do not constrict the demand, but the supply is constricted by costs (Bernardes & Pinillos, 2004, p. 95).

BACKGROUND

At the end of December 2019, a new unspecified disease appeared in Wuhan, China. The outbreak was linked to SARS-CoV and acknowledged as a novel betacoronavirus, a few weeks after, at the beginning of 2020, most of the countries were not well-prepared, for this unknown virus and this can be proven by the overwhelming hospital and COVID-19 patients in China, Italy, UK, Brazil, India, and the US. The mortality rate was very high, and it got quadruple in just a semester (depended on the preparedness of national health system in each country). How responsive each government dealing with COVID-19 transmissions could also be shown through the type of lockdown modes applied by each country.

Further, we may highlight the economic and social shock caused by the COVID-19 from the perspective of the Good, the Bad, and the Ugly terms of COVID-19. For instance, we are highlighting how the economics of a certain country is affected both at macro and micro levels. We might see the perception of the value and the national health system status from the perspective of society. How ready the NHS

– National Health System in each country is perceived by the society, and how the government strengthen their NHS system. Some studies have highlighted this issue and provide us with a helpful guidance.

SUPPLY

Supply is an essential economic theory that designates the total amount of a particular good or service available to consumers. The quantity that is supplied will be influenced by the price obtainable. More products or services will be available to the consumers at higher prices because suppliers will desire to gain more earnings. Not only on the price level, but there are also other economic dynamics, competing goods, the production technology, the quantity available on the market, cost of labor, and other factors of production.

Public goods, in the purest form, have two main characteristics:

- **Non-excludability:** It means that the goods are available to all citizens, cannot exclude a person based on the price, regardless of whether or not they have contributed financially.
- **Non-rival:** Means that when one person uses a good, it does not prevent others from using it.

Differing on these two characteristics, researchers habitually divide entities into four classes (Moon et al., 2017, p. 196); (i) Private goods (e.g., pills and syringes), (ii) Club goods (e.g., knowledge protected by patent), (iii) Common goods (e.g., universal healthcare), and (iv) Public goods (e.g., public information or pandemic preparedness) (Figure 1).

Figure 1. Categories of goods
Source: Moon et al., 2017, p. 196.

	Excludable	Non-excludable
Rivalrous	Private goods	Common goods, common pool resources
Non-rivalrous	Club goods	Public goods

The balance between the supply and demand in the health sector does not follow the same laws as the economy because health is not a good susceptible for direct

Figure 2. Share of cataract surgeries performed as day cases (2000 and 2010)
Source: OECD, 2012, p. 22.

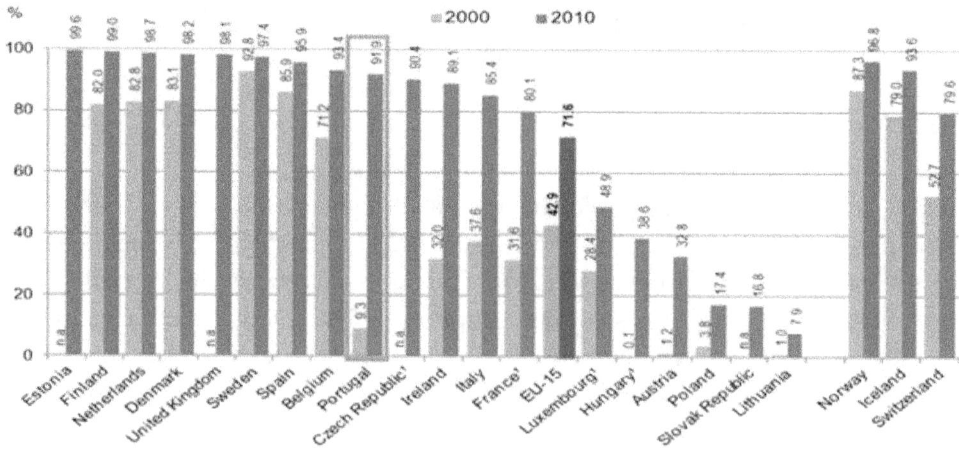

Adapted: OECD, 2012, p. 22.

utilization or exchange. Instead, health corresponds to an ideal constitutional ambition through values such as solidarity, social justice, and equity between citizens and regions. In most OECD countries is beginning to be demanded as a real public good.

The acceptance of health as a social good and universal right by citizens leads consumers to react practically inelastically to price variations. Nevertheless, governments endorse sustainability in co-payments for emergency events, selected medicines, and health diagnostics. These constitutional ideologies engender "free-riders" patients because users can enjoy health privileges without expending effort for paying it or the actual cost of the service. If there are too many free-rider beneficiaries, the resources, facilities, or services tend to be underprovided. Simultaneously, payers may be reluctant to voluntarily fund the service if they know others can free ride on its provision. Therefore, some citizens advocate more efficiency, private insurances, and less tax spending with the public national health system. On the other hand, other citizens promote more equality and health as a public right for all citizens.

In any case, the populations' demand for health certainly increases at an excessive speed, both in the developing countries as in the undeveloped countries. This growth is mainly due to the tremendous explosion of medical knowledge and technology, which generates an increase in life expectancy and reduces diseases' consequences. Observing at tendencies, the number of cataract surgeries accomplished on a same-day basis has intensified very fast in some nations, such as Portugal, from 9,3% in 2000 to 91,9% in 2010 (Figure 2).

In most OECD countries, Bismark and Beveridge's Welfare State principles generated an improvement in health indicators, e.g., reduction of infant mortality, decreased tuberculosis incidents, and reduced mandatory notification diseases associated with vaccination coverage, etc. But these developments had a cost, at the beginning more health staff, then more infrastructures and maintenance, afterward more diagnostics, technology, and medicines.

The more the supply increases, that is, an upsurge in the number of health personnel, technological equipment, and health infrastructures, the more is the demand for healthcare services. This correlation of supply on demand is called the phenomenon of induced demand, along with a more requiring and consumerist society, as well as an increase in the claiming power of citizens.

However, in an environment of limited resources allocated to healthcare provision, the rising cost of sophisticated technology and the high level of demand from citizens increase spending and worsen the national health systems' economic situation.

Tax Revenues

In 2018, tax revenue (including social contributions) in the EU – European Union stood at 40.3% of GDP and accounted for 89.4% of total government revenue. Due to the subprime mortgage crisis, continued growth from its low point of 2009 (Figure 3). The higher tax to GDP ratio, the better the country's financial position will have to improve health, education, and justice, however less available income for families and more pressure on stimulating efficiency and economy in the public sector.

Figure 3. Overall tax-to-GDP ratio in the EU and the euro area (2002-2018)
Source: Eurostat, 2019.

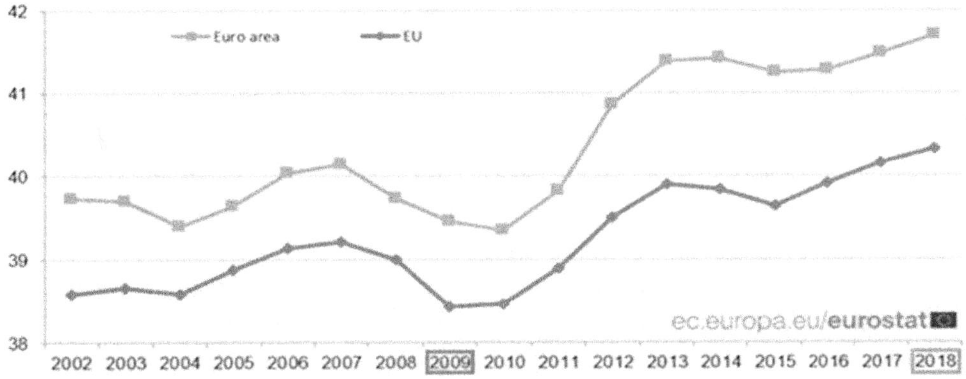

Across OECD countries, a considerable percentage of health spending, 71%, is subsidized by public sources – from government revenues generated from tax income, and social insurance contributions, "the share of public spending on health in total government expenditure has slightly since 2015, up to 14%, reflecting the fact that health plays an increasingly important role in government budgets" (OECD, 2020a, p. 3). This increases sustainability apprehensions because most nations pull resources mostly from public sources. The health system competes for limited resources alongside various sectors such as justice, education, and social assistance. Therefore, the health supply is restricted by the national budget, showing signs of weak elasticity, on the supply side, whenever there is a manifest demand, not satisfied, so expressive in the long waiting lists for hospitalization or in external hospital consultations. However, the evolution of public expenditure in the direction of growth occurs without corresponding improvements in the services provided or a reduction in private expenses.

In the European Union, where member countries' convergence criteria prevent indebtedness from financing increased public spending, and the resistance of public opinion has prevented the increase in taxes (Béresniak & Duru, 1999). They are adding more struggles for the public authorities due to the persistence of a low economic growth rate and the budget.

The COVID-19 pandemic will cause a significant decline in tax revenue in most countries. It can be explained by the economic slowdown and indirectly by tax policy and administration measures taken in response (IMF, 2020). Governments are promoting actions to support the population, enterprises, and the provision of vital public services (CITA, 2020, p. 3). Thus, the fiscal revenues will decrease, and the expenses with public assistance increase; nevertheless, the public revenues' economic sustainability is unsatisfactory to reimbursement public spending. Due to COVID-19 external effects, especially in the economy and social welfare, there is a limitation for increasing more public resources (via taxation or social health insurance) because families and the economy cannot support further surcharge.

Rational and Practical Distribution of Resources

Due to the progressive disproportion between the growth of expenses and resources, health systems were forced to conduct cost-containment policies, aiming to influence the demand or offer health services (Simões, 2004, p. 59). Lessening health system obligations through coverage reduction will promote inequalities in health access, especially for those who cannot afford health insurance or the correct treatment. Besides, most governments contemplate human health as a primary and inalienable need, which constitutes a fundamental right that cannot be dispensed. The way to weaken the obligations that a health system has and bring expenditure back in line with revenue is to reduce coverage. This is the most commonly advocated approach for addressing health system sustainability (Thomson et al., 2009, p. 8).

Not all needs can be met simultaneously, so it is necessary to identify the population's health problems to quantify and typify their needs; classify and prioritize typologies and beneficiaries; trigger public stimulus measures to respond to priorities, and assess the effectiveness of programs. Meanwhile, in practically all European Union countries, co-payment systems are used to control medicines' expenditure, lists of reimbursed medicines were established. Governments handle hospital investments, wages, and staff admissions.

Since 1977, at least, a researcher like Bryant proposes methodologies to promote better sustainability by addressing the health priorities to promote a more rational and practical distribution of public resources. This scholar referred to eight principles as cited by Béresniak (1999, p. 65):

- Number of inhabitants likely to benefit from the health program.
- Number of patients and deaths due to the disease in question, or likely reduction of this number due to the implementation of the program.
- Effectiveness of available techniques or the possibility of launching the program.
- Existence of safe methods to guarantee the maintenance phase.
- The probability that the program's maintenance phase can be reached.
- The actual cost of running the program and its maintenance phase.
- The program's likely effect on the economic development of the covered region.
- Express wishes of the population.

Any decision to increase health care and improve health levels implies renouncing other public expenses, with limited resources, a priori. Consequently, governments must promote transparency. At every moment, society must have precise information to decide how much they are willing to pay to fulfill their public needs such as health, education, justice, or defense.

In most cases, in public services, we encounter a problem of valuing intangible products/services. However, there is a need to assign a cost-benefit analysis that justifies the decisions. This is an old topic; the waiting list for surgeries, appointments, diagnosis is a recurring problem in all national health services, further embracing difficult ethical decisions. Why should a cancer patient wait, and how many beds should be allocated to COVID-19.

The COVID-19 is guilty of increasing waiting lists, has had a considerable impact on core NHS service; the British Medical Association reported millions of patients living with health problems (including life-threatening conditions such as cancer) had been affected, with their treatment postponed or canceled. One point five million fewer elective admissions than usual during April to June, and up to 2.6 million fewer outpatient attendances (BMA, 2020).

There is a lack of information; nevertheless, some countries like Australia reveal COVID-19 impact on the elective surgery waiting list (Figure 4). We should expect a higher number in countries with elevated COVID-19 rates.

Figure 4. Patients on the waiting list at the end of the month (January to June 2020 and 2019)
Source: NWS, 2020, p. 43.

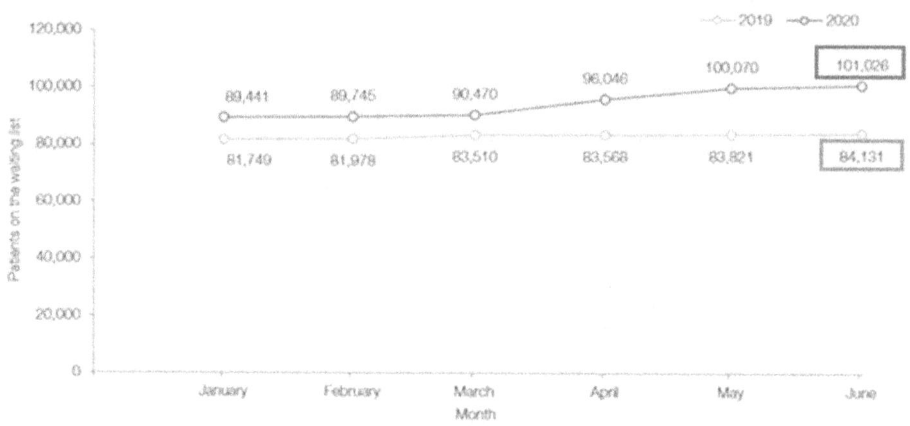

Nevertheless, the COVID-19 cannot be responsible for previous waiting lists before the epidemic. Quoting OECD (2020, p. 46), "long waiting times for health services have been an important policy issue in most OECD countries for many years, waiting times for elective treatment stalled between 2010 and 2019 in many countries, and had started to rise in some countries even before the COVID-19 pandemic. The COVID-19 outbreak is likely to result in at least some temporary increases in waiting times for non-urgent services in all the OECD countries that have been hard hit." Lessening health system obligations through coverage reduction, i.e., increasing waiting lists, may secure fiscal sustainability but does not unscramble the supply problem.

Improving Value

Improving the ability of health systems to generate value can focus on the reform of service delivery or on the reform of financing systems (Thomson et al., 2009, p. 7). Such reforms include increasing primary care network, shifting treatments from hospital to home or fewer cost facilities, liberating beds, remunerating doctors on a capitation (rather than a service fee), upsurge financing based on case-mix (i.e., adjusting for the nature and intensity of treatments undertaken), incentivize the provision of equitable and efficient services (Brick et al., 2010, p. 328). Governments have been attempting these approaches, although there are insignificant reform footprints over the years.

According to the health minister and researcher Campos, the public administration has too many staff and at the same time suffers from a shortage of staff. There are also many people, who cannot dismiss or become available, who cannot dismiss or transfer. Recruitment is heavily conditioned. They are limited by the dynamics of professional careers, by almost automatic promotions, where incompetence and laziness are treated in the same way as capacity and diligence (Campos, 1999, p. 19). Two decades after, according to the last OECD report, health and social systems employ more workers now than at any other time in history, with about one in every ten jobs found in health or social care (OECD, 2020b, p. 11). Shifting tasks from doctors to nurses and other health professionals can alleviate cost pressures and improve efficiency (OECD, 2020b, p. 11).

The doctor-patient relationship features a central and shared objective - enhancing the patient's well-being. Nevertheless, doctors are also motivated by other purposes, including self-interest in several guises. Doctors' decisions about the provision of medical services are also influenced by factors such as clinical uncertainty, remuneration arrangements, the ownership structure of their practices (including linkages with other health care providers), and the more comprehensive institutional and regulatory framework within which they operate (Bickerdyke et al., 2002). Therefore, professional group pressure tends to block some reforms in the name of the patient's well-being.

The health sector has a weak capacity for self-regulation. Coercive cost control has become the most important means that governments have to reduce healthcare spending. There are, however, incentives that allow for some self-regulation of expenditure. However, on the one hand, they remain known, and they demand a new allocation of powers, which is difficult to put into practice by centralized governments (Béresniak & Duru, 1999, p. 103).

Due to the progressive disproportion between spending and resource growth, governments were forced to conduct cost-containment policies to influence the demand or supply of health services (Simões, 2004, p. 60). Three cost-containment measures are presented: the limitation of public resources, the new budgeting techniques, and forms of control.

Governments tend to use ratios, misrepresenting the efficiency of health services. Bernardes & Pinillos (2004) concluded the significant advantages of the econometric frontier approach instead of ratios or regression models: when used systematically, it can contribute to cost containment in hospitals through the reduction of wastes, which can be achieved by reorganizing the service and processes. Based on this information, the hospital administration should distribute its resources to each hospital service by identifying deficiencies that affect their resources and the causes of these deficiencies to initiate corrective actions to eliminate or reduce them. The pertinence of its efforts can also be extended to the political level by stimulating new ways of thinking about the adopted policies and comparing different hospital contexts possible (Bernardes & Pinillos, 2004, p. 99). Sixteen years later, allocative efficiency measures are still lacking in hospitals and health systems in general. Governments use statistics as they want, point them as best fit on their strategies, misleading citizens.

According to WHO's data from national authorities, Denmark, Switzerland, and Cabo Verde had six new deaths in the past seven days (WHO, 2020) at the same period. Media will spread government' data, such as number of cases, number of deaths, and cumulative deaths. For an ordinary spectator, these three countries have the same disease level (six), the remaining data is not presented at all or not in the same headline. Denmark, Switzerland, and Cabo Verde have 5.8 million, 8.5 million, and 0.5 million residents, correspondingly. Countries with a substantial percentage of the elderly population are susceptible to many deaths due to COVID-19. Developed countries have superior per capita testing, whereas testing is less intensive in developing/underdeveloped countries, such as Cabo Verde. Pandemic has been affecting countries rendering income level, health infrastructure, demographics, government policies, and cultural characters of populations.

Therefore, government and media should inform faithful these data, combining different metrics such as population, average life expectancy, number of tests, and fatality rates. Apart from that, the use of homogeneous analysis during this pandemic; the "Good minister" will report Rt is decreasing (a key measure of how fast the virus is growing) therefore let us open the economy, at the same time, the "Bad minister" use cumulative deaths data to force people to use masks.

Before COVID-19, the government reported more doctors on the health system. On the other hand, opposition described more patients on the waiting lists. Each part used the best data available to support their arguments. Nevertheless, they both subscribed to the importance of improving more efficiency and value for the health systems.

DEMAND

As the number of cases of COVID-19 continues to grow, it is possible to realize there is not a pure correlation between population and COVID-19 patients, epidemic outbreaks can take place in small communities, and this can lead to abnormal demand on local health care services before projected to serve normal and typified diseases. Certain hospitals can receive substantial quantities of patients early in an outbreak, though different hospitals may be only mildly affected. This disparity of resources vs. demand is ordinary. Even before COVID-19, health facilities were projected to attend political lobbies and population desire, if enquired all residents would like to have in their neighborhood a hospital, university, and a mix of public services.

Underlying a commitment to provide equal treatment no matter location or individual status, the founders of public health national services proclaim health equity as the primary basis. Pursuing health equity implies striving for the same level of services for all residents, in a permanent attempt, although impossible mission.

The more the supply increases, the more the number of physicians and health facilities available, the more the demand for health care on the population grows (Béresniak & Duru, 1999, p. 81). This is called supplier induced demand (SID) "effect resulting either from physicians or from hospitals shifting the demand for health services in such a way as to increase the demand for their services. This note of caution stems from the presumption that where demand is greater, the quantity supplied will be greater because of the responsiveness of quantity supplied to price, and because increased supply itself will increase quantity demanded in market equilibrium" (Auster & Oaxaca, 1981). The demand for medical care is unlimited. Suppose we define health as a state of physical and moral well-being. In that case, it is added that each medical discovery immediately finds a new field of use, rarely replacing the previous finding. The density of doctors and the population, the ease of access to care, and the offer's sophistication are not the same at all times and in all regions. The proposal does not work homogeneously, and patients' behavior is difficult to study (Béresniak & Duru, 1999, p. 81).

Life Expectancy

Life expectancy at birth has increased worldwide significantly since the nineteenth century (Figure 5), mostly due to progress, better lifestyle, medical advances, childhood immunizations, universal health treatments, along with a better quality of life, in general. These advances are not homogeneous; education, income, equality, and health facilities are essential related topics. In the year of 1901, the life expectancy at birth was nearly 45 years for men and 50 years for women. In the United Kingdom, in 2018, baby boys might expect to live on average to the age 87.6 years old and girls to age 90.2 years, taking into account projected changes in mortality patterns over their lifetime (ONS, 2020). There were slowdown moments in life expectancy, mostly after financial crises, due to austerity, creating more constraints on health, social care, and lifestyle (Kings Fund, 2020).

Figure 5. Trends in life expectancy at birth by gender (1960-2018)
Source: OECD, 2020d, p. 1.

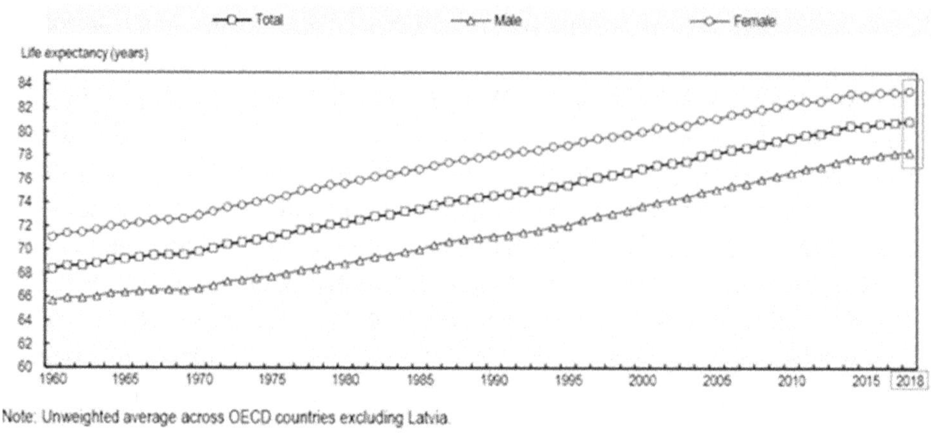

It is difficult to predict the impact of COVID-19 on life expectancy. Nevertheless, the excess of mortality related to COVID-19 will affect. Andrasfay and Goldman (2021) projected a reduced US life expectancy in 2020 by 1.13 years to 77.48 years, valued diminutions for the Black and Latino populations are 3 to 4 times that for Whites. This will continue beyond 2020 because of continued COVID-19 mortality and long-term health, social, and economic impacts of the pandemic. In the period previous to the COVID-19 pandemic, annual improvements in US life expectancy had been minor, i.e., an upsurge from 76.8 y to 78.9 y or an average yearly growth of 0.15 y between 2000 and 2014— nevertheless, global life expectancy has rarely declined, Figure 3, according to these researchers, this is the largest single-year decline in life expectancy in 40 years and is the lowest estimate since 2003 (Andrasfay & Goldman, 2021).

Life expectancy led to concerns about the impact of aging on healthcare systems. Given the almost correlation between age and chronic diseases, morbidity among elderly hospital patients has become more complex. The older patient is "made complex" by having multiple co-occurring medical conditions (Johnson et al., 2018).

Quoting Dixon, "the increasing number of older people will inevitably result in a greater burden of chronic and degenerative diseases, such as cardiovascular diseases, osteoarthritis, cancers, diabetes, cataract and macular degeneration, and dementia syndromes, which will result in an increased demand for health care and hence soaring costs" (Dixon et al., 2004, p. 1). Nevertheless, the average number of bed days spent in hospital in the period before death shows no discernable increase with increasing age. However, the highest amount of costs for intense care are incurred in the final years of life (Dixon et al., 2004).

Longevity is deferring, persistent diseases and mental degradation affecting more and more individuals. The causes are complex, expanding obesity and diabetes, respiratory diseases such as influenza and pneumonia, and horrible health habits due to opioids, alcohol or smoke, heart attacks, stroke, and other circulatory disorders—almost a third of adults living with two or more chronic conditions (Figure 6). Mental ill-health also takes its toll, with an estimated one in two people experiencing a mental health problem in their lifetime (OECD, 2020b, p. 9).

Figure 6. Multiple chronic conditions among people aged 65 and over, by gender (2017)
Source: OECD, 2020b.

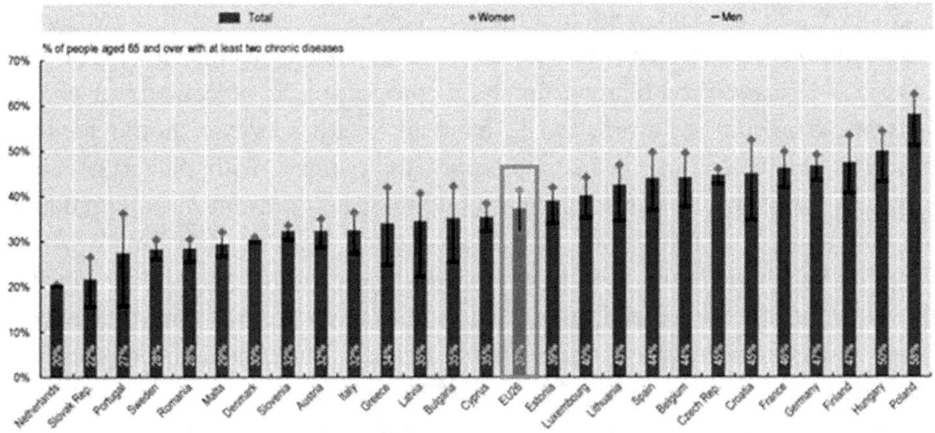

It is people aged 65 and over who, overall, use more health services, whether throughout laboratory analysis, nursing services, medical consultations, and consumptions or hospitalization. This more significant demand can be explained by the fact that the elderly suffer from deterioration of health status, an increasing number of health conditions related to age, and, subsequently, by the increase in life expectancy thanks to technology geriatrics services' progress. For example, in the pharmaceutical field, cardiovascular drugs, analgesics, and anti-inflammatory medicines are mainly consumed by people over 65. In any case, for a similar state of health, the elderly take care of themselves less than the young people. This effect, attributed as a generation effect, can be explained by the fact that numerous diseases are not susceptible to treatment in the elderly, contributing to moderate their demand for care (either because the treatment would be excessively aggressive or because the disease evolves so slowly). This does not constitute a real risk for the elderly, or because, due to the lack of information on the progress of medicine, older people do not look for it but what they could provide them with forty years ago (Giraldes, 1997, p. 84, 152). The increase in total life expectancy should be accompanied by a proportional rise in health and quality of life expectancy, reducing the morbidity into a briefer period, effectively postponing the onset of chronic diseases and associated disabilities. This premise would lower healthcare resources burden (Dixon et al., 2004).

Chronicity and comorbidity influence the risk of COVID-19 infection and the course of the disease. On the other hand, COVID-19 restricts standard treatments, generating a massive disruption worldwide in diagnosing and treating people with deadly but preventable diseases. According to WHO, there is a disruption in healthcare services, including non-communicable diseases diagnosis and treatments in 69 percent of cases. People living with cancer have their health services disrupted by 55% (UN, 2020). The pandemic directly affects patients and will continue to produce indirect outcomes on diseases and lifespan, increasing mortality indirectly.

COVID-19 cannot be blamed for the disproportionate percentage of chronic diseases and mental syndromes. The national health services should focus on preventive healthcare to enhance outcomes for patients with diabetes, cancer, respiratory problems, or cardiovascular conditions and prevent more populations from developing these illnesses. Improving better, healthier life for all people, promoting healthier routines, more gymnastics and exercises, and better nutrition will relieve healthcare expenditures in the future, help diminish the incidence of chronic diseases and improve our resilience against future pandemics. According to Blundell et al. (2020, p. 216) "COVID-19 pandemic has exacerbated existing inequalities and brought to the fore other inequalities that were perhaps less of a concern prior to the pandemic".

"The COVID-19 pandemic and the associated challenges in ensuring quality chronic care have shed light on pre-existing deficiencies in primary care practices. Structural changes in primary care organization are needed to improve general chronic illness management as well as to be resilient to future COVID-19 waves and pandemics" (Danhieux et al., 2020).

Can COVID-19 be accused altogether for excess mortality?

Excess mortality designates the mortality number from all causes during a crisis, like COVID-19, exceeding and beyond the 'normal' circumstances. Even though the mortality amount caused by COVID-19 may be superior, first, some nations eliminate deaths that did not test positive for coronavirus before dying. Second, hospitals and civil registries may not deliver obituary certificates for some days, generating lags and downgrades on the total of COVID-19 deaths. Lastly, the pandemic may have indirectly caused an increase in fatalities from diseases (Economist, 2021). Figure 7 reveals indirect effects from COVID-19 disclose a positive number when compared deaths with normal baseline.

Technology

Technology designates widgets (diagnostic tools, e.g., Positron Emission Tomography – Computed Tomography systems, Magnetic resonance/positron emission tomography systems), discoveries (new drugs, vaccines, e.g., biological agents), therapeutic interventions (e.g., angioplasty, joint replacement), and new management tools (healthcare IT systems, e.g., software, widgets, personal health monitors, telemedicine) by which medical assistance is provided. Although certain new technologies—vaccines, for example— outcome in lower short-term expenditure, technology advances, in general, amplify expenses (Goyen & Debatin, 2009). The growth of health care expenses is mainly due to the utilization of new medical technology. Those expenditures are now growing at an annual rate of 7% a year; the Medicare program, in the US, as a result, is projected to go bankrupt in nine years, and general health care expenditures to go from their present $2.1 trillion annually to $4 trillion in 10 years (Callahan, 2005).

Before COVID-19, research like Neumann & Weinstein in 2001 address the intensifying effect of new technologies, costly items, such as organ transplantation, diagnostic imaging systems, and new biotechnology products attract a significant share of payments.

Five figures about new medical technology, described in Neumann & Weinstein (2001):

1. New technologies improve medical care quality, although it is an average not for every technology in all clinical use.
2. Several new technologies are ineffective or unnecessary and do not improve health outcomes. It is difficult to distinguish between effective and ineffective technologies at the time they are introduced.
3. New technologies increase more expenses, immediately with the purchasing and technical maintenance, nevertheless can diminish expenditures by replacing more expensive equipment or preventing pricey health consequences.
4. Incentives, subventions, and regulations on the health care sector can advance to untimely disseminate technologies, both under dispersion of practical and cost-effective technologies and overdispersion of ineffective and cost-ineffective technologies: grants motivations, legal considerations, and professional compensation.
5. Patients and familiars demand innovation and better treatments, and suppliers are, in general, happy to oblige. We are more eager to capitalize on new advances with diminutive support than to disinvest in technology with evidence for a diminutive or no effectiveness (Hofmann, 2015).

Figure 7. Excess deaths since country or city's first 50 COVID-19 deaths
Source: Economist (2021) - Last updated on January 6th, 17:43 UTC.

COUNTRY / REGION	TIME PERIOD	COVID-19 DEATHS	EXCESS DEATHS	EXCESS DEATHS PER 100K PEOPLE
Peru	Apr 1st-Dec 31st	37,650	86,156	262
Mexico	Mar 29th-Nov 21st	101,357	251,805	211
Ecuador	Mar 1st-Sep 30th	11,355	34,067	198
Russia	Apr 1st-Nov 30th	39,474	269,392	184
Belgium	Mar 18th-Dec 15th	18,299	19,836	174
Spain	Mar 4th-Dec 29th	49,974	69,702	149
Britain	Mar 14th-Dec 18th	82,714	82,146	124
Portugal	Mar 25th-Dec 29th	6,718	12,142	118
United States	Mar 8th-Dec 12th	290,791	375,065	115
Italy	Feb 26th-Oct 27th	36,963	63,645	107
South Africa	Apr 15th-Dec 29th	27,541	58,315	99
Netherlands	Mar 14th-Dec 25th	11,005	15,988	92
Switzerland	Mar 16th-Dec 27th	7,196	7,542	88
Brazil	Mar 22nd-Nov 21st	168,974	184,202	88
France	Mar 11th-Dec 1st	52,094	55,186	85
Sweden	Mar 18th-Dec 15th	8,257	8,333	81
Chile	Apr 8th-Dec 29th	16,444	14,075	80
Austria	Mar 16th-Dec 13th	5,335	6,227	70
Istanbul	Mar 25th-Nov 17th	5,830	8,808	57
Jakarta	Mar 1st-May 31st	520	4,243	39
Germany	Mar 18th-Nov 24th	14,808	17,290	21
Denmark	Mar 25th-Dec 8th	869	362	6
Norway	Apr 1st-Dec 22nd	366	130	2

Citing Cahan et al. (2020), in health care, the innovation disruption is occasional, between 2005 and 2015, more than 75% of all medications receiving new patents were "reissues", representing the previous approvement, and the new patent manifested minor changes to the previously approved formula, meanwhile, the expenses of approved medicines boosted over time, at rates between 4 percent and 7 percent annually. Most performance-enhancing diagnostic tools and therapeutic innovations are inclined to forward restricted / rare illnesses or cancer subtypes, with limited straightforward clinical utility in broader populations. Cahan et al. (2020), mention the recently approved eculizumab, a monoclonal antibody approved for paroxysmal nocturnal hemoglobinuria - affecting 1 in 10 million individuals. At the time of its introduction, eculizimab medicine was rated more than 400,000 USD per year, rendering it the most expensive medication in modern history. For clinical populations with no available alternatives, drugs such as eculizimab may be cost-effective, pending society's willingness to pay, and morally desirable, given a society's values. However, such medicines are certainly not cost-reducing for health services.

Nowadays, the practice of medicine is gradually more reliant on technology, contrastive with other social and economic fields. The medicinal technology expenditures are not declining, and its increasing promotes inequality and an escalation of healthcare budgets. Most of these new technologies are not so new or disruptive, and they add more sensitivity and specificity to preexisting techniques. The growth of new diagnostic equipment often began with better resolution or a small technical improvement. Such innovations "may not result in better diagnostics – we may only see better what we already know" (Hofmann, 2015, p. 1). However, technology has changed the prevalence of disease (Table 1).

COVID-19 critical constraint is not about new technology. The most innovative equipment required to nurse patients was invented 100 years ago, in reaction to polio. Expensive investments in new health technologies will constrain patient treatment's scalability throughout outbreaks of respiratory infections, such as COVID-19 (Cahan et al., 2020).

Patients

It is relevant to mention the conflicts of interest between the different health stakeholders: patients, doctors, administrators, and the state:

- **Patients:** Are unaware of making sensible choices, which makes providers (mainly doctors) their representatives in guiding the demand for care on behalf of patients (this is called an agency relationship). Patient's unawareness of their needs, health position; the best moment of "purchasing", the unheard-of costs (direct and indirect) associated; and how to control the situation; the health care effect used its consequences to patients, family, and society.

Table 1. Examples of conditions where technology has change detection of disease

Condition	Technology	Change
Pulmonary embolism	Pulmonary angiography (1930), ventilation perfusion scintigraphy (1964), computed tomography pulmonary angiography (1998)	80% increase in pulmonary embolism from 1998 to 2006 with little reduction in mortality
Thyroid cancer	Neck ultrasonography (1980), guided biopsy (1990), CT, MRI (1996), ultrasound guided aspiration of thyroid nodules (2002)	Increased detection (and removal) of small papillary cancers/nodules. More patients receive a diagnosis after incidental findings than after evaluation of a symptomatic or palpable nodule
Gestational diabetes	From dual step test to single glucose value with reduced thresholds	New diagnostic criteria triple the prevalence of gestational diabetes with unclear effect on outcomes
Prediabetes	Impaired glucose tolerance by glucose challenge test (1979), impaired glucose tolerance by a fasting plasma glucose test (1997), glycated haemoglobin (2009)	Technological changes combined with lowering threshold results in a twofold to threefold increase in prevalence
Colon cancer	Sigmoidoscopy, colonoscopy, high definition endoscopy with modern enhancement techniques	Serrated polyps are identified and removed, although risky and without knowledge about outcome
Dissection of carotid or vertebral arteries	Doppler sonography, magnetic resonance angiography, CT angiography	3-10 times increase in detection rate
Breast cancer	Clinical examination to (digital) mammography screening	For every 1000 US women aged 50, 490-670 will have at least 1 false alarm, and 3-14 will be overdiagnosed and treated needlessly while 0.3 to 3.2 will avoid a breast cancer death when screened annually from age 40
Chronic kidney disease	Serum creatinine or cystatin C levels (to estimate glomerular filtration rate) and an assessment of kidney damage (eg, from testing albuminuria)	Almost 14% in the US are labelled as having chronic kidney disease
Osteoporosis	Dual energy x ray absorptiometry	Changing the treatment threshold (T score $\leq$2.0) makes more than half of women age $\geq$65 treated as diseased
Prostate cancer	Prostate specific antigen	Proportion of overdiagnosis in screen detected cases varies between 22% and 67%
Hypertension	Blood pressure monitoring	Substantial overdiagnosis when treatment decisions are based on clinic or home blood pressure alone. Without BP measurement, hypertension would not be considered to be a disease
Asthma	Stethoscope, spirometer	30% of people who had asthma diagnosed were overdiagnosed

Source: Hofmann, 2015, p. 5.

There are, therefore, a succession of unknowns, uncertainties in this health care market, which are the cause of the information asymmetry in this sector and are still the main responsible for the existence of failure in the health care market.

- **Doctors:** Are the most powerful group because they recognize what patients need and how to help them. They control the access to their profession, where there is a deficit of clinicians. For these professionals, their fundamental purpose is to treat patients as efficiently when their knowledge and resources allow, though main their job status.
- **Administrators:** Who are responsible for managing resources but are not involved in clinical decisions. Its purpose is to maintain efficiency while reducing costs, increasing pressures to adopt more cost-effective treatment practices.
- **State:** Must ensure universal care; the best example is COVID-19, where the more population is vaccinated, the greater the protection for society. Thus, we assume that health systems exist for society's good to keep people and the community healthier, disregarding all economic and administrative aspects.

Consumers' expectations regarding health are increasing. Citizens with more education and resources (e.g., internet, social networks) become more attentive and informed about the health sector. Many consumers show less agency theory characteristics, patients are increasingly willing to tell treatments and medical procedures to their doctors, and when they disagree, their expert option (doctor).

Patients are using more online resources to get data, now consumers live with personal electric devices (tracking and monitor their health, permanently) and use that data to make new judgments and requirements to doctors, access more hospital personal medical data to reanalyze doctors' decisions and use these medical records, freely, consuming more supplement vitamins and other drugs without prescription.

Technology is shifting consumer behaviors and the health sector. It can decrease health care expenses, increase patient admission, and doctor supervision through online technologies, advance health care and associated diagnoses using patients' health devices. From telehealth work to fast and secure sharing (medical records between doctors and facilities), the breathtaking use of artificial intelligence (AI) makes diagnostics more precise and faster, saving important health and resources.

Consumers demand better health services and infrastructures, free admissions, more technology, more specialists. Studies show that medical care rises with income: as a nation and its population become wealthier, it provides a fertile market for new medical innovations. Consumers also prefer medical care that will help them achieve and maintain good health. Advances in medical technology are perceived as a means to promote those goals. Consumers and medical industry demand are affected by increased public awareness of medical technology through the media, the internet, and direct-to-consumer advertising.

Private health insurances desire to attract more clients by promoting new technologies, more specializations, and medical advances. Encourage the public sector to follow their steps, increasing, indirectly, more pressure on public hospitals and taxpayers. Insurances deliver absolute confidence to technological developers, investigators, and medicinal contractors, safeguarding potential patients and the resources. At some time, encourage, in a utopic contest between private, public, and patients. Privates are willing to pay faster for new medical products, thus enabling research and development. Simultaneously, the promise of better health through improvements in medicine increases the consumers' demand for health insurance, as consumers look for ways to ensure access to the highest level of medical care.

CONCLUSION

There is an added difficulty for the public authorities to implement reforms, faced with a situation of the persistence of a low rate of economic growth caused by COVID-19 and the budgetary impositions of treaties that compromise the UE countries. However, the evolution of public expenditure in the direction of development occurs without that. This corresponds to improvements in the services provided or a reduction in private expenses, or a significant efficiency performance, which is very challenging to do in the health system.

Many individual factors outside the health system influence health status, notably income, education, the physical environment in which an individual lives, and the degree to which people adopt healthy lifestyles. The demographic, economic, and social context also affects the demand for and supply of health services and health status. (OECD, 2020b, p. 13). In the health sector, demand is predominant personal, irregular, and uncertain. Furthermore, as "sellers of health services" acting as representatives of patients, doctors act differently from other professions. Sometimes, they defend their corporation, preventing more providers or competition (restricting access to their job or specialty), otherwise representing their patients and health sector, in general. This, in turn, increases the cost of the services.

Moreover, there are numerous internal problems with the healthcare market, the demand is much higher than supply, there is insufficiency staff (doctors and nurses) in some regions due to population transferences, major cities are getting bigger and more crowded on the contrary, some areas have oversized infrastructures (beds) but without specialists. Technology has become more expensive; medicines are costly to develop and produce. COVID-19 will be tried and condemned for sure; politicians from all sectors will blame this pandemic for the past mistakes, the present occurrences, and the future pretexts. Although there are many historical facts to absolve COVID-19 from particular facts, historical underinvestment in the public health system could avoid or minimize COVID-19 effects. Governments use and exchange scarce resources (taxes); next year's many countries will reinvest, hire and allocate more taxes for the health sector, disclosing education, justice, or social measures.

It is not easy to balance supply and demand, as we had the opportunity to explain throughout this chapter, the imbalance between demand and supply is deteriorating. In the first place, tax revenue pressure increase over taxpayers. Second, the health is just a fragment of governments liabilities, other public segments will demand, and need, more resources. Third, it is challenging to improve value and efficiency, where the population is getting older, with more chronic diseases. Fourth, the doctors, medical staff, and technological manufacturers increase the budgets and rise more expectations on patients. Last, the patients reclaim the best and for free. Consequently, this will be followed only by further failure and more excuses.

REFERENCES

Andrasfay, T., & Goldman, N. (2021). Reductions in 2020 US life expectancy due to COVID-19 and the disproportionate impact on the Black and Latino populations. *Proceedings of the National Academy of Sciences of the United States of America*, *118*(5), e2014746118. Advance online publication. doi:10.1073/pnas.2014746118 PMID:33446511

Béresniak, A., & Duru, G. (1999). *Economia da Saúde*. Climepsi Editores.

Bernardes, O., & Pinillos, M. (2004). *Data Envelopment Analysis and Performance Management*. Aston University.

Bickerdyke, L., Dolamore, R., Monday, L., & Preston, R. (2002). *Supplier-Induced Demand for Medical Services*. Productivity Commission Staff Working Paper, Canberra. https://www.pc.gov.au/research/supporting/ supplier-induced-medical-demand/sidms.pdf

Blundell, R., Dias, C. M., Joyce, R., & Xu, X. (2020). COVID-19 and Inequalities. *Fiscal Studies*, *41*(2), 291–319. doi:10.1111/1475-5890.12232 PMID:32836542

BMA. (2020). *The hidden impact of COVID-19 on patient care in the NHS in England*. https://www.bma.org.uk/media/2841/the-hidden-impact-of-COVID_web-pdf.pdf

Brick, A., Nolan, A., O'Reilly, J., & Smith, S. (2010). Resource allocation, financing and sustainability in health care. *Evidence for the expert group on resource allocation and financing in the health sector*, 1. https://www.esri.ie/system/files?file=media/file-uploads/2015-07/BKMNEXT168.pdf

Cahan, E., Kocher, B., & Bohn, R. (2020). *Why Isn't Innovation Helping Reduce Health Care Costs?* Health Affairs. http:// https://www.healthaffairs.org/do/10.1377/hblog20200602.168241/full/

Callaham, D. (2005). *Health Care Costs and Medical Technology*. https://www.thehast ingscenter.org/briefingbook/health-care-costs-and-medical-technology

CIAT/IOTA/OECD. (2020). *Tax Administration Responses to COVID-19: Measures Taken to Support Taxpayers*. OECD. https://read.oecd-ilibrary.org/view/?ref=126_126478-29c4rprb3y

Danhieux, K., Buffel, V., Pairon, A., Benkheil, A., Remmen, R., Wouters, E., & Van Olmen, J. (2020). *The Impact of COVID-19 on Chronic Care: A Qualitative Study Among Primary Care Practices in Belgium*. doi:10.21203/rs.3.rs-42353/v1

Dixon, T., Shaw, M., Frankel, S., & Ebrahim, S. (2004). Hospital Admissions, Age, and Death: Retrospective Cohort Study. *BMJ (Clinical Research Ed.)*, *328*(7451), 1288. doi:10.1136/bmj.38072.481933.EE PMID:15090442

Economist. (2021). *Tracking COVID-19 excess deaths across countries*. http://www.economist.com/ graphic-detail/coronavirus-excess-deaths-tracker

EUROSTAT. (2019). *Tax revenue statistics*. https://ec.europa.eu/eurostat/documents/2995521/ 10190755/2-30102019-AP-EN.pdf/68739572-f06a-51e4-3a5b-86e660a23376

Giraldes, M. (1997). *Economia da Saúde da teoria à Prática*. Editora Estampa.

Goyen, M., & Debatin, J. (2009). Healthcare costs for new technologies. *European Journal of Nuclear Medicine and Molecular Imaging*, *36*(S1), 139–143. doi:10.100700259-008-0975-y PMID:19104799

Grytten, J., & Sørensen, R. (2001). Type of Contract and Supplier-Induced Demand for Primary Physicians in Norway. *Journal of Health Economics*, *20*(3), 379–393. doi:10.1016/S0167-6296(00)00087-4 PMID:11373837

Hofmann, B. (2015). Too much technology. BMJ, 350. doi:10.1136/bmj.h705

IMF - International Monetary Fund. (2020). Challenges in Forecasting Tax Revenue. *Special Series on Fiscal Policies to Respond to COVID-19*. https://www.imf.org/~/media/Files/ Publications/COVID-19-special-notes/en-special-series-on-COVID-19-challenges-in-forecasting-tax-revenue.ashx

Johnson, H., O'Farrell, A., McKeown, D., Sayers, G., Hayes, C., & Beaton, D. (2018). Is Increasing Life Expectancy Leading To More Complexity? *Irish Medical Journal, 111*, 672. PMID:29869853

Lorenzoni, L., Marino, A., Morgan, D., Murakami, Y., & James, C. (2019). *Health spending projections to 2030*. OECD Health Working Paper N.° 110, OECD Publishing. doi:10.1787/18152015

Moon, S., Røttingen, J., & Frenk, J. (2017). Global public goods for health: Weaknesses and opportunities in the global health system. *Health Economics, Policy, and Law, 12*(2), 195–205. doi:10.1017/S1744133116000451 PMID:28332461

NHS UK - National Health System UK. (2020). *The principles and values of the NHS in England*. https://www.gov.uk/government/publications/the-nhs-constitution-for-england/the-nhs-constitution-for-england

NSW. (2020). COVID-19 Supplement Emergency department, ambulance, admitted patients and elective surgery - January to June 2020. *NSW Bureau of Health Information*. https://www.bhi.nsw.gov.au/__data/assets/pdf_file/0008/603566/BHI_HQ_APR-JUN_2020_COVID-19_Supplement.pdf

OECD. (2012). *Comparing activities and performance of the hospital sector in Europe: how many surgical procedures performed as inpatient and day cases?* OECD Publishing. https://www.oecd.org/health/Comparing-activities-and-performance-of-the-hospital-sector-in-Europe_Inpatient-and-day-cases-surgical-procedures.pdf

OECD. (2020a). *Focus on public-funding-of-health-care*. OECD Publishing. https://www.oecd.org/health/Public-funding-of-health-care-Brief-2020.pdf

OECD. (2020b). *Health at a Glance 2019 - OECD indicators*. OECD Publishing. https://www.oecd-ilibrary.org/docserver/4dd50c09-en.pdf

OECD. (2020c). *Waiting Times for Health Services: Next in Line*. OECD Publishing. https://www.oecd.org/health/waiting-times.htm

OECD. (2020d). *Life expectancy at birth*. OECD Publishing. https://www.oecd.org/els/family/CO_1_2_Life_expectancy_at_birth.pdf

ONS - Office for National Statistics UK. (2020). *National life tables – life expectancy in the UK: 2017 to 2019*. https://www.ons.gov.uk/peoplepopulationandcommunity/birthsdeathsandmarriages/lifeexpectancies/bulletins/nationallifetablesunitedkingdom/2017to2019

Oxley, H., & MacFarlan, M. (1994). *Health Care Reform Controlling Spending and Increasing Efficiency*. OECD Working Papers. N.º 24. Economics Department, OECD Publishing. doi:10.1787/18151973

Rice, T. (1984). Physician-induced demand for medical care: New evidence form the Medicare Program. *Advances in Health Economics and Health Services Research*, *5*, 129–160. PMID:10300352

Simões, J. (2004). *Retrato político da saúde*. Almedina.

Thomson, S., Foubister, T., & Mossialos, E. (2009). *Financing health care in the European Union: challenges and policy responses*. Observatory Studies Series N.º 17, European Observatory on Health Systems and Policies. https://www.euro.who.int/_data/assets/pdf_file/ 0009/9 8307/E92469.pdf

UN - United Nations. (2020). *COVID-19 impact on treatment for chronic illness revealed*. https://news.un.org/en/story/2020/09/1071732

WHO - World Health Organization. (2020). *Coronavirus disease (COVID-19)*. https://www.who.int/ docs/default-source/coronaviruse/situation-reports/20201005-weekly-epi-update-8.pdf

KEY TERMS AND DEFINITIONS

Case-Mix or Patient Mix: Is a term used for adjusting the nature and intensity of treatments undertaken by a group of patients.

Co-Payment: Refers to percentage of the total amount for a service paid by a patient, on their own or by his insurance, to the provider of service before receiving the service.

Elasticity in Demand: Shows the relationship between price and quantity demanded and provides a precise calculation of the effect of a change in price on quantity demanded.

Excess Mortality: Designates the mortality number from all causes during a crisis, exceeding and beyond the 'normal' circumstances.

"Free-Riders": Patients because users can enjoy health privileges without expending effort for paying it or the actual cost of the service.

Non-Excludability: Means that public goods are available to all citizens, cannot exclude a person based on the price, regardless of whether or not they have contributed financially.

Non-Rival: Means that when one person uses a good, it does not prevent others from using it.

Chapter 7
Health Communication During the COVID-19 Pandemic in Hungary

Zoltán Juhász
University of Szeged, Hungary

Erzsébet Hetesi
University of Szeged, Hungary

ABSTRACT

In this chapter, the authors are looking for the answer to how novel coronavirus disease (COVID-19) has influenced health communication in online platforms. The aim was to investigate with a newer qualitative research method (netnography) how the scenes of communication have been changed during the COVID-19 crisis. The content of some popular online public forums was analyzed that came up during the outbreak in Hungary. The participant opinions and attitudes regarding health communication of COVID-19 crisis management were observed. The community acceptance of two measures were investigated: necessity of wearing a mask and the mandatory evacuation of hospital beds. These topics divided the opinion of the citizens. In spite of the efficient COVID-19 outbreak management, there were very extreme and different opinions (skepticism, indignation, accusation, acceptance) in the online community about the accuracy and reliability of health communication. The results may support the future improvement of health crisis management.

DOI: 10.4018/978-1-7998-7263-4.ch007

INTRODUCTION

The novel coronavirus (COVID-19) epidemic, which originated from China at the end of 2019 and then became a pandemic, poses perhaps the greatest challenge for the world in the last century. Healthcare systems have the biggest role in the epidemiological control, reducing morbidity and mortality, and mitigating the economic downturn. Communication has a special place in the organization of fast and efficient healthcare and in the preparation of the population. Communication with the general public and health professionals is primarily aimed at strengthening the sense of security and awareness in the coronavirus pandemic, but solidarity also plays an important role.

Epidemiological measures have brought the transformation of communication channels used in health care. One of the important elements of the measures to slow down the spread of the pandemic is the reduction of personal contacts, the minimization of personal doctor-patient meetings, and the introduction of remote consultation. In the current situation, the Internet has become one of the main arenas of communication, and the role of social media in the dissemination of health information and social communication is becoming more and more important. Reaching the most vulnerable population over the age of 65 in the pandemic requires the use of offline communication channels as well. The delivery of short, focused messages (eg. stay at home, wash your hands) can be facilitated by credible professionals.

As the importance of communication in the COVID-19 pandemic increased worldwide, informing the population about epidemiological measures in Hungary also became a priority, and the main channels of this were the media (TV, radio, online press), which sought to reach out to the authorities and institutions. For this collaboration to be successful, credibility, reliability, comprehensibility, and most importantly, trust are required in communication.

Unfortunately, in connection with COVID-19 outbreak in Hungary, a specific, highly centralized, one-channel communication is typical to still this day, so health communication can only be examined in the light of this. Where healthcare institutions could not independently release data on the number of infected, treated and deceased individuals, where citizens could only be informed about the COVID-19 situation in the country through official channels and only by region, and where military commanders have been appointed to healthcare institutions, there have been uncertainties in institutional communication and among the population on a number of issues.

NOVEL TRENDS IN HEALTHCARE COMMUNICATION

Health communication is important to influence, engage individuals, communities, health professionals, policy makers, facilitates behavioural change and improves health outcome (Schiavo, 2013).

Four milestones can be identified in the evolution of public health communication (Salmon & Poorisat, 2020):

1. early use of mass communication in public health campaigns,
2. monitoring the effects,
3. searching for interdisciplinary explanation, and
4. formal recognition of health communication as a separate field of theory and practice.

Healthcare is a professional service where possession of the adequate amount of information is very important to decrease the perceived risk before and throughout the medical process and influence health behaviour (Vajda et al., 2012).

The personalized empathetic service, patient-centered communication and the involvement of patients into the decision-making are basic elements of the modern healthcare (Wolff, 1989; Volmann, 2008). Donabedian emphasizes the importance of interpersonal relations, the proper communication to improve the quality of healthcare service and increase the patients' satisfaction (Donabedian, 1988). According to World Health Organization (WHO), the following attributes influence the effectiveness of health communication: accuracy, availability, balance, consistency, cultural competence, repetition, timeliness and understandability (WHO, 2017). The scene and mood of the traditional patient-physician interaction has changed substantially in the past decades.

The effective communication in a healthcare institute is determined by health literacy, cultural competency and language barriers. Health literacy enables the individuals to make better healthcare decisions, change their health behaviour, thus improve their health outcomes. Deficiencies in health communication can be a significant cost burden for healthcare institutions (Ratna, 2019).

Young people prefer social media, while older adults are usually informed through the traditional mass media (national evening television, newspapers etc.) (Arnstein, 2020).

Web 2.0 is an ideal platform for information-sharing and interactive communication. Users can interact and collaborate with each other, generate and share content in the virtual community. The online media platforms allow to customize messages, increase the reach to different target groups or the whole population, facilitate the multidirectional communication flow, enable and empower the community

(Ramanadhan et al., 2013; Schein et al., 2010). Social media provides great opportunities to rapidly spread and integrate public health messages with daily online conversations and contributes to the improvement of functional health literacy of the general population. Since the emergence of social media in 2004, a growing number of users apply this technology for health-related purposes (Smailhodzic et al., 2016).

With the introduction of social media websites, the online static information moves to an interactive communication channel. The social media has six types: virtual game worlds (eg. World of Warcraft), collaborative projects (eg. Wikipedia), virtual social worlds (eg. Second Life), blogs and microblogs (eg. Twitter), social networking sites (eg. Facebook), content communities (eg. YouTube) (Kaplan & Haenlein, 2010). Social media has basically changed the way people interact, communicate, share and gather information. The social media is an instantaneous channel with 4 characteristics that have changed the traditional way of communication: user-generated content, community, rapid distribution and opened, two-way dialogue (PwC, 2012). The static health information on websites were followed first by one-to one communication on social media and then replaced by one-to-many or many-to-many (Kaplan & Haenlein, 2010). Social networks (eg. Facebook, Twitter, YouTube) represent a new world for healthcare consumers and providers, as they have a platform to join virtual communities, participate in research, receive support and communicate rapidly and inexpensively (Childs & Martin, 2012; Lambert et al., 2012). The public can actively participate in creating and disseminating influential messages on this platform (Burgess & Green, 2018).

Social media revolutionized the healthcare industry and service, becoming a preferred source of uptodate health information. Patients often join online health communities to express their satisfaction/dissatisfaction with their healthcare professional, share their own experiences and get emotional, informational support from the other members of the network (Rupert et al., 2014). The most common reasons of social media usage for health-related purposes are social support, emotional expression and social comparison. The social media enables a more equal communication between the patient and the healthcare professional (Smailhodzic et al., 2016). Patients may be better prepared for the consultation as they probably know more about their condition. The social support effects of social media increases the likeliness of an active communication with the physician during the service (Bartlett & Coulson, 2011; Oh & Lee, 2012).

In their article, Kim and Kreps (2020) analyze U.S. Governments' communication during the COVID-19 pandemic. In their opinion, ineffective communication by governments has caused widespread confusion and misunderstanding among the public, with disastrous health and social consequences for the population and prolonged the pandemic, particularly in the United States. The U.S. government response to the COVID-19 pandemic demonstrates a breakdown in the system transformation process with slow and haphazard sensemaking and response to the health threat, despite available information that this dangerous new virus had already rapidly infected and killed many people in other countries before spreading to the United States. They also point out that the world has paid innumerable prices for the COVID-19 pandemic, which could have been prevented much more effectively and responded to much more effectively if governments had more sensitive and strategic health risk communication systems (Kim & Kreps, 2020).

Citizens are confronted with an increasing amount of conflicting information, which is difficult to navigate and competes for the public's attention. The implication for public policy is that increasing the amount of official and factual information will not necessarily be more effective unless this content is made more persuasive and delivered to different audiences through their preferred channels and with an understanding of behavioural and psychological biases. This is particularly important for young audiences, who access news primarily through social media (OECD, 2020).

American authors found that the use of social media for health communication was influenced significantly by two factors: year and age. The application of social media to share health information has reduced over time, while the exchange of medical information with a health professional via social media platform has increased. The younger population (18-49 years) had higher percentage of using social media for health communication (Huo et al., 2019).

The expansion of social media between health professionals and patients provides a great oppurtunity for the development of health promotion campaigns, thus the health inequlaities in the society may be reduced. Health communication campaigns that use marketing tools as well as a communication strategy may support health education and social marketing (Huo et al., 2019; Zhao, 2020).

Personal healthcare contributes to faster diagnosis, provides quality care to patients, and involves them in making decisions about their health status. In contrast, virtual healthcare implemented online allows for a reduction in costs and the timely care of patients (Accenture, 2018).

The risks of using social media in healthcare include quality control, conflict of interest, limited reach, lack of anonimity, loss of privacy, damage to professional image, increased switching of doctors and addiction to online resources. Due to the nature of health services, the online communication channels cannot completely replace the offline, face-to-face patient-physician interaction (Ventola, 2014). The social media enhances and supports the role of traditional media in delivering important public health messages and contributes to an effective crisis management (CMA, 2011).

The Centers for Disease Control and Prevention (CDC) has been actively and successfully utilized the advantages of web 2.0 and social media to raise awareness of common public health problems and crises. This includes the swine flu outbreak in 2009 and the novel coronavirus pandemic in 2020. A highly effective social media marketing strategy was developed and innovative approaches were implemented to promote health communication. The CDC has an active presence on Twitter and Facebook to share updates about current public health issues. Real time social media sites are able to provide a rapid and enhanced preparedness for public health emergencies and crises (George et al., 2013).

The three main challenges governments have to face when planning health communication are information overload, information uncertainty and misinformation. These factors are especially important in a public health crisis like the present COVID-19 pandemic (Vraga & Jacobsen, 2020).

In practice, public communication entails providing information for the public interest that is factual, transparent and separate from political communication. In Italy, for instance, a dedicated law requires that institutions can sustain the distinction between public and political communication (ForumPA, 2020, in: OECD).

According to an analysis by the Reuters Institute, 59% of the false information about COVID-19 is to some extent manipulated but based on real information, while 38% is completely fictitious (Brennen et al., 2020).

The fight against the "infodemic" is one of the priority frontlines of managing the coronavirus pandemic (OECD, 2020). The types of problematic information circulating around the virus are becoming more complex. The debate on this issue revolves around three main concepts (Wardle et al., 2017):

- Misinformation – when fales information is shared, but no harm is meant.
- Disinformation – when false information is knowingly shared to cause harm.
- Malinformation – when genuine information is shared to cause harm, often by moving what was designed to stay private into the public sphere.

The true reach of disinformation is also difficult to estimate, as some research suggests people are likelier to share misinformation than they are to believe it (Pennycook et al., 2020).

In order to prevent the circulation of rumors, robust scientific evidence against misinfomation must be presented to the public.

In special situations (like the present COVID-19 pandemic), governments should use recommendations to achieve an effective health communication, for example: communicate with empathy; communicate with openness, frankness, and honesty; recognise that uncertainty is inevitable; proactively fight against misinformation; empower people to act. The long-term success depends on maintaining public trust and cooperation (Hyland-Wood et al., 2021).

HEALTH COMMUNICATION IN THE COVID-19 PANDEMIC

The COVID-19 pandemic and its health and economic consequences have drastically impacted our daily life. The flood of reliable and unreliable information challenges the health communication. In the COVID-19 pandemic, the countries must pursue an effective risk communication strategy in a timely manner to the public so that people can make decisions based on official facts and data, not a hearsay.

The risk communication is necessary to understand the health threats, follow the infection control measurements. Perception and response to risk messaging is influenced by social and cultural factors, personality, immediacy, familiarity, scientific uncertainty, trust in media and institutions (Malecki et al., 2021).

Trust is a key factor in risk communication and the messages should express empathy. Announcing early shows competency, leads to trust, may prevent rumor and speculation (PAHO, 2020). The risks of the COVID-19 infection and preventive measures (eg. lockdowns, vaccination) should be thoroughly explained. The communication should consider the categories of people who must be engaged in order to achieve outbreak control. The key audiences, partners and stakeholders include (IFRC et al., 2020a):

- all people at risk of acquiring COVID-19 (eg. elderly, people with chronic diseases, healthcare workers, travelers)
- healthcare providers
- stakeholders and partners (policy-makers, relevant government sectors, NGO partners, community leaders, international organizations).

By comparing the communication of political/institutional leaders in Italy, Germany, Spain and Sweden, the researchers found that the solutions to the problems caused by COVID-19 pandemic were largely driven by epidemiological considerations. The communication of the heads of state and government was based on the principle that individual citizens had a significant role and responsibility for preventing further spread of the virus. While the German case is clearly about the relationship between democracy and the limits of rights, in most other countries the issue has been different. The relationship between individual autonomy as a democratic right and disciplinary mechanisms was seen as contradictory, and it was pointed out that while the (laudable) aim of state action was to create spaces free of crowns, human and democratic rights were marginalised (Sjölander-Lindqvist et al., 2020).

The general content needed by all stakeholders and all target groups must contain the clinical characteristics of COVID-19 infection, the current status of

COVID-19 infections in the country and globally, the sources of credible, updated and comprehensible information, the steps of prevention.

Channels and forums that might reach broad national audiences should be identified and applicated (eg. mass media, trusted organizations' websites, social media platforms, billboards) (IFRC et al., 2020a).

Due to the strict and wide public health measures, the dramatical decrease of personal contacts, the usage and importance of online platforms has increased.

During the COVID-19 pandemic, governments published information on their official portals, mobile apps, social media platforms. People should be regularly informed on the government's response, practical knowledge on protection, travel restrictions (UN, 2020). Reliable government information helps people to make informed decisions about their daily life, restrictions, build public trust and enables public authorities to act consequently to flatten the epidemic curve (UN, 2020). The involvement of the public is essential in the process of message creation for the effective fight against the virus. The behaviour of the public in this situation (eg. stay home, hand hygiene, social distancing, mask wearing) is basically depends on how they perceived the risk and how they have apprehended the official communication (PAHO, 2020).

The surveillance of public perceptions, knowledge gaps through polling, hotlines or social media may serve as a useful tool to improve the efficiency of communication activity. The continous control of misinformation and disinformation may prevent the emergence of falsehood. The information to the population should be accessible, technically correct, honest, transparent and complete. The presented information should minimize speculation and avoid overinterpretation of data. It should always be declared that the recommendations and obligatory measures may change as we learn more the dynamics of the COVID-19 pandemic (PAHO, 2020).

In the COVID-19 Global Risk Communication and Community Engagement Strategy, international organizations suggest that the one-way, directive communication that characterized the early phase of the COVID-19 response should be changed. Engagament and active participation of communities should be encouraged to effectively control the current outbreak. The efficient risk communication and community engagement is characterized as nationally-led, community-centered, participatory, open and transparent, data-driven, coordinated, accountable, inclusive, integrated and trustworthy. In the upcoming period of the pandemic the main challenges will be: uncertainty, accessibility of vaccines, increasing pandemic fatigue, management of misinformation, community engagement, building trust, increasing economic pressure that foster risk-taking behaviour (IFRC et al., 2020b).

Public health organizations like WHO and CDC, numerous journals, healthcare institutions disseminate information and post guidance during the COVID-19 pandemic accross social media platforms.

Chinese authors found in their research that in Wuhan (China) the delayed decision-making process of local government officials and limited or incoherent dissemination of information are mainly responsible for the ineffective risk communication. The government seemed to fail sharing information in a timely and effective way. This undermined the public perception associated with COVID-19, the authorities failed to treat it. The whole communication process worsened the circulation of rumours and lead to panic. Morover, it may also contributed to the rapid, country-wide spread of the infection (Zhang et al., 2020).

In the USA, the risk perception about the COVID-19 outbreak was surveyed. The responsive, open, respectful communication of public health organization leaders may improve public compliance and safety. It was found that vast majority (69%) of the responders preferred the scientific/public health leadership (CDC director or NIH director), only 14% wanted a political leadership (President, Congress) to lead the response process. The responsive, open and respectful communication may improve the public health compliance and safety. Public health/scientific leadership should be in the forefront of the COVID-19 response (McFadden et al., 2020).

The over-abdundance of information during the current pandemic (the so-called infodemic), especially if it is contradictory and obscure may make it hard for the individuals to make informed decisions. In the longer term, the infodemic may cause mental disorders and results in breaches of lockdowns (Porat et al., 2020).

In Hungary, the health communication was centralized during the COVID-19 crisis and directed mainly towards two target groups: the public and the leaders of health system. The content of the communication was determined by the Operative Board that had been set up quite well before the government declared the State of Emergency in the middle of March 2020.

The Chief Medical Officer of Hungary presents the current health-related topics of COVID-19 in a daily press conference accompanied by two uniformed police officials of the Operative Board.

The management of the outbreak in the first and second phases of the pandemic was basically different in Hungary. While the first phase was characterized by overinsurance, rapid and costly measures, the second phase was dominated by neglect and lately introduced actions. In the second phase, communication related to the national vaccination plan and the announcement of complete lockdown, the distrust of vaccination in the population due to the lack of transparency of the vaccination plan and insufficient communication about the reliability of the Russian and Chinese vaccines are particularly noticeable.

In the first phase of the COVID-19 pandemic, based on the reports of national press, the most important phenomena causing public outrage in connection with pandemic management:

- The need to wear a mask (first it was not necessary, then possible, then mandatory) - we did not know exactly to whom and why.
- Late large-scale testing, late protective measures and testing of healthcare workers and residents of social institutions (resulting in hotspots, about 15% of illnesses were among health workers, almost half of all deaths occurred in nursing homes).
- Mandatory evacuation of 50% (36,000 beds) of all active hospital beds in a week to prepare for the hospital care of COVID-19 patients; many hospital patients were sent home regardless of their health status and social condition; 7,000 intensive care beds were also prepared, which was absolutely unnecessary given the dynamics of the pandemic (this capacity would have been enough perhaps for all COVID-19 patients in Europe). The measure was taken in the form of a command.
- Detailed data on COVID-19 morbidity and mortality were initially not provided.
- Inconsistency between the availability of protective equipment and the government's claim (eg. there were shortages of personal protective equipments in family practices).
- Highly centralized communication, militarized management in healthcare system.
- Acquisition of devices unsuitable for invasive ventilation of COVID-19 patients.

Many studies analysing social platforms have been published, but there are few of them that specifically deal with citizens' opinions on government and health communication. In the next part of the chapter, the authors examine the online communication related to mask wearing and mandatory evacuation of hospital beds.

The spread of COVID-19 in Hungary compared to other European countries (Italy, Spain, Austria) appeared much later, so it would have been time to learn lessons. However, the health and other measures taken in the country still divided the public in several cases, in which the power struggles of the political parties also played a role.

In this qualitative research, the authors captured two topics: mask wearing, evacuation of hospital beds from the opinion-sharing measures. The communication of these were inconsistent in Hungary, were not credible, created distrust in people and thus served as a basis for social and political debates.

METHODOLOGY

Defining the Research Questions

In examining the problems of health communication, it has been already mentioned that it leaves something to be desired even under normal circumstances. While patients have many rights to information, the communication channels, the way of communication, and its content often cause uncertainty. This uncertainty can be even more pronounced in a critical situation, as is the current COVID-19 pandemic, where decision-makers themselves are not sure what is the right path. Exaggerated steps and inconsistent information are confusing the recipients.

The research questions are as follows:

- Can groups with specific attitudes be identified in judging government communication about mask wearing?
- Are there marked differences of opinion on the mandatory evacuation of hospital beds?

To answer these research questions, the authors chose the netnographic qualitative method.

The Antecedent of Netnography is Ethnography

Ethnography has been a popular method of sociology for decades, but opinions are divided on its application, on the precise definition of the method itself, and its definition has undergone several changes. One reason for this is that it is closely related to anthropology and their demarcation is still unclear. Cultural anthropology has long been identified with ethnography, but some still consider it a general human science. However, the methods of anthropology are now much more specific, and the field of interest in anthropology also shows a very colourful picture (Marcus & Fischer, 1996). Ethnography has become one of the means of studying sociocultural relations precisely through its relationship with anthropology, but there is no complete consensus in the broader social science discourse on what exactly we consider ethnography to be. As many people write about it, we find so many definitions. One of the most widely accepted definitions is that ethnography "validates the methodological traditions of cultural anthropology in other social sciences" (Hammersley, 2006, p. 12). Or, as many believe, "ethnography is more than a method, but less than a discipline: a specific research methodology that uses several methods together" (Mészáros, 2014, p. 5). For many, ethnography is synonymous with qualitative, interpretive social science research (Denzin & Lincoln,

2003), more simply: ethnography (fieldwork) can be considered qualitative research (Anderson-Lewitt, 2006). Conceptual confusion is exacerbated by the fact that many do not even separate ethnography from cultural anthropology, and some even consider observational research to be ethnography that does not (or does not necessarily) fall within the scope of cultural anthropology (Dobbert & Kurt-Schai, 1992).

Netnography is the Etnography of Modern Era

Netnography is a qualitative research method that adapts ethnographic research techniques to examine the culture of online communities (Kozinets, 2002). Already in the name, there has been a lot of controversy (cyberanthropology, cyberetnography, virtual ethnography, online ethnography), and it is the subject of further discussion about what qualitative method adaptation we can talk about.

According to Langer and Beckman (2005), netnography is a form of content analysis, while Kozinets (2006) believes that it is not worthwhile to stick to a kind of traditional method, they can be combined because of the possibilities offered by online space, and this is also true for analytical techniques. Based on this, netnography offers a wide range of qualitative research methods and analysis techniques, ie. netnographers also need to use as colorful methods as possible in order to explore the diversity of the online world. Netnography can be conducted online as well as offline. This new and growing qualitative method is essential to online community research and enables the analysis of the enormous amount of data that is archived online (Udenze, 2019).

Due to this flexibility of netnography, the authors decided to use this method in their research in the extremely hectic situation resulting from COVID-19. The authors tried to explore the effects of health communication on the epidemiological situation in Hungary by analyzing online communication. In applying the netnographic method, the authors relied primarily on the study of Kozinets (2002) and followed its steps.

THE RESEARCH PROCESS

Identification of Online Communication Forms to be Involved in the Analysis

The online platform offers many opportunities to find the form of communication that is best for us. These can be forums, blogs, instant messengers, social networks, social networking sites, email lists, game interfaces. In this case, familiar communities specializing in one topic did not develop due to the shortness of time appeared in the online research related to COVID-19 pandemic, so it was difficult to find and select the ones that would have been limited to two topics.

Public opinions were published on almost all existing online platforms, and the authors' choice ultimately fell on wearing masks and the evacuation of hospital care of coronavirus patients. The choice of topic is justified by the fact that in the case of these two topics the central communication was perhaps the most controversial or least understandable, and therefore a very intensive communication activity started in the online communities and forums.

Selecting the Field of Research

For investigating research problems, theoretical sampling in online setting was used, preferring online communities that were relevant to the research, active and interactive, heterogenous and data rich (Kozinets, 2010).

In this research, online news portals and an official government portal were involved to observe and analyze the available public posts on Facebook connected to a defined news.

The following Hungarian news portals and their Facebook websites were chosen for conducting the analysis:

www.index.hu

www.24.hu

www.hvg.hu

www.origo.hu

www.koronavirus.gov.hu

Determining the Level of Participation

Depending on the type of online community studied, research objectives, and characteristics of the research field, two types of access can be distinguished (Addeo et al., 2020):

- Hidden access ("lurking") - the researcher observes the communication activity of the community without the participants knowing about their presence and the research.

- Open access (participant observation) - the researcher informs the members of the community and asks for their consent, often through the community leader / opinion gatekeeper.

During the participatory observation, the researcher's presence in the examined community can be realized at different levels and intensities: following and reading links, rating, commenting, writing responses to members, interviewing in the form of emails, active involvement in online community communication, a kind of expert role (Morton, 2001; Kozinets, 2010). The great advantages of netnography are the less time-consuming data collection, the easier availability, relevance, wider scope, controllability, and heterogeneity of data obtained from online sources (Kozinets, 2010; Addeo et al., 2020).

The method of passive observational netnography was used, the authors did not interact with the observed groups, did not react or comment on any content, hoping that this would also reduce the possible subjectivity during the analysis.

Data Collection and Analysis

The Google search engine was applied to conduct the investigation, using the keywords "mask wear", "recommendation of mask wear", "hospital bed evacuation", "hospital bed emptying" to search for content relevant to the research. The authors focused on online news portals where there were posts on the topic and it was possible for readers to comment on social media and received a significant number (at least 100) of comments. The content analysis was guided by the research questions. The collected comments were analyzed using the Nvivo method.

Kozinets categorized the posters of online messages based on their level of involvement with the online community and the consumption activity into four classes: tourists, minglers, devotees and insiders (Kozinets, 1999). In the present research, due to the special field of investigation, these categories were not applicated, but the analyzed comments of the two topics could be categorized into well-defined groups.

Lurking activity enabled the authors to observe and familiarize with the values, norms and roles of the online community and study the dynamics of the online interaction. As for necessity of wearing a mask, based on the mood of conversation and the attitude of posters, 4 categories of participants were identified within the online community: Acceptors/Advisors, Unsatisfied and disgusted, Blamers/accusers, Skepticals (Figure 1).

Mask Wearing

Figure 1. Categories of online users for the necessity of mask wearing

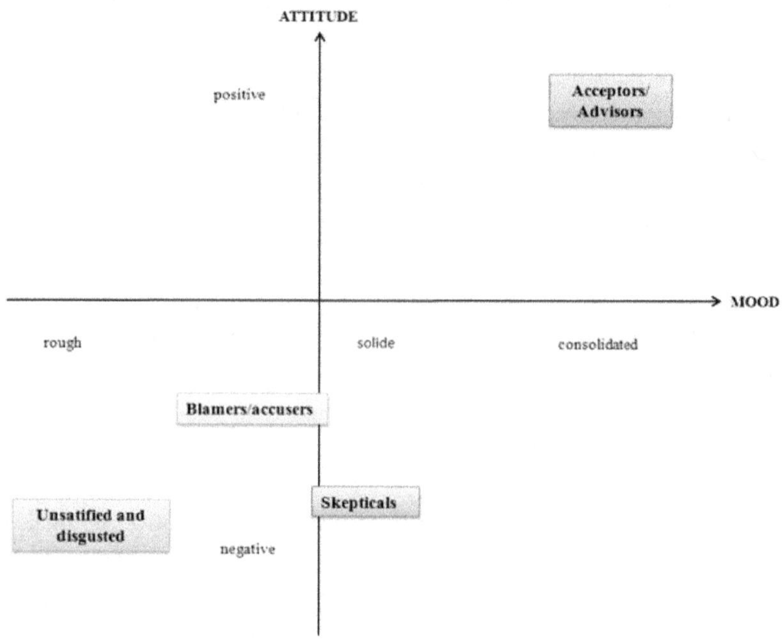

A. **Acceptors/Advisors:** These people agree with wearing a face mask, independently of the government's communication. Their opinion may be based on a professional knowledge. They try to convince others to wear a mask (or a scarf) so as to prevent the spread of the coronavirus infection.

Well, finally! If you don't have a mask and don't get one, make it at home or wear a scarf. And don't forget the gloves. Take care of yourself, take care of each other.

In this case, everyone should act like an infected person. And the mask reduces the chances of transmitting the virus.

If everyone wears it, the spread of virus and its radius will decrease. The infectious disease transmission is reduced. You are less likely to infect the other. Outbreaks can be prevented by reducing the transmission of infection, not the protection of the individual is important, but the community.

It's good to wear a mask now for many other reasons, for example, if two people meet they see the mask on the other, they don't forget there is a pandemic. Awareness!

B. **Unsatisfied and Disgusted:** The users are not satistied with the received information about wearing the mask or not. They think that the government should decide whether to suggest to wear or not wear a mask and who should wear it (healthy or ill individuals?). They feel the communication chaotic and not clear as there are supply shortages of masks in the country.

They seem to be communicating about useless masks where they can't be accessed.

They'd rather say there aren't enough masks, and there won't be. Therefore, we leave them to the doctors (there is no other option). A lot of fake text and constant blurring is already too much.

The problem here is that I shouldn't buy a mask, but the government should give it. An emergency state has been declared !!!!! The people should be taken care of!!?? Rather they say there is no need for it ....

I have no idea whether I'm healthy or not. So I'll put on the mask !!! And I also put on because the public information is as it is. None! I am very angry!

C. **Blamers/Accusers:** They blame the government and/or the members of the Operative Board for the unclear communication and the consequent situation. Their personal attitudes toward wearing a mask is not clearly expressed.

Cecília Müller is a puppet, and the government seems to have no problem with the epidemic. Otherwise, I think there are few masks even now, that is why this "striking" solution was invented.*

State propaganda is lying about not having to wear a mask, because so far it has NOT been! The world pandemic was declared a month ago, but so far they have been unable to obtain masks.

Poor Cecília Müller doesn't think what she's propagating either, but if the Prime Minister still can't show the masks he lied about a week ago that there had been enough, she can't do anything else, she has to persuade the people not to wear a mask.

Only Cecília Müller and the Operational Staff are not suitable for anything.

* *Chief Medical Officer of Hungary*

D. **Skepticals:** This group of users do not understand or agree with wearing a mask. Maybe they are not fully informed and educated about the proper use and role of face mask. Their attitude is neutral.

The majority who wear it are unaware of how to properly put on, wear and then take off the mask.

I think the mask is nonsense anyway. It's not because of the mask you're not going to catch if you're sick or don't go out.

If only patients have to wear it because it doesn't protect from the disease, then why do healthcare workers wear it?

It is certainly not acceptable that half of the country wears it, the other half not...

Hospital Bed Evacuation

Based on the level of competence and the orientation of attitudes in case of mandatory hospital bed evacuation, three types of online users were identified: Skepticals, Disgusted, Supporters/acceptors (Figure 2).

A. **Skepticals:** They do not understand the cause of hospital bed evacuation, the secrecy of the government and try to find out the background of the measurements (eg. reorganization of health system in the future, accepting patients from abroad). Their attitude is instead neutral, they seem to be dilletants.

But seriously: 1695 reported cases. Of those, 199 were healed and 142 died. So there were 1354 active infected. Of which 729 in hospital. So more than half of the confirmed infections are so severe that they need hospital care! According to them, the situation is the worst for us, because in most places it is around 20%! Then we are doing something very wrong!

But there will not be suddenly thousands of patients! Possibly on paper so that they can maintain the state of emergency and carry out their plan. So much.

Figure 2. Categories of online users for the hospital bed evacuation

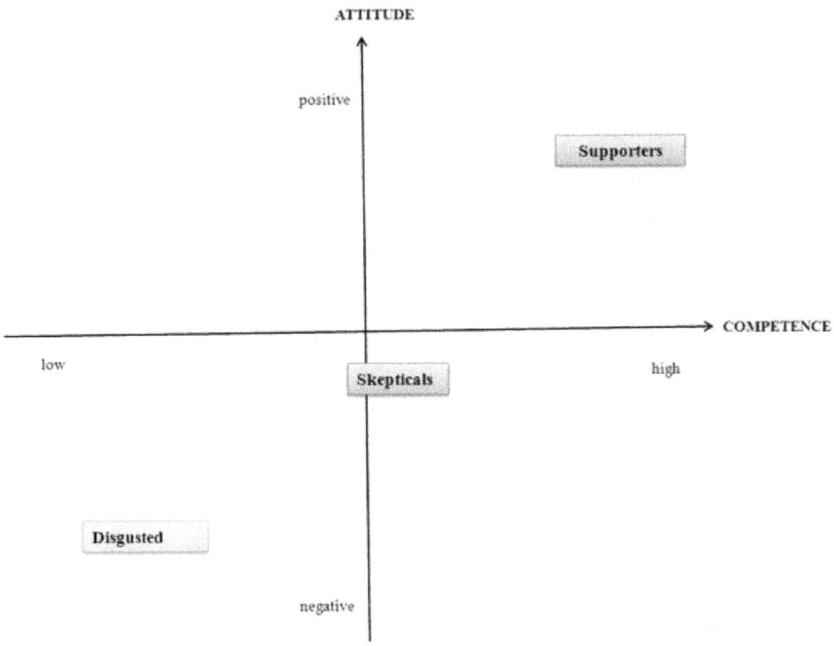

But did Mekk Elek have to free 32,000 beds on the weekend and holidays and send patients home who needed care?! Because there are 730 patients across the country who are in the hospital??? Ridiculous

729 patients across the country and that's why hospitals are shutting down! Then when healthcare starts again I wonder how many years I have to wait for a lab! Don't be sick!

And where are these hundreds of patients, because wherever I ask in the country they are nowhere outside Budapest.

Note, this decision was not about the virus !!!!! But about the transformation of healthcare and not to mention that there is no need to pay hospital care for the patient at home.

I note quietly, do they maybe bring foreign patients?

B. **Disgusted:** The members in this group are searching for the responsible person for this measurement. There is a strong emotional expression. They consider the sudden evacuation of hospital beds disgusting, they worry for the patients, the elderly and families.

Why did they do this with the elderly patients that they were sent home?

There is not and will not be a mass disease, as the virus is especially dangerous for the elderly, sick people. Let everyone over 65 stay at home and the rest go to work! Stop scaring and mindless actions!!!

Coronavirus patients are sent home to their families without prior notification. Incapacitated people who require constant medical supervision were sent in conditions where they surely die.

They send home people who are chronically ill and paralyze their families because their care costs a lot of money. Families who have become unemployed will not be able to solve their care. These people have already payed for healthcare.

C. **Supporters/Acceptors:** They seem to accept/support the measurement and try to give a rational explanation for it, the competence level is high. Their attitude is positive, they find the evacuation of hospital beds necessary to some extent. The users try to convince the others with arguments.

How long have helpless people with dementia been treated in hospital? There is also a place that specializes in that. I also had a helpless relative, the situation is no stranger. And sent home to die? Wow, look at the United States, where you're only in the hospital as long as you need to, you've been sent home smoothly there so far, because honestly, whoever would really leave is why we want to spend 2 weeks. Calculate how much goes into this in a year, not how much they steal.

Don't you think that suddenly there will be thousands of patients? They will need care.

Once upon a time, the elderly were not hospitalized when they could no longer work at home. Today, everyone chooses comfort. My mother had cancer and I worked in 3 shifts. It was not fashionable to put parents in the hospital. In today's world, many forget their parents. You can scold me but that's the truth.

A person in need of care is not the same as a person in need of hospital care. Hospitals should be replaced by an appropriate other care system and adequate social care!

For example, those who are "bedridden" and hospitalized on a different social basis need a different form of care that is not a burden on the healthcare system!

FUTURE RESEARCH DIRECTIONS

In the successful management of the pandemic, the dissemination of credible information to the population is essential, which can be ensured through consistent and cooperative political and health communication. Due to the limitations of this research, many new research directions can be set as goals in the future.

With regard to research issues, a number of new topics may arise.

From a theoretical point of view:

- The question may be how the relationship between health and political communication will develop in the future?
- A future research goal could be to examine how the measures taken in the past are evaluated retrospectively on online platforms after the pandemic, and whether opinions change or not?
- It is worth examining what communication strategies about management of pandemic and vaccination programs have been followed in each country in international comparisons and how they are assessed by citizens.

Following the international literature, it appears that a number of new methodological approaches can be applied in the future to continue the present research.

From a methodological point of view:

- It is advisable to supplement the netnography research with other qualitative methods (eg. focus group, interviews).
- A questionnaire survey covering a large population.

CONCLUSION

The presented research was based on a netnographic approach applied to two important topics in connection with the management of coronavirus outbreak in Hungary. This chapter provided an insight into the opinion of the public referring to the government's COVID-19 outbreak management in Hungary.

There was an intensive communication activity in online communities regarding wearing a mask and the compulsory evacuation of hospital beds preparing the hospitals for the potentially increased number of new coronavirus patients. Based on the results of the qualitative research, the authors concluded that these two neuralgic topic divided the opinion of the citizens. The communication of mask wearing and the evacuation of hospital beds caused markedly different viewpoints. These indicate that in spite of the efficient COVID-19 outbreak management, there are very extreme opinions in the society about the accuracy and reliability of health communication. These do not good for the public opinion about the originally controversial health communication.

The exaggerated and thoughtless prevention steps, which sometimes lacked of professional and scientific grounds, the politically dominated, unsettled communication may have influenced the public trust and resulted in functional anomalies in the country. The improperly drafted health communication can undermine trust in the whole healthcare system. The qualitative research showed that the management of a public health crisis would have required a deeper preparation of the decisions and a consistent communication of the decision-makers. It can be assumed that the social damages of the pandemic may exceed the direct health damage in Hungary.

In this COVID-19 crisis, the health communication should be dominated and managed by health professionals, not by politicians.

REFERENCES

Accenture. (2018). *2018 Consumer survey on digital health*. https://www.accenture.com/t20180306t103559z__w__/us-en/_acnmedia/pdf-71/accenture-health-2018-consumer-survey-digital-health.pdf

Addeo, F., Paoli, A. D., Esposito, M., & Bolcato, M. Y. (2020). Doing social research on online communities: The benefits of netnography. *Athens Journal of Social Sciences*, *7*(1), 9–38. doi:10.30958/ajss.7-1-1

Anderson-Levitt, K. M. (2006). Ethnography. In Handbook of Complementary Methods in Education Research (3rd ed.). American Educational Research Association.

Arnstein, F. (2020). Effective health communication – a key factor in fighting the COVID-19 pandemic. *Patient Education and Counseling*, *103*(5), 873–876. doi:10.1016/j.pec.2020.03.027 PMID:32336348

Bartlett, Y. K., & Coulson, N. S. (2011). An investigation into the empowerment effect of using online support groups and how this affects health professional/patient communication. *Patient Education and Counseling*, *83*(1), 113–119. doi:10.1016/j.pec.2010.05.029 PMID:20599338

Brennen, J., Simon, F., Howard, N., & Nielsen, R. K. (2020). *Types, sources, and claims of COVID-19 misinformation*. https://reutersinstitute.politics.ox.ac.uk/types-sources-and-claims-covid-19-misinformation

Burgess, J., & Green, J. (2018). *YouTube: online video and participatory culture*. Polity.

Childs, L. M., & Martin, C. Y. (2012). Social media profiles: Stiking the right balance. Americal. *Journal of Health System Pharmacy*, *69*(23), 2044–2050. doi:10.2146/ajhp120115 PMID:23172261

CMA. (2011). *Social media and Canadian physicians: Issues and rules of regulations*. Canadian Medical Association – CMA Policy. https://policybase.cma.ca/documents/policypdf/PD12-03.pdf

Denzin, N., & Lincoln, Y. (1994). *Handbook of Qualitative Research*. Sage.

Dobbert, M. L., & Kurt-Schai, R. (1992). Systematic Ethnography: Toward an Evolutionary Science of Education and Culture. In The Handbook of Qualitative Research in Education (pp. 93–159). New York: Academic Press.

Donabedian, A. (1988). The quality of care. How can it be assessed? *Journal of the American Medical Association*, *260*(12), 1743–1748. doi:10.1001/jama.1988.03410120089033 PMID:3045356

Forum, P. A. (2020). *Legge 150 del 2000: cosa prevede la prima (e a tutt'oggi unica) legge quadro sulla comunicazione pubblica*. https://www.forumpa.it/open-government/comunicazione-pubblica/legge-150-del-2000-cosa-prevede-la-prima-e-a-tuttoggi-unica-legge-quadro-sulla-comunicazione-pubblica/

George, D. R., Rovniak, L. S., & Kraschnewski, J. L. (2013). Dangers and oppurtunities for social media in medicine. *Clinical Obstetrics and Gynecology*, *56*(3), 453–462. doi:10.1097/GRF.0b013e318297dc38 PMID:23903375

Hammersley, M. (2006). Ethnography: Problems and Prospects. *Ethnography and Education*, *1*(1), 3–14. doi:10.1080/17457820500512697

Huo, J., Desai, R., Hong, Y. R., Turner, K., Mainous III, A. G., & Bian, J. (2019). Use of social media in health communication: findings from the Health Information National Trends Survey 2013, 2014, and 2017. *Cancer Control: Journal of the Moffitt Cancer Center, 26*(1).

Hyland-Wood, B., Gardner, J., Leask, J., & Ecker, U. K. H. (2021). Toward effective government communication strategies in the era of COVID-19. *Humanities and Social Sciences Communications, 8*(1), 1–11. doi:10.105741599-020-00701-w

IFRC, UNICEF, & WHO. (2020a). *Risk communication & community engagement (RCCE) action plan guide. COVID-19 preparedness & response.* https://www.unicef.org/media/65936/file/Preparedness%20for%20and%20response%20to%20coronavirus%202019%20(COVID-19).pdf

IFRC, UNICEF, & WHO. (2020b). *COVID-19 Global Risk Communication and Community Engagement Strategy.* https://www.who.int/publications/i/item/covid-19-global-risk-communication-and-community-engagement-strategy

Kaplan, M. A., & Haenlein, M. (2010). Users of the world, unite! The challenges and opportunities of social media. *Business Horizons, 53*(1), 59–68. doi:10.1016/j.bushor.2009.09.003

Kim, D. K., & Kreps, G. L. (2020). An Analysis of government communication in the United States during the COVID-19 pandemic: Recommendations for effective government health risk communication. *World Medical & Health Policy, 12*(4), 398–412. doi:10.1002/wmh3.363 PMID:32904935

Kozinets, R. V. (1999). E-Tribalized Marketing? The strategic implications of virtual communities of consumption. *European Management Journal, 17*(3), 252–264. doi:10.1016/S0263-2373(99)00004-3

Kozinets, R. V. (2002). The field behind the screen: Using netnography for marketing research in online communities. *JMR, Journal of Marketing Research, 39*(1), 61–72. doi:10.1509/jmkr.39.1.61.18935

Kozinets, R. V. (2006). Netnography 2.0. In R. W. Belk (Ed.), *Handbook of Qualitative Research Methods in Marketing* (pp. 129–142). Edward Elgar Publishing.

Kozinets, R. V. (2010). *Netnography: redefined* (2nd ed.). Sage.

Lambert, K. M., Barry, P., & Stokes, G. (2012). Risk management and legal issues with the use of social media in the healthcare setting. *Journal of Healthcare Risk Management, 31*(4), 41–47. doi:10.1002/jhrm.20103 PMID:22528403

Langer, R., & Beckman, S. C. (2005). Sensitive research topics: Netnography revisited. *Qualitative Market Research*, *8*(2), 189–203. doi:10.1108/13522750510592454

Malecki, K. M. C., Keating, J. A., & Safdar, N. (2021). Crisis communication and public perception of COVID-19 risks in the era of social media. *Clinical Infectious Diseases*, *72*(4), 699–704. doi:10.1093/cid/ciaa758 PMID:32544242

Marcus, G. E., & Fischer, M. J. M. (1996). *Anthropology as cultural critique* (2nd ed.). The University of Chicago Press.

McFadden, S. A., Malik, A. A., Aguolu, O. G., Willebrand, K. S., & Omer, S. B. (2020). Perceptions of US population regarding the novel coronavirus outbreak. *PLoS One*, *15*(4), e0231808. doi:10.1371/journal.pone.0231808 PMID:32302370

Mészáros, G. (2014). *Subcultures and school education. Narrative, critical pedagogical ethnography (School culture books 48.)*. Thought.

Morton, H. (2001). Computer-mediated communication in Australian anthropology and sociology. *Social Analysis*, *45*(1), 3–11.

OECD. (2020). Transparency, communication and trust: The role of public communication in responding to the wave of disinformation about the new Coronavirus. In *OECD Policy Responses to Coronavirus (COVID-19)*. Paris: OECD Publishing. Https://read.oecd-ilibrary.org/view/?ref=135_135220-cvba4lq3ru&title=Transparency-communication-and-trust-The-role-of-public-communication-in-responding-to-the-wave-of-disinformation-about-the-new-coronavirus

Oh, H. J., & Lee, B. (2012). The effect of computer-mediated social support in online communities on patient empowerment and doctor-patient communication. *Health Communication*, *27*(1), 30–41. doi:10.1080/10410236.2011.567449 PMID:21797714

PAHO. (2020). *COVID-19. Guidelines for communicating about coronavirus disease 2019. A guide for leaders*. Pan American Health Organization.

Pennycook, G., McPhetres, J., Zhang, Y., Lu, J. G., & Rand, D. G. (2020). Fighting COVID-19 misinformation on social media: Experimental evidence for a scalable accuracy nudge intervention. *Psychological Science*, *31*(7), 770–780. doi:10.1177/0956797620939054 PMID:32603243

Porat, T., Nyrup, R., Calvo, R. A., Paudyal, P., & Ford, E. (2020). Public health and risk communication during COVID-19 enhancing psychological needs to promote sustainable behavior change. *Frontiers in Public Health*, *8*, 573397. doi:10.3389/fpubh.2020.573397 PMID:33194973

PwC. (2012). *Social media likes healthcare. From marketing to social business.* PwC Health Research Institute. https://www.pwc.com/us/en/health-industries/health-research-institute/publications/pdf/health-care-social-media-report.pdf

Ramanadhan, S., Mendez, S. R., Rao, M., & Viswanath, K. (2013). Social media use by community-based organizations conducting health promotion: A content analysis. *BMC Public Health, 13*(1), 1–10. doi:10.1186/1471-2458-13-1129 PMID:24313999

Ratna, H. (2019). The importance of effective communication in healthcare practice. *Harvard Public Health Review, 23*, 1–6.

Rupert, D. J., Moultrie, R. R., Read, J. G., Amoozegar, J. B., Bornkessel, A. S., Donoghue, A. C., & Sullivan, H. W. (2014). Perceived healthcare provider reactions to patient and caregiver use of online health communities. *Patient Education and Counseling, 96*(3), 320–326. doi:10.1016/j.pec.2014.05.015 PMID:24923652

Salmon, C. T., & Poorisat, T. (2020). The rise and development of public health communication. *Health Communication, 35*(13), 1666–1677. doi:10.1080/10410236.2019.1654180 PMID:31429307

Schein, R., Wilson, K., & Keelan, J. (2010). *Literature review on effectiveness of the use of social media*. Brampton, Ontario Canada: Region of Peel, Peel. *Public Health*.

Schiavo, R. (2013). *Health Communication: From Theory to Practice*. JohnWiley & Sons.

Sjölander-Lindqvist, A., Larsson, S., Fava, N., Gillberg, N., Marcianò, C., & Cinque, S. (2020). Communicating about COVID-19 in four European countries: Similarities and differences in national discourses in Germany, Italy, Spain, and Sweden. *Frontiers in Communication, 5*, 593325. doi:10.3389/fcomm.2020.593325

Smailhodzic, E., Hooijsma, W., Boonstra, A., & Langley, D. (2016). Social media use in healthcare: A systematic review of effects on their relationship with healthcare professionals. *BMC Health Services Research, 16*(1), 442. doi:10.118612913-016-1691-0 PMID:27562728

Udenze, S. (2019). Challenges of netnography as a qualitative research method. *Journal of Communication and Media Research, 11*(2), 58–63.

UN. (2020). *COVID-19: Embracing digital government during the pandemic and beyond*. United Nations, Department of Economic and Social Affairs. https://www.un.org/development/desa/dpad/publication/un-desa-policy-brief-61-covid-19-embracing-digital-government-during-the-pandemic-and-beyond/

Vajda, B., Horváth, S., & Málovics, É. (2012). Co-decision making as an innovation in the physician-patient relationship. In Regional innovation capacity, competitiveness and sustainability (pp. 336-353). Szeged: JATE Press.

Ventola, C. L. (2014). Social media and health care professionals: Benefits, risks, and best practices. *P&T, 39*(7), 491–499. PMID:25083128

Vollmann, J. (2008). *Patientenselbstbestimmung und Selbstbestimmungsfähigkeit*. Kohlhammer Verlag.

Vraga, E. K., & Jacobsen, K. H. (2020). Strategies for effective health communication during the coronavirus pandemic and future emerging infectious disease events. *World Medical & Health Policy, 12*(3), 233–241. doi:10.1002/wmh3.359

Wardle, C., & Derakshan, H. (2017). *Information disorder: towards an interdisciplinary framework for research and policy making*. Council of Europe.

WHO. (2017). *WHO Strategic Communications Framework for effective communications*. https://www.who.int/mediacentre/communication-framework.pdf

Wolff, H. P. (1989). Arzt und Patient. In H. M. Sass (Ed.), *Medizin und Ethik* (pp. 184–211). Reclam.

Zhang, L., Li, H., & Chen, K. (2020). Effective risk communications for public health emergency: Reflection on the COVID-19 (2019-nCOV) outbreak in Wuhan, China. *Health Care, 8*(1), 64.

Zhao, X. (2020). Health communication campaigns: A brief introduction and call for dialogue. *International Journal of Nursing Sciences, 7*(Suppl 1), S11–S15. doi:10.1016/j.ijnss.2020.04.009 PMID:32995373

ADDITIONAL READING

Abrams, E. M., & Greenhawt, M. (2020). Risk communication during COVID-19. *The Journal of Allergy and Clinical Immunology. In Practice, 8*(6), 1791–1794. doi:10.1016/j.jaip.2020.04.012 PMID:32304834

Benski, C., Goto, A., & Reich, M. R. (2020). Developing health communication materials during a pandemic. *Frontiers in Communication, 5*, 603656. doi:10.3389/fcomm.2020.603656

Cinelli, M., Quattrociocchi, W., Galeazzi, A., Valensise, C. M., Brugnoli, E., Schmidt, A. L., Zola, P., Zollo, F., & Scala, A. (2020). The COVID-19 social media infodemic. *Scientific Reports, 10*(1), 16598. doi:10.103841598-020-73510-5 PMID:33024152

Hauer, M. K., & Sood, S. (2020). Using social media to communicate sustainable preventive measures and curtail misinformation. *Frontiers in Psychology, 11*, 568324. doi:10.3389/fpsyg.2020.568324 PMID:33178073

Nguyen, M. H., Gruber, J., Fuchs, J., Marler, W., Hunsaker, A., & Hargittai, E. (2020). Changes in digital communication during the COVID-19 global pandemic: Implications for digital inequality and future research. *Social Media + Society, 6*(3), 1–6. doi:10.1177/2056305120948255 PMID:34192039

Paulik, L. B., Keenan, R. E., & Durda, J. L. (2020). The Case for Effective Risk Communication: Lessons from a Global Pandemic. *Integrated Environmental Assessment and Management, 16*(5), 552–554. doi:10.1002/ieam.4312 PMID:32881245

Reddy, B. V., & Gupta, A. (2020). Importance of effective communication during COVID-19 infodemic. *Journal of Family Medicine and Primary Care, 9*(8), 3793–3796. doi:10.4103/jfmpc.jfmpc_719_20 PMID:33110769

KEY TERMS AND DEFINITIONS

COVID-19: The abbreviation stands for Coronavirus disease 2019 (COVID-19), which is a contagious airborne infection caused by the severe acute respiratory syndrome coronavirus 2 (SARS-CoV-2). The first case was reported from Wuhan, China, in December 2019. The disease has since spread worldwide, leading to an ongoing pandemic with 114 million cases and 2,5 million deaths by the end of February 2021.

Health Communication: Type of communication that targets individuals, communities, health professionals, policymakers in order to facilitate behavioural changes and improve health outcome. The effectiveness of the communication depends on understandability, repetition, accuracy, consistency, availability, and timeliness.

Infodemic: Exponential increase of the information volume within a short period of time in connection with a specific incident (e.g., COVID-19 pandemic). The credibility of information may be endangered by misinformation, rumors, and manipulation of information. The information may be disseminated very quickly through social networks.

Netnography: A qualitative research method that observes and interprets social interaction within online communities and social media platforms.

Operative Board: Coordination and decision-making committee in Hungary that was set up at the beginning of the COVID-19 pandemic. It is headed by the Interior Minister and the Minister of Human Resources.

Risk: Communication: Interaction process, exchange and dissemination of real-time information to the public about threatening health, social or economic situations. The main purpose of the communication is to support the people at risk and to help informed decisions.

Social Media: Characterized by user-generated content, online community, rapid distribution of information and opened, two-way dialogue. Social media includes virtual game worlds, collaborative projects, virtual social worlds, blogs and microblogs, social networking sites, content communities.

Chapter 8
Colour Theory in Healthcare Corporate Identity

Inês Veiga Pereira
https://orcid.org/0000-0002-7906-612X
ISCAP, Polytechnic Institute of Porto, Portugal

José Duarte Santos
https://orcid.org/0000-0001-5815-4983
Polytechnic Institute of Gaya, Portugal

Inês Nunes de Carvalho
ISCAP, Polytechnic Institute of Porto, Portugal

ABSTRACT

This study aims to analyse the colours associated with Portuguese healthcare units and medical centres—namely the colour of their logo, through environmental colour mapping—and understand if the colour management choices match the desired perception of a healthcare unit and identify new colour combinations that can serve as a differentiation factor and simultaneously get the desired interpretation of the brand. The logos of 24 healthcare centres were randomly selected. The images were collected through the SNS web page dedicated to each facility and were later processed in Adobe Photoshop CC. The colours of each logo were catalogued and sorted according to their hue. It was observed that the majority of the colours used corresponded to blues and greens, which was to be expected considering their symbolism: stability, calm, relaxation, and serenity. Lastly, four new colour schemes were created, which, in addition to being differentiated from the previously identified schemes, are evocative of desirable characteristics for a brand associated with a healthcare unit.

DOI: 10.4018/978-1-7998-7263-4.ch008

iNTRODUCTION

Over the past decade marketing has been paying greater attention to research into the use of colors by brands (Labrecque, 2020).

Human beings interact constantly with the surrounding environment, absorbing sensory stimuli, especially visual stimuli. In some of those interactions, they assume the role of consumers.

Brand interactions are no different than any others – they rely on a complex process of perception and interpretation in which various factors come into play. During these interactions, consumers draw conclusions and create conceptions of what the brand is according to the stimuli it provokes.

In addition to being a core part of the brand's visual identity, color is also a powerful stimulator and information source, that has the capacity to incite emotional and physical responses (Singh, 2006). Throughout history, different meanings have been attributed to different colors, whether by cultural influence or instinct. In turn, these meanings, even if subconsciously, have an influence in the image consumers create about the brand: its values, beliefs, characteristics and personality. Thus, the adequate use of color can positively distinguish a brand in comparison to its competitors, while it contributes to the creation of a relationship between the consumer and the brand (Labrecque, 2010).

The evaluation of color perception is not easy, its measurement depends on the reaction to stimuli. One of the ways researchers go through the three dimensions of color analysis (hue saturation and value) (Labrecque, 2020).

The present study aims to analyse the colors associated with Portuguese healthcare units and hospital centres' logos through the environmental color mapping method and evaluate if the colors used evoke the desired perception of a healthcare service. In addition, this study intends to identify and suggest new color schemes that can serve as a differentiation factor, as well as convey the desired message.

COLOR IN CORPORATE IDENTITY

Brands work as guarantee for consumers – if the consumer associates a brand with an attribute considered relevant in the product category, that brand will be chosen over its competitors (Christodoulides & Chernatony, 2010). For a brand to be successful, it must identify the needs of its target market and come up with a value proposition with the aim of satisfying them. A brand's value proposition is "the set of benefits or values it promises to deliver to consumers to satisfy their needs" (Kotker & Armstrong, 2018). Those values define brand's identity.

One of the brand's fundamental roles is differentiation. It's crucial that the brand is distinct from its competitors – it must design a differentiating identity. Brand's identity is set by the organization, i.e. it is outlined and constructed internally in order to reflect the messages and the values that the brand aims to convey (Mindrut et al., 2015). Brand's identity includes several elements, that must be managed in the interest of creating a cohesive and distinctive brand image.

Brand image, unlike its identity, finds its origin in the consumer. The image is the set of perceptions that a consumer has regarding a product or organization – it results from the associations between the sensory stimuli caused by the brand and the attributes relevant to the evaluation of the product or service in cause (Dubois, 1993). Therefore, the organization must manage its communication efforts in the name of assuring that brand image corresponds to the brand identity.

Clifton and Simmons (2003) claim that brand's identity is constituted by two aspects: visual and verbal identity. These two identity aspects must be cohesively managed in a way that allows the efficient communication of brand's values, mission, vision, beliefs, strategies and characteristics. Verbal identity aims to distinguish the language of a brand and it's composed by its name – and that of its products – its slogan, tone and the way it tells stories.

Visual identity, on the other hand, comprises the graphic components: logos, symbols, colors and fonts. The design and color of the logo, along with the color associated with the brand (which usually coincides), especially, constitute a vital part of visual identity and play a very important role in the brand's communication efforts (Ward et al., 2020). A person's preferred color can influence the perception of a brand (Yu et al., 2018).

Consumers are much more influenced by what they see than any other type of stimuli. In a 2004 study directed by the secretary of the Seoul International Color Expo, 92,6% of the participants claimed that the visual factors were the most important in the purchase decision. Therefore, visual identity plays a key role in a brand's success (Dash, 2018).

Logo and Color

A logo is a "graphic design that a company uses, with or without its name, to identify itself and its products" (Elliot & Maier, 2014). Therefore, the logo is defined by its design and its color. Because of its importance in environmental perception, the logo's color takes on special relevance in contrast with the remaining graphic elements – in fact, color is the element of visual identity that prompts recognition and recollection the most (Henderson & Cote, 1998). Studies developed by *CCICOLOR* – Institute for Color Research, show that people generate conceptions about a person, environment or product within the first 90 seconds of contact, being that 62% to 90%

of that assessment is based on color. A more colorful logo tends to be perceived as friendlier (Nasseraldin et al., 2019). Additionally, a company's logo is more attractive to the consumer when its color – and its adjacent symbolism – matches the brand personality precepted by the consumer (Kumar, 2017).

Brand Personality

A brand's personality can be defined as one, or more, human characteristics attributed to a brand (Aaker & Fournier, 1995). In the same manner that consumers attribute human characteristics to a brand, they also treat the relationship with the brand as human, thus preferring brands whose personality matches their own (Lin, 2010). The perception that the consumers has of brand personality is influenced by all the points of contact between them and the brand (Aaker, 1997). That vision is responsible for about 80% of the information we process, so visual identity is a major factor in brand personality perception.

Aaker (1997) concluded that consumers distinguish five main personality dimensions: sincerity, excitement, competence, sophistication and ruggedness. Sincerity represents an honest, original and joyful brand. Excitement represents a spirituous, young and bold brand. Competence, in contrast, describes an intelligent and reliable brand. Sophistication and ruggedness, in their turn, are not as linearly described as the other dimensions, but can be associated with characteristics such as femininity and masculinity, respectively. In their turn, these five dimensions unfold in a total of forty-two personality features (Table 1), which allow the clear identification and distinction of different brand personalities.

Among these dimensions, the most favourable considering the type of entity being studied, are sincerity and competence, along with the features associated. The association of the brand with sophistication and excitement may also be an advantage, given that sophistication isn't interpreted as unreachable, but rather as a sign of quality treatment, and excitement is perceived as an optimistic feeling, as opposed to an anxiety trigger.

Color Theory

Our perception process can be divided into two phases: (1) sensation, i.e., the recording and processing of externals stimuli by the sense organs and (2) interpretation, i.e., the meaning we attribute to the stimuli. Color, as an ever-present factor in our environment, is intrinsically connected to the way any object is precepted by the human being (Elliot & Maier, 2014).

Color is, fundamentally, an interpretation of the electromagnetic radiation that stimulates the human eye – light. This interpretation depends on the energy

Table 1. Aaker's personality dimensions

Brand Personality (Aaker)				
Sincerity	**Excitement**	**Competence**	**Sophistication**	**Ruggedness**
Down-to-heart: down to earth, family oriented, small Town	Daring: daring, trendy, exciting	Reliability: reliable, hardworking, secure	Class: upper class, good looking, glamorous	Masculinity: outdoorsy, masculine, western
Honesty: honest, sincere, real	Spiritedness: spirited, cool, young	Intelligence: intelligent, technical, corporate	Charm: charming, feminine, smooth	Toughness: tough, rugged
Wholesomeness: wholesome, original	Imaginative: imaginative, unique	Success: successful, leader, confident		
Cheerfulness: cheerful, sentimental, friendly	Contemporary: up-to-date, independent, contemporary			

Source: Authors

(wavelength) and the light quantity. The visible spectrum is situated approximately between 400 nm and 700 nm in the electromagnetic spectrum, being that the lowest wavelength corresponds to what we consider purple and the highest to what we call red.

The color stimuli, and our perception of it, depends on three properties: (1) hue, the way light is reflected according to its wavelength, which determines its classification; (2) saturation, the intensity of the color, i.e., how pigmented it is and (3) brightness, which determines if a color moves towards white (100%) or black (0%) the most (Jacobs & Suess, 1975; Kumar, 2017). These three components constitute the HSB (Hue, Saturation, rightness) system. Any variation in one of these properties alters the cognitive and emotional response from the stimuli receptor (Fairchild, 2013). However, not all these components have the same "weight". Although hue is what determines the color categorization, changes in the levels of saturation and brightness have been shown to alter the emotional response in a much more accentuated fashion.

There are six pure hues: red, orange, yellow, green, blue and purple. These hues mix continuously throughout the color wheel, making each hue correspond to an angle (MacEvoy, 2019a). That being so, "pure" blue, for example, is situated at 240º, while "pure" green is located at 120º. Red both opens and closes the circle.

Hues can be classified as warm or cold. This categorization has, as opposite poles, green-blue hues, which are the coldest and red-orange hues, which are the warmest. Thus, greens and blues that don't contain any visible yellow or red are cold hues and reds, oranges and yellows that don't contain any visible blue or green, are warm hues (MacEvoy, 2019b).

Color Harmony

Color harmony can be defined as "when two or more colors are brought together to produce a satisfying affective response" (Burchett, 2002). There are six mainly recognized color combination techniques that aim to achieve harmony (see Figure 1):

- Complementary: use of opposing colors in the color wheel. These colors have a high contrast and can result in a vibrant combination. Tendentially one of them is chosen as dominant.
- Analogous: use of "neighboring" colors in the color wheel. The color schemes created using this technique are harmonious and pleasing to the eye.
- Triadic: use three equally spaced colors (120º from each other) around the color wheel. These combinations tend to be vibrant, even when low saturated colors are used. It is very popular because it offers a strong visual contrast and is considered by many to be the best of the schemes
- Split-complementary: variation of the complementary technique. Aside from the base color, two adjacent colors to its complementary are used. This color scheme has an equally strong contrast, but a smaller amount of tension.
- Tetrahedral: it uses two complementary color pairs, offering great variation possibilities. It is difficult to harmonize because if all four colors are used in equal quantities, the scheme may seem unbalanced, so the need to choose a color to be the dominant one.
- Rectangle: use of four colors arranged in two pairs of complementary colors. Similar to tetrahedral colors, but with all four colors also spaced on the color wheel. It is the scheme that offers as many combinations as possible, which can be a problem for good harmony between them.

Color Psychology and Symbolism

Along with the aesthetic information, color is also charged with emotional connections – thus, colors go beyond their physical nature and take on a psychological meaning (Gil & Le Bigot, 2014). The field of color psychology studies hues as a determinant of human behavior (Kumar, 2017). The meaning attributed to colors can have two origins: cultural or evolutionary (Elliot & Maier, 2014) – certain color interpretations are considered purely a result of constant associations between a color and a concept.

Figure 1. Color combination

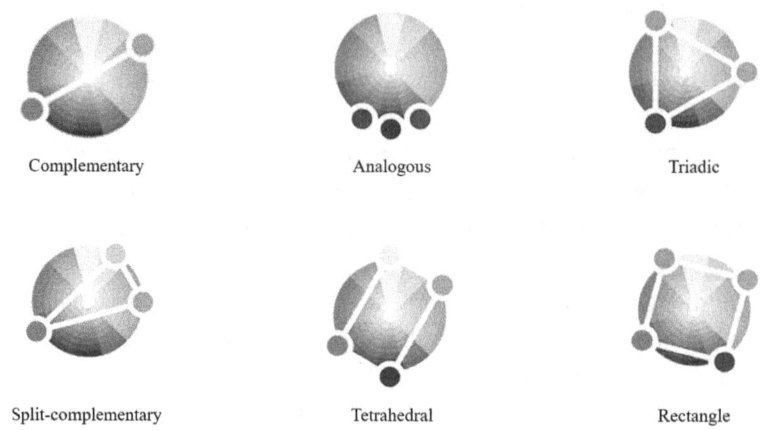

Other, however, derive from our survival instinct, for example, the association of red with danger (Cuthill et al., 1997).

Various studies have demonstrated how color influences our perception, affection and cognition, even in a subconscious manner (Elliot & Maier, 2014).

Pleasure, for example, varies directly with the levels of brightness and saturation, being, nevertheless, more sensitive to brightness alterations. Excitement, on the other hand, is inversely proportional to the brightness level.

Numerous studies dedicated to the physiological response to colors demonstrate that long wavelengths (reds and yellows) are more exciting than short wavelengths (blues and greens) (Valdez & Mehrabian, 1994) which explains the link between warm hues and excitement – and consequently, anxiety – and cold hues and relaxation (Birren, 2006; Jacobs & Suess, 1975).

In addition to this, each pure hue has a meaning generally associated with it:

- Purple: throughout history, purple has acquired a noble a luxurious connotation (Aslam, 2006). Light purple is usually considered romantic, while dark purple is seen as intellectual. Additionally, younger generations tend to interpret it as a happy color. Purple is generally associated with luxury and sophistication, as well as femininity and glamour (Ridgway & Myers, 2014). This color is usually associated with Aaker's sophistication dimension (Hynes, 2009).
- Blue: the symbology associated with blue varies according with its brightness, even if it mainly triggers positive emotional responses. Dark blue is seen as a symbol of trust, dignity and intelligence, while light blue is associated with

cleanness, calm, stability, peace, comfort and serenity. In a study conducted by Hynes, when asked to choose a color for a logo described as "prestigious", "secure", "dynamic", "prosperity" and "protecting", three quarters of the respondents cited blue as the most appropriate color. Blue is also associated with Aaker's competence dimension (Ridgway & Myers, 2014).

- Green: green is usually associated with growth, rebirth and fertility owing to its abundance in nature. It is interpreted as a positive and pleasant color, which symbolizes calm, relaxation, happiness, comfort, peace, hope and promotes creativity. Exposure to green environments has also been shown to improve the mood and reduce fatigue of those practicing exercise (Valdez & Mehrabian, 1994).
- Red: red is considered the color of passion and seduction, while, simultaneously, that of violence and danger (Aslam, 2006). It is also an extremely captivating color, being the second most visible.
- Orange: orange is a vibrant and polarizing color, both in acceptance and symbolism. It symbolizes energy, vitality, excitement and adventure while, on the other hand, it can be interpreted as crass and of poor taste (Aslam, 2006).
- Yellow: yellow is the most luminous color of the spectrum and, consequently, the one that captures the most attention. This color is associated with happiness, optimism and creativity (Aslam, 2006). In a study conducted by Kaya and Epps (2004), yellow obtained an extremely positive emotional response, being only second to green. It can also be considered enthusiastic, spirituous and exciting (Ridgway & Myers, 2014).

Environmental Color Mapping

Environmental color mapping (ECM) is a process through which the color characteristics of natural and artificial elements of an environment are identified and documented. Typically, this process is used to identify and document architectonic color schemes, with the aim to establish an indicator of local identity. In this context, the process is composed of four stages: (1) definition of the environment that's meant to be mapped; (2) identification and collection of samples of natural and/or artificial elements; (3) correspondence of the colors collected to an existent color notation system and (4) creation of a database of the environmental color characteristics (Mikellides & Porter, 2009).

When applied to marketing, however, ECM is used in a not so structured manner and takes on another meaning. Here, the environment represents, for example, a business area instead of an urbanization (O'Connor, 2009). Furthermore – while, when applied to architecture, this method seeks to study the colors of a region with the intention of harmonizing the colors and identity of said region – when applied to marketing, this method aims to find a way to differentiate a brand in terms of color in a visually crowded market. This can be used, for example, in the identification of potential logo color schemes (Kumar, 2017).

The result of the application of this method is a database, usually similar to a grid, of various color samples (O'Connor, 2009).

In the present study, this method will be applied to healthcare institutions, with the purpose of analysing the color scenery of the business area and developing a color scheme that matches the desired characteristics of this type of organizations, while it simultaneously promoting differentiation.

Color Psychology in Health

Color and health have been connected all throughout history. In Ancient Egypt, colored light "baths" were given to patients, because it was a common belief that colors had healing properties (Singh, 2006).

As with any other product or service, the color associated with a healthcare service influences the consumer's perception of it.

When it comes to medication, for example, color is especially important because it can catalyse the creation of a personal connection between the patient and the product, facilitating the treatment. Moreover, patients react better to medication when its color corresponds to the effect it's supposed to have (Meissner & Linde, 2018) which, in its turn, makes the medication more effective, given that color has the capacity to increase the placebo effect. For example, patients tend to have a better reaction to a blue tranquilizer, in comparison to a red one. In addition, some studies have demonstrated that patients that take medication on a regular basis, prefer pills with bright, saturated colors (Morton, 2013?).

In a study conducted by Coad and Coad (2008), to examine the preferences of children and teens regarding the design and color of a hospital environment, the participants stated that the design of a hospital must transmit comfort and that the decoration should be nature related. This study also concluded that – contrarily to what happens with pills – patients prefer a hospital environment with mild to pale colors (medium to low saturation), blue and green being the preferred colors.

RESEARCH AIM AND OBJECTIVES

The present study aims to analyse the most common hues in the visual identities of Portuguese healthcare facilities with the goal of assessing if their use is adequate in the business area context. The image of a healthcare facility must inspire trust, relax and stabilise feelings of anxiety.

RESEARCH METHODOLOGY

In this study, the environmental color mapping method will be applied to the healthcare business area. The application of this method intends to: (1) analyse patterns of similarity in the colors used in the logos of the selected organizations; (2) assess if these patterns make sense according to the literature on color psychology and (3) identify new color schemes that allow for a brand's differentiation while simultaneously creating the desired perception of the service.

To develop this study, the logos of twenty-four randomly selected healthcare entities – namely, public hospital centres and local health units – were collected. These logos compose the environment to which the environmental color mapping method will be applied.

The images were gathered from the sections of the national healthcare system's webpage dedicated to each organization and posteriorly processed in Adobe Photoshop CC. Because the program doesn't have any functionality that allows for the automatic creation of a color palette based on the image, the identification of colors was manually made, resorting to the color picker tool.

The colors of each logo were catalogued and later organized according to their hue, matching each value to the corresponding degree on the hue scale. Only the six pure hues were taken into consideration. In order to categorize each hue based on its degree, the following limits were defined:

- Red: 315° to 15°
- Orange: 16° to 45°
- Yellow: 46° to 75°
- Green: 76° to 180°
- Blue: 181° to 255°
- Purple: 256° to 314°

It's important to note that, given the fact that color interpretation is subjective and that the hues mix all throughout the scale, these limits are arbitrary. These limits were outlined based on the "true" value of each color, supplemented by the visual interpretation of the hues. The geometric distance between the pure hues was also taken into consideration, having used the medium value of the interval between each pure hue as a guide. It is also important to note that, during this stage, the percentages of saturation and brightness were not taken into consideration.

Because this study only seeks to analyse the frequency with which each color is used, the proportion of each color on the corresponding logo wasn't taken into consideration, neither was the background color (white), because it is not an element of the logo itself. Lastly, black wasn't pondered given that it stays unaltered regardless of the hue degree and, being used solely in the text, it's probably used for practical convenience and readability and not symbolic communication.

The colors of each logo were registered according to the HSB system. This system was chosen because it most accurately and intuitively represents the way humans perceive color. The analysis of the three aspects (hue, saturation and brightness) was manually made, i.e., without resorting to quantitative data processing software.

DATA ANALYSIS AND RESULTS

All the logos used were composed of a symbol accompanied by text. In total, 58 colors were identified, having only one be repeated (Color #1 of logos #14 and #15). The vast majority of the logos (62,5%) presents two colors. There are three logos with three or four colors, two with one color and only one with five colors.

Using the table of values corresponding to the HSB system in Table 2 we can verify its application to each of the logos.

According to the color limitations mentioned, the absolute and relative frequency of each hue were calculated and ordered from lowest to highest as we can see in Table 3.

The color map created (Figure 2) serves only as a visual guide because the small scale of the image doesn't allow for a precise display of the colors based on their hue degree. However, it's possible to observe that the prevalent hues are blues (36,2%) and greens (27,6%). This observation is supported by the HSB values. Orange and yellow present very low frequencies, with 10,3% and 6,9% respectively. Purple isn't presented even once in the sample.

The predominant use of blue isn't surprising when taking into account that it is very commonly used in corporate identity (Aslam, 2006) and its symbology: stability, security, serenity, confidence and intelligence. This color is also related to Aaker's competence and sincerity dimensions, which, presumably, patients want to associate with their hospitals. The vast use of green was also to be expected based on the emotions associated with this color: relaxation, calm, good mood.

The prevalent use of cold hues (blue and green) as opposed to warm hues (yellow and red) makes sense when considering the anxiety levels associated with the latter[14,22]. On the other hand, although yellow is a warm hue, and thus, exciting and even associated with feelings of anxiety, it is also considered the "happiest" color, and so, its use could be appropriate in the business area context in question.

Table 2. HSB Values

Logo/Color	Color #1	Color #2	Color #3	Color #4	Color #5
Logo #1	H: 175 S: 49 B: 74	H: 177 S: 92 B: 50			
Logo #2	H: 36 S: 52 B: 87	H: 50 S: 35 B: 98	H: 135 S: 24 B: 80	H: 138 S: 29 B: 64	
Logo #3	H: 2 S: 86 B: 51				
Logo #4	H: 33 S: 78 B: 96	H: 221 S: 65 B: 38			
Logo #5	H: 199 S: 74 B: 87	H: 206 S: 83 B: 71			
Logo #6	H: 15 S: 65 B: 31	H: 87 S: 76 B: 71			
Logo #7	H: 224 S: 62 B: 34	H: 357 S: 83 B: 58			
Logo #8	H: 45 S: 89 B: 89	H: 206 S: 81 B: 74	H: 207 S: 52 B: 84		
Logo #9	H: 5 S: 78 B: 84	H: 142 S: 92 B: 56			
Logo #10	H: 62 S: 93 B: 83	H: 344 S: 92 B: 83			
Logo #11	H: 73 S: 47 B: 82	H: 77 S: 82 B: 74	H: 175 S: 67 B: 38	H: 186 S: 95 B: 57	
Logo #12	H: 64 S: 85 B: 71	H: 189 S: 95 B: 59			
Logo #13	H: 218 S: 8 B: 96	H: 218 S: 27 B: 78	H: 220 S: 80 B: 56		
Logo #14	H: 83 S: 78 B: 72	H: 207 S: 98 B: 63			
Logo #15	H: 83 S: 78 B: 72	H: 179 S: 100 B: 56			
Logo #16	H: 186 S: 83 B: 78	H: 187 S: 97 B: 63			
Logo #17	H: 9 S: 62 B: 62				
Logo #18	H: 213 S: 70 B: 29	H: 358 S: 77 B: 79			
Logo #19	H: 142 S: 84 B: 65	H: 228 S: 68 B: 53	H: 355 S: 79 B: 90		
Logo #20	H: 84 S: 60 B: 75	H: 151 S: 100 B: 40			
Logo #21	H: 0 S: 83 B: 89	H: 19 S: 78 B: 86	H: 193 S: 96 B: 84	H: 201 S: 95 B: 62	
Logo #22	H: 40 S: 89 B: 98	H: 193 S: 62 B: 81			
Logo #23	H: 31 S: 69 B: 96	H: 90 S: 65 B: 65	H: 221 S: 44 B: 64	H: 330 S: 70 B: 62	H: 358 S: 71 B: 88
Logo #24	H: 77 S: 82 B: 74	H: 200 S: 100 B: 62			

Source: Authors

Table 3. Color frequencies

Color	Absolute Frequency	Relative Frequency
Green	16	27,6%
Red	11	19,0%
Orange	6	10,3%
Yellow	4	6,9%
Purple	0	0,0%
Total	58	100%

Source: Authors

Figure 2. Collected color schemes
Source: Authors

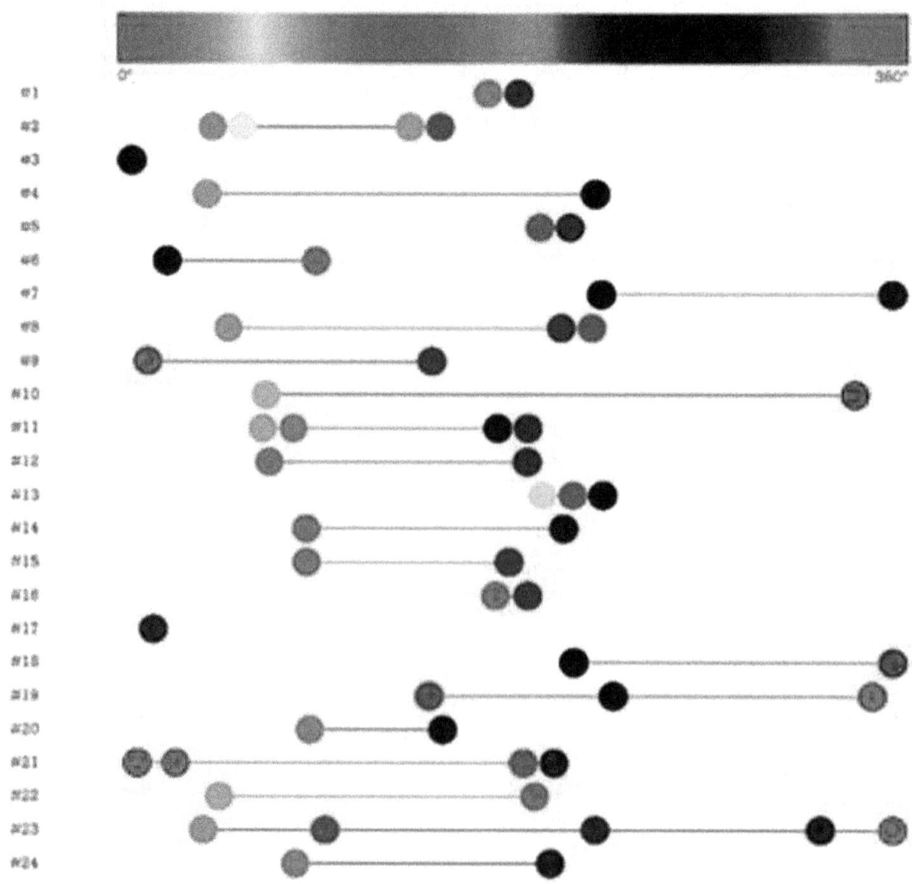

Regarding saturation, it is possible to observe that the majority (86,2%) of the colors present over 50% of saturation, i.e., the use of "intense" colors is more frequent. The highest saturation value registered is 100% on three separate occurrences. Concerning brightness, the results are similar. Only 10,3% of the colors present a brightness level under 50%. The highest brightness value registered is 98% on two separate occurrences.

Suggestions for New Color Schemes

Having analysed the visual identity scenery of the Portuguese healthcare centres in terms of color, this study intends to create new differentiating color schemes, that are able to stand out among the existing ones, but that also convey the desired personality of a healthcare service.

Consequently, in an effort to differ from the current scenery, the hues blue and green will not be used on their own, i.e., there will not be color schemes created using only hues between 76° and 255°. While these colors transmit the desired message by the organizations in this study, the market is, visually, overcrowded and thus, they would not represent a good option to pursue the differentiation goal.

Given that purple wasn't found in the sample, its use would allow for a visual distinction from the remaining entities operating in the area. Purple is associated with wealth and, reliant on the brightness, intellect. Moreover, this color isn't considered cold nor warm – although it may not be considered relaxing, it also won't trigger feelings of anxiety.

Yellow, on the other hand, isn't very frequent in the sample either. Being a happy color, its use can be considered appropriate. Regarding the anxiety caused by warm colors, this can be counterbalanced by an increase in the brightness level, bearing in mind that excitement – a key component of anxiety – varies inversely with the brightness level, while pleasure varies directly. Additionally, because yellow is the most visible color in the spectrum, it is a good option when it comes to capturing attention.

Although orange isn't vastly used either, it is a very polarizing color, and thus, risky. Taking this into account, this color will not be used in the created color schemes.

Lastly, red is a color that can be interpreted in very distinctive ways. Although it is associated with violence and anxiety, it is also associated with passion and love. As with yellow, the negative emotions associated with the color can be counterbalanced by an increase in brightness. The use of a high value of saturation is also adequate, considering that the human being tends to feel more pleased when confronted with more saturated colors. Besides, the use of hues of red between 315° and 0°, i.e., the hues more closely located to purple on the color wheel, may also diminish the negative effects of this color, owing to purple's neutrality.

Taking all this into consideration, four color schemes were conceived (Figure 3), based on four out of the five color harmony techniques: complementary, analogous, triadic and split-complementary.

Figure 3. Created color schemes
Source: Authors

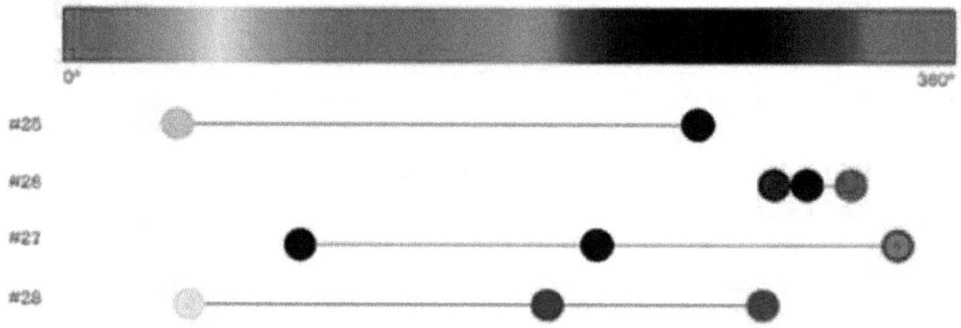

The colors used in these color schemes, like the ones used in the collected logos, were catalogued according to their HSB values (Table 4).

Table 4. HSB values of the created color schemes

Logo/color	Color #1	Color #2	Color #3
Logo #25	H: 48 S: 78 B: 95	H: 262 S: 78 B: 47	
Logo #26	H: 299 S: 77 B: 63	H: 303 S: 79 B: 48	H: 317 S: 64 B: 87
Logo #27	H: 96 S: 100 B: 34	H: 211 S: 77 B: 40	H: 337 S: 79 B: 89
Logo #28	H: 52 S: 76 B: 100	H: 197 S: 60 B: 64	H: 293 S: 48 B: 80

Source: Authors

Logo #25 was created using the complementary technique. This combination was thought of taking into account both colors, in other words, there isn't a defined base color from which the complementary was obtained. The colors used are yellow and purple. The purple hue presents a low brightness level, with the intent of conveying sophistication and intelligence – referencing Aaker's class and intelligence features. Yellow references the excitement dimension.

Logo #26 was obtained using the analogous technique. The chosen color was purple, for the previously mentioned motives, having selected three analogous colors.

Because these purples have higher brightness levels than those used in logo #25, they can be interpreted as more feminine and cheerful. When applied to healthcare, this color combination can be a good alternative for the visual identity of a maternity.

Logo #27, in its turn, was created using the triadic technique. The base color, in this case, was red. This red has high brightness and saturation levels for the previously exposed reasons. The other two ends of the "triangle" are located in degrees of the color wheel corresponding to blue and green. That being the case, very low levels of brightness were used – which in not common in the collected sample – in order to not coincide with the current scenery. The blue and green can be associated with intelligence and security, while red can be considered young and cool.

Lastly, Logo #28 was obtained using the split-complementary technique. Here, the base color used was, again, purple. In this color scheme, a purple with a lower brightness level was chosen, so as to differentiate it from the rest. Being green purple's complementary color, and blue one of green's analogous colors (besides yellow), these colors were used, not assuming, however, the main role in the scheme. The yellow used in this color scheme has very high brightness and saturation levels, making it associated with happiness and cheerfulness.

All these color schemes have differentiation potential when compared to those belonging to the sample. Furthermore, the symbology of these colors goes hand in hand with the desirable precepted personality of a healthcare brand.

DISCUSSION

The impact of color on emotions and physiognomy is undeniable. Color affects perception, humour and even metabolism. The use of color in the healthcare industry is no exception and it is used and managed with a goal in mind. Yet, when analysing the different logos collected for this study, it is possible to observe that certain colors are overused and can, because of the visual saturation caused, make the brand more unattractive to the consumer. Thus, the use of color mapping techniques is recommended in order to identify and select a differentiating visual identity, that allows the brand to stand out and excel.

When analyzing the logos included in the study, it was found that the vast majority of the color schemes included blue and/or green. Blue is associated with trust, dignity and reliability, while green is associated with relaxation and comfort. The meanings associated with these two colors, along with the fact that they're both cold tones – and thus, known to reduce anxiety – make them obvious, and efficient, choices when deciding which colors to include in a healthcare institution's corporate identity. However, it was also found that these colors now saturate the visual identity of healthcare entities throughout Portugal. As such, the newly developed color schemes work as a possible starting point for visual differentiation of future healthcare brands. While the aforementioned colors are not included, others with equally positive connotations take their place - such as the joyful yellow and the sophisticated purple – which will allow for said brands to differentiate themselves while still communicating a sense of trust, well-being and competence.

CONCLUSION

After analysing through ECM 24 logos of Portuguese healthcare units, it was possible to conclude that the colors currently used in the visual identities of healthcare units in Portugal are consistent with what is the ideal symbolism, connotation and personality of a healthcare service and/or brand - which is that of a reliable, responsible and calming institution.

Further, four new color combinations were suggested in order to obtain alternatives which can be distinguished from the existing ones, but also support the desired image. It is important to keep in mind, however, that color and its meaning are subjective – color in itself is just light and as a concept only exists as a result of the human brain's interpretation, which, obviously, varies from person to person, and its meaning differs according to time and space. Despite that, the methodology used has led to four color combinations which can be used in several healthcare units and contexts.

This study did not take into account the role of digital marketing in the influence of the perception of the logo, which may constitute a good opportunity to continue investigating.

REFERENCES

Aaker, J. (1997). Dimensions of Brand Personality. *JMR, Journal of Marketing Research, 34*(3), 347–356. doi:10.1177/002224379703400304

Aaker, J., & Fournier, S. (1995). A Brand as a Character, a Partner and a Person: Three Perspectives on the Question of Brand Personality. *Advances in Consumer Research. Association for Consumer Research (U. S.), 22*, 391–395.

Aslam, M. M. (2006). Are you selling the right color? A cross-cultural review of color as a marketing cue. *Journal of Marketing Communications, 12*(1), 15–30. doi:10.1080/13527260500247827

Birren, F. (2006). *Functional Color: A Book of Facts and Research Meant to Inspire More Rational Methods in the Solution of Color Problems*. Kessinger Publishing, LLC.

Burchett, K. E. (2002). Color harmony. *Color Research and Application*, *27*(1), 28–31. doi:10.1002/col.10004

Christodoulides, G., & Chernatony, L. (2010). Consumer-based brand equity conceptualization and measurement: A literature review. *International Journal of Research in Marketing*, *52*(1), 43–66.

Clifton, R., & Simmons, J. (2003). *Brands and branding*. Bloomberg Press.

Coad, J., & Coad, N. (2008). Children and young people's preference of thematic design and color for their hospital environment. *Journal of Child Health Care*, *12*(1), 33–48. doi:10.1177/1367493507085617 PMID:18287183

Cuthill, I. C., Hunt, S., Cleary, C., & Clark, C. (1997). Color bands, dominance, and body mass regulation in male zebra finches (Taeniopygia guttata). *Proceedings of the Royal Society of London. Series B, Biological Sciences*, *264*(1384), 1093–1099. doi:10.1098/rspb.1997.0151

Dash, S. K. (2018). Role and Importance of Color in Marketing. Vilakshan: *The XIMB. Journal of Management*, *15*(1), 105–112.

Dubois, B. (1993). *Comprendre le Consommateur*. Editions Dalloz.

Elliot, A. J., & Maier, M. A. (2014). Color psychology: Effects of perceiving color on psychological functioning in humans. *Annual Review of Psychology*, *65*(1), 95–120. doi:10.1146/annurev-psych-010213-115035 PMID:23808916

Fairchild, M. D. (2013). *Color Appearance Models*. Wiley Press. doi:10.1002/9781118653128

Gil, S., & Le Bigot, L. (2014). Seeing Life through Positive-Tinted Glasses: Color–Meaning Associations. *PLoS One*, *9*(8), e104291. doi:10.1371/journal.pone.0104291 PMID:25098167

Henderson, P. W., & Cote, J. A. (1998). Guidelines for selecting or modifying logos. *Journal of Marketing*, *62*(2), 14–30. doi:10.1177/002224299806200202

Hynes, N. (2009). Color and meaning in corporate logos: An empirical study. *Journal of Brand Management*, *16*(8), 545–555. doi:10.1057/bm.2008.5

Jacobs, K. W., & Suess, J. F. (1975). Effects of four psychological primary colors on anxiety state. *Perceptual and Motor Skills*, *41*(1), 207–210. doi:10.2466/pms.1975.41.1.207 PMID:1178407

Kaya, N., & Epps, H. H. (2004). Relationship between color and emotion: A study of college students. *College Student Journal, 38*(3), 396–405.

Kotler, P., & Armstrong, G. (2018). *Principles of Marketing* (17th ed.). Pearson Prentice Hall.

Kumar, J. S. (2017). The Psychology of Color Influences Consumers' Buying Behaviour – A Diagnostic Study. *Ushus Journal of Business Management, 16*(4), 1–13. doi:10.12725/ujbm.41.1

Labrecque, L. (2010). *The marketer's prismatic palette: Essays on the importance of color in marketing with implications for brand personality* (Doctoral Dissertation). https://scholarworks.umass.edu/dissertations/AAI3409617

Labrecque, L. (2020). Color research in marketing: Theoretical and technical considerations for conducting rigorous and impactful color research. *Psychology and Marketing, 37*(7), 855–863. doi:10.1002/mar.21359

Lin, L. (2010). The relationship of consumer personality trait, brand personality and brand loyalty: An empirical study of toys and video games buyers. *Journal of Product and Brand Management, 19*(1), 4–17. doi:10.1108/10610421011018347

MacEvoy, B. (2019a). *Light and the eye. Color vision*. http://www.handprint.com/HP/WCL/color1.html#spectrum

MacEvoy, B. (2019b). *Modern color theory (concepts). Color theory*. http://www.handprint.com/HP/WCL/color18a.html

Meissner, K., & Linde, K. (2018). Are Blue Pills Better Than Green? How Treatment Features Modulate Placebo Effects. *International Review of Neurobiology, 139*, 357–378. doi:10.1016/bs.irn.2018.07.014 PMID:30146054

Mikellides, B., & Porter, T. (2009). *Color for Architecture Today*. Taylor & Francis.

Mindrut, S., Manolica, A., & Roman, C. (2015). Building Brands Identity. *Procedia Economics and Finance, 20*, 393–403. doi:10.1016/S2212-5671(15)00088-X

Morton, J. (2013?). *Color Psychology in Medicine*. Color-blog. https://munsell.com/color-blog/color-psychology-medicine-jill-morton/

Nasseraldin, A., Westland, S., & Marsden, J. (2019). *The role of color in a successful logo*. http://stephenwestland.co.uk/pdf/nasseraldin_westland_marsden_AIC2019.pdf

O'Connor, Z. (2009). Environmental color mapping using digital technology: A case study. *Urban Design International, 11*(1), 45-47. doi:10.1057/palgrave.udi.9000161

Ridgway, J., & Myers, B. (2014). A study on brand personality: consumers' perceptions of colors used in fashion brand logos. *International Journal of Fashion Design, Technology and Education, 7*(1), 50-57. doi:10.1080/17543266.2013.877987

Singh, S. (2006) Impact of color on marketing. *Management Decision, 44*(6), 783-789. doi:10.1108/00251740610673332

Valdez, P., & Mehrabian, A. (1994). Effects of color on emotions. *Journal of Experimental Psychology. General, 123*(4), 394–409. doi:10.1037/0096-3445.123.4.394 PMID:7996122

Ward, E., Yang, S., Romaniuk, J., & Beal, V. (2020). Building a unique brand identity: Measuring the relative ownership potential of brand identity element types. *Journal of Brand Management, 27*(4), 393–407. doi:10.105741262-020-00187-6

Yu, L., Westland, S., Li, Z., Pan, Q., Shin, M. J., & Won, S. (2018). The role of individual color preferences in consumer purchase decisions. *Color Research and Application, 43*(2), 258–267. doi:10.1002/col.22180

ADDITIONAL READING

Adams, S. (2017). *The designer's dictionary of color*. Abrams.

Eiseman, L. (2017). *The complete color harmony, pantone edition: expert color information for professional results*. Rockport Publishers Incorporated.

KEY TERMS AND DEFINITIONS

Brand Personality: Attempt to humanize the brand to bring it closer to the communication target.

Color Symbology: Attribution of a feeling, a meaning, a symbology to a color, which can vary according to culture and temporal space.

Corporate Identity: It consists of all elements, including graphics, that allow you to communicate the organizational culture.

Logo: It is a graphic representation composed of one or more elements that must be in harmony and that serves to represent an entity (company, institution, product brand, service).

Visual Identity: Combination of graphics that contribute to the positioning of the institutional brand or product.

Chapter 9
How Social Media Contribute to Autists' Wellbeing:
A Netnographic Analysis of Virtual Communities Content

Wilian Ramalho Feitosa
https://orcid.org/0000-0002-7005-4499
Federal Institute of São Paulo, Brazil

Daniela Silveira
Getulio Vargas Foundation, Brazil

Leticia Prado Andrade
Federal Institute of São Paulo, Brazil

ABSTRACT

Electronic social networks have expanded communication possibilities. This chapter aims to present how such platforms allow the formation of virtual communities to support and exchange information and the inclusion of people with ASD (autism spectrum disorders) by comparing brand virtual communities from two countries, five from Brazil and one from the USA. Among interpretative methods, netnography and manual content analysis considering posts on each community were performed. Also, tweets about Autism Awareness Day were analyzed. As a result, it was possible to see that virtual communities' contribution allows dialogue among autists' relatives, releasing their suffering and sharing acceptable practices. Among contributions, this study helps to know the differences among various virtual communities and content in terms of viralization in health marketing.

DOI: 10.4018/978-1-7998-7263-4.ch009

INTRODUCTION

A challenge for public policies is the inclusion of different people in the production process or the most diverse aspects of life. Communication, for example, is something essential and vital for coexistence. From the dawn of humanity, the human being transmits ideas and desires through various means, including speech, gestures, and expressions, to live in the community.

In recent years, communication has gained new contours with the advent of the internet and written communication through cellular devices. Written language in these media has become more accessible to those who might be excluded from the process of communication and living in society.

It is the case with ASD - autism spectrum disorders. Autism is a term that designates different degrees and types of disorders, including Asperger Syndrome, all linked to the way people communicate and perceive the world. It is a worldwide disorder (WHO, 2017). Individuals with ASDs frequently have issues in communication, for instance, difficulty in understanding non-verbal cues in a conversation in social environments, used have problems in keeping social ties and friends, and, as a result, are vulnerable to depression (Ahmed *et al.*, 2019; Ward *et al.*, 2018).

Patients and relatives need to deal with their Stigma (Ahuja & Williams, 2010; Mirabito *et al.*, 2016; Rusch *et al.*, 2005). Lack of information, suffering, and vulnerable positions turn this a potential area for policymakers' interventions (Yeh *et al.*, 2017). Health services, more than any service, demand empathy and compassion. Probably, mental health services are the most sensible of them. For this, consumers' journey is increasing and sophisticated, including internet searching and the dawn of several informational sharing options (Larson & Bock, 2016). Inclusively, access to the marketplace, helping consumers cope with their conditions is still a gap (Machin *et al.,* 2011). In this way, health campaigns can reduce Stigma, changing implicit worldviews (Meyer *et al.,* 2020). Traditional media can induce people in one-to-many communication. Nevertheless, what can be the contribution of other media? What is the effect of a direct-to-consumer advertisement and the received feedback from consumers? (McKeever, 2014; Spottswood & Wohn, 2019).

Considering that ASD involves different types of patients (Maenner et al., 2013), this study may observe its performance in social networks and verify how social networks help differentiate the different ones, contributing to reducing the risks to which these consumers are subjected in their daily lives. Considering that about 4 billion people around the world (53%) have access to the internet; 3.1 billion (42%) are active users of social networks; 2.9 billion (39%) use social media on their mobile devices, especially smartphones, this is particularly relevant (Hootsuite, 2019). More, unstable social relationships, loneliness, depression, and anxiety are characteristic of the person living with ASD, and it worsens significantly when social relations do not exist (Mazurek, 2014).

Social networks' written language may help solve problems such as the difficulty of individuals with ASD, such as facial recognition of emotions or human interaction, having better relationships mediated by machines and digital platforms (Maia et al., 2012). On the other hand, family members may be the beneficiaries of the process, interacting and receiving emotional and informational support (Ahuja & Williams, 2010; Eisenback et al., 2004; Reinze & Solheim, 2015). For this, digital communication, which includes virtual communities and social media, can help access health products and services communication (Basch & MacLean, 2019; Berry et al., 2016; Huo & Turner, 2019). Social media can help individuals with ASD cope with sadness and increase happiness in moderation cases (Ward et al., 2018). More, patients of several conditions have found on social media the support and health information they need, forming communities of interest in diabetes mellitus, cancer, or hypertension (Greene et al., 2011). Peer-to-peer healthcare is growing up, and 23% of adult internet users in a chronic condition in the USA are in some community (Chretien & Kind, 2013). Online health subcultures, e.g., people seeking weight loss, are among the biggest on social media.

There are gaps in theory about how exactly there can be some gain: quality of life or risk reduction. How would families or individuals with ASD benefit from the process of participating in social networks? Is it possible for companies, entities, or the government to assist in the process?

The following section will discuss the background of this subject, including the research questions after, in the third section, the main focus of the chapter. Methods will be presented, followed by data analysis, and, closing, our conclusions and suggestions to further studies.

BACKGROUND

Consumer well-being is a related to socially responsible business practices that involve business practices designed to support social causes, improve community well-being, and protect the environment (Sirgy & Lee, 2008). It is about goods and services that can enhance the overall quality of life and do it safely – to the consumers themselves. Pancer and Handelman (2012), analyzing the evolution of this concept, show that it results from consumer activism. Singy (2008) shows that it is related to consumers' education and their pursuit of information.

ASD: What Is and How Online Networks Can Help

Autism is a term that designates different degrees and types of disorders. Its symptoms are based on a triad: lack of communication, lack of social interaction, and repetitive and restricted behavior patterns. In addition to the three significant areas mentioned, the first reference was made of the association of ASD with cognitive impairment: more than half of the children studied cognitive deficits, with IQ below 50 (Wing & Gould, 1979) and a slow pace in development (Kohane et al., 2012; Krakowiak et al. 2008,). Some co-morbidity as echolalia and epilepsy, are also related (Ko et al., 2016). Recent data indicate a prevalence of 1 case for every 68 individuals born worldwide (CDC, 2014). Recently, the acronym ASD – Autism Spectrum Disorder started to designate all kinds of conditions, including Asperger Syndrome. Its origins are based on parental genetics. However, there is some controversy about what can increase the odds of children develop Autism, including exposition to environmental issues such as toxins and pollution during pregnancy.

Lack of communication is an aspect that social media can help. Ward et al. (2018) show that moderate uses of social media can increase happiness in ASD patients. However, severe cases may turn illiteracy into a reality, turning communication impossible by written ways to patients. Other hand, efforts to participate in social media can solve issues on social interaction and development.

Technology has supported diverse segments of society, including those with special needs, such as ASD. Odom et al. (2015) review the literature on how technology has helped educate those with Autism. Their studies have shown increased freedom, communication, independence, social competence, and even vocational ability to benefit technology.

More than that, technologies such as electronic social networks can enable the exchange of information, helping people understand the challenges and even the networking of interested parties and the production of the content itself. Moreover, social networks have allowed people to share information about diseases and their conditions, implying healthy issues. More studies about the viralization of health content are needed (Meng et al., 2018, Yang et al., 2018).

Ransbotham et al. (2012) portray this, speaking about content generated collaboratively by social networking users. This content production flows from the producer and the network that forms between itself and the collaborators. The study showed that the more extensive the network, the higher the viralization, which is stronger when the content is more recent. He analyzed data from a website called wikiproject medicine using Markov chain and Bayesian statistics.

The formation of a virtual community, sharing ideas, resources, solutions to problems, collaborating with indications of specialized services and products, and even purchasing clubs.

On the other hand, inclusion may not occur homogeneously, or even an opportunity for action, both for those who suffer from such disorders and their relatives to obtain support, companies, entities, and governments to access and understand how the phenomenon manifests itself. For example, Pechmann et al. (2011) define and a typology of different consumers at risk. Consumers may be at risk, but this risk is real or just perceived. Moreover, its typology presented a scale with four dimensions: level of vulnerability, speed of change required, level of awareness, and focus level. ASD will likely make people more vulnerable, and therefore technology support could reduce this risk through information and support.

Research has sought to identify whether and how electronic social networks improve people's quality of life with autism-related syndromes about communicability and independence. However, what content could produce evidence of improvement? The work of Ozanne et al. (2013), for example, identified that posting photos could be evidence of social transformation generated by social networks. On the other hand, Maenner et al. (2013) presented that different profiles of patients with ASD may have different vulnerability and response levels.

Virtual Communities and Its Engagement

A community is a group of people united by their common interests. Muniz and O'Guinn (2001, p. 412) define a brand community as "a specialized, non-geographically bound community, based on a structured set of social relationships among users of a brand". This definition suggests a relationship between the brand and its customers and between customers (Feitosa *et al.*, 2014). Nowadays, interest communities are increasing due to virtual platforms, forming virtual communities, with features similar to presential communities, even more geographically sparse, using social networking tools. Those tools (e.g., Twitter and Facebook), professional networking sites (e.g., LinkedIn), media sharing sites (e.g., Instagram and YouTube), commerce communities (e.g., Amazon and eBay), blogs (e.g., Blogger and Bloglines), and discussion forums are examples of social media platforms. Social media has changed the way companies have done business over the years (Ramsaran-Fowdar & Fowdar, 2013). As a result, in recent years, social media sites have become essential for users and companies (Maecker et al., 2016; Silva et al., 2020). Even neighbors and families have organized themselves by social media, in WhatsApp groups, for example, exchanging security procedures (Torres, 2017), health information, including COVID19 procedures (Aparicio et al., 2020), and public interest information, increasing the risk of misinformation and fake news (Galhiardi et al., 2020).

One of the primary motivations for participating in virtual communities is the exchange of information (Ridings & Gefen, 2004) among their interacting members, as there is a sense of obligation and duty of the individual to the community as a whole (Bagozzi & Dholakia, 2002; Muniz & O'Guinn, 2001). On the other hand, members' lack of expertise can make them vulnerable to believe in wrong pieces of information (Zarocostas, 2020).

It is also up to the community members themselves to integrate and retain new members and share information about the use of the brand (Muniz & O'Guinn, 2001). Thus, in a community where the ratio of its members' activities to the brand's activities is high - which establishes the proportion with which its members build value on a larger scale - such communities have more significant potential to generate engagement.

Consumer and Patient Communities' Differences

Customer engagement is an evolving concept (Hollebeeck, 2011) about how an actor can be profoundly interested and limited in a company regarding trust, loyalty, commitment, and trust (Moriuchi, 2012). It includes the context B2B (Diba et al., 2019) and B2C (Feitosa et al., 2014; Kesgin & Murthy, 2019). Online engagement can include how someone views, follows, and resends content on social media to the audience, helping a company gain media instead of buying it. This can happen based on the sender's characteristics, such as how reliable someone is (Oeldorf-Hirsch & DeVoss, 2019) or based on the message, for example, how positive or negative they are (Feitosa & Botelho, 2015, 2017; Spottswood & Wohn, 2019). Also, it is based on technology issues, for example, how the message is sent (Zhu, 2019). For Clafey and Bradley (2019), consumer engagement has three elements: cognitive appraisal, affective states, and participation. Their study argues that it is needed to contextualize, personalize, and respond to the consumer's engagement experience to develop engagement.

That engagement can be boosted in several ways. Feitosa and Botelho (2018) have discussed what can motivate people to share knowledge in virtual communities, dividing them into extrinsic and intrinsic reasons. Psychological research has proposed that motivation can be intrinsic – internal reasons, such as interests, satisfaction, emotional status, overall health – or extrinsic – external reasons, such as approvals, rewards, concordances, reactances (Ryan & Deci 2000, p. 61). Even extrinsic motivation is based on internal reasons such as beliefs, culture, and attitudes, but social interactions form. It means that what motivates someone in an online social interaction can vary according to their profile and consider these extrinsic factors. Therefore, an incentive is given by a company to consumers' needs to fit their profiles and take into account different kinds of motivation. In this point, Gazit and Aharoni (2018) say that psychological factors such as social support, extroversion, and narcissism significantly predict the level of participation in WhatsApp groups.

However, they also argue that age, the level of group importance, the group's manager, WhatsApp usage, and the group's subject play a vital role in participation.

Companies have tried different methods of motivating people to spread their content (Godes et al., 2005). First, to consider intrinsic consumer motivation, extra care concerning content creation is necessary. Here, it is essential to consider how the consumer can interpret content to create the right content for the right market segment, such as memes, useful content, homophilous influence consideration, i.e., by choosing the right influencers, and timing. Thus, if companies create excellent and attractive content, they can stimulate people to share it, increasing interest in online social interactions. If the content can improve the sharer's self-image – i.e., make it more likely for him/her to be seen as an intelligent and calm person, motivation will grow.

Second, it is essential to consider extrinsic motivation. Among critical external factors, financial rewards (monetary prizes and discounts) or non-financial (gifts, badges, contest campaigns, and becoming part of a group) are both possibilities.

However, the forms of interaction and community management practices can lead to different results. Practices unite behaviors, performances, and representations through 1) procedures: explicit rules, principles, precepts, and instructions, called "discursive knowledge"; 2) understandings: knowledge of what to say and do skills and know-how; 3) engagements: ends and purposes that contain emotion to the extent that people are committed to them (Warde, 2005). Practices also highlight the brand community's vitality: the number of posts, responses, and hits provide evidence of interest to participants on online sites. The existence, number, and diversity of practices that can be evaluated on brand relationship sites offer additional methods for assessing the brand community's vitality (Schau et al., 2009).

Schau et al. (2009) follow Vargo and Lusch's (2004) logic that the creation of value resides in the actions, interactions, and projects that occur between agents. For these authors, practices are implicit and connected ways of understanding, affirming, and undertaking actions. These practices are the mechanisms by which communities create value. They are not the value itself, but they work together to create value: the user; the community in which the user is inserted; the brand itself; and the company that owns it.

Among those practices, i) evangelization to attract more members to the community, and ii) justification to explain the community's purpose properly are essential in the impression's management. After, it is essential to manage social interactions by welcoming new members, creating empathy, and managing their interaction, for instance, punishing those who had misbehaved or reenforcing good behaviors. The third practice is community governance, where members' documentation, recognition, and titles will be attributed. Participation can be controlled and indicators measured (Schau et al., 2009).

Another approach is made by Kietzmann et al. (2011). They came up with a honeycomb framework that identifies seven functional building blocks of social media management, including virtual communities: i) identify identities, ii) monitoring and comprehending conversations, iii) the stimulation of sharing, iv) the constant presence of the owner, solving doubts and solving conflicts, v) making relationships, vi) managing reputation and vii) creating groups. Each block allows us to unpack and examine a specific facet of Social media user experience and its consequences for companies.

Amongst patients, it is possible to say that all those principles to manage virtual communities are valid. Social and emotional bonds are intense, and a seek for helpful content, in complement to medical advices or to consider alternatives for treatment. Smailhodzic et al. (2016), in a systematic review about patients' behavior on social media, have found that o seven identified types of effects on patients, namely i) improved self-management and control, ii) enhanced psychological well-being, and iii) enhanced subjective well-being, iv) diminished subjective well-being, v) addiction to social media, vi) loss of privacy and vii) being targeted for promotion. Also, patients' social media use was found to affect the healthcare professional and patient relationship by leading to equal communication between the patient and healthcare professional, increased switching of medical assistance.

Patients with ASDs cope with sadness using social media (Ward et al., 2018). More, patients of several conditions have found on social media the support and health information they need, forming communities of interest in diabetes mellitus, cancer, or hypertension (Greene et al., 2011). Peer-to-peer healthcare is growing up, and 23% of adult internet users in a chronic condition in the USA are in some community (Chretien & Kind, 2013). Online health subcultures, e.g., people seeking weight loss, are among the biggest on social media. Twitter has been reported to help women manage their breast cancer situation (Attai et al., 2015). Participants reported overall increased knowledge, survivorship, metastatic breast cancer, cancer types and biology, clinical trials and research, treatment options, breast imaging, genetic testing and risk assessment, and radiotherapy. Moreover, patients reported decreasing anxiety after twitter community participation.

Therefore, this study's research question is: How do virtual communities benefit autistic people and their families? Do they benefit from this, improving their general condition or reducing the risks they are subjected to?

This question will require analyzing virtual communities' content related to the theme in social networks involving Autism, family, and associations dedicated to the theme.

METHOD

This chapter sought to analyze the content of different social media linked to Autism, amongst interpretative methods, netnography (Kozinets et al., 2018), and content analysis (Saura et al., 2020), including manual coding on each community.

The data collection was divided into three phases:

Phase 1) Netnography: The netnographic approach involved being part of the six selected communities on Facebook, interacting, and acting as an ordinary member during the study. The immersion was for four months, between May and August 2017.

The selection of communities took place in two ways: the number of community members on the Facebook platform, their accounts on Twitter, and their appearance in search rankings on Google.

Phase 2) Content analysis on Facebook virtual communities: After the observation and immersion phase, a list of posts from these communities were extracted between June and August 2017, making 300 posts using a web crawler of each virtual community.

Phase 3) Content analysis on Twitter content: After this study, a third phase was performed. We have followed how content was generated in March 2018, during the period before an event known worldwide – the world autism day, by extracting Twitter content on the Netlytic website (netlytic.org). We analyzed the spreading of the word Autism by drawing a graph and content analysis.

DATA ANALYSIS

The largest community among those considered is Asperger and Autism in Brazil, with more fans on its Facebook fan pages. However, what moves their fans the most in generating content with greater reach is Understanding Autism. This community had more interactions and more sharing of its content in total. On the other hand, Asperger and Autism in Brazil had more likes, even with less sharing.

The level of interactions of each community and their engagement will be discussed below, considering engagement by content type.

The content has been categorized in shared links, original text messages, photos, videos, and events for review purposes. It is perceived that in the period considered, Understanding Autism had more text updates, while Overcoming Autism promoted

Figure 1. Data Collection Procedures

more events and focused on transmitting more photos, as well as Understanding Autism, in English.

It is then necessary to evaluate each community's content concerning the type of content posted. It is noticed that the *Autism Understanding* community with a level of commitment far superior to the others, in terms of sharing any content, but mainly with their videos, as a rule, informational with Dr. Brites, one of the responsible activists by the community administration. *Asperger and Autism Brazil* has external, instructional, or motivational content as a link, shared, generating a sizeable tanned volume. *Winning the Autism* community stands out the tannings related to face-to-face events, such as lectures, fairs, and the like. Autism Talk is the biggest and internationalized community. It focuses on pictures and motivational

Table 1. Communities analyzed

Virtual Community Name	Description	Members	Likes	Shares
1) Understanding Autism (UA)	Owned by Dr. Clay Brites, from Londrina/Brazil	106.070	114.514	121.129
2) Asperger and autism in Brazil (AAB)	NGO founded in June/2012	318.153	127.557	20.306
3) Autism and life (AL)	NGO from Porto Alegre/Brazil founded in Set/2010 www.autismoevida.org.br	211.136	882	29
4) Winning the Autism (WA)	NGO from Porto Alegre/Brazil. Founded in nov/2010. www.vencerautismo.org	211.057	45.727	15.218
5) Autism and reality (AR)	NGO from São Paulo/Brazil. Founded in 2010.	204.866	249.149	104.725
6) Autism Talk (AT)	From the USA. Founded in out/2012 by Patienttalk.org www.autismoerealidade.org.	615.165	440.135	125.200

Table 2. Number of posts by type of content in each community

	1 – UA	2 - AAB	3 - AL	4 - WA	5 - AR	6 – AT
Links	46	93	0	37	81	92
Text	9	1	3	6	2	95
Pictures	189	107	56	198	194	4.168
Vídeos	56	98	6	53	21	0
Events	0	1	0	6	2	5

content. On Twitter, it is possible to see their centrality of discussion about Autism; for instance, look at Figure 2.

Table 3. Means of likes (a) and shares (b) by communities (a; b)

	1 – UA	2 – AAB	3 - AL	4 - WA	5 - AR	6 – AT
Links	316,7; 370,5	516,8; 142,4	0	114,2; 62,1	470,0; 204,1	420; 130
Text	95,6; 10,3	49; 5	0,3; 0	16,7; 5,7	939,0; 601,5	1302; 905
Pictures	245,6; 235,9	386,1; 61,3	0,5; 15,5	162,8; 62,8	1050,9; 440,8	40033; 2333
Vídeos	940,4; 1060,7	388,9; 5,2	3; 0	167,3; 8,4	252,2; 70,1	0
Events	0	0	0	49; 0	13,5; 0,5	45; 55

Support, Motivation, and Exchange of Information

Virtual communities related to Autism were created to encourage support and enlightenment to those in need. Some of them are maintained with the support of hospitals, clinics, or laboratories, supporting the disclosure of these brands directly, by offering specialized products, or indirectly, through public relations, with the appearance of doctors directly, clarifying doubts of potential patients or through sponsorship of events or even the NGO's website.

Thus, "take your doubts with the doctor" is content that is highly shared and is among those that have more significant repercussions and engagement. Content that generates clarification and eliminates myths that the commonplace cultivates.

Although it was not among the ones that generate more engagement, the motivational content is the one that exists in greater quantity. Most shared photos and images seek to promote self-acceptance, relief, and the feeling that the relative weight of the situation is less because of the self's power. It is an attempt to demystify the disease and empower everyone.

Figure 2. Autism network on Twitter in March 2018

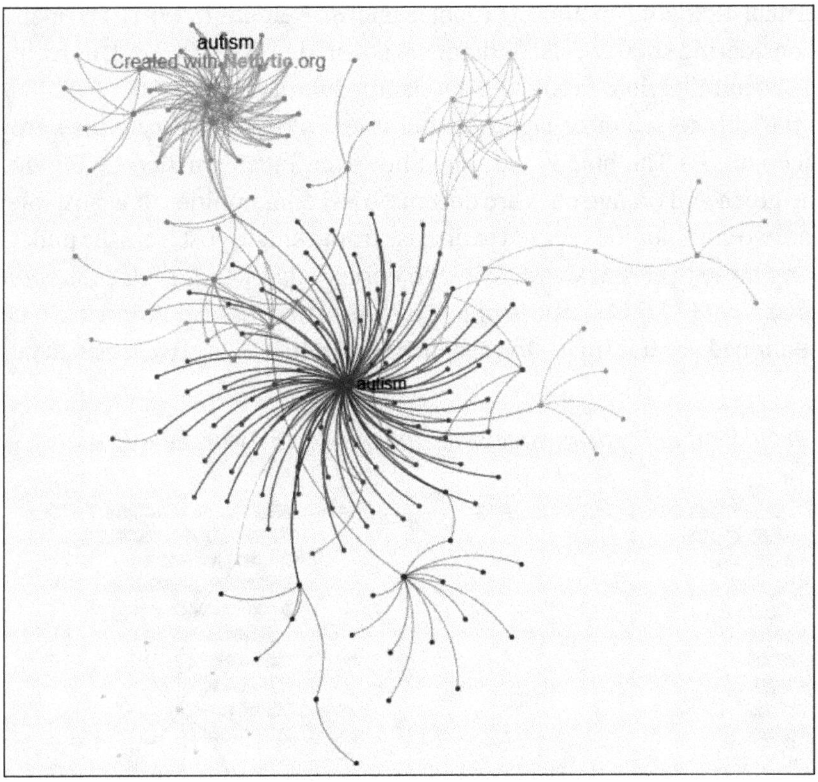

Importance of Events on Promoting Well-Being

Social media is a valuable marketing tool for events (Harb et al., 2019). In March 2018, all virtual communities distributed motivational content promoting world autism day. It was possible to verify that its viralization was more significant during this period. These contents promote a sense of affiliation and proximity, acceptance, relief, and awareness. At these events, people seek pieces of information and interact with new members, helping each other.

A graph was generated to understanding how this event could mobilize and make the information spread. Graphs are a structure amounting to a set of objects in which some pairs of objects are in some sense related. The objects correspond to mathematical abstractions called vertices (also called nodes or points), and each of the related pairs of vertices is called an edge (Kolaczyk & Csardi, 2020; Trudeau, 1991). In online communications, a graph represents a sender/receiver online interaction.

This graph in figure 2 represents interactions during the autism world awareness day in March 2018. Netlytic.org generated it. It is possible to see how the word

Autism was spread on the Twitter social network. The graph was generated by the Fruchterman-Reingold method (Fruchterman & Reingold, 1991; Herman et al., 2000), considering 1000 tweets. Its diameter is 4, its density, 0.002784, its reciprocity: 0.007273, centralization: 0.109200, and its modularity: 0.856900.

It is possible to see three significant clusters: a) the pink one comes from one single account. B) The blue is the same; however, much smaller. C) On the other hand, the green and orange ones are decentralized communities. It is possible to see that these two communities started to discuss from a single post from the pink cluster.

Among these tweets, it was possible to observe that words such as *support* (139 times), *amazing* (137 times), and *people* (169 times) were used more times. Some users were mentioned several times, for instance, *@asdinfowales*, five times mentioned.

Figure 3. Content analysis of tweets on Autism World Awareness Day

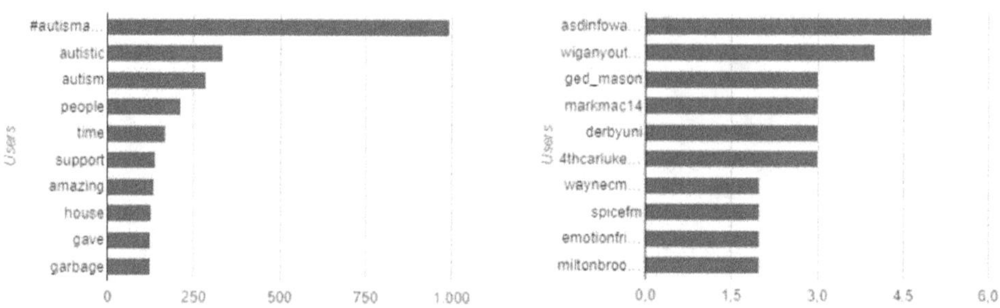

Finally, information sharing or even brainstorming, crowdfunding, crowdsourcing, and shared shopping are among actions that are potentially engaging if they do not generate engagement statistics.

Among the promotion of products and services, t-shirts, gifts, and other motivational goods could be found amongst publications. However, medical services used to be recommended amongst members.

Some Findings on Selected Virtual Communities Management about Autism

About motivation, it was possible to identify virtual communities' intrinsic motivation (Ryan & Deci, 2000), sometimes looking for some support, self-confidence, coping with anxiety, or reinforcing their practices to handle their situation. The extrinsic motivation was less frequent, but it was present, for instance, when members tried to get a free consultation or get some advices from the doctors. Following Schau et

Figure 4. Examples of motivational or support pictures or interactions

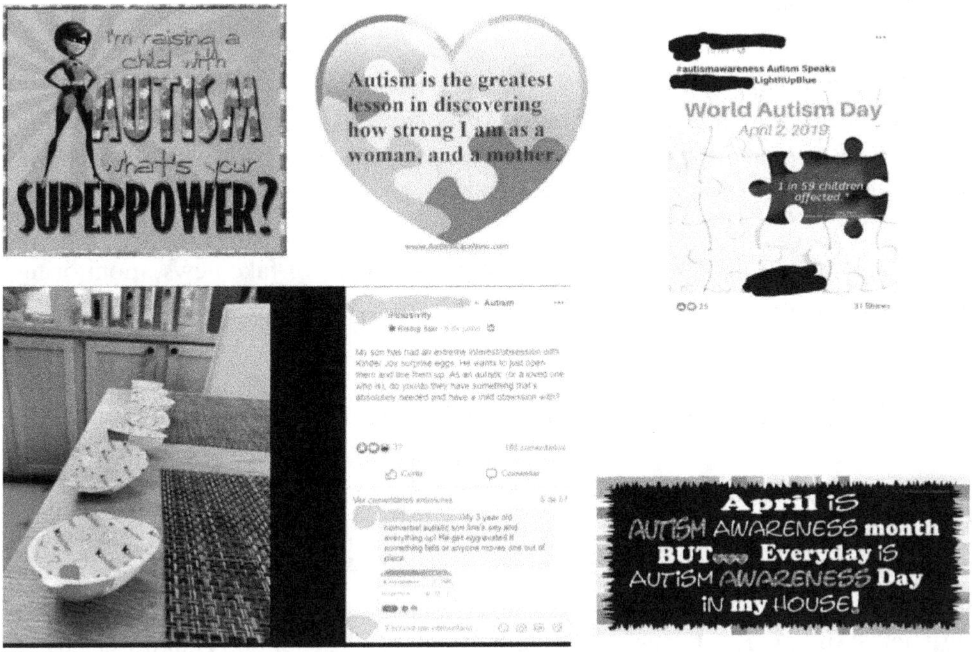

al. (2009) practices, welcoming was a common practice; however, it is possible to see that interactions were not so frequent – in general, the communication is non-bidirectional. Probably, the community Understanding autism has a higher level of interactions. Following Kietzmann et al. (2011) model, the stimuli of sharing by providing several figures and motivational texts are the most critical aspect of those communities.

The low rate of reciprocity in the autism awareness day (Figure 2) indicates that moderators and group managers have central importance on information flow. Probably, this is a psychological motivation factor - social support, extroversion, and narcissism can predict the level of participation in this case. This, aligned to personal importance, is usually the patient's relatives – and the economic factor plays an essential role in the participation level.

Considering the economic factor and the fact that many people with similar interests find each other in virtual communities, a potential risk is the drugs or treatments self-prescription. It is essential to say that any analyzed content could indicate a trace of that misbehavior. However, people used to ask for indications. More than this, they can mobilize resources to ask for changes to policymakers (Seltzer et al., 2017).

Moreover, virtual communities can be exposed to fake news. Galhardi et al. (2020) argue that it refers to

the production and massive spread of false news, to intentionally distort facts, in order to attract audiences, deceive, misinform, mislead, manipulate public opinion, discredit or exalt an institution or a person on a specific subject, to obtain economic and political advantages (Galhardi et al.,2020).

Virtual communities need to manage the occurrence of fake news, monitoring, punishing, and excluding those members who spread it.

SOLUTIONS AND RECOMMENDATIONS

Posts by famous autistics are also very prone to get viral. The story of the artist Marcos Mion (a Brazilian TV show presenter) about his autistic son stands out in several posts that are among the most viralized. A survey of Google's organic search for Autism also reinforces this strand. There are many searches for "Messi autistic", "Autistic Bill Gates" and others. As in the Croisier and Handford (2012)' study, it is possible to verify a "consumer journey" in these communities, with emotional reasons.

Also noteworthy are the inspirational/motivational posts related to the recovery of the autistic and their families' self-esteem. The difficult conviviality with the disease and its symptoms of social inadequacy and the constant judgments made by those who do not know these families' issues relate to these posts.

Movies, videos, novels, texts, and books on Autism are other types of posts entirely shared. Frequent content with awareness campaigns about the disease shows family members' efforts to spread information, sometimes exercising unconsciously media advocacy.

They are family members of the disease who become activists for the protection of the vulnerable. Because it is a disease that impedes social relations immensely, making its bearer an inappropriate individual for the common sense of relationships, it presents a great potential of transformation in the families.

Parents may also be perceived as inappropriate by the impotence to contain repetitive movements, echolalia, inappropriate laughter, and exacerbated reactions of their autistic.

Many autistic parents report exhaustion to sidestep and socially justify these behaviors of their autistic children in many posts and comments.

Talks between parents from autistic people seem to have a code of their own. Phrases like "parents of autistic will understand" "only for parents of autistic" are highlighted. Social networks have given a voice, not only to autistic children with an extraordinary commitment in their social relations but especially to parents who seek to defend their children from the many aggressions they already suffer. Among the concerns of the community members are still: early diagnosis, better treatments, school inclusion, social inclusion, laws that guarantee rights to autistic. It is similar to Morahan-Martin's (2004) findings, however, on a new scale.

Also, this study is aligned to Smailhodzic et al. (2016) results because it was possible to see the emotional support and esteem. On the other hand, this study differs from focusing measure the centrality of social media data.

Finally, emotional support is a motivational cue that these communities offer their members, making them more welcomed, informed, and identified with their peers. A future study for the deepening of these communities' psychological complexity and their members is in perspective.

Vulnerable consumers need additional support from policymakers. Whether the second does not supply all the support needed, the first will look for easy and fast solutions. Unfortunately, this can put them at risk.

FUTURE RESEARCH DIRECTIONS

As suggestions for future studies, study in-depth the relationship between autistic, the community, and their family members to understand the nuances of these relationships, possibly using the ethnographic approach. A survey can also be made to indicate which values are associated with participation in online groups linked to Autism or to study the most viralized posts, including the case of Dr. Clay Brites. Future studies may also consider engagement in the relationship with the subject's valence and line of each comment, post, and likes. In the case of Facebook, consider each reaction's positive or negative valence since harmful valence content may have different engagement positive valence. A quantitative study could assess the self-prescription propensity in virtual communities. More, how could vulnerable consumers be more fragile to self-prescription based on online information? Could that be based on misinformation or fake news, such as on COVID19 (Galhardi et al., 2020)?

Finally, future studies could consider how to use and maintain Instagram for health purposes. To analyze the causes of some events to have more significant repercussions than others and, if they are negative, what is the organ's position to preserve its image and solve these problems. More, health misinformation can spread on social media. Further studies can consider how this happens.

Another opportunity for future research is using a different methodology such as content analysis or discourse analysis to study the relationship between ADS, inclusion, and social platforms (Reyes-Menendez et al., 2020a, 2020b). Sentiment analysis using machine learning can be included in future research methodology (Saura et al., 2018).

CONCLUSION

This chapter aimed to understand how social networks can contribute to ASD and how users and their families can benefit from the content analysis of virtual communities related to the topic on Facebook. The communities analyzed found that among the most viralized posts are those with predominantly emotional content.

We highlight stories of success and overcoming autistic. The most liked post among all analyzed communities has 44,118 likes, about an autistic who has become "the youngest researcher of astrophysics in the world" (at the time of the posting).

Among contributions, this study helps to know the differences among various virtual communities and contents in terms of viralization in social marketing. Health marketing and the diffusion of health information on social media need to be studied, and this study brings light to how these communities spread information (Dimiris, 2006; Huo & Turner, 2019). Vulnerable consumers need additional support from policymakers. Whether the second does not supply all the support needed, the first will look for easy and fast solutions. Unfortunately, this can put them at risk.

REFERENCES

Ahmed, S., Hossain, M. F., Price, K., Pranger, C., Hossain, M. M., & Sharmin, M. (2019, July). A Tale of the Social-Side of ASD. In *2019 IEEE 43rd Annual Computer Software and Applications Conference (COMPSAC)* (Vol. 1, pp. 644-652). IEEE 10.1109/COMPSAC.2019.00098

Ahuja, A. S., & Williams, R. (2010). Telling Stories: Learning from Patients' and Families' Experiences of Specialist Child and Adolescent Mental Health Services. *International Journal of Consumer Studies*, *34*(5), 603–609. doi:10.1111/j.1470-6431.2010.00904.x

Aparicio, M., Bilbao, S., Saenz Valenzuela, M., & Barán Attias, T. (2020). Entre barbijos, ollas populares y grupos de WhatsApp: Mujeres, salud y cuidados ante el COVID-19 en los barrios del Gran Buenos Aires, Argentina. *Tessituras*, *8*(1), 279–301.

Attai, D. J., Cowher, M. S., Al-Hamadani, M., Schoger, J. M., Staley, A. C., & Landercasper, J. (2015). Twitter social media is an effective tool for breast cancer patient education and support: Patient-reported outcomes by survey. *Journal of Medical Internet Research, 17*(7), e188. doi:10.2196/jmir.4721 PMID:26228234

Bagozzi, R., & Dholakia, U. (2002). Intentional social action in virtual communities. *Journal of Interactive Marketing, 16*(2), 2–21. doi:10.1002/dir.10006

Barry, A. E., Bates, A. M., Olusanya, O., Vinal, C. E., Martin, E., Peoples, J. E., Jackson, Z. A., Billinger, S. A., Yusuf, A., Cauley, D. A., & Montano, J. R. (2016). Alcohol marketing on Twitter and Instagram: Evidence of directly advertising to youth/adolescents. *Alcohol and Alcoholism (Oxford, Oxfordshire), 51*(4), 487–492. doi:10.1093/alcalc/agv128 PMID:26597794

Basch, C. H., & MacLean, S. A. (2019). Colorectal Cancer on Instagram: A Content Analysis. *Journal of Consumer Health on the Internet, 23*(4), 378–383. doi:10.1080/15398285.2019.1684149

CDC – Center for Disease Control and Prevention. (2014). Prevalence of autism spectrum disorder among children aged 8 years - Autism and developmental disabilities monitoring network, 11 sites, United States, 2010. *MMWR. Surveillance Summaries, 63*(2), 1–21. PMID:24670961

Chretien, K., & Kind, T. (2013). Social Media and Clinical Care - Ethical, Professional, and Social Implications. *Circulation, 127*(13), 1413–1421. doi:10.1161/CIRCULATIONAHA.112.128017 PMID:23547180

Clafey, E., & Bradley, M. (2019). An empirical study of the impact of consumer emotional engagement and affective commitment in firm-hosted virtual communities. *Journal of Marketing Management, 35*(11-12), 1047–1079. doi:10.1080/0267257X.2019.1601125

Crosier, A., & Handford, A. (2012). Customer Journey Mapping as an Advocacy Tool for Disabled People: A Case Study. *Social Marketing Quarterly, 18*(1), 67–76. doi:10.1177/1524500411435483

Diba, H., Vella, J., & Abratt, R. (2019). Social media influence on the B2B buying process. *Journal of Business and Industrial Marketing, 34*(7), 1482–1496. doi:10.1108/JBIM-12-2018-0403

Dimiris, G. (2006). The diffusion of virtual communities in health care: Concepts and challenges. *Patient Education and Counseling, 62*(2), 178–188. doi:10.1016/j.pec.2005.10.003 PMID:16406472

Eysenbach, G., Powell, J., Englesakis, M., Rizo, C., & Stern, A. (2004). Health related virtual communities and electronic support groups: Systematic review of the effects of online peer to peer interactions. *BMJ (Clinical Research Ed.)*, *328*(7449), 1166. doi:10.1136/bmj.328.7449.1166 PMID:15142921

Feitosa, W. R., & Botelho, D. (2015). O Papel da Excitação no Engajamento de Defensores da Marca: Suas Reações a Notícias Positivas e Negativas no Ambiente Virtual. *Revista Economia & Gestão*, *15*(40), 117–141.

Feitosa, W. R., & Botelho, D. (2017). Online Brand Content Sharing on Social Networks – an Experiment Assessing the Role of Emotions on News and Advertising Online Sharing. *LA - Latin American. Advances in Consumer Research. Association for Consumer Research (U. S.)*, *4*, 155–158.

Feitosa, W. R., & Botelho, D. (2018). Mechanisms for incentivizing and encouraging online social interactions - an experiment analysing the role of recommendations and rewards on advertisement sharing behaviour. In B. Rishi & S. Bandyopadhyay (Eds.), *Contemporary Issues in Social Media Marketing*. Routledge. doi:10.4324/9781315563312

Feitosa, W. R., Botelho, D., & Lourenço, C. E. (2014). Comunidades virtuais de marca de produtos de consumo e criação de engajamento: Uma investigação qualitativa. *Revista Eletrônica Gestão e Serviços*, *5*(1), 827–848. doi:10.15603/2177-7284/regs.v5n1p827-848

Fruchterman, T. M., & Reingold, E. M. (1991). Graph Drawing by Force-directed Placement. *Software, Practice & Experience*, *21*(11), 1129–1164. doi:10.1002pe.4380211102

Galhardi, C., Freire, N., Minayo, M., & Fagundes, M. (2020). Fato ou Fake? Uma análise da desinformação frente à pandemia da Covid-19 no Brasil. *Ciencia & Saude Coletiva*, *25*(suppl 2), 4201–4210. doi:10.1590/1413-812320202510.2.28922020 PMID:33027357

Gazit, T., & Aharony, N. (2018). Factors explaining participation in WhatsApp groups: An exploratory study. *Aslib Journal of Information Management*, *70*(4), 390–413. doi:10.1108/AJIM-03-2018-0053

Godes, D., Mayslin, D., Chen, Y., Das, S., Dellarocas, C., Pfeiffer, B., ... Verlegh, P. (2005). The firm's management of social interactions. *Marketing Letters*, *16*(3), 415–428. doi:10.100711002-005-5902-4

Greene, J. A., Choudhry, N. K., Kilabuk, E., & Shrank, W. H. (2011). Online social networking by patients with diabetes: A qualitative evaluation of communication with Facebook. *Journal of General Internal Medicine*, *26*(3), 287–292. doi:10.100711606-010-1526-3 PMID:20945113

Harb, A., Fowler, D., Jung, H., & Alakaleek, W. (2019). Social media as a marketing tool for events. *Journal of Hospitality and Tourism Technology*, *10*(1), 28–44.

Herman, I., Melancon, G., & Marshall, M. (2000). Graph visualization and navigation in information visualization: A survey. *IEEE Transactions on Visualization and Computer Graphics*, *6*(1), 24–43. https://doi.org/10.1109/2945.841119

Hollebeek, L. (2011). Exploring customer brand engagement: definition and themes. *Journal of Strategic Management*, *11*(7), 555–573.

Hollebeek, L. D., Andreassen, T. W., Smith, D. L., Grönquist, D., Karahasanovic, A., & Marquez, A. (2018). Epilogue – service innovation actor engagement: An integrative model. *Journal of Services Marketing*, *32*(1), 95–100. https://doi.org/10.1108/JSM-11-2017-0390

Hootsuite. (2019). *We Are Social, Digital In 2019*. Available in: https://wearesocial.com/global-digital-report-2019

Huo, J., & Turner, K. (2019). Social Media in Health Communication. In J. Bian, Y. Guo, Z. He, & X. Hu (Eds.), *Social Web and Health Research* (pp. 53–82). Springer.

Keen, D., & Ward, S. (2004). Autistic Spectrum Disorder: A Child Population Profile. *Autism*, *8*(1), 39–48. https://doi.org/10.1177/1362361304040637

Kesgin, M., & Murthy, R. S. (2019). Consumer engagement: The role of social currency in online reviews. *Service Industries Journal*, *39*(7-8), 609–636. https://doi.org/10.1080/02642069.2018.1553237

Kietzmann, J. H., Hermkens, K., McCarthy, I., & Silvestre, B. (2011). Social media? Get serious! Understanding the functional building blocks of social media. *Business Horizons*, *54*(3), 241–251.

Ko, C., Kim, N., Kim, E., Song, D. H., & Cheon, K. A. (2016). The effect of epilepsy on autistic symptom severity assessed by the social responsiveness scale in children with autism spectrum disorder. *Behavioral and Brain Functions*, *12*(1), 1–9.

Kohane, I. S., McMurry, A., Weber, G., MacFadden, D., Rappaport, L., Kunkel, L., ... Churchill, S. (2012). The co-morbidity burden of children and young adults with autism spectrum disorders. *PLoS One*, *7*(4), e33224.

Kolaczyk, E., & Csárdi, G. (2020). *Statistical Analysis of Network Data with R*. Springer.

Kozinets, R., Scaraboto, D., & Parmentier, M. A. (2018). Evolving netnography: How brand auto-netnography, a netnographic sensibility, and more-thanhuman netnography can transform your research. *Journal of Marketing Management*, *34*(3-4), 231–242. https://doi.org/10.1080/0267257X.2018.1446488

Krakowiak, P., Goodlin-Jones, B. E. T. H., Hertz-Picciotto, I. R. V. A., Croen, L. A., & Hansen, R. L. (2008). Sleep problems in children with autism spectrum disorders, developmental delays, and typical development: A population-based study. *Journal of Sleep Research*, *17*(2), 197–206.

Larson, L., & Bock, E. (2016). Consumer Search and Satisfaction with Mental Health Services. *Journal of Services Marketing*, *30*(7), 736–748.

Machin, J. E., Adkins, N., Crosby, E., Ferrell, J., & Mirabito, A. (2019). The Marketplace, Mental Wellbeing, and Me: Exploring Self-Efficacy, Self-Esteem, and Self-Compassion in Consumer Coping. *Journal of Business Research*, *100*, 410–420.

Maecker, O., Barrot, C., & Becker, J. U. (2016). The effect of social media interactions on customer relationship management. *Journal of Business Research*, *9*(1), 133–155.

Maenner, M., Smith, L., Hong, J., Makuch, R., Greenberg, J., & Mailick, M. (2013). Evaluation of an activities diary living scale for adolescents and adults with developmental disabilities. *Disability and Health Journal*, *6*(1), 8–17.

Maia, I., Magalhães, L., Lencastre, J., Monteiro, A., & Bilimória, H. (2012). E-moções: avaliação heurística a um jogo multimédia em m-learning para crianças com perturbações do espetro do autismo. In *Atas do Encontro sobre Jogos e Mobile Learning*. Braga: CIEd.

Mazurek, M. (2014). Loneliness, friendship, and well-being in adults with autism spectrum disorders. *Autism*, *18*(3), 223–232. https://doi.org/10.1177/1362361312474121

McKeever, R. (2014). Thinking Outside the Medicine Cabinet: A Comparative Content Analysis of Direct-to-Consumer Advertisements for Prescription Drug Treatments. *Health Marketing Quarterly*, *31*(4), 353–369.

Meng, J., Peng, W., Tan, P., Liu, W., Cheng, Y., & Bae, A. (2018). Diffusion size and structural virality: The effects of message and network features on spreading health information on twitter. *Computers in Human Behavior*, *89*, 111–120.

Meyer, J., Ruyter, K., Grewal, D., Cleeren, K., Keeling, D., & Motyka, S. (2020). Categorical Versus Dimensional Thinking: Improving Anti-Stigma Campaigns by Matching Health Message Frames and Implicit Worldviews. *Journal of the Academy of Marketing Science*, *48*(2), 222–245.

Mirabito, A. M., Otnes, C., Crosby, E., Wooten, D., Machin, J., Pullig, C., ... Velagaleti, S. (2016). The Stigma Turbine: A Theoretical Framework for Conceptualizing and Contextualizing Marketplace Stigma. *Journal of Public Policy & Marketing*, *35*(2), 170–184.

Morahan-Martin, J. (2004). How Internet Users Find, Evaluate, and Use Online Health Information: ACross-Cultural Review. *Cyberpsychology & Behavior*, *7*(5), 497–510.

Moriuchi, E. (2019). Okay, Google!: An empirical study on voice assistants on consumer engagement and loyalty. *Psychology and Marketing*, *36*(5), 489–501. https://doi.org/10.1002/mar.21192

Muniz, A., & O'guinn, T. (2001). Brand community. *The Journal of Consumer Research*, *27*(4), 412–432.

Odom, S., Thompson, J., Hedges, S., Boyd, B., Dykstra, J., Duda, M., Szidon, M., Smith, L., & Bord, A. (2015). Technology-Aided Interventions and Instruction for Adolescents with Autism Spectrum Disorder. *Autism Dev Disord*, *45*, 3805-3819. doi:10.100710803-014-2320-6

Oeldorf-Hirsch, A., & DeVoss, C. L. (2019). Who Posted That Story? Processing Layered Sources in Facebook News Posts. *Journalism & Mass Communication Quarterly*, *97*(1), 141–160. https://doi.org/10.1177/1077699019857673

Ozanne, J., Moscato, E., & Kunkel, D. (2013). Transformative Photography: Evaluation and Best Practices for Eliciting Social and Policy Changes. *Journal of Public Policy & Marketing*, *32*(1), 45–65.

Pancer, E., & Handelman, J. (2012). The evolution of consumer well-being. *Journal of Historical Research in Marketing*, *4*(1), 177–189.

Pechmann, C., Moore, E., Andreasen, A., Connell, P., Freeman, D., Gardner, M., Heisley, D., Lefebvre, R., Pirouz, D., & Soster, R. (2011). Navigating the Central Tensions in Research on At-Risk Consumers: Challenges and Opportunities. *Journal of Public Policy & Marketing*, *30*(1), 23–30.

Ramsaran-Fowdar, R., & Fowdar, S. (2013). The implications of Facebook marketing organizations. *Contemporary Management Research*, *9*(1), 73–84.

Ransbotham, S., Kane, G., & Lurie, N. (2012). Network Characteristics and the Value of Collaborative User-Generated Content. *Marketing Science, 31*(3), 387–405. https://dx.doi.org/10.1287/mksc.1110.0684

Reinke, J., & Solheim, C. (2015). Online Social Support Experiences of Mothers of Children with Autism Spectrum Disorder. *Journal of Child and Family Studies, 24*(8), 2364–2373.

Reyes-Menendez, A., Saura, J. R., & Filipe, F. (2020a). Marketing challenges in the# MeToo era: Gaining business insights using an exploratory sentiment analysis. *Heliyon, 6*(3), e03626.

Reyes-Menendez, A., Saura, J. R., & Thomas, S. B. (2020b). Exploring key indicators of social identity in the# MeToo era: Using discourse analysis in UGC. *International Journal of Information Management, 54*, 102129.

Ridings, C., & Gefen, D. (2004). Virtual community attraction: Why people hang out online. *Journal of Computer-Mediated Communication, 10*(1).

Rüsch, N., Angermeyer, M. C., & Corrigan, P. W. (2005). Mental Illness Stigma: Concepts, Consequences, and Initiatives to Reduce Stigma. *European Psychiatry, 20*(8), 529–539.

Ryan, R. M., & Deci, E. L. (2000). Intrinsic and extrinsic motivations: Classic definitions and new directions. *Contemporary Educational Psychology, 25*(1), 54–67.

Saura, J. R., Reyes-Menendez, A. R., & Sánchez, P. R. P. (2018). A Sentiment Analysis on Twitter with Machine Learning: Identifying sentiment about #BlackFriday deals. *Revista Espacios, 39*(42), 16.

Saura, J. R., Reyes-Menendez, A. R., & Sánchez, P. R. P. (2020). Innovación Docente y Redes Sociales: Twitter como herramienta de comunicación docente a través de comunidades digitales. In El uso de las TIC en la Innovación Docente (pp. 15-27). Dykinson.

Schau, H. J., Muñiz, A., & Arnould, E. (2009). How Brand Community Practices Create Value. *Journal of Marketing, 73*(1), 30–51.

Seltzer, E., Horst-Martz, E., Lu, M., & Merchant, R. (2017). Public sentiment and discourse about Zika virus on Instagram. *Public Health, 150*, 170–175.

Silva, S. C., Feitosa, W., Duarte, P., & Vasconcelos, M. (2020). How to Increase Engagement on Social Media Using the Honeycomb Model: A case Study in a Portuguese HR Company. *Revista de Gestão, 27*(2), 153–167.

Sirgy, M. J. (2008). Ethics and Public Policy Implications of Research on Consumer Well-Being. *Journal of Public Policy & Marketing*, *27*(2), 207–212.

Sirgy, M. J., & Lee, D. (2008). Well-being Marketing: An Ethical Business Philosophy for Consumer Goods Firms. *Journal of Business Ethics*, *77*(4), 377–403.

Smailhodzic, E., Hooijsma, W., Boonstra, A., & Langley, D. J. (2016). Social media use in healthcare: A systematic review of effects on patients and on their relationship with healthcare professionals. *BMC Health Services Research*, *16*, 442. https://doi.org/10.1186/s12913-016-1691-0

Spottswood, E., & Wohn, D. Y. (2019). Beyond the Like: How People Respond to Negative Posts on Facebook. *Journal of Broadcasting & Electronic Media*, *63*(2), 250–267. https://doi.org/10.1080/08838151.2019.1622936

Torres, P. (2017). Seguridad y separación clasista en Córdoba: Grupos de Whatsapp y aplicaciones de asistencia ciudadana para la gestión de la conflictividad. *Astrolabio*, *18*(6), 9–33.

Trudeau, R. J. (1993). *Introduction to Graph Theory*. Dover Pub.

Vargo, S., & Lusch, R. (2004). Evolving to a new dominant logic for marketing. *Journal of Marketing*, *68*(1), 18–27.

Ward, D. M., Dill-Shackleford, K. E., & Mazurek, M. O. (2018). Social media use and happiness in adults with autism spectrum disorder. *Cyberpsychology, Behavior, and Social Networking*, *21*(3), 205–209.

Warde, A. (2005). Consumption and theories of practice. *Journal of Consumer Culture*, *5*(2), 131–153.

Wing, L., & Gould, J. (1979). Severe impairments of social interaction and associated abnormalities in children: Epidemiology and classification. *Journal of Autism and Developmental Disorders*, *9*(1), 11–29.

World Health Organization. (2017). *Depression and Other Common Mental Disorders: Global Health Estimates*. World Health Organization. http://apps.who.int/iris/bitstream/10665/254610/1/WHO-MSD-MER-2017.2-eng.pdf

Yang, Q., Tufts, C., Ungar, L., Guntuku, S., & Merchant, R. (2018). To Retweet or Not to Retweet: Understanding What Features of Cardiovascular Tweets Influence Their Retransmission. *Journal of Health Communication*, *23*(12), 1026–1035. https://doi.org/10.1080/10810730.2018.1540671

Yeh, M. A., Jewell, R., & Thomas, V. (2017). The Stigma of Mental Illness: Using Segmentation for Social Change. *Journal of Public Policy & Marketing*, *36*(1), 97–116.

Zarocostas, J. (2020). How to fight an infodemic. *Lancet*, *395*(10225), 676.

Zhu, Y. (2019). Social media engagement and Chinese international student recruitment: Understanding how UK HEIs use Weibo and WeChat. *Journal of Marketing for Higher Education*, *29*(2), 173–190.

KEY TERMS AND DEFINITIONS

ASD: Autism Spectrum Disorder.

Engagement: It is the level of participation and involvement that someone has in a Community (Muniz & OGuinn, 2001). It is how an actor can be profoundly interested and limited in a company in terms of the trust, loyalty, commitment, and trust (Moriuchi, 2012).

Evangelization: It is a practice to invite and keep new members to a virtual Community (Schau et al., 2009).

Influentials: An influential person has several contacts, social ties, credibility, and social capital. They can influence people to decide in one direction. Influentials are essential to boost the spreading of content (Muniz & OGuinn, 2001).

Netnography: A research method on the researcher gets into the data intensely during a period, acting as a community member and becoming some of them (Kozinets et al., 2018).

Social Media: It is an application that allows people to get along and follow friends and institutions. It is replacing some traditional media and becoming a way to someone be informed about the world.

Virtual Community: It is a set of people bounded by an interest, taste, or attitude. Virtual Communities used to have some organization and be together on a fan page, such as on Facebook. Patients are reunited in several communities (Chretien & Kind, 2013).

Viralization: It is the total spreading of content on social media. It results from several shares done by people (Meng et al., 2018; Yang et al., 2018).

Well Being: It is a set of feelings and states that make someone full of health and good living conditions.

Chapter 10
The Role of Technologies in Relationship Management and Internal Marketing:
An Approach in the Health Sector

Eduarda Mendes
Polytechnic Institute of Cávado and Ave, Portugal

Bruno Barbosa Sousa
https://orcid.org/0000-0002-8588-2422
Polytechnic Institute of Cávado and Ave, Portugal & CiTUR, Portugal & UNIAG, Portugal

Márcia Gonçalves
ISAG – European Business School, Portugal

ABSTRACT

In health, as in any other industry, technology adoption, if used appropriately, is an important asset and a success factor for a company. Nowadays, it is no longer feasible to talk about health without addressing the role of technology. In this context, the present study aims to understand the impact and role of technologies in a hospital context (e.g., Hospital de Braga) and in the relationship management from an internal perspective (internal marketing). Based on a qualitative approach, the research also aims to analyze how internal communication is made between employees and between employees and managers in the Hospital of Braga. Semi-structured interviews were conducted with five employees of the health institution, and a focus group with eight employees as well (four nurses, one computer technician, one administrative, one operational assistant, and a technical/administrative assistant). The results show that this technology is successful, but there are still some points to point out. The results also provide some discontent regarding internal marketing.

DOI: 10.4018/978-1-7998-7263-4.ch010

INTRODUCTION

In a society in constant evolution, and in an era marked by rapid technological advancement and by its affirmation and imposition, it is imperative for institutions to adjust to this new reality. The health area is by no means an exception to this rapid evolution, in recent decades there have been several technological investments in hospitals in order to facilitate the work of health professionals and consequently the care provided to patients. With the development of Information and Communication Technologies, health organizations had to adapt to new methods of operation.

The technology implemented at the Hospital de Braga has stood out positively, in the elaboration of the functions of a large part of its employees. The health institution in the North stands out at a technological level when compared to other Portuguese public hospitals, being considered one step ahead with regard to technology. As one of the best and most efficient hospitals in the NHS, with Private Public Partnership (PPP), it held its management until August 31, 2019, under the responsibility of the Melo Group, passing on September 1 of that same year for Public Business Entity (EPE), now the state takes over its management. The main objectives that this investigation set out were to understand the degree of dependence on the use of Technologies in a hospital context, to understand how technologies in a hospital context facilitate the tasks of employees, to understand the evolution of technologies over the years in the Braga Hospital, understand how technologies facilitate internal communication, and finally, understand the importance of internal marketing strategies for employee satisfaction and motivation.

Data collection was carried out through interviews and a focus group on real dependencies and current needs. Based on the qualitative analysis of the interviews and the focus group, carried out on the employees of Hospital de Braga, it is understood that the dependence on technologies is increasing. The article concludes by discussing the main conclusions and provides final observations, limitations, and possibilities for potential research.

HEALTH INFORMATION TECHNOLOGIES AND SYSTEMS

In a health organization, the use of IT is essential, and this is true both in the public and private sectors (Pollitt, 1993). With the advent of computers, devices have emerged, such as the computer, increasingly sophisticated, allowing greater speed in getting and using information (Barra et al., 2006). It is advocated in the OCDE Report (2010), "Improving Health Sector Efficiency: The Role of Information and Communication Technologies", the use of ICT in the health sector. Its use helps to reduce operating costs and clinical services by improving tasks and the way they are performed, saving time with data processing, and reducing the need to deal with paper and other documents (OCDE, 2010). In the last few years, several information systems have been developed, implemented, and updated, currently, more than 60 IS are available in primary health care and hospital care. The objective is to improve the quality of health care provision and management, increase efficiency and technologically update health institutions, improving public services, with repercussions for citizens and health professionals (Ministry of Health, 2018).

The impact of IT on the NHS began to occur in 2010, but it was in 2011 that this was most significant, starting the electronic prescription of medicines, with the objective of facilitating the citizen's access to medicines, so that he did not have to pass throughout the administrative circuit that happened until then. This advancement in health has brought benefits to doctors, pharmacists, citizens, and to the health system in general, with great cost reduction and simplification of procedures (Ministry of Health, 2018). In 2012, nationwide files were created, containing health data, using information technologies, and within the framework of the NHS. This same year, it was also marked by the launch of the health data platform, developed by the commission for clinical computerization and by the shared services of the Ministry of Health (Ministry of Health, 2018). The health data platform aims to bring people closer to the NHS and is characterized as a privileged instrument of information on health and access to services (Ministry of Health, 2013). It allows health professionals to access users' clinical information anywhere in the country and allows direct contact between the user and their family doctor (Ministry of Health, 2015). All information can be consulted and shared on the user's portal, this portal is an online platform, available since 2012, that allows consulting all the information from the NHS, with the aim of bringing citizens, health professionals, and NHS institutions closer together. In addition to the previously mentioned electronic drug prescription initiative, there was also a dematerialization of the processes associated with electronic death certificates and sick leave. Portugal was distinguished in 2017, by the European health systems observatory, as an example of good practice, being referred to as the first European country with an electronic death certificate (Ministry of Health, 2018).

Another major digital transformation in the SNS was telehealth, it is now possible to have access to the provision of health care through teleconsultations, which makes it possible to take the SNS to all citizens, regardless of geographical barriers. The SNS contact center (SNS 24), in addition to providing information and administrative services, also provides screening services, counseling whenever possible, and also makes the necessary referrals, with the aim of improving access, by releasing urgencies and hospitals (Ministry of Health, 2018). All the clinical information of each citizen, (exams, diagnoses performed, date of the last consultations, prescribed medication, among other relevant and important information on the health of the user) is now registered so that it can be shared between the user, health professionals and health service providers (Ministry of Health, 2018).

Technological advances in hospitals have been growing noticeably, and technologies have become a fundamental part of the smooth functioning of any hospital entity. On the one hand, the health professional, on the other the citizen, and between both, the information technologies.

INTERNAL MARKETING AND INTERNAL COMMUNICATION

Communicating within an organization is synonymous with motivating, estimating, integrating, improving the relationship between employees and between employee and employer, in addition to encouraging inclusion (Skwara, et al., 2012). Communication between the management of an organization and its employees is one of the elements of internal marketing and mass communication should promote information about new marketing strategies involving the use of newsletters and other sources (Tansuhaj et al., 1988). Internal communication must be made from leaders to employees and in the opposite direction, about all aspects of the company and people as a whole. Piercy (1995) adds that there must be formal meetings, reports, presentations, and good communication and response by managers to their employees. Kalla (2005), identifies four types of communication within internal communication: business communication, which is concerned with the communication skills of employees, management communication, which focuses on the management of competences and communication skills, corporate communication, where the focus is on formal communication, and finally on organizational communication, focused on philosophical and theoretical issues (Ballantyne, 2003; Bush et al, 2009).

Currently, there are several forms of internal communication, coming from the new information technologies as a means of communication, and nowadays, it is easier and faster to transmit all important information within an organization. According to Chiavenato (2014), new information technologies result in internal communication support, such as electronic mail, newsletter, video conference, and intranet. The same author argues that the sharing of information thus acquires new characteristics and becomes the main source of energy for the organization, occupying less space, less time, and greater contact between employees and management. In the near future, there were few companies that had their newsletters to communicate with external customers, and even fewer those that had internal newsletters to communicate with their employees (Carrera, 2012). As communication is valued within the organization, due to the possibilities of contact with all stakeholders, new resources and new practices are being adopted that change the structure and redefine the way in which organizations work in the 21st century (Huber et al., 1999). In the same sense, Elias and Mascaray (2003) maintain that ICT can promote a new relational life between the organization and its employees, developing a greater production capacity.

Internal communication is processed and affirmed through a multiplicity of means and instruments, but the intranet stands out as an instrument of excellence for the consolidation of an internal communication policy, which is intended to generate positive participation through a motivational reinforcement of all employees, by providing clarification on the path that the organization intends to follow and involving them in this project (Brandão, 2014). The intranet is seen as a direct channel between the organization and its employees, they are local computer networks that are connected to each other, and where only authorized persons can access (Aloy et al., 2005). The internet and intranets provide employees with power, influence communication, and collaboration, accelerate access to information, with immediate return on investment. Unlike physical installations and their functionalities, on the Intranet the space is virtually infinite, and the functionalities are only limited by the imagination (Carrera, 2012). This same author, advises the organization, to never forget to go back to the beginning, to never forget to start over, stating that an intranet is never finished, and if it is considered completed, it is because it is dead or inadequate to reality.

Thus, Information and Communication Technologies enable various forms of communication in an organization, present content exchange models, and communication between all people who are part of the company is valued, and this is fundamental to encourage integration, increase motivation and enhance the active cooperation of employees (Brandão, 2014).

INTERNAL MARKETING AND INTERNAL COMMUNICATION IN HEALTH ORGANIZATIONS

Marketing in healthcare organizations is a relatively recent practice, and that said, for IM practices to work properly in healthcare, it is necessary that it follow the philosophy of business management, (Azêdo & Alves, 2013).

In the health area, internal marketing is mainly concerned with the way in which the organization's management develops its educational teachings, the way it communicates the organization's perspectives and creates reward systems that improve the capacity and satisfaction of its employees, (Tsai, 2014). Organizations whose main objective is to teach their employees should shape their learning culture accordingly. To that end, Watkins and Ellinger (1998) suggest that dialogue, interaction, and the exchange of knowledge between members of different departments be encouraged.

If the leaders of an organization are able to positively guide the teachings and consequently the attitudes of their professionals, this can, in turn, increase the level of service provided to patients. Organizational commitment and job satisfaction, therefore, influence the quality of service, and thus Tsai, (2014), in his empirical study, identified some hypotheses for the question of behavioral changes on the part of nurses in their daily work, to that the results can be as positive as possible, and so that the commitment to the organization is increasingly greater and better, such as creating training influenced by internal marketing in organizations, encourage continuous learning, highlighting the way in which leaders can empower their employees, creating an organization that learns to influence organizational commitment, and using internal marketing as a mediator between creating a learning organization and commitment organizational (Ammenwerth et al., 2003, 2004). Also in relation to new employees, it is important that in a first stage, they are provided with ways to get to know the new job, the company, its internal functioning, the functional relations that it establishes with other services and bodies, that is essential both for the development of the new employee and for their motivation (Monteiro et al., 2020).

A health organization that cares about its employees, that cares about its continuous teaching, may be able to guarantee a stable provision of quality health care, and in turn patient satisfaction. The use of internal marketing, consequently, makes the employees of a hospital transmit the objectives of a hospital abroad (Tsai, 2014).

Motivation

He great challenge for organizations is to motivate their employees, that is, to make them stimulated, committed, confident, and above all that they are happy and motivated in their daily tasks. Motivation is born as a strategy for MI, instilled in promoting success in the company's results, with the active partnership of all employees (Azêdo & Alves, 2013). An employee, when valued in an organization, tends to perform his duties better, and this has positive consequences for an organization. An employee tends to be motivated more easily when he realizes that there is a reward in response to his effectiveness at work or when the organization offers him professional possibilities and expectations (Cruz, 2012). According to Kotler et al., (2006), motivation is necessary to initiate any action, maintain it, or end it. The motivation is contained within the people themselves and can be largely influenced by external sources or by the employee's own work in the company (Chiavenato, 2014). With motivated internal customers, the results will be as expected, productivity increases and the company is able to achieve the desired success. It is also important to note that with motivation related to individual needs, expectations, incentives, and objectives, positive reinforcements, decision making, and acknowledgments, many of the IM actions adopted by the managers of organizations in order to motivate their employees. employees must also go through reducing the distance between the hierarchical level and the employees (Monteiro et al., 2020). The IM challenge is thus, in any organization, to motivate its employees, making them determined, confident, committed, and enthusiastic in the development of their work, to achieve the organization's objectives (Chiavenato, 2014).

Motivation is undoubtedly very important for the good functioning of organizations, and one of the main steps for achieving success.

Satisfaction

Internal marketing, in the first phase, was explored as a driver of satisfaction and motivation of employees, where it was found that they are subject to fluctuations in performance, as they are emotional beings (Rafiq & Ahmed, 2000). Rodrigues et al. (2016) affirm thus, that the satisfaction of an employee at work can be explained by a positive or pleasant emotional state, which comes from the experiences lived in the workplace. Different levels of performance can result in a variation in the quality of the work produced (Varey, 2001). Internal marketing is important to attract, develop, motivate, and retain qualified employees, through the design of jobs as products that meet their needs (Berry & Parasuraman, 2001). The same authors state that internal marketing is the philosophy of treating employees like customers and is the strategy of modeling / creating work products to meet human needs. These authors insist that the focus of any company should be the satisfaction of its employees. Lings (2004) also states that highly satisfied and motivated employees are the main success factors for companies. One of the theories related to job satisfaction is the theory of Herzberg the two-way theory. In this theory, two factors are identified: motivational factors and hygiene factors. Motivational factors are related to challenging work, recognition, and responsibility, and in turn, hygiene factors are related to job security, remuneration, and benefits. Although these factors alone are not sufficient to promote employee satisfaction, the lack of them can, however, contribute to their dissatisfaction (Ewen, 1964). It is also possible that a company can measure the satisfaction of its workers through the use of surveys (an effective way) so that they can identify attitudes and opinions, verify what is good and what is less well, and review current policies of the company, for the satisfaction of its employees (Tso et al., 2014). It is important for managers to realize that satisfying and motivating their employees is a fundamental task so that they can prevent them from looking for other safer work opportunities, avoiding the loss of very valuable employees (Akroush et al., 2012).

TECHNOLOGY AT BRAGA HOSPITAL

In recent years, several information systems and technologies have been developed, implemented, and updated in health institutions. The objective is to improve the quality of healthcare provision and management, increase efficiency and technologically update institutions, improving public services, with repercussions for citizens and professionals.

According to technological evolution, the IS in health has developed rapidly, so that the information is used in the most efficient way in the management processes of health services, allowing efficient use of resources involved in the provision of care of health (Andrade & Falk, 2001). Information technologies (IT) and information systems (SI) are spread in different ways, in hospital entities, among the simplest communication and information applications, to the most sophisticated equipment for diagnosis and disease screening, and in relation to all this, Braga Hospital is no exception. Freixo and Rocha, (2014), also state those information systems are more than an advantage, they are a requirement and should be experienced by organizations as a constant concern. "Since 2014, Hospital de Braga has been considered the best hospital in the country, for obtaining the best national classification in clinical excellence in the national health assessment system (SINAS), developed by the health regulatory authority. Since 2015, it has won first place in the group of best medium / large hospitals in the National Health Service in the following prizes: TOP 5 - Hospital Excellence, promoted by IASIST - multinational hospital benchmarking company (Hospital de Braga, 2019b). Among the various distinctions achieved to date, the following awards stand out in terms of the technology implemented at Hospital de Braga (Hospital de Braga, 2019a):

- Hospital do Future Award (2013), is an initiative of the hospital of the future forum and aims to highlight people and organizations that contributed to the development of Health organizations in Portugal. This distinction was due to the quality management system implemented Braga Hospital.
- Sustainable health award (2015), is an initiative of business newspaper and Sanofi and aims to distinguish, disseminate, and encourage good practices and health sustainability in Portugal. The prize was awarded in relation to clinical quality and health results, taking into account the user's experience, environmental responsibility, innovation and technology in health and economic and financial sustainability.
- Award for excellence in the health sector (2016), it is an award recognized by the Minister of Health attributed to health services, departments or units, with high competencies in the provision of health care in clinical situations that require highly differentiated technical and technological resources,

due to the low prevalence of the disease, the complexity of its diagnosis or treatment and its high costs. This distinction was attributed to the area of adult oncology, more specifically to the treatment of cancer of the rectum by the general surgery service.

Braga Hospital has several types of technology, information systems, equipment with technology considered to be first-rate, to help provide health care to around 1.2 million people in the districts of Braga and Viana do Castelo. Currently, several general computer applications are in use in the health organization, such as (Hospital de Braga, 2018):

- SI CTH - a Computer System for Consultation in Time and Hours;
- SIGLIC - a Computer System for Managing Registrant Lists for Surgery;
- GESTCARE CCI - an IT System for registration and monitoring of the National Network of Integrated Continuous Care;
- RNU - National Registry of Users;
- PDS - a Health Data Platform (safe surgery registration, electronic prescription and others);
- SIM @ SNS - a National Health Service Monitoring Information System with three components: SDM @ SNS, SIARS and MIM @ UF;
- SICA - a Contracting and Monitoring Information System;
- SIMH - an Information System for Hospital Morbidity.

In addition to these general computer applications, there is also a specific computer system in use at Hospital de Braga, with the name glintt, used by administrative and clinical areas, for hospital and patient management. The use of health information systems has ceased to be sporadic and has become a rule for hospitals, to allow the reduction of data processing and processing and to guarantee the validity and timely availability of all information. health information (Lippeveld et al., 2000).

Braga Hospital has been worthy of great prizes, demonstrating the quality of its care, which without the aid of technology, would make a large part of these results impossible to achieve.

METHODOLOGY

This study used a case analysis research project to investigate the propositions, semi-structured interviews were conducted with five employees of the health institution (two nurses, a lawyer, a data analyst and a computer technician), and a focus group with eight elements, also professionals from Hospital de Braga (four nurses, a computer technician, an administrative assistant, an operational assistant, and a technical / administrative assistant), to try to understand the degree of dependence on technologies and the impact within the institution. This study provides a basis for the systematic study of subjectivity, such as a person's opinions, opinions, or attitudes. The main constructs are extracted from empirical surveys among employees of Hospital de Braga, in which data analysis was carried out along a qualitative analysis. Qualitative research methodologies are inspired, among others, by the assumptions of the constructivist paradigm (Guba & Lincoln, 1994). The reality is, according to the principles of this paradigm, socially constructed and perceived as a mental and intangible construction, with a social and experiential basis, predicting the existence of multiple realities (Denzin & Lincoln, 2000). The investigator and the object of investigation are linked to each other (Guba & Lincoln, 1994). The qualitative paradigm is the most used in the scope of research, it covers several ways to plan an investigation, and may eventually contribute to a better understanding of the sources (Bell, 1993). In this type of investigation, the roles of the researcher and the investigated have similar characteristics in that both are at the same time, interpreters and knowledge builders according to their socio-cultural schemes, in a process of the double search for meaning, which is called "hermeneutic duo" (Usher, 1996, cited by Coutinho, 2011). It is a method of collecting information that consists of oral, individual, or group conversations, with several carefully selected people, whose degree of relevance, validity, and reliability is analyzed from the perspective of the objectives of collecting information (De Ketele & Roegiers, 1999). This type of instrument facilitates the interviewees' sharing of perspectives and experiences on the phenomenon observed by the interviewer (Wahyuni, 2012).

The focus group is one of the qualitative research techniques and is considered to be one of the most important. This technique is known for the elaboration of an interview in an unstructured and natural way, regulated by the researcher, with a minimum of 8 participants and a maximum of 12, it is not advisable to be less than 8 and more than 12, as the sample can insufficient or excessive working. The main objective is "to obtain an in-depth view by listening to a group of people talking about problems of interest to the researcher" (Malhotra, 2002, p. 156). The importance of this technique is in the unexpected results that can be obtained in a "free discussion". The realization of a focus group can be very beneficial at the stage of data collection in an investigation. In the present investigation, the participants in the focus group were chosen from a non-probabilistic sample, which means that they were purposely selected by the researchers to collect the necessary information (Wahyuni, 2012). The criteria for the selection of stakeholders, related to the specific context of the study, focused on the fact that individuals work at Braga Hospital, trying to have some diversity in the ages of the stakeholders so that there was a slightly different opinion about the study problem. The technique used was always content analysis.

With the research of several researchers dedicated to technology and IM, more specifically, to technology and marketing in health, the concept has been deepening, and IM is still a novelty in the health area. Finally, some employees from some branches of Hospital de Braga were selected and interviews and a focus group were conducted. It is concluded that, in general, Braga Hospital is one step ahead of the other Portuguese hospitals in relation to technology, and consequently its employees are more dependent on the implemented technologies. This came, in general, to make life easier for health professionals, and most of them no longer see themselves working without it. In turn, the IM still needs to be worked on, because in relation to this matter the Hospital is still far below what was expected by its collaborators.

Sample

The interviewees were selected with the aim of a better interpretation of the subject matter of the study, representing the employees of the Hospital de Braga. It was observed that, on several occasions, the interviewees also easily placed themselves in the role of the user, allowing them to enrich the content of the interview. Five interviews were carried out (Table 1), and a focus group with 8 participants (Table 2). To maintain confidentiality, a table was drawn up where the interviewees were listed and characterized. For the analysis of the study, there was an interview script, between eighteen to twenty-two questions, some questions being asked only to some employees, considering their specific areas. Five observation themes were devised: theme 1 (Understanding the degree of dependence on the use of Technologies in the hospital context), theme 2 (Understanding how IT in the hospital context facilitates the tasks of employees), theme 3 (Understanding which the evolution of IT over the years at Hospital de Braga), theme 4 (Understanding how IT facilitates internal communication), and theme 5 (Understanding the importance of internal marketing strategies for employee satisfaction and motivation).

The interviews started with questions related to the use of technologies used by the interviewees and their dependence on each other's daily lives. The target participants of the study showed evidence that led us to conclude that there is indeed a great technological dependence, and their daily use is a fact among them. There is, on their part, a clear awareness of the value that technology brings and the help it offers, without it, everything would be different (negatively), more complicated and for some, the information sought would be much longer and sometimes impossible in due time (Table 3).

In the second phase, we wanted to understand how the digitization of documentation in the hospital context is seen by its professionals. There is a great deal of subjection in relation to technologies, and to return to the age of paper is generally unthinkable among the interviewees. Digitization is viewed favorably, and for nurses not having

Table 1. Five interviews in the context of the study conducted at Braga Hospital

Interviewee	Genre	Position occupied by the respondent
A	Female	Nurse
B	Male	Nurse
C	Male	IT technician
D	Female	Data Analyst
E	Male	Lawyer

Source: Authors

Table 2. Eight participants in the focus group in the context of the study conducted at Braga Hospital

Interviewee	Genre	Position occupied by the respondent	Professional experience
A	Male	Nurse	5 years
B	Feminine	Nurse	26 years
C	Male	Nurse	10 years
D	Feminine	Nurse	1 year
E	Male	Computer technician	8 years
F	Feminine	Administrative	6 years
G	Feminine	Operational Assistant	2 years
H	Feminine	Technical / Administrative Assistant	2 years

Source: Authors

the patient's history digitized and easily accessible on the computer, it is already unthinkable. If there is a computer stop, the hospital generally stops, no one can work like that. However, the general idea that technologies are beneficial and help in the daily life of each employee, is questioned by nurses, when talking about the

Table 3. Sample of illustrative phrases from the interviews in the context of the study conducted at Hospital de Braga

	Illustrative phrases
Participant B	*"(...) of course, now practically everything is done with the help of technology, and what is not, has to be transcribed there (...)."*
Participant C	*I always use technology, the opposite didn't even make sense. "*
Participant E	*"I practically always use technology, but there are things in my area that have yet to be done and consulted on paper (…)"*

Source: Authors

computer system they use, the glintt, who claim to force them to lose a lot of time recording unnecessary things. It was also questioned the existence of training courses for adapting to technology and consequently its updates, which we found that new professionals, depending on the area, can count on training, or with the support and explanation of colleagues in the service, so that, adapt to all the technology implemented and necessary for the elaboration of their functions. We realized that using technology, as a work tool at Braga Hospital, is, in general, a facilitator in the execution of tasks, you can save a lot of time by being able to access everything through a computer. We also found that the information that is passed on the patient is now, in the age of technology, more accurate and secure.

Table 4. Sample of illustrative phrases from the interviews in the context of the study conducted at Hospital de Braga

	Illustrative phrases
Participant D	*"Glintt really requires us to spend a lot of time with it, and that time is taken away from the patient."*
Participant C	*"(...) If we went back to the paper in general, here in the hospital, most of them, not to mention all the employees, were unable to work (...)."*
Participant D	*"And whenever there is a change, we can request training. The duration of the training is never very long, it takes a few hours, and it always depends on the importance of the system and its importance for our practice."*

Source: Authors

Even though Braga Hospital is a highly developed hospital in relation to technologies, part of its collaborators does not use the latest communication technologies as a first option, preferring and valuing personal communication between co-workers. The use of email happens when the matter is not urgent and does not need an immediate response. However, some professionals stress that, in addition to the importance of being able to exchange information in person, or by telephone, the latest technologies have brought other facilities and amenities these days. Technology (email) brings employees closer to managers and vice versa, creating facilities to communicate and deal with many matters between superiors and employees.

In the face of the Hospital's employees, there is discontent about the lack of concern on the part of their superiors and the institution to motivate them and keep them satisfied.

It is concluded that the Hospital de Braga is quite developed with regard to technology, and investments in this regard are notorious, however, there is still a lot of work ahead, with regard to the motivation and satisfaction of its employees.

Table 5. Sample of illustrative phrases from the interviews in the context of the study conducted at Hospital de Braga

	Illustrative phrases
Participant B	*"No motivation, no satisfaction. Nobody cares if you are tired, unmotivated if our hours are excessive…"*
Participant G	*"Motivation?! Satisfaction?! Who cares about that?! The bosses are certainly not."*

Source: Authors

FINDINGS

The technology was implemented in the healthcare organization about 21 years ago, and since then, continuous efforts have been made in relation to its implementation and modification, so that the results can be the best and fastest possible. It was always implemented at the right time, which leads us to conclude that the Braga Hospital, in addition to being one step ahead of many other hospitals in terms of innovation, invests in this direction in a very thoughtful way. The new technologies introduced a set of new organizational aspects, increased the capacity to archive documentation, analyze and transmit large volumes of complex information, in a more secure, flexible, reliable, and immediate way. Braga Hospital is one of the most technologically advanced hospitals in the country, and as it becomes more digital, consequently its employees become more dependent on this technology. This fact is known and made aware of among professionals, and the ease with which they are now able to access all information is unquestionable.

It is felt among the employees of Hospital de Braga, the appreciation and dependence in relation to access to information in an easy and quick way. The dependence is so great that, in the event of an interruption in the system, some professionals even refuse to work, even going so far as to send the sick away. The truth is that the age of paper is moving towards the end, and the need to adapt to this new reality is perceived and felt among the participants. Increasingly, technology provides them with security in what they do, everything is recorded, everything they do every day is pointed out, and no one can question their work. It is undeniable that technology is a great help in the area of health, no one doubts that nowadays diagnoses are faster and more accurate, that there is greater agility in consultation and information exchange. However, despite all this dependency, there are still areas in the hospital, which do not use only technology, and sporadically, there is still something or other that has to be done using paper, as is the case with nurses.

Braga Hospital, has made continuous efforts in relation to the implementation and modification of technology, and all these efforts are generally recognized and valued by its collaborators, they have very positive opinions regarding the impact of digitization, which in addition reducing the loss of information, gives them more confidence and reliability. The fact that the information is now more accurate, and its tampering more difficult to happen, is also an added value and security for the user himself. In addition to all the advantages, there was an annoyance on the part of nursing professionals regarding the information system with which they work daily, the glintt, testifying to the fact that it is still far from meeting the needs of professionals who if they are forced to work with him. From the outset, it seems to us a necessary condition that the elaboration and definition of an information system incorporate the collaboration of all the people involved in all areas and not only the technical area of the institution (Berg, 2001), thus reducing the probability of dissatisfaction with part of its users towards the IS and managing to overcome this problem experienced by nurses at Braga Hospital. Health professionals may feel that the system does not fit and is not appropriate for their work routines, and this is because they are not free to give their opinion and contribution to the elaboration of the same. Regarding the reliability of the information systems, implemented at Braga Hospital, the lack of concern is notorious, due to the almost inexistence of failures at the technical level, which leads us to conclude that they work close to perfection, in relation to possible failures. The Hospital provides training to its employees about the technology implemented so that they understand its operation and can use it in the most positive way possible. Regarding the glintt information system, there are also training courses on how it works, but in this case, its duration is continuous. The health institution also values the integration of its new employees, who can count on training, so that they can adapt to all the technology implemented and necessary for the elaboration of their functions. However, that on the part of the Braga Hospital, there is a preference to hire professionals who have already interned in the health unit, so that the integrations are no longer a "headache", and the training is unnecessary so that this charge is not necessary. However, there is a motto of mutual assistance towards new professionals, being accompanied and supported by older colleagues.

TIC facilitated the various forms of internal communication and the exchange of content, came to enhance communication between all the people who are part of a company, and all this is fundamental to encourage integration, increase motivation and enhance the active cooperation of employees (Brandão, 2014). However, some of the professionals at the Braga Hospital may not always use technology as a means of communication, as their profession does not allow it.

The nursing area requires special and attentive care towards the patient in almost all situations, and, consequently, it has to use what allows it to communicate in a faster and safer way, always in favor of the patient, which is understandable because a minute can save a life. When it comes to caring for people, when human life is at stake, new technologies are not always the most beneficial form of communication between nursing professionals, as they need an immediate exchange of information, which leads them to give priority and to value personal communication with co-workers. Relevant information is always passed orally between colleagues in the same unit when making the shift, and only in case of doubt do they use the computer system. The use of email happens when the matter is not urgent and does not need an immediate response. However, other hospital areas do not require close proximity to the user, which allows them to take greater advantage of new communication technologies, and in addition to using the phone with some frequency, it is by email that most part of internal communications. The fact that they have some margin of response time, and that they can reach several people at the same time, regardless of distance, are some of the advantages of using new communication technologies. That said, there is thus a distinct way of prioritizing the various forms of communication within the Braga Hospital, in the different areas of study. As for the internal communication between managers and collaborators, collaborators, and managers, technology, more specifically email, emerged to create a greater "rapprochement" between them, there is now ease in communicating and dealing with many matters between superiors and collaborators. The email is seen as a reminder and sometimes security of what was treated. However, there is an interest on the part of some managers in selecting the subjects that they think are pertinent to be registered, which ends up not giving freedom to the collaborators to deal with all the matters that they think opportune by email. Although, it is also necessary not to fall into the facilitation of technologies, because sometimes there is a lack of care on the part of some professionals, and they end up using the media in an excessive way, which ends up being harmful in internal relations of the health organization, leading to everything being dealt with in a more virtual way, and ignoring the need to create some types of bonds necessary for the good functioning of the hospital. Technologies, if used properly, with awareness, can be a good communication strategy within an organization. Since the challenge of MI, in any organization, is to motivate its employees, making them decisive, confident, committed and enthusiastic in the development of their work, in order to achieve the organization's objectives (Chiavenato, 2014), we analyze whether internal marketing principles are being adopted in the best way by Braga Hospital, and we try to understand if they have an impact on the satisfaction and motivation of its employees. Although some participants feel that these initiatives, referring to the existence of training, events, among other things, most of them, demonstrated that there is no concern on the part of the superiors and the institution to motivate and keep them satisfied. We were also able to conclude, after being asked about this topic, that nursing professionals feel a great deal of dissatisfaction in terms of salaries, schedules, exhaustive work, and, until there may be some initiative on the part of the hospital with the intention of to motivate them, this will never be enough if it is not an initiative that directly affects them, and in relation to the needs that they have been demanding.

However, Braga Hospital shows a little concern with the satisfaction and motivation of its employees, but within what he (hospital) thinks is relevant. As for the acknowledgments on the part of the managers, in relation to the efforts and work of the employees of Braga Hospital, these are not felt, and the testimonies given by the participants convey the demotivation and dissatisfaction on the subject, the opposite of what is intended when one speaks of IM. It is notorious, after hearing all the participants, that the concern on the part of the health institution, about the principles of internal marketing, is quite reduced. It is felt, in general, the discontent of the participants in relation to the valorization of their efforts.

DISCUSSION

Braga Hospital is one of the most technologically advanced hospitals in the country, it was the first hospital in Portugal, which in 2011 introduced a "paper-free" information system platform, with the aim of ensuring better productivity and service efficiency. In the health sector, organizations need information systems that ensure timely and necessary information for different health professionals (Sousa, 2005). We know that in the past all user information was passed on to paper, its organization and filing was a lengthy process, in which chronological order was often the only criterion for the organization.

If for Bürkle et al. (2001) an SI when compared to the records in paper format, are more complete, achieving better and faster accessibility, better organization, and ease in interpreting what is there writing, for the nurses at the Braga Hospital, it's not like that. Although they are not indifferent to all the benefits of technology, they do not overlook the fact that SI Glint does not suit their work needs in the best way, and they criticize it several times during the interview. It is noteworthy that, in addition to the discontent with the time that they are obliged to have towards the computer system used, the participants, affirm that if they could, they changed the way the responsible people face the information systems, making them responsible for the waste of time that these imply. The implementation of an information system in the health area is a process whose success depends on several types of activities, one of which is the teaching of users, training them and teaching them about their use (Tan, 1995), so that the search for information can thus be faster, and there is no lack of knowledge at this level. Since digitization transmits more precision and security to health professionals, we must not forget that data are entered by people, people who are susceptible to error, and therefore, one should not always have all the information for certain, yet moreover, when they are health-related issues, where a small mistake can sometimes have big consequences. Questioning, and communicating, in certain cases, should be considered important. Another reality, and no less important, is the fragility of computer systems, which, however careful they may be, can be the target of a computer attack, and confidential information can inevitably pass abroad. Despite the evident concerns in responding to advances in technology, there is a point, that Hospital de Braga, also does not do without - the integration of new employees in relation to the technology used. The new professionals, depending on the area, can count on training, or with the support and explanation of colleagues in the service, so that they can adapt to all the technology implemented and necessary for the elaboration of their functions.

Communicating within an organization is synonymous with motivating, estimating, integrating, improving the relationship between employee and employer, it means encouraging inclusion (Skwara et al., 2012). Having good internal communication, between colleagues, and between employees and managers, is a challenging task today, and in this matter, Braga Hospital does not seem to fall short of expectations. Although technologies are not always the most appropriate means of communication between health professionals, they still have them available, and whenever justified they can use them. Keeping employees motivated and satisfied is one of the fundamental objectives for a company to achieve satisfactory results. Finding out what the needs of its workers are, favoring professional growth, offering benefits, are some of the aspects that a company must consider when it intends to achieve success (Parasuraman et al., 1985). There is a certain concern, on the part of Braga Hospital, with the satisfaction of its employees, and care in motivating them, with prizes, training, and initiatives aimed at their interaction, among other things. However, there is clearly, on the part of the nurses interviewed, dissatisfaction with the heads, and with the hospital in general, this class of health workers is so dissatisfied, in terms of excessive hours, in terms of salary, which clearly conveys discontent in this regard. An employee tends to be motivated more easily when he realizes that there is a reward in response to his effectiveness at work or when the organization offers him professional possibilities and expectations (Cruz, 2012).

Every year, a satisfaction survey is carried out to the employees of the Braga Hospital, where in addition to asking several questions to understand the level of satisfaction, it is also possible to make pertinent suggestions in this matter, this practice goes against the defended by Tso et al., (2014), the use of surveys should be used so that one can identify attitudes and opinions and see what is good and what is less well. The impact of this survey is little felt or practically nil, there is no clear feedback regarding the surveys answered.

CONCLUSION AND FUTURE RESEARCH

Braga Hospital employees are really dependent on the technologies implemented, and if, on the one hand, they are obliged to use them, "*we are obliged to use the technologies on a daily basis (...)*" (participant D), since the technologies are essential for the health institution, (Sousa, 2005), on the other hand, when they temporarily come without them, they are no longer able to work, "*(...), they feel completely lost, (...)*" (participant C). The implemented technologies are thus, facilitating the daily tasks of the employees of Braga Hospital, "*We have access to everything in a more easy way*" (participant F), but, nevertheless, there is a need to improve the SI glint, claimed during the entire interview by nurses. The improvement of the IS, and its evaluation, must be considered in any hospital institution (Gable et al., 2008), even more so, when a professional class such as nursing, demonstrates discontent in this sense.

Braga Hospital, like other hospitals, needs to ensure timely and necessary information for its professionals, and in this regard, this hospital institution has made several and thoughtful investments "*It is a hospital that is always innovating, this does not for, there are always new things*" (participant C). As in the entire health area, in the northern health organization, the implementation of technology is a process whose success depends on various types of activities, including the teaching of its users, training them and teaching them about its use (Tan, 1995), an aspect that this hospital shows not to do without.

The role of technology is very important in the internal communication of Braga Hospital, and regardless of whether there are health professionals who can only use it in a timely manner, this is, in general, quite important in that it allows employees to get closer to each other and also in relation to bosses, Baptista (2009), thus facilitating his communication, "*Bring everyone together, now it is easier to discuss a matter with superiors, (...).*".The challenge of IM is in any organization, to motivate its employees, making them determined, confident, committed and enthusiastic in the development of their work, in order to achieve the organization's objectives (Chiavenato, 2014), and for that very reason, Braga Hospital, should reflect better on its IM challenges, taking into account the discontent felt, "*Nobody cares about our satisfaction and if we are motivated.*" (participant A), and rethink the best way to achieve them, always prioritizing the motivation and satisfaction of its employees.

This study followed an entirely qualitative approach, using semi-structured interviews, and the development of a focus group. However, it will also be important in future work to consider a quantitative approach (i.e., administering surveys by questionnaire) that allows researchers to increase the strength of the data collection instruments and thereby improve the quality of the results obtained.

There was a difficulty in generalizing the results obtained since the sample was non-probabilistic and subject to a certain context of an investigation. The range of professions of the focus group and interview participants should be larger and more diverse, focusing on ages over 35, so that one could have a better conclusion about the study. It is also suggested a study extended to other public hospitals in the country, in order to be able to make data comparability.

REFERENCES

Akroush, M. N., Abu, E. L., & Samen, A. A. (2012). An empirical investigation of the mediating role of relationship marketing skills on the relationship between customer satisfaction and customer loyalty. *International Journal of Internet Marketing and Advertising*, *7*(1), 1–30. doi:10.1504/IJIMA.2012.044956

Aloy, J. A., Delgado, M. R., & Pérez, X. R. (2005). *Comunicación Interna en la empresa*. Editorial UOC.

Alves, G. M., Sousa, B. M., & Machado, A. (2020). The Role of Digital Marketing and Online Relationship Quality in Social Tourism: A Tourism for All Case Study. In J. D. Santos & Ó. L. Silva (Eds.), *Digital Marketing Strategies for Tourism, Hospitality, and Airline Industries* (pp. 49–70). IGI Global. doi:10.4018/978-1-5225-9783-4.ch003

Ammenwerth, E., Brender, J., Nykänen, P., Prokosch, H., Rigby, M., & Talmon, J. (2004). Visions and strategies to improve evaluation of health information systems Reflections and lessons based on the HIS-EVAL workshop in Innsbruck. *International Journal of Medical Informatics*, *73*(6), 479–491. doi:10.1016/j.ijmedinf.2004.04.004 PMID:15171977

Ammenwerth, E., Gräber, S., Herrmann, G., Bürkle, T., & König, J. (2003). Evaluation of health information systems - Problems and challenges. *International Journal of Medical Informatics*, *71*(2-3), 125–135. doi:10.1016/S1386-5056(03)00131-X PMID:14519405

Andrade, D. G., & Falk, J. A. (2001). Eficácia de Sistemas de Informação e Percepção de Mudança Organizacional: Um Estudo de Caso. *Revista de Administração Contemporanêa*, *5*(3), 53–84. doi:10.1590/S1415-65552001000300004

Azêdo, D. F., & Alves, M. H. (2013). Práticas de marketing interno nas organizações de saúde e a sua influência na motivação dos colaboradores. *Revista Portuguesa de Saude Publica*, *31*(2), 201–212. doi:10.1016/j.rpsp.2013.05.003

Ballantyne, D. (2003). A relationship-mediated theory of internal marketing. *European Journal of Marketing, 37*(9), 1242–1260. doi:10.1108/03090560310486979

Barra, D., Nascimento, E., Martins, J., Albuquerque, G., & Erdmann, A. (2006). Evolução histórica e impacto da tecnologia na área da saúde e da enfermagem. *Revista Eletrónica de Enfermagem, 8*(3), 422–430.

Berg, M. (2001). Implementing information systems in health care organizations: Myths and challenges. *International Journal of Medical Informatics, 64*(2-3), 143–156. doi:10.1016/S1386-5056(01)00200-3 PMID:11734382

Berry, L. L., & Parasuraman, A. (2001). *Marketing Services: Competing Through Quality*. Simon and Schuster.

Brandão, N. (2014). A importância da Comunicação Interna para a motivação e participação em Organizações Positivas. In M. Artur (Org.), Gestão de Recursos Humanos. Escolar Editora.

Bürkle, T., Ammenwerth, E., Prokosch, H., & Dudeck, J. (2001). Evaluation of clinical information systems. What can be evaluated and what cannot? *Journal of Evaluation in Clinical Practice, 7*(4), 373–385. doi:10.1046/j.1365-2753.2001.00291.x PMID:11737529

Bush, M., Lederer, A., Li, X., Palmisano, J., & Rao, S. (2009). The alignment of information systems with organizational objectives and strategies in health care. *International Journal of Medical Informatics, 78*(7), 446–456. doi:10.1016/j.ijmedinf.2009.02.004 PMID:19307148

Carrera, F. (2012). *Marketing Digital na Versão 2.0 – O que não pode ignorar* (2nd ed.). Edições Sílabo.

Chiavenato, I. (2014). *Gestão de pessoas: O novo papel dos recursos humanos nas organizações*. Manole.

Coutinho, C. P. (2011). *Metodologia de Investigação em Ciências Sociais e Humanas: Teoria e Prática*. Edições Almedina.

Cruz, C. A. (2012). A Importância da Motivação e da Liderança nas organizações. *Revista Interfaces Científicas-Humanas e Sociais, 1*(1), 73–79. doi:10.17564/2316-3801.2012v1n1p73-79

De Ketele, J. M., & Roegiers, X. (1999). *Metodologia de Recolha de Dados. Fundamentos dos métodos de observações, de questionários, de entrevistas e de estudo de documentos*. Instituto Piaget.

Denzin, N. K., & Lincoln, Y. S. (2000). *Handbook of qualitative research*. SAGE Publications.

Elias, J., & Mascaray, J. (2003). *Más allá de la comunicación interna: La intracomunicación*. Ediciones Gestión 2000.

Ewen, R. B. (1964). Some determinants of job satisfaction: A study of the generality of Herzberg's theory. *The Journal of Applied Psychology*, *48*(3), 161–163. doi:10.1037/h0048383

Freixo, J., & Rocha, Á. (2014). Arquitetura de Informação de Suporte à Gestão da Qualidade em Unidades Hospitalares. *Revista Ibérica de sistemas e Tecnologias de Informação, 14*, 1-15.

Gable, G. G., Sedera, D., & Chan, T. (2008). Re-conceptualizing Information System Success: The IS-Impact Measurement Model. *Journal of the Association for Information*, *9*(7), 377–408. doi:10.17705/1jais.00164

Guba, E. G., & Lincoln, Y. S. (1994). Competing paradigms in qualitative research. In N. K. Denzin & Y. S. Lincoln (Eds.), *Handbook of qualitative research* (pp. 163–194). SAGE Publications.

Hospital de Braga. (2018). *Relatório anual sobre o acesso a cuidados de saúde*. Author.

Hospital de Braga. distinções. (2019a). *O Hospital: distinções do Hospital de Braga*. https://www.hospitaldebraga.pt/hospital/distincoes-do-hospital-de-braga

Hospital de Braga. Sobre nós. (2019b). *O Hospital: sobre nós*. https://www.hospitaldebraga.pt/hospital/sobre-nos

Huber, G. P., Sutcliffe, K. M., Miller, C., & Glick, W. (1993). Understanding and predictingorganizational change. In G. Huber & W. H. Glick (Eds.), *Organizational Change and redesing* (pp. 215–254). Oxford University Press.

Kalla, H. K. (2005). Integrated internal communications: A multidisciplinary perspective. *Corporate Communications*, *10*(4), 302–314. doi:10.1108/13563280510630106

Kotler, P. (1991). *Marketing management analysis, planning, implementation, and control*. Prentice-Hall.

Kotler, P., & Keller, K. (2006). Administração de marketing. Academic Press.

Lings, I. N. (2004). Internal Market Orientation. Construct and Consequences. *Journal of Business Research*, *57*(4), 405–413. doi:10.1016/S0148-2963(02)00274-6

Lippeveld, T., Sauerborn, R., & Bodart, C. (2000). *Design and implementation of health information systems*. World Health Organization.

Malhotra, N. K. (2002). Pesquisa de Marketing: Uma orientação aplicada. *The Bookman*.

Ministry of Health. (2013). *Relatório Anual Sobre o Acesso a Cuidados de Saúde nos Estabelecimentos do SNS e Entidades Convencionadas*. https://www.sns.gov.pt/wp-content/uploads/2016/07/20140724_RA_Acesso_2013V12.pdf

Ministry of Health. (2015). *Relatório Anual Sobre o Acesso a Cuidados de Saúde nos Estabelecimentos do SNS e Entidades Convencionadas*. https://www.sns.gov.pt/wp-content/uploads/2016/11/Relat%C3%B3rio-Anual-sobre-o-Acesso-a-Cuidados-Sa%C3%BAde-no-SNS-2015-MS.pdf

Ministry of Health. (2018). *Retrato da Saúde*. https://www.sns.gov.pt/retrato-da-saude-2018/

Monteiro, B., Santos, V. P., Reis, I., Sampaio, M., Sousa, B., Martinho, F., Sousa, M. J., & Au-Young-Oliveira, M. (2020). Employer Branding Applied to SMEs: A Pioneering Model Proposal for Attracting and Retaining Talent. *Information (Basel)*, *11*(12), 574. doi:10.3390/info11120574

Parasuraman, A., Zeithaml, V. A., & Berry, L. L. (1985). A conceptual model of service quality and its implications for future research. *Journal of Marketing*, *49*(4), 41–50. doi:10.1177/002224298504900403

Piercy, F. N. (1995). Customer satisfaction and the internal market; marketing our customers to our employees. *Journal of Marketing Practice: Applied Marketing Science*, *1*(1), 22–44. doi:10.1108/EUM0000000003878

Pollitt, C. (1993). *Managerialism and the Public Services: Cuts or Cultural Change*. Blackwell Publishers.

Rafiq, M., & Ahmed, P. K. (2000). Advances in the internal marketing concept: Definitions, synthesis and extension. *Journal of Services Marketing*, *14*(4), 449–462. doi:10.1108/08876040010347589

Rodrigues, A., Queirós, A., & Pires, C. (2016). A influência do marketing interno nas atitudes e comportamentos dos colaboradores: Aplicacão a uma organizacão de cuidados sociais e de saúde. *Revista Portuguesa de Saude Publica*, *34*(3), 292–304. doi:10.1016/j.rpsp.2016.08.001

Shortliffe, E. H., & Cimino, J. J. (2006). *Biomedical Informatics: Computer Applications in Health Care and Biomedicine*. Springer Science. doi:10.1007/0-387-36278-9

Skwara, A. S., Panella, C., Mendonça, D., Garcia, H., Cremonine, I., Goulart, L., & Glogowski, M. (2012). *Caderno de Comunicação Organizacional: por que investir em comunicação interna*. Abracom.

Sousa, B. M., & Alves, G. M. (2019). The role of relationship marketing in behavioural intentions of medical tourism services and guest experiences. *Journal of Hospitality and Tourism Insights*, *2*(3), 224–240. doi:10.1108/JHTI-05-2018-0032

Tan, J. (2019). *Adaptive Health Management Information Systems*. Jones & Bartlett Learning.

Tansuhaj, P., Randall, D., & McCullough, J. (1988). A services marketing management model: Integrating internal and external marketing functions. *Journal of Services Marketing*, *2*(1), 31–38. doi:10.1108/eb024714

Tsai, Y. (2014). Learning organizations, internal marketing, and organizational commitment in hospitals. *BMC Health Services Research*, *14*(1), 1–8. doi:10.1186/1472-6963-14-152 PMID:24708601

Usher, R. (1996). A critique to the neglected epistemological assumptions of educational research. In D. Scott & R. Usher (Eds.), *Understanding educational research* (pp. 17–40). Psychology Press.

Wahyuni, D. (2012). The research design maze: Understanding paradigms, cases, methods and methodologies. *Journal of Applied Management Accounting*, *10*(1), 69–80.

Watkins, K. E., & Ellinger, A. D. (1998). Building Learning Organization: New Roles for Managers and Human Resource Developers. In *IFTDO Conference*. Dublin: Professors Forum.

KEY TERMS AND DEFINITIONS

Consumer Behavior: The study of individuals, groups, or organizations and all the activities associated with the purchase, use, and disposal of goods and services, including the consumer's emotional, mental, and behavioral responses that precede or follow these activities.

E-Satisfaction: The contentment of a consumer concerning his or her prior purchasing experiences with a given retail-oriented website.

E-WOM: Is any positive or negative statement made by a potential, actual, or former customer which is available to a multitude of people via the internet.

Internal Marketing: Is the promotion of a company's objectives, products and services to employees within the organization. The purpose is to increase employee engagement with the company's goals and fostering brand advocacy.

Marketing Tools: The techniques and materials used by those who are involved in the promotion of goods and services.

Relationship Marketing: Relationship marketing corresponds to marketing work focused on the relationship with customers and suppliers.

Social Media: Is the collective of online communications channels dedicated to community-based input, interaction, content-sharing, and collaboration (e.g., websites and applications, forums, microblogging, social networking, social bookmarking, social curation, and wikis are among the different types of social media).

Chapter 11
KPIs for Mobile Apps and Digital Data Management in Healthcare

Rebeca Antolín-Prieto
Rey Juan Carlos University, Spain

Nuria Ruiz-Lacaci
Rey Juan Carlos University, Spain

Ana Reyes-Menendez
https://orcid.org/0000-0003-0636-9573
Rey Juan Carlos University, Spain

ABSTRACT

This study aimed to identify quantitative and qualitative KPIs for the implementation of apps and use of digital data in healthcare management. To this end, a systematic review of the literature was undertaken to analyze relevant scientific articles downloaded from reputed scientific databases (Scopus, PubMed, PsyINFO, ScienceDirect, and WOS). The databases were searched using the following keywords: "Big Data," "Artificial Intelligence," "Mobile Technologies," "APP," "Disease," "Geolocation," and "Health." Subsequently, 25 qualitative and quantitative KPI values, as rating, product quality, or unique users, were identified for the successful preparation and management of healthcare based on apps and the use of digital data.

INTRODUCTION

Today, due to people's ubiquitous use of mobile devices, smartphones have become

DOI: 10.4018/978-1-7998-7263-4.ch011

a key element of any business strategy (Reyes-Menendez et al., 2020). According to the Global Mobile Market Report (2019), the number of mobile devices worldwide is also growing exponentially (see Table 1).

Table 1. Global smartphone users

Ranking	Country	Smartphones users (millions)		
		2017	2018	2019
1	China	747M	800M	851M
2	India	241M	291M	346M
3	Asia Pacific	381M	426M	472M
4	Middle East and Africa	328M	364M	403M
5	Eastern Europa	202M	212M	220M
6	Western Europe	298M	306M	313M
7	Latin America	230M	259M	288M
8	North America	268M	278M	288M

Source: Global Mobile Market Report (2019)

From the years 2017 to 2019, the number of smartphone users worldwide has increased from 2.7 billion to 3.2 billion (The Global Mobile Market Report, 2019). According to the aforementioned report, assuming an increase of 7.8%, by 2022, the number of smartphone users will reach 3.9 billion. This growth has important consequences for all business sectors.

Considering these data, it is necessary to carry out an analysis based on the KPIs for mobile apps and the digital data management in the healthcare sector. To this end, this section will present relevant data on the use of smartphones, mobile applications in general and more specifically those related to health, as well as the possible implications and applications that should be taken into account from the marketing area and the main trends in the field of mhealth.

While smartphone users use their devices for multiple purposes, mobile applications—also known as apps—are used particularly frequently. The first mobile applications date back to the late 1990s; however, apps' development has been spectacular in the last decade. Accordingly, companies need to adapt their strategies based on this new trend (Allen, et al., 2010). Popularity of apps also open new venues for market research.

Smartphones support the installation of mobile applications that perform specific and predetermined functions on the terminal (Lin et al., 2014). The global increase in the use of smartphones (Agrebi & Jallais, 2015), improvements in the infrastructure of the mobile network, and the global growth of the demand for mobile applications have dramatically transformed the way in which the content and value of the apps are delivered, distributed, and consumed (Basole & Karla, 2012).

In this sense, we can see how far the use of mobile apps in our daily bases has been established that we have different apps installed in our smartphones for different purposes. These purposes can range from banking applications, social networks to personal care and health apps.

Related to the health area and according to the results of a survey conducted by Accenture (2019), the patient expectations respect to the digital capabilities of a medical provider are increasing, in fact, the 70% of the patients surveyed choose a medical provider that offers follow-up via email or text and a 53% will choose a provider that offer remote or telemonitoring devices (see Figure 1).

Figure 1. Consumers increasingly will choose medical providers who offer digital capabilities
Source: Accenture (2019)

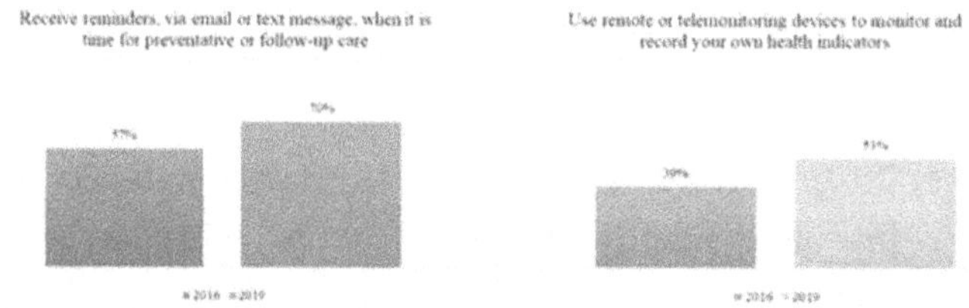

Today, people live in the era of hyperconnectivity that invades the society: since users have over 100,000 information impacts per day, it has been a challenge for companies to attract their customers (Zunzarren & Gorospe, 2012). Another concern is that, since users permanently and actively connect through multiple mobile platforms, we can speak about merging of personal time with professional time (Alegre, 2016.)

As revealed by the Ditrendia (2020) Mobile report in Spain and in the world, in 2019, there was a 6% increase in downloads of mobile applications (apps) as compared to the previous year, and the number of mobile app downloads reached 204 billion. Interestingly, the report also showed that users spend 91% of their time using applications, as compared to 9% of the time spent using browsers. Furthermore, in 2019, users accessed the Internet through a smartphone in 50.1% of cases, which suggests that half of users' online time is spent using mobile devices. By 2027, the share of the mobile applications market is expected to reach US $ 55,420 million (Global Biometrics Market Revenue, 2018-2027).

ICT and Hyperconectivity

In recent years, Information and Communication Technologies (ICT) have integrated into people's daily life to such an extent that there are few areas that have not undergone digital transformation. Accordingly, human relations in social areas, such as culture, economy, education, politics, or communications, have evolved adapting to market demands of today's digital age. These changes in communication processes—where the Internet is has become the place of work, leisure, training, consumption or advertising, and where technology is omnipresent and access to information is unlimited and uninterrupted—have dramatically changed the ways people related to each other (Rus-Arias et al., 2021). This hyperconnection affects people's relationships and their way of creating new social ties and new forms of affiliation (Zapatero et al., 2017).

Of note, there are many types of connected devices beyond smartphones that have Internet access and are thus relevant to the present study. Connected devices have a digital interconnection with everyday objects, which opens new opportunities for the improvement of users' quality of life (Xia et al., 2012). Among the ICTs linked to mobile devices, the Internet of Things (IOT), which refers to technology, remote monitoring and control, as well as to application of these technologies, is worth mentioning (Holler et al., 2014). The IoT products are present in homes in the form of devices for surveillance, space control, analysis of energy consumption, or home automation (Marques et al., 2020). In the health field, the IoT promotes the development of intelligent and predictive solutions for daily life or the hospital environment (Rahmani et al., 2018).

Mobile Apps in the Health / Wellness Sector: Transforming the Health Industry

In the context of digital invasion, the mobile application market has expanded to cover all aspects of people's daily lives—from product sales to contracting services, transport reservation, leisure, as well as health and wellness. Accordingly, hundreds of applications have emerged on the market. These apps allow users to perform diverse functions, including health monitoring, data recording, setting reminders, getting advice, and so forth. The increase in these types of applications is evidenced by the growing number of smartphone users who have access to these types of applications to store their medical history data or monitor their health status.

At the same time, extensive effort has been invested into improving the performance and credibility of these mobile applications, and this trend is completely transforming the health industry. This transformation has become particularly noticeable since the outbreak of the COVID-19 pandemic that brought about the urgent need for remote healthcare services. The increase in popularity of health-related apps and portable health technologies has also been driven by the globally growing number of patients with chronic diseases, such as diabetes, cardiovascular disorders and obesity. Overall, there is evidence that mobile health applications can help patients to lead healthy lifestyles, improve their access to medical care, and positively impact the productivity of health personnel (Zhang et al., 2014).

Due to the expansion of mobile applications, numerous relevant guidelines have emerged. One of them, entitled "Mobile Medical Applications Guidance for Industry and Food and Drug Administration Staff", was published the Food and Drug Administration (FDA, 2013). This guide not only provides an understanding of the mobile applications in health, but also reviews how the use of mobile devices and apps affects the health of users. In this guide, manufacturers, distributors, and other entities are informed about the FDA regulations concerning mobile medical apps. The 2013 report of the FDA also highlights the risks related to the misuse of mobile health applications and outlines the following four strategic areas of action: 1) raising awareness among payers and providers, as well as regulators and legislators, about the role performed by apps in the health area; 2) ensuring security and privacy among providers, patients, and app developers; 3) conducting periodic reviews of the apps to inform users of their proper use; and 4) integration of apps into other aspects of patient care.

In general, the use of medical apps continues to increase. In the last quarter of 2020, a 1.68% increase in downloads, as compared to the previous period, was observed, resulting in a total of 47,140 mobile health applications available for download (Statista, 2020). Similarly, the COVID-19 pandemic caused a significant increase in the number of downloads of mobile health applications (Sharma & Bashir, 2020).

By 2025, the mobile health applications market is expected to exceed 300,000 million US dollars. However, an important concern is that, given the high number of mobile health applications available for download, users have questions about which application would best meet their expectations and needs. According, many users end up not downloading any app (van Velsen et al., 2013)

With regard to measuring patient satisfaction with the use of mobile health apps, the annual Telehealth satisfaction study conducted by Power (2020) quantified 15 performance metrics and the relative weight of each metric on user satisfaction and loyalty. This study identified the dominant factors driving patient satisfaction, as well as measured patient perceptions of the apps' ability to meet their expectations. The study also identified Key Performance Indicators (KPIs), which are metrics used to measure the effectiveness of marketing strategies from a management point of view in order to optimize the results of campaigns (Reyes-Menendez et al., 2018). The top five KPIs identified in Power's (2020) study are listed below.

Figure 2. Evolution of mHealth app downloads in Google Play (2015-2020)
Source: Sharma and Bashir (2020)

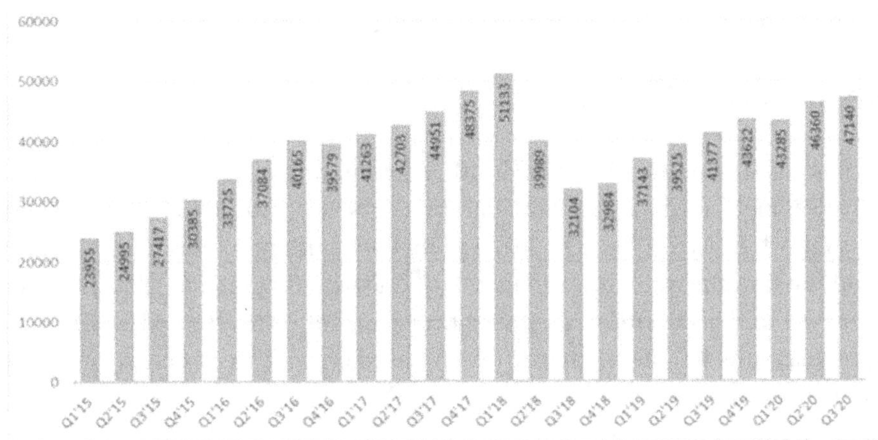

1. Invested time invested was sufficient to receive quality care
2. Medical concern resolved on first visit
3. Follow-up after the first visit
4. Online: question / problem solved in the first contact
5. Phone: question / answer resulted in the first contact

From the list above, it can be concluded that, above all, users appreciated the apps' ease of use and their ability to solve problems.

Mobile Health

As defined by the Policy on mHealth (Mobile Health) of the Shaping Europe's digital future introduced by European Commission (2020), mHealth is a sub-section of eHealth that covers the use of mobile communication devices and mobile apps for information and service purposes related to health or wellness. As of now, over 100,000 relevant applications are available in the market. This suggests that mHealth apps have a strong potential to participate in the transformation of healthcare and increase its quality and efficiency. Since, through the autonomous management of their health afforded by the apps, patients can have more active and independent lives, mHealth is also said to contribute to empowering patients. In addition, mHealth helps healthcare professionals to more effectively treat patients, as mobile apps can encourage patients' adherence to a healthy lifestyle (European Commission, 2020).

In summary, mHealth can perform various health-related tasks, such as improving users' lifestyle, providing fitness and meditation exercises, as well as helping medical professionals to prevent, identify, and even diagnose patients remotely.

mHealth and Marketing

Due to the growing popularity of mHealth, corresponding apps have become a very attractive segment for investors and entrepreneurs. According to the Research and Markets report, by 2027, the size of the global mHealth market is expected to hit $ 316.8 billion. Similarly, Sharma and Bashir (2020) predict that, by 2025, this figure will increase to $ 333 billion. At present, the market of health and wellness apps incorporates more and more applications focused on specific diseases or those that complement medical practice. This suggests that the market is still far from being oversaturated and rapidly changes and progresses.

mHealth apps can turn smartphones into laboratories that constantly evaluate users' physiological parameters, behavior, social context, and the environment (Kumar et al. 2013; Reyes-Menendez et al. 2018). Therefore, along with benefits, these types of apps can have an adverse impact on the relationship between the patient and medical care (Tyer, 2013). Among other concerns, the health sector has to face challenges such as the treatment of the patients' personal data, confidential diagnoses, as well as other sensitive information. In this context, users who intend to download mHealth apps may have concerns related to security, privacy, data encryption, as well as integrations or APIs between multiple devices and channels (Reyes-Menendez et al., 2019).

In this context, it becomes important to design apps with a close consideration of the opinions and preferences of those apps' end users (Matthew-Maich et al., 2016). As these apps become increasingly more complex in their design, there is an urgent need for a close collaboration among different teams involved in their development and users in order to better understand users' needs (Kumar et al., 2013; Reyes-Menendez et al., 2018).

mHealth Trends

One of the key factors underlying in the development of mobile apps in the health sector is the recent technological development (Reyes-Menendez et al. 2019). These technological advances include current trends in AI (Artificial Intelligence), Blockchain, VR and AR (virtual reality and augmented reality), or the IoT (Internet of things). All these new developments made it possible to elaborate personalized medical software, which benefits both patients, on the one hand, and medical personnel and institutions, on the other hand.

AI assists in medical tasks, such as diagnosing diseases, structuring data, analyzing medical records, prescribing treatments, identifying patients who need urgent care. AI is also used in viewing ultrasound images, computed tomography, magnetic resonance imaging, as well as in creating medications with specific formulas, monitoring the movement of doctors and patients in medical institutions, planning the work of hospitals and clinics, and so forth. Furthermore, AI algorithms are also employed in application chatbots, since these algorithms can be used to collect primary information, ask questions, and offer response variants. In this way, AI helps to connect patients with doctors in the most initial stages, facilitating an adequate subsequent follow-up process.

In its turn, Blockchain can also be meaningfully used applied in the mHealth environment in management of electronic medical records, remote monitoring of patients, medical data analysis, clinical and biomedical investigations, as well as in the improvement of insurance and billing procedures.

Furthermore, VR and AR also have a wide range of application in mHealth, such as surgeons' training, diagnosis, or assisting patients with mental problems. In previous studies, mHealth apps were used to investigate insomnia (Taylor & Roane, 2010), migraines (Nestoriuc et al., 2008), chronic pain (Palermo et al., 2010), and diabetes. This body of research convincingly demonstrated the strong potential of specific mobile applications for the prevention, monitoring, and control of these conditions (Peng et al., 2016).

Specifically, applications of the IoT in mHealth was documented to lead to a reduction in economic investment and time, both of which are highly valued among patients, as well as in substantial improvements in accompaniment of the elderly, monitoring, alerts that can be sent directly to the corresponding medical personnel, and registration of medical results (Slathia & Nagamalai, 2016)

However despite its many advantages, mHealth has to face several important challenges. First, as concerns security, there is an urgent need to ensure that the system through which information is sent to the user is valid and adequate (Palos -Sanchez et al., 2019). Security also includes reliability of the data shown to the user depending on the previous selection of criteria. Another important challenge of mHealth is efficacy, which refers to the validity of the corresponding devices and their capacity to generate reproducible measurements and results. Yet another crucial challenge of mHealth is privacy patient data that can be threatened due to the use of different sensors, way of transmitting data and operating, as well as many parties involved in the entire technical process (Kumar et al., 2013).

In view of the challenges briefly reviewed above, it is essential to systematically evaluate all available techniques in terms of their functionality and to establish a roadmap for companies that want to improve their marketing and competitiveness through the use of mobile apps in the health sector. In this context, the present study aims to identify quantitative and qualitative KPIs for the implementation of apps and use of digital data in the healthcare sector.

The remainder of this paper is structured as follows. Upon a systematic review of the literature, we describe the methodology used in the present study. This is followed by the analysis of the results. The paper concludes with a discussion of implications of our findings for further research on the use of apps in the healthcare sector.

BACKGROUND

Previous research analyzed the use of mobile health applications in various contexts, including healthy adults, chronic diseases (Loo, 2009), and lifestyle (Fukuoka et al., 2011). Other authors focused on classifying different mobile health apps according to different criteria. In addition, previous research analyzed different stages of apps development, such as conception, implementation, integration, and operation (Khoja et al., 2013).

Another large body of work analyzed the characteristics of the apps. For instance, Handel (2011) reviewed 35 mHealth mobile apps based on user ratings for ease of use, reliability, quality, reach, and aesthetics. Furthermore, using MARS (Mobile App Rating Scale) as a quality rating tool for mHealth apps, Stoyanov et al. (2015) elaborated a multidimensional, reliable, and flexible quality rating scale system for mobile health apps using KPIs such as engagement, functionality, aesthetics, information quality, and subjective quality.

In another relevant study, Mosa et al. (2012) analyzed 83 mobile health applications, of which 57 were intended for health professionals, 11 for medical and nursing students, and 15 for patients. Within these three groups of apps, different applications were analyzed. The authors concluded that health professionals, including medical and nursing students, found that the apps for disease diagnosis, drug reference, and medical calculators were the most useful.

According to the IMS Health Report (2013), most health applications aimed at the patient are focused on the general well-being of an individual related to diet and exercise. Such apps offer patients useful tools for a healthy lifestyle, as well as increase availability of health professionals, diagnoses, information and recipes. Such apps also provide a possibility of self-diagnosis through verification of symptoms. Using such apps, patients can get informed through text, photo or video; train through instructions in the app; register their data, view information, obtain a guide with information, diagnoses or consultation; finally, app users can also receive alerts or reminders, communicate with the medical team, or share information on social networks.

Overall, mHealth apps aim to "improve the well-being and health of people by being able to continuously monitor their condition, quickly diagnose conditions, recognize behaviors and provide timely interventions in the user's mobile environment" (Kumar et al., 2013) Accordingly, exponential growth in the use of these apps in recent years (Marques et al., 2020) has been due to the advantages offered by smartphones, which provide access to information at any time and place (Stoyanov et al., 2015), as well as to the benefits of the apps that measure physical activity, sleep, or movement, as well as can improve patients' quality of patient care or reduce patient care costs (Wu & Luo, 2019).

Furthermore, many previous studies evaluated the usability of mobile health apps (Rahmani et al., 2018; Sharma & Bashir, 2020). In one such study by the Health Care Information and Management Systems Society (mHIMSS, 2012), each evaluation criterion was rated on a Likert scale from "Totally agree" to "Totally disagree".

While there have been many attempts to classify KPIs of the apps, there is a general consensus that a correct evaluation should be based on multiple KPIs (Pernici et al., 2018). Therefore, regardless of the specific use or purpose of mobile health apps, it is necessary to establish their performance indicators or KPIs to define appropriate marketing strategies (Ntalkos et al., 2015). This is particularly important in the context of the rapid growth of the mobile app market where it is essential to use digital marketing techniques (Reyes-Menendez et al., 2020).

MAIN FOCUS OF THE CHAPTER

Issues, Controversies, Problems

Following Kazakov and Predvoditeleva (2015), the present study aimed to provide a state-of-the-art overview of previous research on KPIs for mobile apps in the health industry. To this end, the analysis focused on both qualitative and quantitative KPIs.

Available literature on KPIs of mobile technologies in the health industry was carefully examined. The following two main topics were considered in the analysis: (i) mobile technologies; (ii) health. Following Sherman et al. (2005) and Banerjee et al. (2015), a randomized controlled process to select the main topics and keywords was used.

Relevant publications were collected in the following scientific databases: Scopus, PubMed, PsyINFO, ScienceDirect, and Web of Science. The keywords used for the searchers were as follows: "Big Data", "Artificial Intelligence", "Mobile Technologies", "App", "Disease", "Geolocation", and "Health". In searching the publications by "Title" in Web of Science, only one article met the search requirements; the title of this article contained both search terms.

In the process of article selection, following Reyes-Menendez et al. (2019), priority was given to papers that focused on health and mobile technologies. The search returned a total of 321 articles; after filtering (see Fig. 3), 22 studies were retained in the database. The results were optimized by using the Boolean operator AND. Only the articles that met all inclusion criteria were retained in the dataset. The subsequent qualitative analysis of the selected papers was performed using the AMSTAR tool that helps to evaluate the quality of articles based on their abstracts (Shea et al., 2009). This was done to ensure the inclusion of only high-quality studies. The process of article selection followed the recommendations outlined in Van den Bosch and Ode Sang (2017), such as keyword search in several databases, a clear set of inclusion criteria, and data extraction based on the keywords.

Specifically, following Reyes-Menendez et al. (2019), the researchers sued the Preferred Reporting Items for Systematic reviews and Meta-Analyses (PRISMA) 2009 Flow Diagram. Initially proposed by Moher et al. (2009), this approach specifies guidelines for the development of systematic reviews and meta-analyses. Among the initial phases of the PRISMA Flow Diagram is removing the articles that contain inadequate or inconclusive terms, such as studies that can initially correspond to the keywords, but later appear to be beyond the scope of a study.

The variables accounted for in the AMSTAR tool to evaluate the quality of the systematic review and used in the present study were as follows: (i) the relationship of the research question to the formulated criteria; (ii) data extraction performed by at least two independent researchers; (iii) the quality of the literature review, (iii) identification and definition of relevant concepts; and (iv) quality of conclusions.

Results

The overarching goal of the present study was to provide researchers, companies, and consumers with in-depth knowledge necessary to develop successful marketing and management strategies. Accordingly, to get a clear picture of the use of mobile applications in the health sector, both quantitative and qualitative KPIs were used.

The identification of KPIs, which was the main aim of the present study, was complemented by scientometric analysis. This analysis was performed to establish a thematic and quantitative line of research on the previously published research on mobile apps and health.

Exploratory Analysis of Results

a. **Scientometric Analysis**

Figure 3. PRISMA 2009 flow diagram
Source: Authors

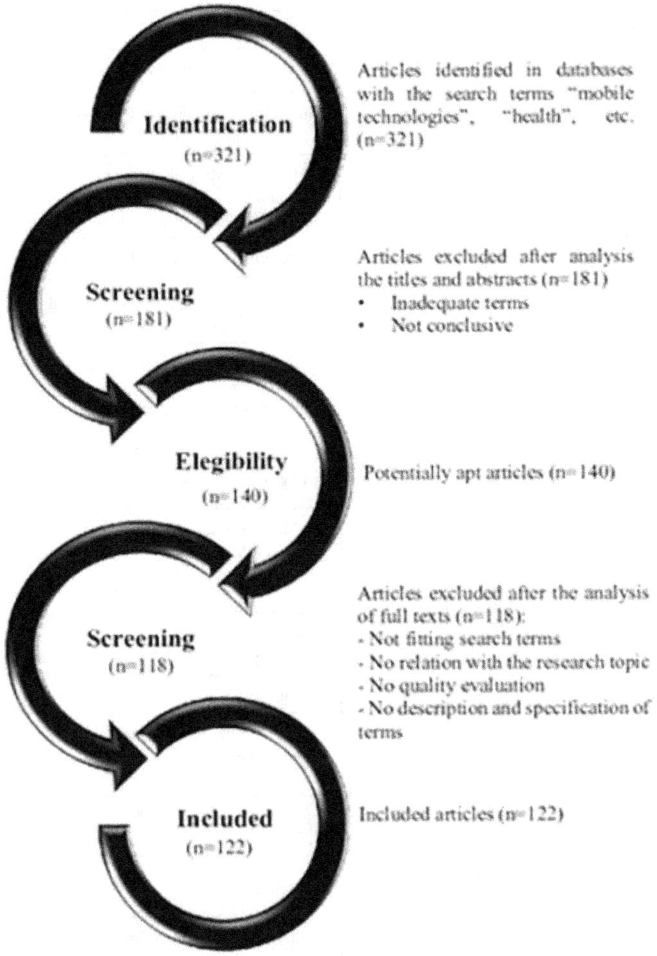

Following previous research (Reyes-Menendez et al., 2019), in order to better understand which research areas are involved in the analysis of mobile health apps, a scientometric analysis was performed. The results of this analysis are summarized in Table 2 that shows relevant journals, the number of articles published in each of them, category, and the quartile classified by Web of Science when (applicable).

The main categories obtained in the analyses were as follows: Public, Environmental & Occupational Health, Engineering, Multidisciplinary, Mathematics, Interdisciplinary Applications, Mathematical & Computational Biology, Health Care Sciences & Services, Medical Informatics, Computer Science and Psychology. The

Table 2. Scientometric analysis

Journal	Total findings	Category	Quartile
JMIR Medical Informatics	1	Emerging	/
International Journal of Health Geographics	1	Public, Environmental & Occupational Health in SSCI edition Public, Environmental & Occupational Health in SCIE edition	Q1
Hindawi Mathematical Problems in Engineering	2	Engineering, Multidisciplinary Mathematics, Interdisciplinary Applications Mathematical & Computational Biology	Q3
Global Health Action	1	Public, Environmental & Occupational Health in SSCI edition Public, Environmental & Occupational Health in SSCI edition	Q2
Translational Behavioral Medicine	1	Public, Environmental & Occupational Health in SSCI edition Public, Environmental & Occupational Health in SCIE edition	Q1 Q2
Journal of Rehabilitation and Assistive Technologies Engineering	1	Emerging	/
JMIR mHealth and uHealth	5	Health Care Sciences & Services Medical Informatics Emerging	Q1 Q1 /
Journal of Medical Internet Research (JMIR)	2	Health Care Sciences & Services Medical Informatics Emerging	Q1 Q1 /
JMIR Formative Research	1	Emerging	/
Journal of Biomedical Informatics	1	Computer Science Interdisciplinary Applications Medical Informatics	Q2
Online Journal of Public Health Informatics (OJPHI)	1	Emerging	/
P & T: a peer-reviewed journal for formulary management	1	Emerging	/
Health Informatics Journal	1	Health Care Sciences & Services Medical Informatics	Q2
BMJ Global Health	1	Public, Environmental & Occupational Health in SSCI edition Public, Environmental & Occupational Health in SCIE edition	Q1
Professional Psychology: Research and Practice	1	Psychology, Multidisciplinary	Q2
Clinical infectious diseases: an official publication of the Infectious Diseases Society of America	1	Emerging	/
Total	22		

Source: Authors

categories with the highest number of publications were Health Care Sciences & Services and Medical Informatics (9 articles). Of these 9 articles, 7 were published by JMIR—specifically, 5 papers in JMIR MHEALTH AND UHEALTH and 2 in the Journal of Medical Internet Research.

Considering the number of articles, the next category is Emerging Sources from Web of Science, with 8 articles distributed in different Journals, as can be seen in Table 2.

Other journals that explored the topic of mobile apps in health were classified as follows: Public, Environmental & Occupational Health (4), Engineering, Multidisciplinary, Mathematics, Interdisciplinary Applications, Mathematical & Computational Biology (2), Computer Science, Interdisciplinary Applications, Medical Informatics (1) and Psychology, Multidisciplinary (1).

Importantly, in terms of the identified categories, relevant publications mostly belonged to the development part of the application itself, rather than to the marketing and management approach. This highlights the importance of the present study that helps to identify important gaps in previous research.

The development of mobile apps related to health for private use by users is an area that continuously grows and develops. The number of diseases that can be controlled and monitored through these types of apps is constantly growing, which necessitates patients' permanent remote contact with medical professionals Accordingly, in the data, 11 of the 22 analyzed articles explored mobile health applications in relation to mental diseases such as Alzheimer's, dietary control, smoking cessation, or well-being, while another five articles focused on the design, analysis, or aspects related to the security of these apps.

Most of the analyzed articles fall into the category of Health Care Sciences & Services and Medical Informatics. This highlights health care and medical information require users' interactions with their mobile health apps. Despite the growing number of different apps, it is only several years ago that the healthcare sector started to be interested in this type of technology to stay connected with patients (Sharma & Bashir, 2020)

Interestingly, 9 of the 22 articles used included in the present systematic review of the literature were extracted from the JMIR Publications, which is the leading peer-reviewed journal for digital medicine and health and health care in the Internet age. The remaining articles were distributed more or less evenly among all other journals.

As concerns the distribution of the quartiles, and taking the scale provided by Web of Science as a reference, the results in Table 2 suggest that four articles were in quartile 1, while all other papers belonged to quartiles 2, 3 or "no quartile" for the papers in the emerging category.

b. Qualitative Variables: In-Depth Analysis

In addition to quantitative analysis reported above, the content of the 22 articles published between 2014 and 2020 was analyzed using qualitative exploratory analysis (Reyes-Menendez et al. 2018; 2019). The aim of this analysis was to find the factors that determine the success of the use the apps and digital data in the management of healthcare and medical care.

First, we followed Reyes-Menendez et al. (2019) in which the authors conduct a systematic literature review that is an exploratory methodology in which they collect and re-analyze available findings. The, following Sherman et al. (2005), Banerjee et al. (2015) and Reyes-Menendez et al. (2019) we used a randomized controlled process to identify qualitative and quantitative KPIs.

Based on the two types of analysis, both quantitative and qualitative KPIs were identified. All KPIs were organized in two tables, with quantitative (measurable) variables and qualitative (non-measurable) variables (see Tables 3-4). Both tables provide the name of the variable, description, and author(s) of the corresponding publication. The classification of the variables was performed following the present authors' previous research on KPIs: namely, identifying the performance class indicators for marketing strategies in mobile applications (Reyes-Menendez et al., 2020) and relating the Big Data technical and business performance indicators (Pernici et al., 2018).

Table 3 provides a summary of qualitative key performance indicators. The following variables were identified: App title / name, Screenshots, App icon, Feature chart, Record type, User flow, Customer satisfaction, Trust, Functionality, Personalization, Platform security, Feedback and design. Each identified variable, its description, and authors of the corresponding publications are summarized in the table.

c. Quantitative Variables: In-Depth Analysis

Table 4 shows the quantitative KPIs. The following variables were identified: Cost reduction, Time efficiency, Product / service quality, Launch of new products / services, Business Model innovation, Ratings, User opinions, Traffic, Time spent per visit, Unique users, Total download and price-value. Each identified variable, its description, and authors of the corresponding publications are summarized in the table.

Table 3. Qualitative KPIs

Variable	Description	Author
App title / name	The name or title that appears in the app store. Some names include the keyword and improve its visibility when users search for an application by category.	Antezana et al. (2020); Mehdi et al. (2020); Ming et al. (2020)
App icon	It can draw users' attention, so where colors and shape are very important.	Antezana et al. (2020); Mehdi et al. (2020)
Client satisfaction	Big Data and analytical application to product management.	Akdur & Akdur (2020); Antezana et al. (2020); Faieta et al. (2020); Maged et al. (2014); Mehdi et al. (2020); Stoyanov et al. (2015)
Design	To measure the relevance, rigor, and design that influence the quality of the app.	Antezana et al. (2020); Dehling et al. (2015); Faieta et al. (2020); Mehdi et al. (2020); Schnall et al. (2016); Stoyanov et al. (2015)
Feedback	Follow-up by health professionals to the patient: with objectives and feedback (real-time comments and mapping).	Gowarty et al. (2020); Logie et al. (2020); Ming et al. (2020); Reichberg et al. (2020); Stoyanov et al. (2015); Zhao et al. (2016)
Flow of users	The study of how users behave in the application. Step-by-step analysis of each diagram of user actions from the moment of opening the application.	Antezana et al. (2020); Logie et al. (2020); Mehdi et al. (2020); Schnall et al. (2016); Stoyanov et al. (2015)
Function graphs	Each of the graphical components of the application can attract users' attention and improve visibility.	Mehdi et al. (2020); Schnall et al. (2016); Stoyanov et al. (2015); Zhao et al. (2015)
Functionality	Utility of regular reminder visits, medical care, diagnostic download. Optimization: less time consumption and more clarity of information.	Maged et al. (2014); Stoyanov et al. (2015); Zhao et al. (2016)
Personalization	Individualized content adaptation, user-centered usability. Application to support changes in habits (adaptation, optimization and clinical support to be effective)	Akdur & Akdur (2020); Antezana et al. (2020); Carroll et al. (2017); Faieta et al. (2020); Gowarty et al. (2020); Logie et al. (2020); Maged et al. (2014); Ming et al. (2020); Stoyanov et al. (2015); Ventola (2014); Zhao et al. (2016)
Security	To measure the degree of confidentiality and level of security and privacy breaches, as well as the path of user information (i.e., if the app has access to valuable information from third parties, the probability increases).	Akdur & Akdur (2020); Dehling et al. (2015); Logie et al. (2020); Maged et al. (2014); Marshall et al. (2020); Mehdi et al. (2020); Ming et al. (2020); Reichberg et al. (2020); Schnall et al. (2016); Stoyanov et al. (2015); Ventola (2014); Wahl et al. (2018)
Screenshots	Screenshot of the apps that appears in the app stores. It visually shows the main functionalities of the application and can serve as a call for users to download the application.	Antezana et al. (2020); Mehdi et al. (2020)
Trust	Confidence building due to the quality of information about the app by the doctor.	Dehling et al. (2015); Logie et al. (2020); Maged et al. (2014); Mehdi et al. (2020); Ming et al. (2020)
Type of register	The type of registration that users make, and their analysis can help marketing. They increase the understanding of each user and their behavior in the application.	Antezana et al. (2020); Dehling et al. (2015); Mehdi et al. (2020); Schnall et al. (2016)

Source: Authors

SOLUTIONS AND RECOMMENDATIONS

In the present study, KPIs were identified to measure efficiency and understand the factors that determine the success of the use of apps and digital data in the management of mHealth healthcare and medical care from the marketing and management perspectives.

In the context of the rapid growth in the use of mobile devices and fast advances in technology, it is necessary to conduct a systematic review of available research so that to identify both good practices and gaps in current research. This is exactly the contribution of the present study to previous research and theories.

In the present study, the following qualitative KPIs were identified: Name / title of the application, Screenshots, Application icon, Function chart, Type of record, User flow, Customer satisfaction, Trust, Functionality, Personalization, Platform Security, Feedback, and Design. In addition, the quantitative KPIs included Cost reduction, Time efficiency, Product / service quality, Launch of new products / services, Business model innovation, Ratings, Opinions of users, Traffic, Time spent per visit, Unique users, Total download, and Price-value.

According with the results of the Qualitative KPIs variables, we can develop the order of importance of these variables in relation with the summatory of times that each variable was named in those 22 papers analyzed: in first place the variable of the personalization (in 12 papers of the 22 papers analyzed appears this variable) with the variable of the Security (also in 12 papers appears this variable); in second place is the variable of Design which appears in 7 papers; the third place is for several variables as Client Satisfaction and Feedback, and both appears in 6 papers; in fourth place is the Flow of Users, Trust, and Functionality, and the three variables appears in a total of 5 papers; in fifth place the variables as Function Graphs, and the Type of Register, and this two appears in 4 papers; in last place the variables as App Name/Title with 3 papers, and the variables screenshots and App Icon which appears only in 2 papers.

In other hand, and according with the results of the Quantitative KPIs variables, we can develop the order of importance of these variables in relation with the summatory of times that each variable was named in those 22 papers analyzed: in first place the variable of Customer Reviews appears in 14 papers of the 22;in second place is the variable Time spent per visit which appears in 8 papers; in the third place there are the variables Time Efficiency and Price-value which both appears in 7 papers; in fourth place the variable traffic, which appears in 6 papers; in fifth place the variable launch of new products/services which appears in 5 papers; and in the las place we have several variables as Total Downloads and product/service quality (both appears in 3 papers), the variable unique users and also the business

Table 4. Quantitative KPI

Variable	Description	Author
Cost reduction	Scope of use of Big Data and analytics for decision making in the optimization task, which has application in the sales part.	Shu et al. (2020)
Time efficiency	Scope of use of apps, Big Data and analytics for data-driven business processes, which has application in the part of customer service and support.	Carroll et al. (2017); Jeong et al. (2020); Lakerveld et al. (2020); Ming. et al. (2020); Schnall et al. (2016): Shijie &Tang (2020); Shu et al. (2020)
Product / service quality	Scope of use of Big Data and Analytics for data orientation, digital transformation, and device connectivity standards, which has application in IT and data operation	Jeong et al. (2020); Lakerveld et al. (2020); Maged et al. (2014);
Launch of new products / services	Use of Big Data and analytics in the application to logistics and maintenance.	Lakerveld et al. (2020); Logie et al. (2020); Ming et al. (2020); Shu et al. (2020); Ventola (2014)
Business model innovation	Use of Big Data and Analytics in the application to marketing	Schnall et al. (2016); Shu et al. (2020)
Ratings	They allow users to rate apps between 1 and 5 stars based on their level of satisfaction with the app and its features. It is a quantitative marketing indicator that reflects user satisfaction with the mobile app.	Akdur & Akdur (2020); Antezana et al. (2020); Carroll et al. (2017); Maged et al. (2014); Mehdi et al. (2020); Ming et al. (2020); Schnall et al. (2016); Stoyanov et al. (2015)
Customer reviews	A review is a written response in which users leave comments. They can be positive or negative. Application platforms are beginning to use software text analysis to determine its quality and volume.	Akdur & Akdur (2020); Antezana et al. (2020); Carroll et al. (2017); Faieta et al. (2020); Jeong et al. (2020); Logie et al. (2020); Maged et al. (2014); Marshall et al. (2020); Mehdi et al. (2020); Ming et al. (2020); Schnall et al. (2016); Stoyanov et al. (2015); Ventola (2014); Zhao et al. (2016)
Traffic	The total number of users who have used the application at any given time.	Antezana et al. (2020); Maged et al. (2014); Mehdi et al. (2020); Ming et al. (2020); Schnall et al. (2016); Stoyanov et al. (2015)
Time spent per visit	Total amount of time that users spend using the application. Determines interests and habits of users within the application, among other parameters.	Carroll et al. (2017) Maged et al. (2014); Mehdi et al. (2020); Ming et al. (2020); Schnall et al. (2016); Stoyanov et al. (2015); Zhao et al. (2016)
Unique users	Total number of unique users the application has in a given period of time. This KPI allows the quantification of the total number of users based on the time horizon.	Carroll et al. (2017); Mehdi et al. (2020)
Total downloads	It quantifies the total number of app downloads and differs from the total number of uninstalled files.	Antezana et al. (2020); Carroll et al. (2017); Mehdi et al. (2020)
Price-value	Free or paid subscription, as recommended by Health Care Provider (HCP).	Akdur & Akdur (2020); Antezana al. (2020); Dehling et al. (2015); Maged et al. (2014); Mehdi et al. (2020); Ming et al. (2020); Stoyanov et al. (2015)

Source: Authors

model innovation (both appears in 2 papers), and the variable Cost Reduction which appears only in 1 of the papers analyzed.

In total, these results explains that the most important KPIs variables are the Customer Reviews (quantitative variable, which appears in 14 papers), the Personalization (qualitative variable, which appears in 12 papers) and the Security (qualitative variable, which appears in 12 papers).

Both researchers and professionals in the healthcare sector can use these indicators to qualitatively and quantitatively evaluate the efficiency of the use, application, and management of digital data of mobile apps in the field of health care and medical care. Further research could also focus on the development of marketing strategies supported by qualitative KPIs to gain greater marketing performance.

Another key point identified in the present study is that the advances in mobile health apps have been explored not only from the marketing perspective, but also from the point of view of programming point (Sharma & Bashir, 2020).

FUTURE RESEARCH DIRECTIONS

The results of the present study provide meaningful implications for further research. Specifically, the identified quantitative and qualitative KPIs can be used develop, measure, and analyze the efficiency of apps in the mHealthcare sector. Furthermore, in recent years, mobile apps and digital data (Big Data, geolocation, UGC, eWOM) have received attention not only from the scientific community, but also from users. Therefore, although the scope of past research on these topics is not even a decade old, the present investigation managed to identify the main journals that published relevant studies in this field. The results provide a valuable perspective on current research trends and topics of interest to the scientific community. Future studies can focus on identifying other relevant KPIs in the proposed framework. In addition, the present results can be used to increase scientific relevance in the environment of health care management and medical care to better understand the factors that determine the success of use of mobile apps and digital data in healthcare.

CONCLUSION

In recent years, the sector of mobile apps and digital data (Big Data, geolocation, UGC, eWOM) has experienced exponential growth. Along with the development of 5G coverage of mobile phones and new technologies in the mHealth environment (such as IoT, Blockchain, as well as VR and AR), recent changes and improvements in app use economize time and cost—the two aspects that are salient to both users and companies. The rapid growth and development of this sector highlights the need for future synergies and changes to better adapt the performance of apps to the target audience.

Since past research on mobile apps in the health sector has focused more on programming aspects, rather than viewed the apps from the perspective of marketing and management, it is necessary to continue investigating major quantitative and qualitative KPIs that allow to analyze the development of these applications from another perspective. It was observed, quantified and described that the most studied KPIs variables were the Customer Reviews (quantitative variable) and Personalization and the Security (both qualitative variables), but it is necessary more researching in order to appreciate better the rest of variables described. We encourage to analyze more and further the qualitative variables KPIs as Design, Client Satisfaction and Feedback, Flow of Users, Trust, Functionality, Function Graphs, Type of Register, App Name/Title, screenshots and App Icon; in the quantitative variables KPIs is necessary to study further the Time spent per visit, Time Efficiency, Price-value, Traffic, launch of new products/services, Total Downloads and product/service quality, unique users, the business model innovation, and Cost Reduction.

Such quantitative and qualitative analysis would allow companies and health researchers to improve the competitiveness and performance in the sector. Finally, it is necessary to emphasize the importance of measuring the strategies developed for mobile apps and the use of digital data with the use of qualitative and quantitative KPIs in mHealth, as well as the importance of evaluating efficiency in other strategic categories of digital marketing. Since there is evidence that the behavior of users of mobile apps and digital data differs from the behavior of users of desktop devices, there is a need to apply specific metrics to each of these two modalities. In summary, the results of the present study are relevant to both academics and professionals in the mHealth sector.

REFERENCES

Accenture. (2019). *Digital Health Consumer Survey.* https://www.accenture.com/t20190208t144039z__w__/us-en/_acnmedia/pdf-94/accenture-2019-digital-health-consumer-survey.pdf

Akdur, G., Aydin, M. N., & Akdur, G. (2020). Adoption of Mobile Health Apps in Dietetic Practice: Case Study of Diyetkolik. *JMIR mHealth and uHealth*, *8*(10), e16911. doi:10.2196/16911 PMID:33006566

Alegre, A. M. (2016). El Crossumer: La evolución del consumidor mediada por las tecnologías sociales y la hiperconectividad móvil. *MÉI: Métodos de Información, 7*(12), 5–16. doi:10.5557/IIMEI7-N12-005016

Allen, S., Graupera, V., & Lundrigan, L. (2010). *Pro smartphone cross-platform development: iPhone, blackberry, windows mobile and android development and distribution*. Apress. doi:10.1007/978-1-4302-2869-1

Antezana, G., Venning, A., Blake, V., Smith, D., Winsall, M., Orlowski, S., & Bidargaddi, N. (2020). An evaluation of behaviour change techniques in health and lifestyle mobile applications. *Health Informatics Journal*, *26*(1), 104–113. doi:10.1177/1460458218813726 PMID:30501364

Banerjee, S., Chua, A. Y., & Kim, J. J. (2015, January). Using supervised learning to classify authentic and fake online reviews. In *Proceedings of the 9th international conference on ubiquitous information management and communication* (pp. 1-7). 10.1145/2701126.2701130

Boudreaux, E. D., Waring, M. E., Hayes, R. B., Sadasivam, R. S., Mullen, S., & Pagoto, S. (2014). Evaluating and selecting mobile health apps: Strategies for healthcare providers and healthcare organizations. *Translational Behavioral Medicine*, *4*(4), 363–371. doi:10.100713142-014-0293-9 PMID:25584085

Boulos, M. N. K., Brewer, A. C., Karimkhani, C., Buller, D. B., & Dellavalle, R. P. (2014). Mobile medical and health apps: State of the art, concerns, regulatory control and certification. *Online Journal of Public Health Informatics*, *5*(3), 229. PMID:24683442

Carroll, J. K., Moorhead, A., Bond, R., LeBlanc, W. G., Petrella, R. J., & Fiscella, K. (2017). Who uses mobile phone health apps and does use matter? A secondary data analytics approach. *Journal of Medical Internet Research*, *19*(4), e125. doi:10.2196/jmir.5604 PMID:28428170

Dehling, T., Gao, F., Schneider, S., & Sunyaev, A. (2015). Exploring the far side of mobile health: Information security and privacy of mobile health apps on iOS and Android. *JMIR mHealth and uHealth*, *3*(1), e8. doi:10.2196/mhealth.3672 PMID:25599627

Ditrendia. (2020). *Mobile en España y en el Mundo 2020*. https://ditrendia.es/informe-mobile-2020/

European Commission. (2020). *Shaping Europe's digital future*. https://ec.europa.eu/digital-single-market/en/mHealth

Faieta, J., Hand, B. N., Schmeler, M., Onate, J., & Digiovine, C. (2020). Health App Review Tool: Matching mobile apps to Alzheimer's populations (HART Match). *Journal of Rehabilitation and Assistive Technologies Engineering*, *7*. doi:10.1177/2055668320938604 PMID:33014412

FDA. (2013). *Mobile medical applications: guidance for industry and food and drug administration staff.* U.S. Food and Drug Administration. https://www.fda.gov/downloads/MedicalDevices/.../UCM263366.pdf

Fukuoka, Y., Kamitani, E., Bonnet, K., & Lindgren, T. (2011). Real-time social support through a mobile virtual community to improve healthy behavior in overweight and sedentary adults: A focus group analysis. *Journal of Medical Internet Research*, *13*(3), e49. doi:10.2196/jmir.1770 PMID:21752785

Gowarty, M. A., Kung, N. J., Maher, A. E., Longacre, M. R., & Brunette, M. F. (2020). Perceptions of Mobile Apps for Smoking Cessation Among Young People in Community Mental Health Care: Qualitative Study. *JMIR Formative Research*, *4*(10), e19860. doi:10.2196/19860 PMID:33006560

Handel, M. J. (2011). mHealth (mobile health)-using apps for health and wellness. *Explore (New York, N.Y.)*, *7*(4), 256–261. doi:10.1016/j.explore.2011.04.011

mHIMSS. (2012). *Selecting a mobile app: Evaluating the usability of medical applications*. http://s3.amazonaws.com/rdcms-himss/files/production/public/HIMSSguidetoappusabilityv1mHIMSS.pdf

Holler, J., Tsiatsis, V., Mulligan, C., Karnouskos, S., Avesand, S., & Boyle, D. (2014). *Internet of Things*. Academic Press.

Health, I. M. S. (2013). *Patient apps for improved healthcare: from novelty to mainstream*. IMS Institute for Healthcare Informatics.

Power, J. D. (2020). *U. S. Telehealth Satisfaction Study*. https://www.jdpower.com/business/healthcare/us-telehealth-satisfaction-study

Jeong, S. H., Lee, T. R., Kang, J. B., & Choi, M. T. (2020). Analysis of Health Insurance Big Data for Early Detection of Disabilities: Algorithm Development and Validation. *JMIR Medical Informatics*, *8*(11), e19679. doi:10.2196/19679 PMID:33226352

Kazakov, S., & Predvoditeleva, M. (2015). *How travelers use online and social media channels to make hotel choice decisions. A comparative study of Russian Federation and American tourists' online consumer behavior.* Higher School of Economics Research Paper No. WP BRP 44/MAN/2015.

Khoja, S., Durrani, H., Scott, R. E., Sajwani, A., & Piryani, U. (2013). Conceptual framework for development of comprehensive e-health evaluation tool. *Telemedicine Journal and e-Health*, *19*(1), 48–53. doi:10.1089/tmj.2012.0073 PMID:22957502

Kumar, S., Nilsen, W., Pavel, M., & Srivastava, M. (2012). Mobile health: Revolutionizing healthcare through transdisciplinary research. *Computer*, *46*(1), 28–35. doi:10.1109/MC.2012.392

Lakerveld, J., Wagtendonk, A., Vaartjes, I., & Karssenberg, D. (2020). Deep phenotyping meets big data: The Geoscience and hEalth Cohort COnsortium (GECCO) data to enable exposome studies in The Netherlands. *International Journal of Health Geographics*, *19*(1), 1–16. doi:10.118612942-020-00235-z PMID:33187515

Li, S., & Tang, Y. (2020). A Simple Framework of Smart Geriatric Nursing considering Health Big Data and User Profile. *Computational and Mathematical Methods in Medicine*. PMID:33149759

Logie, C., Okumu, M., Abela, H., Wilson, D., & Narasimhan, M. (2020). Sexual and reproductive health mobile apps: Results from a cross-sectional values and preferences survey to inform World Health Organization normative guidance on self-care interventions. *Global Health Action*, *13*(1), 1796346. doi:10.1080/16549716.2020.1796346 PMID:32778000

Loo, J. (2009). *Acceptance of health services on mobile phones* (Doctoral Dissertation). University of North Carolina.

Marques, G., Miranda, N., Kumar Bhoi, A., Garcia-Zapirain, B., Hamrioui, S., & de la Torre Díez, I. (2020). Internet of Things and enhanced living environments: Measuring and mapping air quality using cyber-physical systems and mobile computing technologies. *Sensors (Basel)*, *20*(3), 720. doi:10.339020030720 PMID:32012932

Marshall, J. M., Dunstan, D. A., & Bartik, W. (2020). Smartphone psychology: New approaches towards safe and efficacious mobile mental health apps. *Professional Psychology, Research and Practice*, *51*(3), 214–222. doi:10.1037/pro0000278

Matthew-Maich, N., Harris, L., Ploeg, J., Markle-Reid, M., Valaitis, R., Ibrahim, S., Gafni, A., & Isaacs, S. (2016). Designing, implementing, and evaluating mobile health technologies for managing chronic conditions in older adults: A scoping review. *JMIR mHealth and uHealth*, *4*(2), e29. doi:10.2196/mhealth.5127 PMID:27282195

Mehdi, M., Stach, M., Riha, C., Neff, P., Dode, A., Pryss, R., Schlee, W., Reichert, M., & Hauck, F. J. (2020). Smartphone and Mobile Health Apps for Tinnitus: Systematic Identification, Analysis, and Assessment. *JMIR mHealth and uHealth, 8*(8), e21767. doi:10.2196/21767 PMID:32808939

Ming, L. C., Untong, N., Aliudin, N. A., Osili, N., Kifli, N., Tan, C. S., Goh, K. W., Ng, P. W., Al-Worafi, Y. M., Lee, K. S., & Goh, H. P. (2020). Mobile health apps on COVID-19 launched in the early days of the pandemic: Content analysis and review. *JMIR mHealth and uHealth, 8*(9), e19796. doi:10.2196/19796 PMID:32609622

Moher, D., Liberati, A., Tetzlaff, J., & Altman, D. G. (2009). Preferred reporting items for systematic reviews and meta-analyses: The PRISMA statement. *Journal of Clinical Epidemiology, 62*(10), 1006–1012. doi:10.1016/j.jclinepi.2009.06.005 PMID:19631508

Mosa, A. S. M., Yoo, I., & Sheets, L. (2012). A systematic review of healthcare applications for smartphones. *BMC Medical Informatics and Decision Making, 12*(67), 1–31. doi:10.1186/1472-6947-12-67 PMID:22781312

Nestoriuc, Y., Martin, A., Rief, W., & Andrasik, F. (2008). Biofeedback treatment for headache disorders: A comprehensive efficacy review. *Applied Psychophysiology and Biofeedback, 33*(3), 125–140. doi:10.100710484-008-9060-3 PMID:18726688

Noel, M., Petter, M., Parker, J. A., & Chambers, C. T. (2012). Cognitive behavioral therapy for pediatric chronic pain: The problem, research, and practice. *Journal of Cognitive Psychotherapy, 26*(2), 143–156. doi:10.1891/0889-8391.26.2.143

Ntalkos, L., Kambourakis, G., & Damopoulos, D. (2015). 'Let's meet! A participatory-based discovery and rendezvous mobile marketing framework. *Telematics and Informatics, 32*(4), 539–563. doi:10.1016/j.tele.2014.12.002

Palermo, T. M., Eccleston, C., Lewandowski, A. S., Williams, A. C. D. C., & Morley, S. (2010). Randomized controlled trials of psychological therapies for management of chronic pain in children and adolescents: An updated meta-analytic review. *Pain, 148*(3), 387–397. doi:10.1016/j.pain.2009.10.004 PMID:19910118

Palos-Sanchez, P., Reyes-Menendez, A., & Saura, J. R. (2019). Modelos de Adopción de Tecnologías de la Información y Cloud Computing en las Organizaciones. *Información Tecnológica, 30*(3), 3–12. doi:10.4067/S0718-07642019000300003

Peng, W., Yuan, S., & Holtz, B. E. (2016). Exploring the challenges and opportunities of health mobile apps for individuals with type 2 diabetes living in rural communities. *Telemedicine Journal and e-Health, 22*(9), 733–738. doi:10.1089/tmj.2015.0180 PMID:26982017

Pernici, B., Francalanci, C., Geronazzo, A., Lucia, P., Stefano, R., Leonardo, R., . . . Todor, I. (2018). Relating big data business and technical performance indicators. In Conference of the Italian Chapter of AIS (pp. 1-12). Academic Press.

Rahmani, A. M., Gia, T. N., Negash, B., Anzanpour, A., Azimi, I., Jiang, M., & Liljeberg, P. (2018). Exploiting smart e-Health gateways at the edge of healthcare Internet-of-Things: A fog computing approach. *Future Generation Computer Systems*, *78*, 641–658. doi:10.1016/j.future.2017.02.014

Reichberg, S. B., Mitra, P. P., Haghamad, A., Ramrattan, G., Crawford, J. M., Berry, G. J., Davidson, K. W., Drach, A., Duong, S., Juretschko, S., Maria, N. I., Yang, Y., & Ziemba, Y. C.Northwell COVID-19 Research Consortium. (2020). Rapid emergence of SARS-CoV-2 in the greater New York metropolitan area: Geolocation, demographics, positivity rates, and hospitalization for 46 793 persons tested by northwell health. *Clinical Infectious Diseases*, *71*(12), 3204–3213. doi:10.1093/cid/ciaa922 PMID:32640030

Reyes-Menendez, A., Saura, J. R., & Palos-Sánchez, P. (2018). Crowdfunding y financiaci6n 2.0. Un estudio exploratorio sobre el turismo cultural. *International Journal of Information Systems and Tourism*, *3*(1), 23–34.

Reyes-Menendez, A., Saura, J. R., & Filipe, F. (2019). The importance of behavioral data to identify online fake reviews for tourism businesses: A systematic review. *PeerJ. Computer Science*, *5*, e219. doi:10.7717/peerj-cs.219 PMID:33816872

Reyes-Menendez, A., Saura, J. R., & Palos-Sanchez, P. (2020). Identifying key performance indicators for marketing strategies in mobile applications: A systematic literature review. *International Journal of Electronic Marketing and Retailing*, *11*(3), 259–277. doi:10.1504/IJEMR.2020.108126

Rus-Arias, E., Palos-Sanchez, P. R., & Reyes-Menendez, A. (2021). The Influence of Sociological Variables on Users' Feelings about Programmatic Advertising and the Use of Ad-Blockers. *Informatics (MDPI)*, *8*(1), 5. doi:10.3390/informatics8010005

Saura, J. R., Palos-Sánchez, P. R., & Reyes-Menéndez, A. (2017). Marketing a través de aplicaciones móviles de turismo (m-tourism): un estudio exploratorio. *International Journal of World of Tourism, 4*(8), 45-56.

Schnall, R., Rojas, M., Bakken, S., Brown, W., Carballo-Dieguez, A., Carry, M., Gelaude, D., Mosley, J. P., & Travers, J. (2016). A user-centered model for designing consumer mobile health (mHealth) applications (apps). *Journal of Biomedical Informatics*, *60*, 243–251. doi:10.1016/j.jbi.2016.02.002 PMID:26903153

Sharma, T., & Bashir, M. (2020). Use of apps in the COVID-19 response and the loss of privacy protection. *Nature Medicine*, *26*(8), 1165–1167. doi:10.103841591-020-0928-y PMID:32457443

Shea, B. J., Hamel, C., Wells, G. A., Bouter, L. M., Kristjansson, E., Grimshaw, J., & Boers, M. (2009). AMSTAR is a reliable and valid measurement tool to assess the methodological quality of systematic reviews. *Journal of Clinical Epidemiology*, *62*(10), 1013–1020. doi:10.1016/j.jclinepi.2008.10.009 PMID:19230606

Sherman, K. J., Cherkin, D. C., Erro, J., Miglioretti, D. L., & Deyo, R. A. (2005). Comparing yoga, exercise, and a self-care book for chronic low back pain: A randomized, controlled trial. *Annals of Internal Medicine*, *143*(12), 849–856. doi:10.7326/0003-4819-143-12-200512200-00003 PMID:16365466

Shu, Y., Lin, L., & Hu, Y. (2020). A Study on the Health Output Effect of Chinese Medical Service Industry Agglomeration Based on Big Data Analysis. *Mathematical Problems in Engineering*, 2020.

Slathia, R., & Nagamalai, J. (2016). *Internet of things in mobile health care (IoT-m health)*. Academic Press.

Statista. (2020). *mHealth-Statistics & Facts*. https://www.statista.com/topics/2263/mHealth/

Stoyanov, S. R., Hides, L., Kavanagh, D. J., Zelenko, O., Tjondronegoro, D., & Mani, M. (2015). Mobile app rating scale: A new tool for assessing the quality of health mobile apps. *JMIR mHealth and uHealth*, *3*(1), e27. doi:10.2196/mhealth.3422 PMID:25760773

Taylor, D., & Roane, B. (2010). Treatment of Insomnia in Adults and Children: A Practice-Friendly Review of Research. *Journal of Clinical Psychology*, *6*(11), 1137–1147. doi:10.1002/jclp.20733 PMID:20890946

Tyer, D. (2013). *Mobile health apps - still a novelty?* http://www.pmlive.com/blogs/digital_intelligence/archive/2013/november/mobile_health_apps_-_still_a_novelty

Van den Bosch, M., & Sang, Å. O. (2017). Urban natural environments as nature-based solutions for improved public health–A systematic review of reviews. *Environmental Research*, *158*, 373–384. doi:10.1016/j.envres.2017.05.040 PMID:28686952

van Velsen, L., Beaujean, D. J. M. A., & van Gemert-Pijnen, J. E. W. C. (2013). Why mobile health app overload drives us crazy, and how to restore the sanity. *BMC Medical Informatics and Decision Making*, *13*(23), 1–5. doi:10.1186/1472-6947-13-23 PMID:23399513

Ventola, C. L. (2014). Mobile devices and apps for health care professionals: Uses and benefits. *P&T*, *39*(5), 356. PMID:24883008

Wahl, B., Cossy-Gantner, A., Germann, S., & Schwalbe, N. R. (2018). Artificial intelligence (AI) and global health: How can AI contribute to health in resource-poor settings? *BMJ Global Health*, *3*(4), e000798. doi:10.1136/bmjgh-2018-000798 PMID:30233828

Wu, M., & Luo, J. (2019, Fall). Wearable technology applications in healthcare: A literature review. *On-Line Journal of Nursing Informatics*, *23*(3). https://www.himss.org/ojni

Xia, F., Yang, L. T., Wang, L., & Vinel, A. (2012). Internet of things. *International Journal of Communication Systems*, *25*(9), 1101–1102. doi:10.1002/dac.2417

Zapatero, M. D. C., Señán, G. B., & Román, J. A. R. S. (2017). Sociabilidad virtual: la interacción social en el ecosistema digital. *Historia y Comunicación Social, 22*(1), 233-247.

Zhang, C., Zhang, X., & Halstead-Nussloch, R. (2014). Assessment Metrics, Challenges, and Strategies for Mobile Health Apps. *Issues in Information Systems, 15*(2).

Zhao, J., Freeman, B., & Li, M. (2016). Can mobile phone apps influence people's health behavior change? An evidence review. *Journal of Medical Internet Research, 18*(11), e287. doi:10.2196/jmir.5692 PMID:27806926

Zunzarren, H., & Gorospe, B. (2012). *Guía del Social Media Marketing: ¿cómo hacer gestión empresarial 2.0 a través de la aplicación de Inteligencia Digital?* ESIC.

KEY TERMS ANS DEFINITIONS

APP: A computer application that allows, through a mobile device, to execute tasks to manage professional activities, access information or communicate, among other services.

Disease: Disturbance of the normal functioning of the organism leading to a deterioration of the organism.

Geolocation: The process of determining the geographic position or specific location of a person or object through the GPS system of a mobile device, an IP address, or a postal code, among others.

Health: State in which a living being is in a state of complete physical, mental and social well-being and free from disease.

KPI: Key Performance Indicator is a unit of measurement that allows to assess if the company is reaching the objectives.

mHealth: Is a branch of digital Health in which the practice of health care is supported by mobile devices.

Mobile: A wireless phone device, if the device has access to the internet it is commonly referred to as smartphone.

Chapter 12
Positive Technology:
A Growing Market With a Potential to Rebuild a Resilient Society During and After the COVID-19 Crisis

Anuragini Shirish
https://orcid.org/0000-0001-8199-2889
Université Paris-Saclay, France & Université d'Évry, France & LITEM, IMT-BS, France

ABSTRACT

Given the crucial need to bridge the mental health service divide, the author examines the emerging trends in digital well-being management by focusing on the mobile health market. Using a bottom-up perspective and leveraging literature from positive technology and generalized unsafety theory of stress, the author conceptualizes how positive technology as a mobile health solution can help end users to respond effectively to different kinds of stressors during a crisis. It is further argued that the use of positive technology can positively reverse the automatic route to mental ill health that is plausible in the absence of safety perceptions. The chapter offers a theory-driven conceptualization of digital coping through positive technology. By showing how a simple, scalable, and sustainable positive technology design can cater to different user segments, the author urges policymakers, entrepreneurs, and healthcare service providers to participate in the design, propagation, adoption, and diffusion of such holistic positive technologies for fostering societal resilience.

INTRODUCTION

The crisis and its associated management strategies that involve quarantines and

DOI: 10.4018/978-1-7998-7263-4.ch012

lockdowns has affected how individuals can cope with this pandemic at the physical, social, emotional and spiritual levels. Individuals find the need to preserve the old and they may need to adapt to the new normal (Lazarus & Folkman, 1984). In either way, individuals would resort to sense making mechanisms to cope with the imminent impact of the pandemic on their life and that of their loved ones (Christianson & Barton, 2020). The World Health Organization (WHO) defines health as a "State of complete physical, mental, and social well-being, and not merely the absence of disease or infirmity" (WHOa, 1948). The WHO expects elevated rates of stress or anxiety amongst the population: both the frontline workers, old people, people with prior health conditions and amongst public if there is a lack of access to basic services and if lock down measures continue (WHOb, 2020). Stress can be defined as the inability of a person to cope with internal or environmental demands. Stress is therefore not a stimulus or a reaction to a stimulus but it is a process of adaptation between a person and a specific environment (Lazarus & Folkman, 1984). Table 1 below depicts the current stress creating situation.

Table 1. Dynamic and ongoing events affecting well-being during the COVID-19 crisis

Preservation of Old	Adaptation to the New
Keep our usual routine going	Adjust to work-life conflict
Keep our activities going	Adjust to technology overload
Keep our livelihoods intact	Adjust to the unknown threat to life

Source: Author

Although coping is an essential element to handle adversities, there are differences between coping and resilience (Fletcher & Sarkar 2013). In this study, we follow the view that resilience relates to positive adaptation despite the presence of risk or adversity; it has both protective and promote factors encapsulated in the notion of a trait and a process (Fletcher & Sarkar 2013; Sarkar & Hilton, 2013). Recent study defines resilience as "the role of mental processes and behavior in promoting personal assets and protecting an individual from the potential negative effect of stressors" (Fletcher & Sarkar, 2013, p. 16). Further, individual and collective resilience can be built over time (Sarkar & Hilton, 2020).

As of January 2021, we note that several countries such as France, UK, Japan, Germany are thinking about imposing their third lock down measures to handle the pandemic situation. It is predicted that we will witness higher levels of loneliness, depression, harmful alcohol and drug use, and self-harm or suicidal behaviors. They estimated depression and anxiety to be 1 trillion in 2019 (Sime, 2019) and this number will only multiple in 2020 and 2021 showing the lack of collective and individual resilience to manage the multitude stressors posed by the pandemic. Prior studies have shown implications to management as well as to marketing domains when individuals and collectives use digital means to cope with complex societal problems (Reyes-Menendez et al., 2020). Further, health care systems of governments all around the world have failed to keep up with this surge in mental health services in these tough times (Barton et al., 2020).

Given this scenario, we can notice that well-being interventions are offered either expressly or impliedly by several actors in the society (Wilson, 2020). As more and more population, all over the global abundantly rely on mobile devices and other wearable devices (Digital Wellbeing Statistics, 2020) we see the emergence of digital health market with tele health and mobile health (mHealth) resorted to as a rescue measure by individuals for digital coping.

Telehealth refers to delivery of health care services, where patients and providers are separated by distance(WHO, 2016). The use of mobile wireless technologies for public health is termed as mHealth (WHO, 2018b). mHealth is an integral part of eHealth, which refers to the cost-effective and secure use of information and communication technologies in support of health and health-related fields (WHO, 2018b). The term digital health refers to both eHealth and mHealth (e.g. telemedicine, electronic health records and wearable sensors) as well as developing areas such as the use of advanced computing sciences in the fields of big data and artificial intelligence, robotic (WHO, 2018a). Tele health measures have not become the mainstream model for medical care services yet. We often view it as an ad hoc crisis management measure (Smith et al., 2020), therefore its market growth is uncertain. Telemedicine is a regulated industry whereas mHealth providing well-being oriented services whether catering to individuals, corporates and medical professionals are less regulated. Thus these activities may or may not be ethical and legal in all countries (Nittari et al., 2020). In this chapter, we provide an overview of the global mHealth market that is the predominant feature of digital health domain as per a recent review article (Fatehi et al., 2020) and we underline its main opportunities and challenges. We finally aim to offer a model paper that can depict the relevance and relationship of mHealth digital technologies in developing individual resilience by enhancing their well-being (MacInnis, 2011). This chapter also offers several implications that help integrate both mHealth and eHealth marketing and management. An holistic understanding about the psychological and behavioral aspects concerning the dynamics of stressor and its interpretations in general will enable organization involved in providing digital behavioral interventions in an engaging and effective manner (Maher et al., 2014; Ryan et al., 2017; Short et al., 2018). It can provide further insights for undertaking effective and user centric social marketing for the promotion of public health campaigns that has been missing in the literature so far (Patel & Arya, 2017).

The remainder of the chapter is structured as follows. In section 2 we expand on the current context and connect the literature on mHealth, positive technologies, stress and well-being. We do this by specifically examining the evolution and the potential of positive technologies embedded in the mHealth context in empowering individuals to digitally cope with the several technology-induced stressors pertaining to the crisis. In Section 3, we elaborate on our conceptual modeling by introducing the theoretical lens used to generate our conceptual model that integrates the concept of positive technology to effectively manage stress responses of individuals and collectives during a crisis from a bottom up perspective. This extends prior literature and calls to further increase the understanding of customers of digital health services and products from a user centric health management and marketing perspective. In section 4, we conclude by providing our conceptual model and the desired positive technology design strategy that can effectively enhance the coping self-efficacy of an individual increasing the resilience during and beyond a crisis situation. In section 5, we offer future perspectives and limitations of the study. In the final section, we conclude by highlighting how the conceptual model adds to the current understanding of positive technologies that have the potential to bridge the mental health service divide in a scalable and sustainable manner. The propositions can contribute towards digital resilience building efforts and can guide digital innovations, marketing and management of health services at a global level.

CONTEXT AND LITERATURE

MHealth Market: An Overview

The mere presence of media technology has known to ease loneliness symptoms (Hughes, 2020). We can see that as per a French study, tele health sector has easy access to market but takes a longer time for maturing as several behavioral changes and legislative hurdles need to be removed before creating and capturing business value in this sector (Le Goff-Pronost & Krychowski, 2020). Despite these challenges, we cannot ignore that mobile health (mHealth) services are expected to raise up to USD 144.4 billion in 2020, and its annual growth is said to be 27.7% per year. Combined with both the market segment needs and proliferation of digital devices in the world, we can predict that the market for digital wellbeing products and services will continue to rise.

Emerging technologies to support mHealth have revolutionized the healthcare industry. The adoption of mHealth has been significant in the recent years

(Koumpouros & Georgoulas, 2020) but traditional technology adoption model are not known to directly apply to mHealth adoption as user profiles and developmental stages of the country are contextual differences that need empirical testing prior to rolling out of such services (Alam et al., 2020). According to a recent report, over 325,000 mHealth apps are available for apple and android smartphones (GM Insights, 2020). Rising acceptance of mHealth as a primary source of information during sense making has contributed to a positive market growth. Europe is leading in this domain through funding several research initiatives on mHealth (Koumpouros & Georgoulas, 2020). Recent global surveys show that health apps are mostly downloaded by Indian, Chinese, Indonesian and the North American populations (See Figure 1).

Figure 1. mHealth app usage statistics
Source: Statista

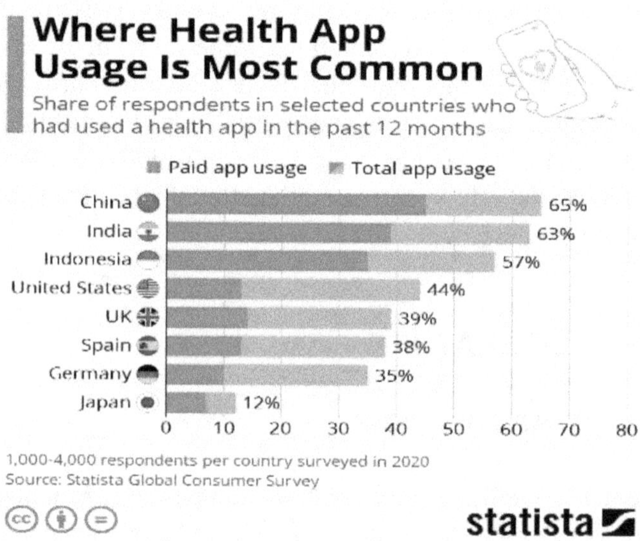

As per prior literature, mHealth services refer to those health services which are delivered through the use of mobile communication technology (Free et al., 2013; Guo et al., 2016; Silva et al., 2015; Silva et al., 2019). Mobile health applications are mostly used for preventive measures, the discovery of health problems, and diagnosis or treatments of diseases amongst others (Bipat et al., 2018). Its use for preventive mental health through social media conversational agents are also on the rise (Meske et al., 2020). mHealth apps and tools are known for their low-cost, high-quality and efficiency (Sun & Feng, 2020; Zhang et al., 2014). However, individuals'

acceptance of mHealth is still low as most offerings are not user centric both in design and in usage parameters (Pan & Zhao, 2018; Zhao et al., 2018). There are several policy issues arising due to political, environmental, economic, organizational, and technology disparities across nations acting as a significant impediment to developing mHealth products and services for global deployment. Payment methods, excessive governmental scrutiny, global resource scarcity are unresolved even at the global levels (Malvey & Slovensky, 2017). eHealth business models are often not sustainable for business as they fail to adopt a customer-centric view, where direct tangible benefits of interventions are identified and communicated effectively (Gorski et al., 2016). Further, its economic value may dependent upon geography and type of intervention it focuses, which can range from diseases management to behavioral change management (Iribarren et al., 2017). Many mHealth projects are not scalable in developing countries where health service divide may be more pronounced (Malvey & Slovensky, 2017; Srivastava & Shainesh, 2015).

There are few other crucial managerial and governance questions surrounding mHealth markets. These are related to safety of mHealth apps, concerns over the use of their data, technology spatial intrusion, the lack of interoperability among solutions, the lack of stakeholder knowledge of the legal requirements applicable to lifestyle and wellbeing apps, such as compliance with data protection rules and whether these apps are medical devices and need to get specific licensing. (Chandra et al., 2020; Silva et al., 2015). Lack of trust among citizens, education, public funding and global health service provider's lack of collaborative sprit add to the many roadblocks to mHealth development and scalability (Malvey & Slovensky, 2017; Ricciardi et al., 2019).

Despite the negatives, several researchers as looking at ways and means to persuade users to use these services, especially in mandatory context such as vaccination or other public health concerns. For example, researchers are looking at how coping appeals are perceived by mHealth service users so that appropriate level of fear can be induced in health related communication delivered through mHealth tools (Sun & Feng, 2020). Similarly, recent studies look at priming effects of short ecological momentary surveys provided to home monitored patients to undertake the required physical activity through digital nudges (Sengupta et al., 2020). Others have looked at adoption and resistance of mHealth tools (Samhan, 2017; Zhang et al., 2017; Zhao et al., 2018). We can see the need for such services, especially in the COVID-19 pandemic as more people are suffering from ill health issues that are directly affecting their quality of life (Riva et al., 2020b). Therefore understanding the specific challenges individuals face during the crisis is therefore an essential element in designing the appropriate mHealth technology. Figure 2 provides an overview of mHealth market.

Figure 2. MHealth market
Source: Adapted from GMInsights, 2020

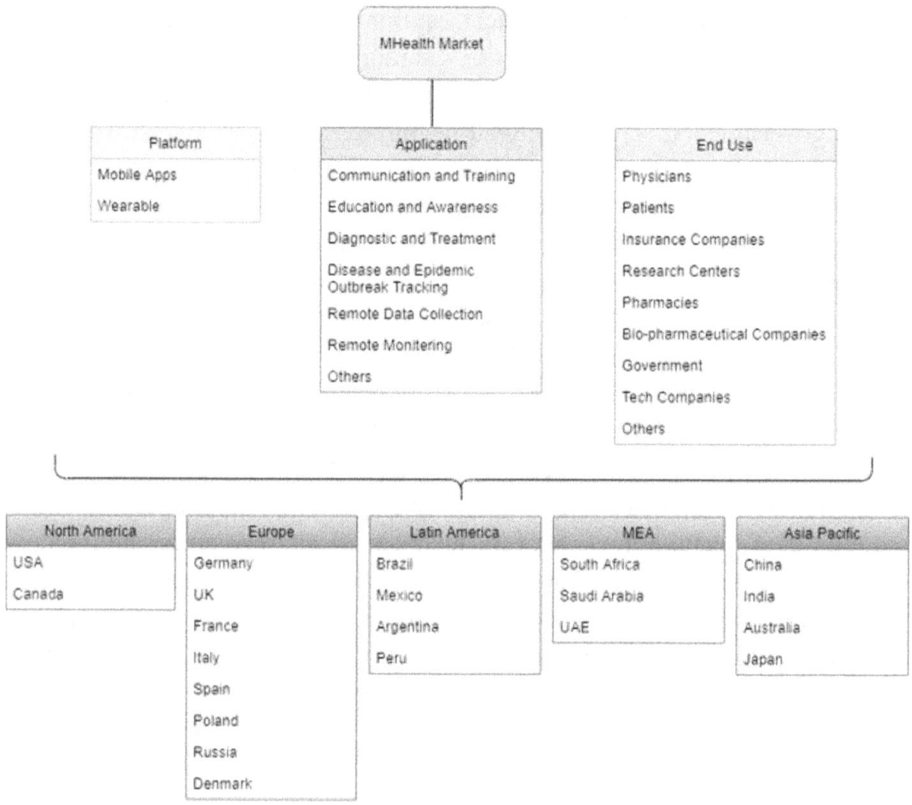

Crisis and Technology Induced Challenges Influencing Well-Being and Health

As shown above, there is an imminent need to address the mental health (good and ill) concerns of the population during the pandemic times. This issue can affect all age groups. Research states that 75 percent of all mental health diagnosis have their onset before the age of 24 (Fitzpatrick et al., 2017). Teenagers are vulnerable population to suffer from this crisis (Meske et al., 2020). Localized measures for treating mental health is superior, but we cannot ignore the accessibility offered by mHealth and internet based social media solutions to manage health services at scale. Hence adequate measures for both prevention and diagnosis of mental health issues become crucial. Introducing technology to help inculcate a positive mind set also becomes very essential to overcome the long-term effects of the crisis on the society.

Positive technologies are profitable and useful in bridging this service divide (Srivastava & Shainesh, 2015) as it can enhance self-management of mental health and well-being (Riva et al., 2020b) and is usually deployable at scale. We can see that several manifestations of mental health issues typify the situation we face during the COVID-19 crisis and these are said to linger on for years. Some of these are challenges are technology induced and are specifically discussed below. However, other issues that may not be technology induced would also require examination.

Technology induced stressors have risen in the past years and new ways of working such as information communication technology (ICT) based mobile working have augmented this phenomenon during crisis. Remote working preferences has caused wellbeing concerns, increasing the demand for technostress prevention and coping (Shirish, 2020) which is proven to cause burn out (Ayyagari, 2012; Srivastava et al., 2015; Srivastava & Shainesh, 2015). The ubiquitous and pervasive nature of digital technologies disrupts the natural balance or the homeostasis of an individual's technostress perceptions of five kinds - techno-overload, techno-invasion, techno-complexity, techno-insecurity, and techno uncertainty (Tarafdar et al., 2010). Some research sheds light on how these demands are coped with by different individuals of various personalities (Srivastava et al., 2015) and others focus on cognitive and the affective process of coping (Chandra et al., 2020; Shirish, 2020a). Techno-overload describes situations where use of new technologies forces individual to work more and faster. Techno-invasion describes being "always exposed" and reachable anywhere, anytime. It also includes the perceptions of the need to be constantly connected because of work. Techno-complexity describes situations where the complex technology used for work, drives individual to spend time and effort in learning and understanding new applications, forcing them to update their skills constantly. Techno-insecurity arises in situations where the individuals feels threatened about losing his/her job to those who have better ICT skills. Techno-uncertainty relates to the sense of helplessness in the face of rapidly changing computer knowledge and skills that require constant adaptation (Shirish, 2020a).

Researchers are grappling with interventions even at the organizational levels to contain techno stressor related consequences (Tarafdar et al., 2019), thus at a societal level, this issue is ill governed requiring a scalable solution such as positive technologies to be adopted to counteract stress-strain prevention and management by creating an organizational safety culture (Brivio et al., 2018). However, empirical research in the area is lacking, there is need to offer solutions to tackle techno overload phenomenon as well.

Another area of concern stemming from technology use is work life conflict and spill overs. Research shows that technology-driven challenge and hindrance stressors experienced at work affect the relationship between employees and their partners. Technology driven hindrance stressors are negatively related to partnership satisfaction when they go through negative affect. Technology driven challenge stressors are positively related to partnership satisfaction, as they do through positive affect. Work–home role integration capability of an individual and perceived organizational support are viewed as important work–home boundary management capabilities that moderate the stress response process (Benlian et al., 2020). Other studies have also shown that affect towards ICT use is another important mediator that can change the negative influences from cognitive appraisal stage to a positive one, attenuating any technology induced negative outcomes or positively contributing well-being outcomes (Shirish, 2020a). Thus, we can see that technology affective frames and technology cognitive frames both are important elements to experience safety perceptions when faced with demands mediated by technology (Shirish, 2020a). However, a detail examination of how to cope with work life conflict induced by technological interruptions are unclear.

In the below section we discuss the root cause of stress to understand the user segment and their problems. Thus following a bottom up conceptualization of mHealth products and services can address these global challenges of techno stressors including techno overload, work life conflict and mental health concerns.

CONCEPTUAL MODELING

Conceptual research work can follow several research designs from theory synthesis, theory adaptation, typology, and model (Jaakkola, 2020). This chapter uses the model approach, where we attempt to build a theoretical framework that predicts relationships between constructs (Jaakkola, 2020). We do this for identifying novel connections based on past literature and theories, as well as for explaining why a sequence of events leads to an outcome (Jaakkola, 2020). We elaborate further on the above literature and leverage psychological theories to develop a novel model of positive technology for resilience during the context of the pandemic.

Safety, Stress and Coping

Crisis has triggered a sense of generalized unsafety perceptions amongst population of all ages and in all countries. We see the rise of prolonged and chronic stress responses that are not adequately managed at the family, company or the society levels sufficiently (Christianson & Barton, 2020). As per past research, the number of people whose mental health is affected is greater than the number of people affected by the infection. The impact on mental health lasts longer even after the end of the pandemic itself as they have a ripple effect on the psychosocial and economic aspects. Leading to a mental ill health curve (Staglin, 2020). Coping self-efficacy is said to mediate the impact between coping resources and stress responses during a crisis situation (Benight & Bandura, 2004; Benight et al., 1999)

As per the generalized unsafety theory of stress (Brosschot et al., 2018), the stress response is a default response, it is 'always there'; it is not generated by a specific stressor but dis-inhibited. It is present when there is a **generalized perception of unsafety (GU).** This default response is dis-inhibited by prefrontal functions of our brain as long as we perceive safety. We learn the conditions of safety during our lifetime. The more we have controlled any stressor in the past, the more we can control future stressors. Chronic stress responses are because of this GU perceptions and not because of the stressors in specific. GU is present in many other conditions including (1) a compromised body: low fitness caused by obesity, old age, illness. These are linked to feeling of safety; (2) a compromised social network: Increased feeling of loneliness. A personal social network will provide the feeling of safety; (3) a compromised context: An employee that has experienced harassments at work. He/she would now consider the entire work context stressful, even though the harassment episodes may be one or two in a year. Humans sometimes cannot recognize the objective context as safe. Although some amount of stress is good, the ability of the individual to cope with the stress is a crucial need (Chandra et al., 2019).

Habitual mal adaptive stress responses can lead to early aging as it can alter our DNAs. Research proposes a model describing how meditation training may impact acute and habitual stress responses as pathways to improved cell aging, contributing to telomere regulation in individuals (Conklin et al., 2019). Thus digital tools that offer meditation as a solution can be viewed as one kind of positive technology that can have positive impact on how safety perceptions can be felt by individuals daily including health care professionals or frontline workers (Amarnath et al., 2017; Cohen et al., 2015; Downey, 2015; Thimmapuram et al., 2017; Thimmapuram et al., 2020). To delve in to the mechanism of how positive technology can play a role in well-being, it is imperative to understand the stress and coping phenomenon.

Stress can take the form of acute stress or chronic stress. Acute stress are generated by onetime stressful events such as speaking in public. Hurt to one's ego may cause momentary or short time unsafe feelings or anger towards an event. Similarly, we may have short-term responses or longer responses to these events. Chronic stress occurs when there is a repeated exposure to conditions that are unsafe. Those can be threats, demands, structural constraints, under reward, complexity, uncertainty, conflict, restriction of choice, resource deprivation (Gottlieb, 1997). The present pandemic conditions give rise to both types of stressors as they both have the potential to be perceived as generalized unsafety condition, causing us to display 'always on' stress response which can be harmful to us. Therefore understanding how to respond better to stress perceptions that trigger automatic responses is important. Moreover, knowing how to improve our coping self-efficacy or skills is another consequential question to address. So what do we require to do to address the 'always turned on' stress response? We can see that individuals during the pandemic are in search of safety signals in their environment in order to remain stress free and healthy lifestyle (Srivastava et al. 2021). Therefore, positive technology use is often resorted to as a way for sense making and continuous coping with stress.

Positive Technologies and Resilience

Positive technology is a scientific and applied approach for improving the quality of our personal experience with the goal of increasing wellness, generating strengths and resilience in individuals, organizations, and society (Botella et al., 2012). Derived from positive psychology that argues that positive emotions, engagement, and connectedness promote adaptive behaviors and positive functioning in individuals (Riva et al., 2020a). Positive technology therefore can provide vitality, meaning, and purpose additionally offer a sense of connectedness. We mention three types of positive technology in literature that can offer a range of changes that support our wellbeing (physical, mental and social) (Botella et al., 2012; Stibe & Cugelman, 2019). Thus, positive technologies can meet hedonic, social and eudaimonic needs of a large population during this tough time of pandemic and offer a unique opportunity to self-manage their mental health and wellbeing effectively (Riva et al., 2012; Riva et al., 2020a).

In prior literature, we see that mobile applications as positive technology have been used by individuals as well as health care providers as treatment interventions to improve mental wellbeing among diverse population (Meske et al., 2020; Sengupta et al., 2020). Some features of these applications include monitoring, participant engagement, tailoring, gamification, adherence, social component, guidance, stimulation possibilities, apps linked to internet of things (IoT) devices (Diefenbach, 2018; Kitson et al., 2018; Mirkovic et al., 2018; Montana et al., 2019; Perez-Marcos et al., 2018; Quesnel & Riecke, 2018; Villani et al., 2018). It has also been used for life skills education to increase resilience amongst younger population (Gabrielli et al., 2020) and to provide stress management possibilities to immigrants (Recupero et al., 2018) and employees to fight against techno stress (Brivio et al., 2018). However, its efficacy is questioned (Weisel et al., 2019). Wearables are another enormous market that has a potential to provide well-being services at scale to larger segments of society. Germany is one of rare countries to have provided legitimacy to introduce wearables as public health measure through legislation (Heidel & Hagist, 2020). We see that both mobile and wearable markets to increase health and well-being (Heidel & Hagist, 2020).

Researchers recommend that before rolling out any digital services as a standalone intervention, it could be useful to consider user-driven and solution-focused offerings.

Designing such solutions using bottom up approach by incorporating comments and feedback from app developers, researchers and clinicians in the process is proposed as the way forward (Weisel et al., 2019). We can use ICT enabled design thinking as one of the innovation management solutions that relies on bottom up mechanism that can lead to an efficient mHealth and wearables solution collaboratively (Farao et al., 2020; Shirish et al., 2019). Thus enabling better user engagement one of preoccupations of marketing (Short et al., 2020)

Further, persuasive technologies or design by intention has been important domains to address the inefficiency in the mobile health app market. However, the success of these apps and wearables depend on user engagement (Weisel et al., 2019). Therefore it is important to understand adherence motivations, user profile specificity, and usage pattern so that these digital self-management solutions actually contribute to resilience of the society i.e., a society with good mental health and well-being. For example, older adults and younger ones may respond to digital mHealth technologies differently (Jaana & Paré, 2020; Meske et al., 2020). We should take care that we inflict no unintended or intended negative consequences upon vulnerable user groups through the digital mHealth solutions as organizations battle to increase the user engagement (Shirish, 2018).

It is clear that positive technologies can offer a mass solution to handle the mental health crisis during the pandemic and beyond by increasing the coping self-efficacy perceptions of different users. Table 2 provides a table that classifies positive technologies based on coping strategies that it might trigger. With hedonic positive technology, we can see that it caters to the enjoying self that is looking for safety. The coping that is used through the use of these technologies can be referred to as transactional. Thus it is term it as "transactional coping". The hedonic technology is usually resorted to as a temporary measure to handle a temporary yet specific stressful context. These technological solutions offer positive emotional experience and positive sensorial experiences. They are often easily available and accessed.

The most important aspect to consider in this type of positive technology is that the digital artefact provides affordances that can alter an individual's mood or transitory perceptions from a negative to a positive one. However, it is contended that in such case of coping, coping self-efficacy does not develop to a great extent. Therefore, it only contribute to a short term coping scenario and does not help the individual or the society to move towards collective coping resilience.

With social positive technology, we can see that it caters to the shared self that is looking for safety (Botella et al., 2012). The coping that is used through the use of these technologies can be referred to as transitory. Thus, it is termed as "transitory coping". The social technology is usually resorted to for a finite period to handle a transitory stressful event or episode such as confinement during the COVID-19 lockdown measures imposed by countries. They design these technological solutions to offer a shared positive emotions. They can also offer well-being trainings. They may even be pro-social in nature and help set shared significant goals with specific type of people in their community (Botella et al., 2012). These positive technologies fulfill motivational needs of an individual.

The most important aspect to consider in this type of positive technology is that the digital artefact provides affordances that can alter an individual's sense of connectedness to others. However, it is contended that in such cases, the individual may develop context dependent coping that may not be transferable to other settings easily but builds one's resilience to similar stressful events in the future. Therefore, it only contribute to a midterm coping scenario and helps the individual or the society to move towards collective coping resilience to some extent.

Table 2. Positive technology and coping classification

Hedonic	Social (Includes Interpersonal)	Eudaimonic
The enjoying self, looking for safety	The shared self, looking for safety	The growing self, looking for safety
Transactional coping	Transitory coping	Transformation coping
Temporary- in specific context	Defined term -in specific context	Timeless -in any context
Positive emotional experience and positive sensorial experience	Shared positive emotions, wellbeing training, developing and sharing strengths, setting shared signification goals, prosocial activities	Positive mood induction, life training and setting significant goals, wellbeing training
Usually economical	Usually motivational	Usually spiritual
Technology can offer mood altering positive experience	Technology can create the feeling of connectedness	Technology can offer an engaging and self-actualizing experience
Coping self efficacy does not develop to a great extent	Develops context dependent coping self efficacy	Develops long terms coping self efficacy

Source: Adapted from Shirish, 2020b

With eudaimonic technology, we can see that it caters to growing self that is looking for safety (Botella et al., 2012). The coping that is used through the use of these technologies can be referred to as transformational. Thus, it is termed as "transformational coping". The eudaimonic technology is timeless and thus useful for many stressful situations and events, as it is non-contextual. They design eudaimonic technological solutions, to offer well-being training; positive mood induction. It concerns itself with life trainings and helps one set significant life goals. These positive technologies fulfill spiritual needs of an individual.

The most important aspect to consider in this type is that the digital artefact provides affordances that can provide engaging and self-actualizing experience, the highest goal sought after by human kind, especially for younger generations (Buie, 2016; Gabrielli et al., 2020; Shirish et al., 2016). Some contend that in such case of coping, the individual may develop long term coping self-efficacy that can come in handy during any crisis or stressful situation. Significantly building long term coping scenarios and helps the individual or the society to move towards collective coping resilience to a great extent. Table 3 provides the types and few examples under each type.

Table 3. Positive technology types and their examples

Hedonic Positive Technology	Social Positive Technology	Eudaimonic Positive Technology
Generic examples: Listening to online music, watching TV or playing video games at times of stress, fact checking for right news, health trackers to monitor health goals, tools that offer help in relaxation, etc	Generic examples: Contributing to Wikipedia, social networking platforms and websites, youtube, maintaining a blog to share experiences, etc	Generic examples: Tools that provide a flow experience, self-growing tools such as meditation Apps, mindfulness training, listening to speeches of learned masters online, using ICT to work on meaningful personal projects.
Specific example: Fitbit watch used for monitoring stress levels and sleep levels to help relax and rest better.	Specific example: Facebook App more specifically, the COVID Support and Recovery a private facebook group created for New York city that has approximately 40 thousand members who share their experience to support each other throughout the pandemic.	Specific example: Meditation apps like Calm, HeadScape for learning to meditate each having millions of users.

Source: Author

RESULTS AND DISCUSSION

Presenting the Conceptual Model

In this sub-section, we provide our conceptual model on how positive technology especially social and eudaimonic technologies such as mobile apps or wearables can contribute to individual resilience through reduced stress responses and mal adaptive coping of crisis or stress. The figure 3 below provides the conceptual model taking crisis as an example to show how positive technologies can help build individual resilience, which will undoubtedly contribute to societal resilience. The example provides instances that are very general, however these can provide further insights to user experience designers of positive technology and mHealth to customize them to respective user segments using the concept of "personas".

We can see that an individual can experience individual stressors stemming from **intermittent situation** that are embedded in specific context and may be different for each individual in the course of their day to day life. They can also experience **collective environmental stressors** that can be **prolonged** and influence their life domains constantly. In the example of COVID-19 crisis, we can imagine certain **environmental context** such as social distancing; limited contact with nature for some individuals depending upon restrictions placed on movement; fear of infection; isolation; uncertain economic conditions; high technology dependence as common features that can **alter an individual's safety perceptions.**

Figure 3. Impact of Positive Technologies on Well-Being at time of COVID-19 crisis
Source: Shirish, 2020b

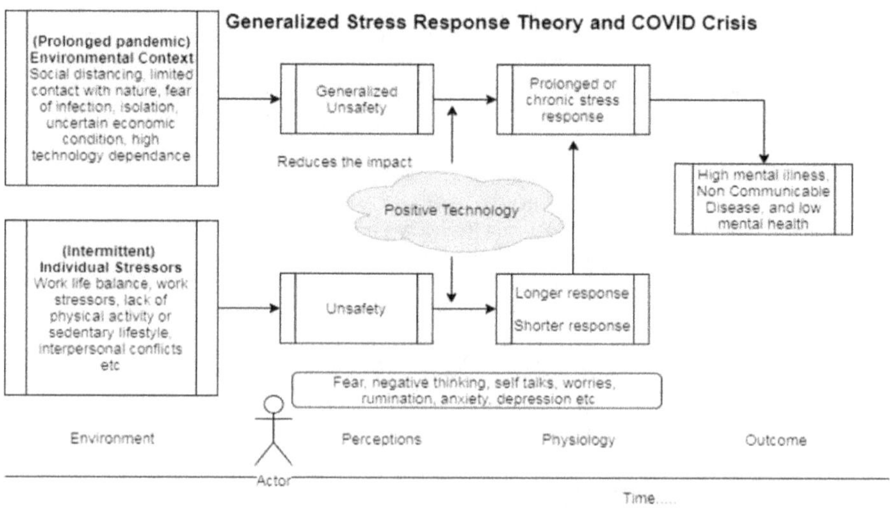

We can imagine other intermittent individual stressors that are likely to exist among many individuals as we adapt to the novel ways of working, new routines, and life in general. They can be new demands for increased work life balance; work stressors; lack of physical activity or sedentary lifestyle; increase of interpersonal conflicts etc. These issues can also trigger **a sense of unsafe perception** in individuals that triggers **stress responses** that vary in type and duration. They that could **be longer or shorter** in nature. These stress responses can also manifest in a **generalized form** or it can transform into **prolonged or chronic stress responses** as per the generalized stress response theory.

Other stress responses can include **fear, negative thinking, self-talks, worries, rumination, anxiety, depression etc**. Based on the promise of positive technology to alter the stress responses to a positive one, we can contend that it can act as a moderator between (generalized) unsafety perceptions and stress responses (long, short, prolonged or chronic), thereby positively contributing to mental well-being and reducing non-communicable diseases in end-users of these technologies.

Holistic Positive Technology: An Illustration

During the pandemic, we have seen the rise of many digital offerings that fall under the scope of techno-spiritual designs that are offered by non-traditional and not-for-profit organizations in the society. They may aim to offer stress management to self-transcendental experience to citizens from diverse countries. Mindfulness and Heartfulness mediation and related practices have gained considerable attention in the recent times. It has shown to provide physical, emotional and social well-being to several types of populations undergoing different stressors in their life. (Amarnath et al., 2017; Anderson-Ross, 2020; Arya et al., 2017; Daugherty, 2014; Iyer & Iyer, 2019; Karmarkar et al., 2020; Léonard et al., 2019; Murphy-Shigematsu, 2018; Niemiec, 2017; Sylapan et al., 2020; Thimmapuram et al., 2020; Voci et al., 2019). Heartfulness based digital offerings have the potential to appeal to one of the three types of users discussed above: the pleasing self, connected self or the growing self (Botella et al., 2012). It can also speak to all the three holistically for a design perspective. For example, we provide here the HeartsApp as an example to show the potential of positive technology to develop individual and collective resilience (Heartfulness Institute, 2020). This positive technology is a simple mobile application provided by a not-for-profit global organization that offers simple relaxation techniques that can provide transitory coping abilities when faced with stressors 24/7. The app offers the possibility to contribute to voluntary activities or join in a group meditation as a family with a remote mediation trainer from anywhere in the globe. The app also offers the features that allow users to learn and sharpen the practice of meditation to deepen the transcendental experience felt by meditators by offering them several possibilities to schedule one to one remote meditation sessions with Heartfulness trainers. Affordances that nudge users to involve in self-reflective behaviors such as journal writing, encouraging retreats and digital detox practices can help users to develop transformational coping self-efficacy in a self-paced manner. This example shows a powerful yet simple positive technology that can appeal to masses. Supporting the adoption and wide spread use in schools, corporates and hospitals such holistic positive technology design solutions as a public health measure can build collective resilience and create lasting positive change in the society at large.

FUTURE PERSPECTIVES AND LIMITATIONS

This study offers a conceptual model that has attempted to propose interesting novel connections to the psychological notions of stress and coping during pandemic and the how positive technology can help in building coping self-efficacy and resilience in society. More research is needed in validating this model in settings where behavioral health interventions are undertaken in scale. This will allow us to better understand how to promote and increase engagement using health interventions during a pandemic from an empirical stand point. Further research can take this model to test the differences between each type of positive technology to extend a nuanced understanding of resilience building. Moreover, there is lack of research on holistic positive technology and the role of non-profit organizations in building societal resilience. This is a ripe area for future research. Information system design and behavioral aspects of technology use are other areas can also leverage this model. A longitudinal study using system data or ecological momentary surveys or social media analysis could be suitable methods to establish the transformative potential of positive technology in the health domain. This study has attempted to integrate interdisciplinary concepts into one unique framework, there could be other theoretical lens that can be used to develop a conceptual model. Moreover, the study does not undertake a systematic review of literature of underlining concepts. The chapter is conceptual and we do not claim any immediate practical implication of this work to the marketing and health domain but we do believe further research can contribute to this goal using this study as a starting point.

CONCLUSION

The COVID-19 pandemic has put well-being and health at the center of societal resilience and progress. Populations suffering from mental health and well-being have increased manifold in the last one year exposing gaps in the public health systems in providing and maintaining a resilience in society. As a complementary strategy, mHealth service providers (commercial and non-commercial) have sprung up to bridge the health service divide at a global scale. Individuals have taken to digital self-management to handle stressful situations during the crisis. This has sped up the demand and supply of eHealth services and solutions recently. MHealth including wearable devices are areas that have shown significant promise because of accessibility to various positive technology that have altered the mental well-being of several end users. In this chapter, we show the need for bridging a health service divide in the society through positive technologies as a way forward to build a resilient society. We introduce the various stressors that have triggered the need for active coping amongst populations. We also classify positive technologies based on their potency to contribute to coping self-efficacy. Finally, we conclude by introducing a nuanced theory-driven understanding on how users may handle stressors so that positive technologies with eudaimonic and social features can act as digital coping mechanism, negatively moderating the impact of unsafety perceptions and stress responses. The conceptual model can inform marketing and management of health care by informing how engagement can be increased when using positive technology. Health promotional and marketing campaigns can be designed in a more user centric perspective looking through the lens of positive technology and resilience model as proposed in this chapter. Although several issues still needs to be addressed to make positive technology adoption ubiquitous, it is believed that its potential to contribute to rebuilding a resilient society during and after the COVID-19 pandemic is undeniable. Whereas, positive technology is under mobilized by health care providers, investors, entrepreneurs and governments to tackle global health demands.

ACKNOWLEDGMENT

The author would like to acknowledge the editorial support provided by Dr. José Duarte Santos and the two anonymous reviewers for their pertinent and constructive comments that have helped in improving the manuscript. The author also acknowledges the intellectual encouragement provided by member of the research lab LITEM, University Paris Saclay, France. The author also acknowledges Aswinikumar Tandalam Kumaraswamy a philosopher, motivational writer, publisher, editor and a media expert for reading and commenting on the first version of the manuscript.

REFERENCES

Alam, M. Z., Hoque, M. R., Hu, W., & Barua, Z. (2020). Factors influencing the adoption of mHealth services in a developing country: A patient-centric study. *International Journal of Information Management*, *50*, 128–143. doi:10.1016/j.ijinfomgt.2019.04.016

Amarnath, G. R., Prasanthi, J., Sharma, N., Jenitha, S., & Rajan, C. (2017). Efficacy of heartfulness meditation in moderating vital parameters-A comparison study of experienced and new meditators. *International Journal of Medical Research & Health Sciences*, *6*(7), 70–78.

Anderson-Ross, K. (2020). We Are What We Think: Downregulating the Chronic Stress Response with Technology-Assisted Mindfulness Meditation. *Journal of Restorative Medicine*, *9*(1), 12–18. doi:10.14200/jrm.2019.0116

Arya, N. K., Singh, K., & Malik, A. (2017). Effect of Heartfulness Spiritual Practice based program on mental and physical health indicators. *Int J Res Manage Soc Sci*, *5*, 91–103.

Ayyagari, R. (2012). Impact of information overload and task-technology fit on technostress. *Proceedings of the southern association for information systems conference*.

Barton, M. A., Christianson, M., Myers, C. G., & Sutcliffe, K. (2020). *Resilience in action: leading for resilience in response to COVID-19*. BMJ Leader.

Benight, C. C., & Bandura, A. (2004). Social cognitive theory of posttraumatic recovery: The role of perceived self-efficacy. *Behaviour Research and Therapy*, *42*(10), 1129–1148. doi:10.1016/j.brat.2003.08.008 PMID:15350854

Benight, C. C., Ironson, G., Klebe, K., Carver, C. S., Wynings, C., Burnett, K., Greenwood, D., Baum, A., & Schneiderman, N. (1999). Conservation of resources and coping self-efficacy predicting distress following a natural disaster: A causal model analysis where the environment meets the mind. *Anxiety, Stress, and Coping*, *12*(2), 107–126. doi:10.1080/10615809908248325

Benlian, A., Klumpe, J., & Hinz, O. (2020). Mitigating the intrusive effects of smart home assistants by using anthropomorphic design features: A multimethod investigation. *Information Systems Journal*, *30*(6), 1010–1042. doi:10.1111/isj.12243

Bipat, S., Sneller, L., Visser, J., & Rouwelaar, H. T. (2018). *The impact of culture on the business value of it–an examination from two sectors*. Academic Press.

Botella, C., Riva, G., Gaggioli, A., Wiederhold, B. K., Alcaniz, M., & Banos, R. M. (2012). The present and future of positive technologies. *Cyberpsychology, Behavior, and Social Networking*, *15*(2), 78–84. doi:10.1089/cyber.2011.0140 PMID:22149078

Brivio, E., Gaudioso, F., Vergine, I., Mirizzi, C. R., Reina, C., Stellari, A., & Galimberti, C. (2018). Preventing Technostress Through Positive Technology. *Frontiers in Psychology*, *9*, 2569. doi:10.3389/fpsyg.2018.02569 PMID:30618986

Brosschot, J. F., Verkuil, B., & Thayer, J. F. (2018). Generalized unsafety theory of stress: Unsafe environments and conditions, and the default stress response. *International Journal of Environmental Research and Public Health*, *15*(3), 464. doi:10.3390/ijerph15030464 PMID:29518937

Buie, E. (2016). Transcendhance: A game to facilitate techno-spiritual design. *Proceedings of the 2016 CHI Conference Extended Abstracts on Human Factors in Computing Systems.*

Chandra, S., Shirish, A., & Srivastava, S. C. (2019). Does technostress inhibit employee innovation? Examining the linear and curvilinear influence of technostress creators. *Communications of the Association for Information Systems*, *44*(1), 19.

Chandra, S., Shirish, A., & Srivastava, S. C. (2020). Theorizing technological spatial intrusion for ICT enabled employee innovation: The mediating role of perceived usefulness. *Technological Forecasting and Social Change*, *161*, 120320. doi:10.1016/j.techfore.2020.120320

Christianson, M. K., & Barton, M. A. (2020). Sensemaking in the Time of COVID-19. *Journal of Management Studies.*

Cohen, M., Downey, L., & Laxton, L. (2015). Well-being and Technology: Exploring Technology-Supported Meditation. *AMCIS.*

Conklin, Q. A., Crosswell, A. D., Saron, C. D., & Epel, E. S. (2019). Meditation, stress processes, and telomere biology. *Current Opinion in Psychology*, *28*, 92–101. doi:10.1016/j.copsyc.2018.11.009 PMID:30553080

Daugherty, A. (2014). *From Mindfulness to Heartfulness.* Archway Publishing.

Diefenbach, S. (2018). The potential and challenges of digital well-being interventions: Positive technology research and design in light of the bitter-sweet ambivalence of change. *Frontiers in Psychology*, *9*, 331. doi:10.3389/fpsyg.2018.00331 PMID:29593625

Digital Wellbeing Statistics. (2020). *Digital Wellbeing Statistics from Humane Tech Even.* Retrieved 20 October 2020 from https://digitalwellbeing.org/digital-wellbeing-statistics-from-humane-tech-event/

Downey, L. (2015). *Well-being technologies: Meditation using virtual worlds.* Nova Southeastern University Repository.

Farao, J., Malila, B., Conrad, N., Mutsvangwa, T., Rangaka, M. X., & Douglas, T. S. (2020). A user-centred design framework for mHealth. *PLoS One*, *15*(8), e0237910. doi:10.1371/journal.pone.0237910 PMID:32813711

Fatehi, F., Samadbeik, M., & Kazemi, A. (2020). What is Digital Health? Review of Definitions. *Studies in Health Technology and Informatics*, *275*, 67–71. PMID:33227742

Fitzpatrick, K. K., Darcy, A., & Vierhile, M. (2017). Delivering cognitive behavior therapy to young adults with symptoms of depression and anxiety using a fully automated conversational agent (Woebot): A randomized controlled trial. *JMIR Mental Health*, *4*(2), e19. doi:10.2196/mental.7785 PMID:28588005

Fletcher, D., & Sarkar, M. (2013). Psychological resilience. *European Psychologist*, *18*(1), 12–23. Advance online publication. doi:10.1027/1016-9040/a000124

Free, C., Phillips, G., Watson, L., Galli, L., Felix, L., Edwards, P., Patel, V., & Haines, A. (2013). The effectiveness of mobile-health technologies to improve health care service delivery processes: A systematic review and meta-analysis. *PLoS Medicine*, *10*(1), e1001363. doi:10.1371/journal.pmed.1001363 PMID:23458994

Gabrielli, S., Rizzi, S., Carbone, S., & Donisi, V. (2020). A Chatbot-Based Coaching Intervention for Adolescents to Promote Life Skills: Pilot Study. *JMIR Human Factors*, *7*(1), e16762. doi:10.2196/16762 PMID:32130128

Gorski, I., Bram, J. T., Sutermaster, S., Eckman, M., & Mehta, K. (2016). Value propositions of mHealth projects. *Journal of Medical Engineering & Technology*, *40*(7-8), 400–421. doi:10.1080/03091902.2016.1213907 PMID:27687907

Gottlieb, B. H. (1997). Conceptual and measurement issues in the study of coping with chronic stress. In *Coping with chronic stress* (pp. 3–40). Springer. doi:10.1007/978-1-4757-9862-3_1

Guo, X., Zhang, X., & Sun, Y. (2016). The privacy–personalization paradox in mHealth services acceptance of different age groups. *Electronic Commerce Research and Applications*, *16*, 55–65. doi:10.1016/j.elerap.2015.11.001

Heartfulness Institute. (2020). *Heartfulness Offerings*. Retrieved 25 December 2020 from https://www.heartfulnessinstitute.org/experience

Heidel, A., & Hagist, C. (2020). Potential benefits and risks resulting from the introduction of health apps and wearables into the German statutory health care system: Scoping review. *JMIR mHealth and uHealth*, *8*(9), e16444. doi:10.2196/16444 PMID:32965231

Hughes, S. (2020). *Study Reveals Everyday Technology Helps Fight Loneliness*. https://phys.org/news/2019-06-reveals-everyday-technology-loneliness.html

GM Insights. (2020). *Healthcare & Medical Devices Market Research Reports*. Healthcare & Medical Devices Market Research Reports | Global Market Insights. gminsights.com

Iribarren, S. J., Cato, K., Falzon, L., & Stone, P. W. (2017). What is the economic evidence for mHealth? A systematic review of economic evaluations of mHealth solutions. *PLoS One, 12*(2), e0170581. doi:10.1371/journal.pone.0170581 PMID:28152012

Iyer, R. B., & Iyer, B. N. (2019). The impact of heartfulness-based elective on middle school students. *American Journal of Health Behavior, 43*(4), 812–823. doi:10.5993/AJHB.43.4.14 PMID:31239023

Jaakkola, E. (2020). Designing conceptual articles: four approaches. *AMS Review*, 1-9.

Jaana, M., & Paré, G. (2020). Comparison of Mobile Health Technology Use for Self-Tracking Between Older Adults and the General Adult Population in Canada: Cross-Sectional Survey. *JMIR mHealth and uHealth, 8*(11), e24718. doi:10.2196/24718 PMID:33104517

Karmarkar, Y., Ravi, M., Vaidya, S., & Bhise, K. (2020). Training To Cope-Up With Aggression. *Attention Span And Nurture Wellbeing Through 'Heartfulness'–An Experimental Study On School Children.*

Kitson, A., Prpa, M., & Riecke, B. E. (2018). Immersive interactive technologies for positive change: A scoping review and design considerations. *Frontiers in Psychology, 9*, 1354. doi:10.3389/fpsyg.2018.01354 PMID:30123161

Koumpouros, Y., & Georgoulas, A. (2020). A systematic review of mHealth funded R&D activities in EU: Trends, technologies and obstacles. *Informatics for Health & Social Care, 45*(2), 168–187. doi:10.1080/17538157.2019.1656208 PMID:31743060

Lazarus, R. S., & Folkman, S. (1984). *Stress, appraisal, and coping*. Springer publishing company.

Le Goff-Pronost, M., & Krychowski, C. (2020). *MédecinDirect–L'adaptation d'un business modèle pionnier à une nouvelle donne réglementaire*. Academic Press.

Léonard, A., Clément, S., Kuo, C.-D., & Manto, M. (2019). Changes in heart rate variability during heartfulness meditation: A power spectral analysis including the residual spectrum. *Frontiers in Cardiovascular Medicine, 6*, 62. doi:10.3389/fcvm.2019.00062 PMID:31139634

MacInnis, D. J. (2011). A framework for conceptual contributions in marketing. *Journal of Marketing, 75*(4), 136–154. doi:10.1509/jmkg.75.4.136

Maher, C. A., Lewis, L. K., Ferrar, K., Marshall, S., De Bourdeaudhuij, I., & Vandelanotte, C. (2014). Are health behavior change interventions that use online social networks effective? A systematic review. *Journal of Medical Internet Research, 16*(2), e40. doi:10.2196/jmir.2952 PMID:24550083

Malvey, D. M., & Slovensky, D. J. (2017). Global mHealth policy arena: Status check and future directions. *mHealth, 3*, 41. doi:10.21037/mhealth.2017.09.03 PMID:29184893

Meske, C., Amojo, I., & Thapa, D. (2020). Understanding the Affordances of Conversational Agents in Mental Mobile Health Services. *International Conference on Information Systems Hydrabad (Virtual).*

Mirkovic, J., Jessen, S., Kristjansdottir, O. B., Krogseth, T., Koricho, A. T., & Ruland, C. M. (2018). Developing technology to mobilize personal strengths in people with chronic illness: Positive codesign approach. *JMIR Formative Research, 2*(1), e10774. doi:10.2196/10774 PMID:30684404

Montana, J. I., Tuena, C., Serino, S., Cipresso, P., & Riva, G. (2019). Neurorehabilitation of spatial memory using virtual environments: A systematic review. *Journal of Clinical Medicine, 8*(10), 1516. doi:10.3390/jcm8101516 PMID:31547137

Murphy-Shigematsu, S. (2018). *From mindfulness to heartfulness: Transforming self and society with compassion*. Berrett-Koehler Publishers.

Niemiec, R. M. (2017). On heartfulness. In *Future Directions in Well-Being* (pp. 123–128). Springer. doi:10.1007/978-3-319-56889-8_22

Nittari, G., Khuman, R., Baldoni, S., Pallotta, G., Battineni, G., Sirignano, A., Amenta, F., & Ricci, G. (2020). Telemedicine practice: Review of the current ethical and legal challenges. *Telemedicine Journal and e-Health, 26*(12), 1427–1437. doi:10.1089/tmj.2019.0158 PMID:32049608

Pan, A., & Zhao, F. (2018). User acceptance factors for mHealth. *International Conference on Human-Computer Interaction.*

Patel, S., & Arya, M. (2017). The BUS Framework: A comprehensive tool in creating an mHealth app utilizing behavior change theories, user-centered design, and social marketing. *Journal of Mobile Technology in Medicine, 6*(1), 39.

Perez-Marcos, D., Bieler-Aeschlimann, M., & Serino, A. (2018). Virtual reality as a vehicle to empower motor-cognitive neurorehabilitation. *Frontiers in Psychology, 9*, 2120. doi:10.3389/fpsyg.2018.02120 PMID:30450069

Quesnel, D., & Riecke, B. E. (2018). Are you awed yet? How virtual reality gives us awe and goose bumps. *Frontiers in Psychology*, *9*, 2158. doi:10.3389/fpsyg.2018.02158 PMID:30473673

Recupero, A., Triberti, S., Modesti, C., & Talamo, A. (2018). Mixed reality for cross-cultural integration: Using positive technology to share experiences and promote communication. *Frontiers in Psychology*, *9*, 1223. doi:10.3389/fpsyg.2018.01223 PMID:30065690

Reyes-Menendez, A., Saura, J. R., & Filipe, F. (2020). Marketing challenges in the# MeToo era: Gaining business insights using an exploratory sentiment analysis. *Heliyon*, *6*(3), e03626. doi:10.1016/j.heliyon.2020.e03626 PMID:32258475

Ricciardi, W., Pita Barros, P., Bourek, A., Brouwer, W., Kelsey, T., Lehtonen, L., Anastasy, C., Barros, P., Barry, M., Bourek, A., Brouwer, W., De Maeseneer, J., Kringos, D., Lehtonen, L., McKee, M., Murauskiene, L., Nuti, S., Ricciardi, W., Siciliani, L., & Wild, C. (2019, October 1). How to govern the digital transformation of health services. *European Journal of Public Health*, *29*(Supplement_3), 7–12. doi:10.1093/eurpub/ckz165 PMID:31738442

Riva, G., Baños, R. M., Botella, C., Wiederhold, B. K., & Gaggioli, A. (2012). Positive technology: Using interactive technologies to promote positive functioning. *Cyberpsychology, Behavior, and Social Networking*, *15*(2), 69–77. doi:10.1089/cyber.2011.0139 PMID:22149077

Riva, G., Mantovani, F., & Wiederhold, B. K. (2020a, September). Positive Technology and COVID-19. *Cyberpsychology, Behavior, and Social Networking*, *23*(9), 581–587. doi:10.1089/cyber.2020.29194.gri PMID:32833511

Riva, G., Mantovani, F., & Wiederhold, B. K. (2020b). Positive Technology and COVID-19. *Cyberpsychology, Behavior, and Social Networking*, *23*(9), 581–587. doi:10.1089/cyber.2020.29194.gri PMID:32833511

Ryan, J., Edney, S., & Maher, C. (2017). Engagement, compliance and retention with a gamified online social networking physical activity intervention. *Translational Behavioral Medicine*, *7*(4), 702–708. doi:10.100713142-017-0499-8 PMID:28523603

Samhan, B. (2017). Patients' resistance towards health information technology a perspective of the dual factor model of IT usage. *Proceedings of the 50th Hawaii International Conference on System Sciences*. 10.24251/HICSS.2017.412

Sarkar, M., & Fletcher, D. (2013). How should we measure psychological resilience in sport performers? *Measurement in Physical Education and Exercise Science*, *17*(4), 264–280. doi:10.1080/1091367X.2013.805141

Sarkar, M., & Hilton, N. K. (2020). Psychological Resilience in Olympic Medal–Winning Coaches: A Longitudinal Qualitative Study. *International Sport Coaching Journal*, *7*(2), 209–219. doi:10.1123/iscj.2019-0075

Sengupta, A., Bhattacherjee, A., & Dutta, K. (2020). Information Technology Interventions in Cardiac Rehabilitation: A Theory Driven Approach. *ICIS*.

Shirish, A. (2018). Shadow Side of Social Media Marketing: A User's Perspective. In Social Media Marketing (pp. 63-79). Springer. doi:10.1007/978-981-10-5323-8_5

Shirish, A. (2020a). Cognitive-affective appraisal of technostressors by ICT-based mobile workers and their impacts on technostrain. *Human Systems Management*, 1–21. doi:10.3233/HSM-200979

Shirish, A. (2020b). *Individual coping at times of COVID crisis: role of positive technology for well being. International webinar on Perspectives of Health Hygiene, Sanitation, Immunity & Social Distancing with Digital Media as per Current Scenario of COVID-19.*

Shirish, A., Boughzala, I., & Srivastava, S. C. (2016). Adaptive use of social networking applications in contemporary organizations: Examining the motivations of Gen Y cohorts. *International Journal of Information Management*, *36*(6), 1111–1123. doi:10.1016/j.ijinfomgt.2016.04.002

Shirish, A., Boughzala, I., & Srivastava, S. C. (2019). Does technology enabled design-thinking influence digital innovation? An innovation affordance perspective. *Proceedings of the 52nd Hawaii International Conference on System Sciences*. 10.24251/HICSS.2019.040

Short, C. E., DeSmet, A., Woods, C., Williams, S. L., Maher, C., Middelweerd, A., Müller, A. M., Wark, P. A., Vandelanotte, C., Poppe, L., Hingle, M. D., & Crutzen, R. (2018). Measuring engagement in eHealth and mHealth behavior change interventions: Viewpoint of methodologies. *Journal of Medical Internet Research*, *20*(11), e292. doi:10.2196/jmir.9397 PMID:30446482

Silva, B. M., Rodrigues, J. J., de la Torre Díez, I., López-Coronado, M., & Saleem, K. (2015). Mobile-health: A review of current state in 2015. *Journal of Biomedical Informatics*, *56*, 265–272. doi:10.1016/j.jbi.2015.06.003 PMID:26071682

Silva, E. H., Lawler, S., & Langbecker, D. (2019). The effectiveness of mHealth for self-management in improving pain, psychological distress, fatigue, and sleep in cancer survivors: A systematic review. *Journal of Cancer Survivorship: Research and Practice*, *13*(1), 97–107. doi:10.100711764-018-0730-8 PMID:30635865

Sime, C. (2019). The Cost Of Ignoring Mental Health In The Workplace. *Forbes*. https://www.forbes.com/sites/carleysime/2019/04/17/the-cost-of-ignoring-mental-health-in-the-workplace/?sh=6bcd3f503726

Smith, A. C., Thomas, E., Snoswell, C. L., Haydon, H., Mehrotra, A., Clemensen, J., & Caffery, L. J. (2020). Telehealth for global emergencies: Implications for coronavirus disease 2019 (COVID-19). *Journal of Telemedicine and Telecare*.

Srivastava, S. C., Chandra, S., & Shirish, A. (2015). Technostress creators and job outcomes: Theorising the moderating influence of personality traits. *Information Systems Journal*, *25*(4), 355–401. doi:10.1111/isj.12067

Srivastava, S. C., & Shainesh, G. (2015). Bridging the Service Divide Through Digitally Enabled Service Innovations: Evidence from Indian Healthcare Service Providers. *Management Information Systems Quarterly*, *39*(1), 245–267. doi:10.25300/MISQ/2015/39.1.11

Staglin, G. (2020). *Flattening The Mental Health Curve*. Retrieved 20 October 2020 from https://www.forbes.com/sites/onemind/2020/03/30/flattening-the-mental-health-curve/?sh=34d7bfa52d31

Stibe, A., & Cugelman, B. (2019). Social influence scale for technology design and transformation. *IFIP Conference on Human-Computer Interaction*.

Sun, Y., & Feng, Y. (2020). *Persuasion Matters: Investigating the Role of Fear Appeal and Coping Appeal in Mobile Health Technology Adoption*. PACIS.

Sylapan, B. S., Nair, A. K., Jayanna, K., Mallipeddi, S., Sathyanarayana, S., & Kutty, B. M. (2020). Meditation, well-being and cognition in heartfulness meditators–A pilot study. *Consciousness and Cognition*, *86*, 103032. doi:10.1016/j.concog.2020.103032 PMID:33096504

Tarafdar, M., Cooper, C. L., & Stich, J. F. (2019). The technostress trifecta-techno eustress, techno distress and design: Theoretical directions and an agenda for research. *Information Systems Journal*, *29*(1), 6–42. doi:10.1111/isj.12169

Tarafdar, M., Tu, Q., & Ragu-Nathan, T. (2010). Impact of technostress on end-user satisfaction and performance. *Journal of Management Information Systems*, *27*(3), 303–334. doi:10.2753/MIS0742-1222270311

Thimmapuram, J., Pargament, R., Sibliss, K., Grim, R., Risques, R., & Toorens, E. (2017). Effect of heartfulness meditation on burnout, emotional wellness, and telomere length in health care professionals. *Journal of Community Hospital Internal Medicine Perspectives*, *7*(1), 21–27. doi:10.1080/20009666.2016.1270806 PMID:28634520

Thimmapuram, J., Yommer, D., Tudor, L., Bell, T., Dumitrescu, C., & Davis, R. (2020). Heartfulness meditation improves sleep in chronic insomnia. *Journal of Community Hospital Internal Medicine Perspectives*, *10*(1), 10–15. doi:10.1080/20009666.2019.1710948 PMID:32128052

Villani, D., Carissoli, C., Triberti, S., Marchetti, A., Gilli, G., & Riva, G. (2018). Videogames for emotion regulation: A systematic review. *Games for Health Journal*, *7*(2), 85–99. doi:10.1089/g4h.2017.0108 PMID:29424555

Voci, A., Veneziani, C. A., & Fuochi, G. (2019). Relating mindfulness, heartfulness, and psychological well-being: The role of self-compassion and gratitude. *Mindfulness*, *10*(2), 339–351. doi:10.100712671-018-0978-0

Weisel, K. K., Fuhrmann, L. M., Berking, M., Baumeister, H., Cuijpers, P., & Ebert, D. D. (2019). Standalone smartphone apps for mental health—A systematic review and meta-analysis. *NPJ Digital Medicine*, *2*(1), 1–10. doi:10.103841746-019-0188-8 PMID:31815193

WHO. (2016). *Global difusion of eHealth: making universal health coverage achievable. Report of the third global survey on eHealth* (Licence: CC BY-NC-SA 3.0 IGO). WHO.

WHO. (2018a). *Digital technologies: shaping the future of primary health care.* Retrieved 9 May 2021 from https://www.who.int/docs/default-source/primary-health-care-conference/digital-technologies.pdf?sfvrsn=3efc47e0_2(accessed#:~:text=Digital%20technologies%20have%20already%20opened,of%20communication%2C%20empowerment%20and%20engagement

WHO. (2018b). mHealth: Use of appropriate digital technologies for public health. Seventy First World Health Assembly, World Health Organization.

WHOa. (1948). *WHO Constitution.* Retrieved 20 October 2020 from https://www.who.int/about/who-we-are/constitution

WHOb. (2020). *Mental Health and COVID-19.* Retrieved 28 December 2020 from https://www.euro.who.int/en/health-topics/health-emergencies/coronavirus-covid-19/publications-and-technical-guidance/noncommunicable-diseases/mental-health-and-covid-19

Wilson, N. (2020). *While Covid Has Taken A Blow At Mental Health, Inclusive Capitalism Offers A Form Of Support*. Retrieved 20 October 2020 from https://www.forbes.com/sites/nigelwilson/2020/10/22/while-covid-has-taken-a-blow-at-mental-health-inclusive-capitalism-offers-a-form-of-support/?sh=716d8c67ef08

Zhang, X., Guo, X., Lai, K., Guo, F., & Li, C. (2014). Understanding gender differences in m-health adoption: A modified theory of reasoned action model. *Telemedicine Journal and e-Health*, *20*(1), 39–46. doi:10.1089/tmj.2013.0092 PMID:24161004

Zhang, X., Han, X., Dang, Y., Meng, F., Guo, X., & Lin, J. (2017). User acceptance of mobile health services from users' perspectives: The role of self-efficacy and response-efficacy in technology acceptance. *Informatics for Health & Social Care*, *42*(2), 194–206. doi:10.1080/17538157.2016.1200053 PMID:27564428

Zhao, Y., Ni, Q., & Zhou, R. (2018). What factors influence the mobile health service adoption? A meta-analysis and the moderating role of age. *International Journal of Information Management*, *43*, 342–350. doi:10.1016/j.ijinfomgt.2017.08.006

KEY TERMS AND DEFINITIONS

Coping Self-Efficacy: An individual's or collective's ability to undertake the process of adaptation to stressors present in the environment or to chronic stress situation. It can be developed through prior experiences of successful adaptations that gave rise to an intermittent or prolonged sense of safety perceptions.

Digital Health: The term digital health refers to both eHealth and mHealth (e.g. telemedicine, electronic health records and wearable sensors) as well as developing areas such as the use of advanced computing sciences in the fields of big data and artificial intelligence, robotic dedicated towards health services.

Digital Self-Management: Voluntary use of digital tools and services as a supplement, complement, or as a substitute for health services with an intention to increase one's health and well-being.

Holistic Positive Technology: A kind of positive technology that is conceived for a wider population undergoing varying stressors or suffering from chronic stress, aimed at simultaneously improving physical, emotional, spiritual, and social well-being levels. It can be seen in digital tools or services that rely on techno-spiritual designs such as those found in the application called 'HeartsApp' which is posited to enhance the resilience of individuals, and societies in a reliable manner by instilling a sense of safety perception amongst the users of this application.

Mobile Health: Mobile Health or mHealth is an integral part of eHealth, which refers to the cost-effective and secure use of information and communication technologies, including mobile phones and wearables in support of health and health-related fields.

Positive Technology: It is a scientific and applied approach for improving the quality of our personal experience using digital goods and services with the goal of increasing wellness, generating strengths and resilience in individuals, organizations, and society.

Resilience: Resilience relates to positive adaptation despite the presence of risk or adversity, it can be both protective and promotive. It can be undertaken individually or collectively.

Stress: It is the inability of a person to cope with internal or environmental demands. It can be chronic, in the form of generalized perception of unsafety that is always present only to be dis-inhibited by safety perceptions. It can also take the acute form, when it is triggered by specific stressors.

Technostress: The inability of an individual to cope with technology related demands in the environment. The demands may be perceived as techno-overload, techno-uncertainties, techno-insecurity, techno-invasion, and techno-complexity.

Well-Being: A state of complete health at physical, mental, spiritual, and social levels.

Compilation of References

Aaker, D. A. (1996). *Building strong brands*. Free Press.

Aaker, D. A. (2004). *Brand portfolio strategy: creating relevance, differentiation, energy, leverage, and clarity*. Free Press.

Aaker, D. A. (2011). *Brand relevance: making competitors irrelevant* (1st ed.). Jossey-Bass.

Aaker, D. A., & Biel, A. L. (1993). *Brand equity &advertising: advertising's role in building strong brands*. Lawrence Erlbaum Associates.

Aaker, D. A., & Joachimsthaler, E. (2000). *Brand leadership*. Free Press.

Aaker, D. A., & Keller, K. L. (1990). *Consumer evaluations of brand extensions*. Marketing Science Institute.

Aaker, J. (1997). Dimensions of Brand Personality. *JMR, Journal of Marketing Research, 34*(3), 347–356. doi:10.1177/002224379703400304

Aaker, J., & Fournier, S. (1995). A Brand as a Character, a Partner and a Person: Three Perspectives on the Question of Brand Personality. *Advances in Consumer Research. Association for Consumer Research (U. S.), 22*, 391–395.

Accenture. (2018). *2018 Consumer survey on digital health*. https://www.accenture.com/t20180306t103559z__w__/us-en/_acnmedia/pdf-71/accenture-health-2018-consumer-survey-digital-health.pdf

Accenture. (2019). *Digital Health Consumer Survey*. https://www.accenture.com/t20190208t144039z__w__/us-en/_acnmedia/pdf-94/accenture-2019-digital-health-consumer-survey.pdf

Addeo, F., Paoli, A. D., Esposito, M., & Bolcato, M. Y. (2020). Doing social research on online communities: The benefits of netnography. *Athens Journal of Social Sciences, 7*(1), 9–38. doi:10.30958/ajss.7-1-1

Ahmed, S., Hossain, M. F., Price, K., Pranger, C., Hossain, M. M., & Sharmin, M. (2019, July). A Tale of the Social-Side of ASD. In *2019 IEEE 43rd Annual Computer Software and Applications Conference (COMPSAC)* (Vol. 1, pp. 644-652). IEEE 10.1109/COMPSAC.2019.00098

Ahuja, A. S., & Williams, R. (2010). Telling Stories: Learning from Patients' and Families' Experiences of Specialist Child and Adolescent Mental Health Services. *International Journal of Consumer Studies*, *34*(5), 603–609. doi:10.1111/j.1470-6431.2010.00904.x

Akdur, G., Aydin, M. N., & Akdur, G. (2020). Adoption of Mobile Health Apps in Dietetic Practice: Case Study of Diyetkolik. *JMIR mHealth and uHealth*, *8*(10), e16911. doi:10.2196/16911 PMID:33006566

Akroush, M. N., Abu, E. L., & Samen, A. A. (2012). An empirical investigation of the mediating role of relationship marketing skills on the relationship between customer satisfaction and customer loyalty. *International Journal of Internet Marketing and Advertising*, *7*(1), 1–30. doi:10.1504/IJIMA.2012.044956

Alam, M. Z., Hoque, M. R., Hu, W., & Barua, Z. (2020). Factors influencing the adoption of mHealth services in a developing country: A patient-centric study. *International Journal of Information Management*, *50*, 128–143. doi:10.1016/j.ijinfomgt.2019.04.016

Alderson, W. (1957). *Marketing behavior and executive action; a functionalist approach to marketing theory*. R. D. Irwin.

Alegre, A. M. (2016). El Crossumer: La evolución del consumidor mediada por las tecnologías sociales y la hiperconectividad móvil. *MÉI: Métodos de Información*, *7*(12), 5–16. doi:10.5557/IIMEI7-N12-005016

Al-Kwifi, S., Ahmed, Z. U., & Yammout, D. (2014). Brand switching of high-technology capital products: How product features dictate the switching decision. *Journal of Product and Brand Management*, *23*(4-5), 322–332. doi:10.1108/JPBM-12-2013-0473

Allen, S., Graupera, V., & Lundrigan, L. (2010). *Pro smartphone cross-platform development: iPhone, blackberry, windows mobile and android development and distribution*. Apress. doi:10.1007/978-1-4302-2869-1

Aloy, J. A., Delgado, M. R., & Pérez, X. R. (2005). *Comunicación Interna en la empresa*. Editorial UOC.

Alves, G. M., Sousa, B. M., & Machado, A. (2020). The Role of Digital Marketing and Online Relationship Quality in Social Tourism: A Tourism for All Case Study. In J. D. Santos & Ó. L. Silva (Eds.), *Digital Marketing Strategies for Tourism, Hospitality, and Airline Industries* (pp. 49–70). IGI Global. doi:10.4018/978-1-5225-9783-4.ch003

Amarnath, G. R., Prasanthi, J., Sharma, N., Jenitha, S., & Rajan, C. (2017). Efficacy of heartfulness meditation in moderating vital parameters-A comparison study of experienced and new meditators. *International Journal of Medical Research & Health Sciences*, *6*(7), 70–78.

Ammenwerth, E., Brender, J., Nykänen, P., Prokosch, H., Rigby, M., & Talmon, J. (2004). Visions and strategies to improve evaluation of health information systems Reflections and lessons based on the HIS-EVAL workshop in Innsbruck. *International Journal of Medical Informatics*, *73*(6), 479–491. doi:10.1016/j.ijmedinf.2004.04.004 PMID:15171977

Ammenwerth, E., Gräber, S., Herrmann, G., Bürkle, T., & König, J. (2003). Evaluation of health information systems - Problems and challenges. *International Journal of Medical Informatics*, *71*(2-3), 125–135. doi:10.1016/S1386-5056(03)00131-X PMID:14519405

Anderson-Levitt, K. M. (2006). Ethnography. In Handbook of Complementary Methods in Education Research (3rd ed.). American Educational Research Association.

Anderson-Ross, K. (2020). We Are What We Think: Downregulating the Chronic Stress Response with Technology-Assisted Mindfulness Meditation. *Journal of Restorative Medicine*, *9*(1), 12–18. doi:10.14200/jrm.2019.0116

Andrade, D. G., & Falk, J. A. (2001). Eficácia de Sistemas de Informação e Percepção de Mudança Organizacional: Um Estudo de Caso. *Revista de Administração Contemporanêa*, *5*(3), 53–84. doi:10.1590/S1415-65552001000300004

Andrasfay, T., & Goldman, N. (2021). Reductions in 2020 US life expectancy due to COVID-19 and the disproportionate impact on the Black and Latino populations. *Proceedings of the National Academy of Sciences of the United States of America*, *118*(5), e2014746118. Advance online publication. doi:10.1073/pnas.2014746118 PMID:33446511

Antal, Z. L. (2018). *A gyógyítás társadalmi beágyazottsága*. Argumentum Kiadó.

Antezana, G., Venning, A., Blake, V., Smith, D., Winsall, M., Orlowski, S., & Bidargaddi, N. (2020). An evaluation of behaviour change techniques in health and lifestyle mobile applications. *Health Informatics Journal*, *26*(1), 104–113. doi:10.1177/1460458218813726 PMID:30501364

Aparicio, M., Bilbao, S., Saenz Valenzuela, M., & Barán Attias, T. (2020). Entre barbijos, ollas populares y grupos de WhatsApp: Mujeres, salud y cuidados ante el COVID-19 en los barrios del Gran Buenos Aires, Argentina. *Tessituras*, *8*(1), 279–301.

Argouslidis, P. C., & Indounas, K. (2010). Exploring the role of relationship pricing in industrial export settings: Empirical evidence from the UK. *Industrial Marketing Management*, *39*(3), 460–472. doi:10.1016/j.indmarman.2009.09.001

Arnstein, F. (2020). Effective health communication – a key factor in fighting the COVID-19 pandemic. *Patient Education and Counseling*, *103*(5), 873–876. doi:10.1016/j.pec.2020.03.027 PMID:32336348

Arya, N. K., Singh, K., & Malik, A. (2017). Effect of Heartfulness Spiritual Practice based program on mental and physical health indicators. *Int J Res Manage Soc Sci*, *5*, 91–103.

Ashforth, B. E., & Humphrey, R. H. (1995). Emotion in the workplace: Reappraisal. *Human Relations*, *48*(2), 97–125. doi:10.1177/001872679504800201

Ashkanasy, N. M. (2003). Emotions in organizations: A multilevel perspective. *Research in Multi-Level Issues, 2*, 9-54.

Aslam, M. M. (2006). Are you selling the right color? A cross-cultural review of color as a marketing cue. *Journal of Marketing Communications*, *12*(1), 15–30. doi:10.1080/13527260500247827

Attai, D. J., Cowher, M. S., Al-Hamadani, M., Schoger, J. M., Staley, A. C., & Landercasper, J. (2015). Twitter social media is an effective tool for breast cancer patient education and support: Patient-reported outcomes by survey. *Journal of Medical Internet Research, 17*(7), e188. doi:10.2196/jmir.4721 PMID:26228234

Ayyagari, R. (2012). Impact of information overload and task-technology fit on technostress. *Proceedings of the southern association for information systems conference.*

Azêdo, D. F., & Alves, M. H. (2013). Práticas de marketing interno nas organizações de saúde e a sua influência na motivação dos colaboradores. *Revista Portuguesa de Saude Publica, 31*(2), 201–212. doi:10.1016/j.rpsp.2013.05.003

Backhaus, K., Steiner, M., & Lügger, K. (2011). To invest, or not to invest, in brands? Drivers of brand relevance in B2B markets. *Industrial Marketing Management, 40*(7), 1082–1092. doi:10.1016/j.indmarman.2011.09.002

Bagozzi, R., & Dholakia, U. (2002). Intentional social action in virtual communities. *Journal of Interactive Marketing, 16*(2), 2–21. doi:10.1002/dir.10006

Bakker, A. B., & Demerouti, E. (2007). The job demands-resources model: State of the art. *Journal of Managerial Psychology, 22*(3), 309–328. doi:10.1108/02683940710733115

Balamohan, P., Tech, M., & Gomathi, S. (2015). Emotional intelligence–It's importance and relationship with individual performance, team-effectiveness, leadership and marketing effectiveness. *Mediterranean Journal of Social Sciences, 6*(1), 120.

Ballantyne, D. (2003). A relationship-mediated theory of internal marketing. *European Journal of Marketing, 37*(9), 1242–1260. doi:10.1108/03090560310486979

Banerjee, S., Chua, A. Y., & Kim, J. J. (2015, January). Using supervised learning to classify authentic and fake online reviews. In *Proceedings of the 9th international conference on ubiquitous information management and communication* (pp. 1-7). 10.1145/2701126.2701130

Barra, D., Nascimento, E., Martins, J., Albuquerque, G., & Erdmann, A. (2006). Evolução histórica e impacto da tecnologia na área da saúde e da enfermagem. *Revista Eletrônica de Enfermagem, 8*(3), 422–430.

Barry, A. E., Bates, A. M., Olusanya, O., Vinal, C. E., Martin, E., Peoples, J. E., Jackson, Z. A., Billinger, S. A., Yusuf, A., Cauley, D. A., & Montano, J. R. (2016). Alcohol marketing on Twitter and Instagram: Evidence of directly advertising to youth/adolescents. *Alcohol and Alcoholism (Oxford, Oxfordshire), 51*(4), 487–492. doi:10.1093/alcalc/agv128 PMID:26597794

Bartlett, Y. K., & Coulson, N. S. (2011). An investigation into the empowerment effect of using online support groups and how this affects health professional/patient communication. *Patient Education and Counseling, 83*(1), 113–119. doi:10.1016/j.pec.2010.05.029 PMID:20599338

Barton, M. A., Christianson, M., Myers, C. G., & Sutcliffe, K. (2020). *Resilience in action: leading for resilience in response to COVID-19*. BMJ Leader.

Basch, C. H., & MacLean, S. A. (2019). Colorectal Cancer on Instagram: A Content Analysis. *Journal of Consumer Health on the Internet*, *23*(4), 378–383. doi:10.1080/15398285.2019.1684149

Başoğul, C., & Özgür, G. (2016). Role of emotional intelligence in conflict management strategies of nurses. *Asian Nursing Research*, *10*(3), 228–233. doi:10.1016/j.anr.2016.07.002 PMID:27692253

Benight, C. C., & Bandura, A. (2004). Social cognitive theory of posttraumatic recovery: The role of perceived self-efficacy. *Behaviour Research and Therapy*, *42*(10), 1129–1148. doi:10.1016/j.brat.2003.08.008 PMID:15350854

Benight, C. C., Ironson, G., Klebe, K., Carver, C. S., Wynings, C., Burnett, K., Greenwood, D., Baum, A., & Schneiderman, N. (1999). Conservation of resources and coping self-efficacy predicting distress following a natural disaster: A causal model analysis where the environment meets the mind. *Anxiety, Stress, and Coping*, *12*(2), 107–126. doi:10.1080/10615809908248325

Benlian, A., Klumpe, J., & Hinz, O. (2020). Mitigating the intrusive effects of smart home assistants by using anthropomorphic design features: A multimethod investigation. *Information Systems Journal*, *30*(6), 1010–1042. doi:10.1111/isj.12243

Béresniak, A., & Duru, G. (1999). *Economia da Saúde*. Climepsi Editores.

Berg, M. (2001). Implementing information systems in health care organizations: Myths and challenges. *International Journal of Medical Informatics*, *64*(2-3), 143–156. doi:10.1016/S1386-5056(01)00200-3 PMID:11734382

Bernardes, O., & Pinillos, M. (2004). *Data Envelopment Analysis and Performance Management*. Aston University.

Berry, L. L. (1983). Relationship marketing. *Emerging Perspectives on Services Marketing*, *66*(3), 33-47.

Berry, F. S., Brower, R. S., Choi, S. O., Goa, W. X., Jang, H. S., Kwon, M., & Word, J. (2004). Three Traditions of Network Research: What the Public Management Research Agenda Can Learn from Other Research Communities. *Public Administration Review*, *64*(5), 539–552. doi:10.1111/j.1540-6210.2004.00402.x

Berry, L. L. (2002). Relationship Marketing of Services Perspectives from 1983 and 2000. *Journal of Relationship Marketing*, *1*(1), 59–77. doi:10.1300/J366v01n01_05

Berry, L. L., & Parasuraman, A. (2001). *Marketing Services: Competing Through Quality*. Simon and Schuster.

Bickerdyke, L., Dolamore, R., Monday, L., & Preston, R. (2002). *Supplier-Induced Demand for Medical Services*. Productivity Commission Staff Working Paper, Canberra. https://www.pc.gov.au/research/supporting/ supplier-induced-medical-demand/sidms.pdf

Bierly, P. E. III, & Gallagher, S. (2007). Explaining alliance partner selection: Fit, trust and strategic expediency. *Long Range Planning*, *40*(2), 134–153. doi:10.1016/j.lrp.2007.03.001

Bilal, A. (2017). The Role of Emotional Dissonance and Emotional Intelligence on Job-Stress, Burnout, and Well-being. In Academy of Management Proceedings (Vol. 2017, No. 1, p. 12770). Briarcliff Manor, NY: Academy of Management.

Biong, H. (2013). Choice of subcontractor in markets with asymmetric information: Reputation and price effects. *Journal of Business and Industrial Marketing*, *28*(1), 60–71. doi:10.1108/08858621311285723

Bipat, S., Sneller, L., Visser, J., & Rouwelaar, H. T. (2018). *The impact of culture on the business value of it–an examination from two sectors*. Academic Press.

Birks, Y. F., & Watt, I. S. (2007). Emotional intelligence and patient-centred care. *Journal of the Royal Society of Medicine*, *100*(8), 368–374. doi:10.1177/014107680710000813 PMID:17682030

Birren, F. (2006). *Functional Color: A Book of Facts and Research Meant to Inspire More Rational Methods in the Solution of Color Problems*. Kessinger Publishing, LLC.

Blombäck, A., & Axelsson, B. (2007). The role of corporate brand image in the selection of new subcontractors. *Journal of Business and Industrial Marketing*, *22*(6), 418–430. doi:10.1108/08858620710780181

Blundell, R., Dias, C. M., Joyce, R., & Xu, X. (2020). COVID-19 and Inequalities. *Fiscal Studies*, *41*(2), 291–319. doi:10.1111/1475-5890.12232 PMID:32836542

BMA. (2020). *The hidden impact of COVID-19 on patient care in the NHS in England*. https://www.bma.org.uk/media/2841/the-hidden-impact-of-COVID_web-pdf.pdf

Bochatay, N., Bajwa, N. M., Cullati, S., Muller-Juge, V., Blondon, K. S., Perron, N. J., Maitre, F., Chopard, P., Kim, S., Savoldelli, G. L., Hudelson, P., & Nendaz, M. R. (2017). A Multilevel Analysis of Professional Conflicts in Helath Care Teams: Insight for Future Training. *Academic Medicine*, *92*(11S), S84–S92. doi:10.1097/ACM.0000000000001912 PMID:29065028

Borchers, U., & Evans, M. (2011). Das "nutzerorientierte" Krankenhaus–Chance und Herausforderung für die Gesundheitswirtschaft. *Zeitschrift Fuer Evidenz. Fortbildung Und Qualitaet Im Gesundheitswesen*, *105*(8), 616–623. doi:10.1016/j.zefq.2011.07.019

Borger, J. (2021). US declares support for patent waiver on COVID-19 vaccines. *The Guardian*. https://www.theguardian.com/world/2021/may/05/us-declares-support-for-patent-waiver-on-covid-19-vaccines

Bortolotti, T., Boscari, S., & Danese, P. (2015). Successful lean implementation: Organizational culture and soft lean practices. *International Journal of Production Economics*, *160*, 182–201. doi:10.1016/j.ijpe.2014.10.013

Botella, C., Riva, G., Gaggioli, A., Wiederhold, B. K., Alcaniz, M., & Banos, R. M. (2012). The present and future of positive technologies. *Cyberpsychology, Behavior, and Social Networking*, *15*(2), 78–84. doi:10.1089/cyber.2011.0140 PMID:22149078

Boudreaux, E. D., Waring, M. E., Hayes, R. B., Sadasivam, R. S., Mullen, S., & Pagoto, S. (2014). Evaluating and selecting mobile health apps: Strategies for healthcare providers and healthcare organizations. *Translational Behavioral Medicine*, *4*(4), 363–371. doi:10.100713142-014-0293-9 PMID:25584085

Boulos, M. N. K., Brewer, A. C., Karimkhani, C., Buller, D. B., & Dellavalle, R. P. (2014). Mobile medical and health apps: State of the art, concerns, regulatory control and certification. *Online Journal of Public Health Informatics*, *5*(3), 229. PMID:24683442

Boyatzis, R. E., Goleman, D., & Rhee, K. (2000). Clustering competence in emotional intelligence: Insights from the Emotional Competence Inventory (ECI). Handbook of Emotional Intelligence, 99(6), 343-362.

Brackett, M. A., Rivers, S. E., Shiffman, S., Lerner, N., & Salovey, P. (2006). Relating emotional abilities to social functioning: A comparison of self-report and performance measures of emotional intelligence. *Journal of Personality and Social Psychology*, *91*(4), 780–795. doi:10.1037/0022-3514.91.4.780 PMID:17014299

Brandão, N. (2014). A importância da Comunicação Interna para a motivação e participação em Organizações Positivas. In M. Artur (Org.), Gestão de Recursos Humanos. Escolar Editora.

Brennen, J., Simon, F., Howard, N., & Nielsen, R. K. (2020). *Types, sources, and claims of COVID-19 misinformation.* https://reutersinstitute.politics.ox.ac.uk/types-sources-and-claims-covid-19-misinformation

Brick, A., Nolan, A., O'Reilly, J., & Smith, S. (2010). Resource allocation, financing and sustainability in health care. *Evidence for the expert group on resource allocation and financing in the health sector*, 1. https://www.esri.ie/system/files?file=media/file-uploads/2015-07/BKMNEXT168.pdf

Brivio, E., Gaudioso, F., Vergine, I., Mirizzi, C. R., Reina, C., Stellari, A., & Galimberti, C. (2018). Preventing Technostress Through Positive Technology. *Frontiers in Psychology*, *9*, 2569. doi:10.3389/fpsyg.2018.02569 PMID:30618986

Brosschot, J. F., Verkuil, B., & Thayer, J. F. (2018). Generalized unsafety theory of stress: Unsafe environments and conditions, and the default stress response. *International Journal of Environmental Research and Public Health*, *15*(3), 464. doi:10.3390/ijerph15030464 PMID:29518937

Brown, B. P., Zablah, A. R., Bellenger, D. N., & Johnston, W. J. (2011). When do B2B brands influence the decision making of organizational buyers? An examination of the relationship between purchase risk and brand sensitivity. *International Journal of Research in Marketing*, *28*(3), 194–204. doi:10.1016/j.ijresmar.2011.03.004

Buie, E. (2016). Transcendhance: A game to facilitate techno-spiritual design. *Proceedings of the 2016 CHI Conference Extended Abstracts on Human Factors in Computing Systems.*

Burchett, K. E. (2002). Color harmony. *Color Research and Application*, *27*(1), 28–31. doi:10.1002/col.10004

Burgess, J., & Green, J. (2018). *YouTube: online video and participatory culture*. Polity.

Bürkle, T., Ammenwerth, E., Prokosch, H., & Dudeck, J. (2001). Evaluation of clinical information systems. What can be evaluated and what cannot? *Journal of Evaluation in Clinical Practice*, *7*(4), 373–385. doi:10.1046/j.1365-2753.2001.00291.x PMID:11737529

Burton, D. (2002). Consumer education and service quality: Conceptual issues and practical implications. *Journal of Services Marketing*, *16*(2), 125–142. doi:10.1108/08876040210422673

Bush, M., Lederer, A., Li, X., Palmisano, J., & Rao, S. (2009). The alignment of information systems with organizational objectives and strategies in health care. *International Journal of Medical Informatics*, *78*(7), 446–456. doi:10.1016/j.ijmedinf.2009.02.004 PMID:19307148

Cahan, E., Kocher, B., & Bohn, R. (2020). *Why Isn't Innovation Helping Reduce Health Care Costs?* Health Affairs. http:// https://www.healthaffairs.org/do/10.1377/hblog20200602.168241/full/

Callaham, D. (2005). *Health Care Costs and Medical Technology*. https://www.thehast ingscenter.org/briefingbook/health-care-costs-and-medical-technology

Campos, A. L. N. (2014). *Modelagem de Processos com BPMN* (2nd ed.). Brasport.

Caro, F. C. (2020). *La calidad del medicamento*. Revista Panacea. http://www.revistapanacea.com/la-calidad-del-medicamento/

Carrasco, L. (2020). *¿Quién ha financiado las vacunas contra la covid?* VozPopuli Sanitatem, 16/12/2020. https://www.vozpopuli.com/sanidad/financiacion-vacunas-covid-pfizer-moderna-oxford_0_1419758359.html

Carrera, F. (2012). *Marketing Digital na Versão 2.0 – O que não pode ignorar* (2nd ed.). Edições Sílabo.

Carricano, M. (2014). Pricing myopia: Do leading companies capture the full value of their pricing strategies? *Management Decision*, *52*(1), 159–178. doi:10.1108/MD-03-2013-0184

Carroll, J. K., Moorhead, A., Bond, R., LeBlanc, W. G., Petrella, R. J., & Fiscella, K. (2017). Who uses mobile phone health apps and does use matter? A secondary data analytics approach. *Journal of Medical Internet Research*, *19*(4), e125. doi:10.2196/jmir.5604 PMID:28428170

Čater, T., & Čater, B. (2010). Product and relationship quality influence on customer commitment and loyalty in B2B manufacturing relationships. *Industrial Marketing Management*, *39*(8), 1321–1333. doi:10.1016/j.indmarman.2010.02.006

Cavanaugh, M. A., Boswell, W. R., Roehling, M. V., & Boudreau, J. W. (2000). An empirical examination of self-reported work stress among US managers. *The Journal of Applied Psychology*, *85*(1), 65–74. doi:10.1037/0021-9010.85.1.65 PMID:10740957

CDC – Center for Disease Control and Prevention. (2014). Prevalence of autism spectrum disorder among children aged 8 years - Autism and developmental disabilities monitoring network, 11 sites, United States, 2010. *MMWR. Surveillance Summaries*, *63*(2), 1–21. PMID:24670961

Chakraborty, S., & Dobrzykowski, D. D. (2013). Supply Chain Practices for Complexity in Healthcare: A Service-Dominant Logic View. *The IUP Journal of Supply Chain Management*, *10*(3), 53–75. doi:10.1016/S2212-5671(14)00233-0

Chandra, S., Shirish, A., & Srivastava, S. C. (2019). Does technostress inhibit employee innovation? Examining the linear and curvilinear influence of technostress creators. *Communications of the Association for Information Systems*, *44*(1), 19.

Chandra, S., Shirish, A., & Srivastava, S. C. (2020). Theorizing technological spatial intrusion for ICT enabled employee innovation: The mediating role of perceived usefulness. *Technological Forecasting and Social Change*, *161*, 120320. doi:10.1016/j.techfore.2020.120320

Chiavenato, I. (2014). *Gestão de pessoas: O novo papel dos recursos humanos nas organizações*. Manole.

Childs, L. M., & Martin, C. Y. (2012). Social media profiles: Stiking the right balance. Americal. *Journal of Health System Pharmacy*, *69*(23), 2044–2050. doi:10.2146/ajhp120115 PMID:23172261

Chopra, S., & Meindl, P. (2011). *Gestão da cadeia de suprimentos: estratégia, planejamento e operações*. Pearson.

Chretien, K., & Kind, T. (2013). Social Media and Clinical Care - Ethical, Professional, and Social Implications. *Circulation*, *127*(13), 1413–1421. doi:10.1161/CIRCULATIONAHA.112.128017 PMID:23547180

Christiansen, N. D., Janovics, J. E., & Siers, B. P. (2010). Emotional Intelligence in Selection Contexts: Measurement method, criterion-related validity, and vulnerability to response distortion. *International Journal of Selection and Assessment*, *18*(1), 87–101. doi:10.1111/j.1468-2389.2010.00491.x

Christianson, M. K., & Barton, M. A. (2020). Sensemaking in the Time of COVID-19. *Journal of Management Studies*.

Christodoulides, G., & Chernatony, L. (2010). Consumer-based brand equity conceptualization and measurement: A literature review. *International Journal of Research in Marketing*, *52*(1), 43–66.

Chumpitaz Caceres, R., & Paparoidamis, N. G. (2007). Service quality, relationship satisfaction, trust, commitment and business-to-business loyalty. *European Journal of Marketing*, *41*(7/8), 836–867. doi:10.1108/03090560710752429

CIAT/IOTA/OECD. (2020). *Tax Administration Responses to COVID-19: Measures Taken to Support Taxpayers*. OECD. https://read.oecd-ilibrary.org/view/?ref=126_126478-29c4rprb3y

Ciorciari, J., Pfeifer, J., & Gountas, J. (2019). An EEG study on emotional intelligence and advertising message effectiveness. *Behavioral Sciences (Basel, Switzerland)*, *9*(8), 88. doi:10.3390/bs9080088 PMID:31443219

Clafey, E., & Bradley, M. (2019). An empirical study of the impact of consumer emotional engagement and affective commitment in firm-hosted virtual communities. *Journal of Marketing Management*, *35*(11-12), 1047–1079. doi:10.1080/0267257X.2019.1601125

Clarke, N. (2006). Developing emotional intelligence through workplace learning: Findings from a case study in healthcare. *Human Resource Development International*, *9*(4), 447–465. doi:10.1080/13678860601032585

Claro, D. P., & Ramos, C. (2018). Sales intrafirm networks and the performance impact of sales cross-functional collaboration with marketing and customer service. *Journal of Personal Selling & Sales Management*, *38*(2), 172–190. doi:10.1080/08853134.2018.1437353

Clifton, R., & Simmons, J. (2003). *Brands and branding*. Bloomberg Press.

CMA. (2011). *Social media and Canadian physicians: Issues and rules of regulations*. Canadian Medical Association – CMA Policy. https://policybase.cma.ca/documents/policypdf/PD12-03.pdf

Coad, J., & Coad, N. (2008). Children and young people's preference of thematic design and color for their hospital environment. *Journal of Child Health Care*, *12*(1), 33–48. doi:10.1177/1367493507085617 PMID:18287183

Cohen, M., Downey, L., & Laxton, L. (2015). Well-being and Technology: Exploring Technology-Supported Meditation. *AMCIS*.

Conklin, Q. A., Crosswell, A. D., Saron, C. D., & Epel, E. S. (2019). Meditation, stress processes, and telomere biology. *Current Opinion in Psychology*, *28*, 92–101. doi:10.1016/j.copsyc.2018.11.009 PMID:30553080

Cooper, R. K. (1997). Applying emotional intelligence in the workplace. *Training & Development*, *51*(12), 31–39.

Cooper, R. K., & Sawaf, A. (1998). *Executive EQ: Emotional intelligence in leadership and organizations*. Penguin.

Copperman, K., Lee, J., Barritt, J., Gruber, R., Gutmann, J., Arredondo, F., & Copperman, A. B. (2012). A Multi-Center Analysis of Emotional Intelligence (EI) in Infertility Practices: A Comprehensive Self-Assessment. *Fertility and Sterility*, *97*(3), S15. doi:10.1016/j.fertnstert.2012.01.032

Coutinho, C. P. (2011). *Metodologia de Investigação em Ciências Sociais e Humanas: Teoria e Prática*. Edições Almedina.

Crosier, A., & Handford, A. (2012). Customer Journey Mapping as an Advocacy Tool for Disabled People: A Case Study. *Social Marketing Quarterly*, *18*(1), 67–76. doi:10.1177/1524500411435483

Cruz, C. A. (2012). A Importância da Motivação e da Liderança nas organizações. *Revista Interfaces Científicas-Humanas e Sociais, 1*(1), 73–79. doi:10.17564/2316-3801.2012v1n1p73-79

Csupor, É., Kuna, Á., Pintér, J. N., Kaló, Z., & Csabai, M. (2017). Konfliktustípusok és konfliktus kezelés magyar egészségügyi dolgozók körében [Conflict types and conflict management among Hungarian healthcare workers]. *Orvosi Hetilap*. doi:10.1556/650.2017.30736

Cuthill, I. C., Hunt, S., Cleary, C., & Clark, C. (1997). Color bands, dominance, and body mass regulation in male zebra finches (Taeniopygia guttata). *Proceedings of the Royal Society of London. Series B, Biological Sciences, 264*(1384), 1093–1099. doi:10.1098/rspb.1997.0151

D'Andreamatteo, A., Ianni, L., Lega, F., & Sargiacomo, M. (2015). Lean in healthcare: A comprehensive review. *Health Policy (Amsterdam), 119*(9), 1197–1209. doi:10.1016/j.healthpol.2015.02.002 PMID:25737260

da Silva Xavier, C. M., da Silva Xavier, L. F., Xavier, A. C., & da Rocha Paranhos, R. P. (2016). *Gerenciamento de Projetos de Mapeamento e Redesenho de Processos: uma adaptação da metodologia*. Basic Methodware. Brasport.

Dacin, M. T., Ventresca, M. J., & Beal, B. D. (1999). The Embeddedness of Organizations: Dialogue & Directions. *Journal of Management, 25*(3), 317–356. doi:10.1177/014920639902500304

Dalgic, T., & Leeuw, M. (1994). Niche Marketing Revisited: Concept, Applications and Some European Cases. *European Journal of Marketing, 28*(4), 39–55. doi:10.1108/03090569410061178

Damasio, A. R. (1994). *Descartes' error: Emotion, rationality and the human brain*. Putnam.

Danhieux, K., Buffel, V., Pairon, A., Benkheil, A., Remmen, R., Wouters, E., & Van Olmen, J. (2020). *The Impact of COVID-19 on Chronic Care: A Qualitative Study Among Primary Care Practices in Belgium*. doi:10.21203/rs.3.rs-42353/v1

Dash, S. K. (2018). Role and Importance of Color in Marketing. Vilakshan: *The XIMB. Journal of Management, 15*(1), 105–112.

Daugherty, A. (2014). *From Mindfulness to Heartfulness*. Archway Publishing.

De Ketele, J. M., & Roegiers, X. (1999). *Metodologia de Recolha de Dados. Fundamentos dos métodos de observações, de questionários, de entrevistas e de estudo de documentos*. Instituto Piaget.

de Pádua, E. M. M. (2007). *Metodologia da Pesquisa* (13th ed.). Papirus Editora.

de Regge, M., Gemmel, P., & Meijboom, B. (2019). How operations matters in healthcare standardization. *International Journal of Operations & Production Management, 39*(9/10), 1144–1165. doi:10.1108/IJOPM-03-2019-0227

Dehling, T., Gao, F., Schneider, S., & Sunyaev, A. (2015). Exploring the far side of mobile health: Information security and privacy of mobile health apps on iOS and Android. *JMIR mHealth and uHealth, 3*(1), e8. doi:10.2196/mhealth.3672 PMID:25599627 della Volpi, Y., & Paulino, S. R. (2018). The sustainability of services: Considerations on the materiality of accommodation services from the concept of life cycle thinking. *Journal of Cleaner Production, 192*, 327–334. doi:10.1016/j.jclepro.2018.04.166

Denzin, N. K., & Lincoln, Y. S. (2000). *Handbook of qualitative research*. SAGE Publications.

Denzin, N., & Lincoln, Y. (1994). *Handbook of Qualitative Research*. Sage.

Deutsch, M., Coleman, P. T., & Marcus, E. C. (Eds.). (2006). *The Handbook of Conflict Resolution: Theory and Practice* (2nd ed.). Wiley Publishing.

Diba, H., Vella, J., & Abratt, R. (2019). Social media influence on the B2B buying process. *Journal of Business and Industrial Marketing, 34*(7), 1482–1496. doi:10.1108/JBIM-12-2018-0403

Diefenbach, S. (2018). The potential and challenges of digital well-being interventions: Positive technology research and design in light of the bitter-sweet ambivalence of change. *Frontiers in Psychology, 9*, 331. doi:10.3389/fpsyg.2018.00331 PMID:29593625

Digital Wellbeing Statistics. (2020). *Digital Wellbeing Statistics from Humane Tech Even*. Retrieved 20 October 2020 from https://digitalwellbeing.org/digital-wellbeing-statistics-from-humane-tech-event/

Dimiris, G. (2006). The diffusion of virtual communities in health care: Concepts and challenges. *Patient Education and Counseling, 62*(2), 178–188. doi:10.1016/j.pec.2005.10.003 PMID:16406472

Ditrendia. (2020). *Mobile en España y en el Mundo 2020*. https://ditrendia.es/informe-mobile-2020/

Dixit, A., Routroy, S., & Dubey, S. K. (2019a). Analysis of government-supported health-care supply chain enablers: A case study. *Journal of Global Operations and Strategic Sourcing, 13*(1), 1–16. doi:10.1108/JGOSS-02-2019-0011

Dixit, A., Routroy, S., & Dubey, S. K. (2019b). A systematic literature review of healthcare supply chain and implications of future research. *International Journal of Pharmaceutical and Healthcare Marketing, 13*(4), 405–435. doi:10.1108/IJPHM-05-2018-0028

Dixon, T., Shaw, M., Frankel, S., & Ebrahim, S. (2004). Hospital Admissions, Age, and Death: Retrospective Cohort Study. *BMJ (Clinical Research Ed.), 328*(7451), 1288. doi:10.1136/bmj.38072.481933.EE PMID:15090442

Dobbert, M. L., & Kurt-Schai, R. (1992). Systematic Ethnography: Toward an Evolutionary Science of Education and Culture. In The Handbook of Qualitative Research in Education (pp. 93–159). New York: Academic Press.

Donabedian, A. (1988). The quality of care. How can it be assessed? *Journal of the American Medical Association, 260*(12), 1743–1748. doi:10.1001/jama.1988.03410120089033 PMID:3045356

Downey, L. (2015). *Well-being technologies: Meditation using virtual worlds*. Nova Southeastern University Repository.

Dubois, B. (1993). *Comprendre le Consommateur*. Editions Dalloz.

Economist. (2021). *Tracking COVID-19 excess deaths across countries*. http://www.economist.com/ graphic-detail/coronavirus-excess-deaths-tracker

Ekman, P. (1992). Facial expressions of emotion: An old controversy and new findings. *Philosophical Transactions of the Royal Society of London. Series B, Biological Sciences*, *335*(1273), 63–69. doi:10.1098/rstb.1992.0008 PMID:1348139

Elias, J., & Mascaray, J. (2003). *Más allá de la comunicación interna: La intracomunicación*. Ediciones Gestión 2000.

Elliot, A. J., & Maier, M. A. (2014). Color psychology: Effects of perceiving color on psychological functioning in humans. *Annual Review of Psychology*, *65*(1), 95–120. doi:10.1146/annurev-psych-010213-115035 PMID:23808916

Erickson, R. J., & Grove, W. J. (2008). Emotional labor and health care. *Sociology Compass*, *2*(2), 704–733. doi:10.1111/j.1751-9020.2007.00084.x

Erigüç, G., & Köse, S. D. (2013). Evaluation of emotional intelligence and communication skills of health care manager candidates: A structural equation modeling. *International Journal of Business and Social Science*, *4*(13), 115–123.

Etzioni, A. (1988). *The Moral Dimension*. The Free Press. doi:10.1002/hrm.3930270407

European Commission. (2020). *Official Website*. https://ec.europa.eu

European Commission. (2020). *Shaping Europe's digital future*. https://ec.europa.eu/digital-single-market/en/mHealth

EUROSTAT. (2019). *Tax revenue statistics*. https://ec.europa.eu/eurostat/documents/2995521/10190755/2-30102019-AP-EN.pdf/68739572-f06a-51e4-3a5b-86e660a23376

Ewen, R. B. (1964). Some determinants of job satisfaction: A study of the generality of Herzberg's theory. *The Journal of Applied Psychology*, *48*(3), 161–163. doi:10.1037/h0048383

Eysenbach, G., Powell, J., Englesakis, M., Rizo, C., & Stern, A. (2004). Health related virtual communities and electronic support groups: Systematic review of the effects of online peer to peer interactions. *BMJ (Clinical Research Ed.)*, *328*(7449), 1166. doi:10.1136/bmj.328.7449.1166 PMID:15142921

Faieta, J., Hand, B. N., Schmeler, M., Onate, J., & Digiovine, C. (2020). Health App Review Tool: Matching mobile apps to Alzheimer's populations (HART Match). *Journal of Rehabilitation and Assistive Technologies Engineering*, *7*. doi:10.1177/2055668320938604 PMID:33014412

Fairchild, M. D. (2013). *Color Appearance Models*. Wiley Press. doi:10.1002/9781118653128

Farao, J., Malila, B., Conrad, N., Mutsvangwa, T., Rangaka, M. X., & Douglas, T. S. (2020). A user-centred design framework for mHealth. *PLoS One*, *15*(8), e0237910. doi:10.1371/journal.pone.0237910 PMID:32813711

Fatehi, F., Samadbeik, M., & Kazemi, A. (2020). What is Digital Health? Review of Definitions. *Studies in Health Technology and Informatics*, *275*, 67–71. PMID:33227742

FDA. (2013). *Mobile medical applications: guidance for industry and food and drug administration staff.* U.S. Food and Drug Administration. https://www.fda.gov/downloads/MedicalDevices/.../UCM263366.pdf

Feather, R. (2009). Emotional intelligence in relation to nursing leadership: Does it matter? *Journal of Nursing Management*, *17*(3), 376–382. doi:10.1111/j.1365-2834.2008.00931.x PMID:21456323

Feitosa, W. R., & Botelho, D. (2015). O Papel da Excitação no Engajamento de Defensores da Marca: Suas Reações a Notícias Positivas e Negativas no Ambiente Virtual. *Revista Economia & Gestão*, *15*(40), 117–141.

Feitosa, W. R., & Botelho, D. (2017). Online Brand Content Sharing on Social Networks – an Experiment Assessing the Role of Emotions on News and Advertising Online Sharing. *LA - Latin American. Advances in Consumer Research. Association for Consumer Research (U. S.)*, *4*, 155–158.

Feitosa, W. R., & Botelho, D. (2018). Mechanisms for incentivizing and encouraging online social interactions - an experiment analysing the role of recommendations and rewards on advertisement sharing behaviour. In B. Rishi & S. Bandyopadhyay (Eds.), *Contemporary Issues in Social Media Marketing*. Routledge. doi:10.4324/9781315563312

Feitosa, W. R., Botelho, D., & Lourenço, C. E. (2014). Comunidades virtuais de marca de produtos de consumo e criação de engajamento: Uma investigação qualitativa. *Revista Eletrônica Gestão e Serviços*, *5*(1), 827–848. doi:10.15603/2177-7284/regs.v5n1p827-848

Fernandez, C. S., Peterson, H. B., Holmstrőm, S. W., & Connolly, A. (2012). Developing emotional intelligence for healthcare leaders. In A. Di Fabio (Ed.), *Emotional intelligence–New perspectives and applications* (pp. 239–260). InTech., doi:10.5772/31940

Fitzpatrick, K. K., Darcy, A., & Vierhile, M. (2017). Delivering cognitive behavior therapy to young adults with symptoms of depression and anxiety using a fully automated conversational agent (Woebot): A randomized controlled trial. *JMIR Mental Health*, *4*(2), e19. doi:10.2196/mental.7785 PMID:28588005

Fitzsimmons, J. A., & Fitzsimmons, M. J. (2014). *Administração de Serviços-: Operações, Estratégia e Tecnologia da Informação*. Amgh Editora.

Fletcher, D., & Sarkar, M. (2013). Psychological resilience. *European Psychologist*, *18*(1), 12–23. Advance online publication. doi:10.1027/1016-9040/a000124

Flick, U. (2009). *An introduction to qualitative research* (4th ed.). Sage Publications.

Flippo, E. B. (1968). Integrative schemes in management theory. *Academy of Management Journal*, *11*(1), 91–98.

Fortin, C., Neustaedter, C., & Hennessy, K. (2014). Posting for community and culture: Considerations for the design of interactive digital bulletin boards. In *Proceedings of the SIGCHI Conference on Human Factors in Computing Systems*. Association for Computing Machinery. 10.1145/2556288.2556970

Forum, P. A. (2020). *Legge 150 del 2000: cosa prevede la prima (e a tutt'oggi unica) legge quadro sulla comunicazione pubblica*. https://www.forumpa.it/open-government/comunicazione-pubblica/legge-150-del-2000-cosa-prevede-la-prima-e-a-tuttoggi-unica-legge-quadro-sulla-comunicazione-pubblica/

Foster, K., Fethney, J., Kozlowski, D., Fois, R., Reza, F., & McCloughen, A. (2018). Emotional intelligence and perceived stress of Australian pre-registration healthcare students: A multi-disciplinary cross-sectional study. *Nurse Education Today*, *66*, 51–56. doi:10.1016/j.nedt.2018.04.001 PMID:29665505

Fredrickson, B. L. (1998). What good are positive emotions? *Review of General Psychology*, *2*(3), 300–319. doi:10.1037/1089-2680.2.3.300 PMID:21850154

Free, C., Phillips, G., Watson, L., Galli, L., Felix, L., Edwards, P., Patel, V., & Haines, A. (2013). The effectiveness of mobile-health technologies to improve health care service delivery processes: A systematic review and meta-analysis. *PLoS Medicine*, *10*(1), e1001363. doi:10.1371/journal.pmed.1001363 PMID:23458994

Freixo, J., & Rocha, Á. (2014). Arquitetura de Informação de Suporte à Gestão da Qualidade em Unidades Hospitalares. *Revista Ibérica de sistemas e Tecnologias de Informação, 14*, 1-15.

Freshman, B., & Rubino, L. (2002). Emotional intelligence: A core competency for health care administrators. *The Health Care Manager*, *20*(4), 1–9. doi:10.1097/00126450-200206000-00002 PMID:12083173

Frijda, N. H. (1986). Studies in emotion and social interaction. The emotions. Cambridge University Press.

Fruchterman, T. M., & Reingold, E. M. (1991). Graph Drawing by Force-directed Placement. *Software, Practice & Experience*, *21*(11), 1129–1164. doi:10.1002pe.4380211102

Fukuoka, Y., Kamitani, E., Bonnet, K., & Lindgren, T. (2011). Real-time social support through a mobile virtual community to improve healthy behavior in overweight and sedentary adults: A focus group analysis. *Journal of Medical Internet Research*, *13*(3), e49. doi:10.2196/jmir.1770 PMID:21752785

Gable, G. G., Sedera, D., & Chan, T. (2008). Re-conceptualizing Information System Success: The IS-Impact Measurement Model. *Journal of the Association for Information*, *9*(7), 377–408. doi:10.17705/1jais.00164

Gabrielli, S., Rizzi, S., Carbone, S., & Donisi, V. (2020). A Chatbot-Based Coaching Intervention for Adolescents to Promote Life Skills: Pilot Study. *JMIR Human Factors*, *7*(1), e16762. doi:10.2196/16762 PMID:32130128

Galán-Ladero, M. M., & Galán-Ladero, M. Á. (2020). La Responsabilidad Social Corporativa (RSC) de las Empresas Farmacéuticas: Beneficio Económico vs. Beneficio Social. *II Congreso AIMPN-LATAM – II Congreso Latinoamericano de Marketing Social.*

Galhardi, C., Freire, N., Minayo, M., & Fagundes, M. (2020). Fato ou Fake? Uma análise da desinformação frente à pandemia da Covid-19 no Brasil. *Ciencia & Saude Coletiva, 25*(suppl 2), 4201–4210. doi:10.1590/1413-812320202510.2.28922020 PMID:33027357

Gazit, T., & Aharony, N. (2018). Factors explaining participation in WhatsApp groups: An exploratory study. *Aslib Journal of Information Management, 70*(4), 390–413. doi:10.1108/AJIM-03-2018-0053

George, D. R., Rovniak, L. S., & Kraschnewski, J. L. (2013). Dangers and oppurtunities for social media in medicine. *Clinical Obstetrics and Gynecology, 56*(3), 453–462. doi:10.1097/GRF.0b013e318297dc38 PMID:23903375

Gilmartin, M. J., & D'Aunno, T. A. (2007). 8 Leadership research in healthcare: A review and roadmap. *The Academy of Management Annals, 1*(1), 387–438. doi:10.5465/078559813

Gil, S., & Le Bigot, L. (2014). Seeing Life through Positive-Tinted Glasses: Color–Meaning Associations. *PLoS One, 9*(8), e104291. doi:10.1371/journal.pone.0104291 PMID:25098167

Giraldes, M. (1997). *Economia da Saúde da teoria à Prática*. Editora Estampa.

Glaser, B. G., & Strauss, A. L. (1967). *The Discovery of Grounded Theory: Strategies for Qualitative Research.* Aldine.

GM Insights. (2020). *Healthcare & Medical Devices Market Research Reports*. Healthcare & Medical Devices Market Research Reports | Global Market Insights. gminsights.com

Godes, D., Mayslin, D., Chen, Y., Das, S., Dellarocas, C., Pfeiffer, B., ... Verlegh, P. (2005). The firm's management of social interactions. *Marketing Letters, 16*(3), 415–428. doi:10.100711002-005-5902-4

Goleman, D. (1995). *Emotional Intelligence*. Bantam Books, Inc.

Goleman, D. (2000). Leadership that gets results. *Harvard Business Review, 78*(2), 4–17.

Gomes, M., Fernandes, T., & Brandão, A. (2014). The Role of Branding in a B2B Purchasing Context. *4th Conference of the International Network of Business and Management Journals.*

Gomes, M., Fernandes, T., & Brandão, A. (2016). Determinants of brand relevance in a B2B service purchasing context. *Journal of Business and Industrial Marketing, 31*(2), 193–204. doi:10.1108/JBIM-08-2014-0151

Gonzalez, M. E. (2019). Improving customer satisfaction of a healthcare facility: Reading the customers' needs. *Benchmarking, 26*(3), 854–870. doi:10.1108/BIJ-01-2017-0007

Gorski, I., Bram, J. T., Sutermaster, S., Eckman, M., & Mehta, K. (2016). Value propositions of mHealth projects. *Journal of Medical Engineering & Technology*, *40*(7-8), 400–421. doi:10.1080/03091902.2016.1213907 PMID:27687907

Gottlieb, B. H. (1997). Conceptual and measurement issues in the study of coping with chronic stress. In *Coping with chronic stress* (pp. 3–40). Springer. doi:10.1007/978-1-4757-9862-3_1

Gowarty, M. A., Kung, N. J., Maher, A. E., Longacre, M. R., & Brunette, M. F. (2020). Perceptions of Mobile Apps for Smoking Cessation Among Young People in Community Mental Health Care: Qualitative Study. *JMIR Formative Research*, *4*(10), e19860. doi:10.2196/19860 PMID:33006560

Goyen, M., & Debatin, J. (2009). Healthcare costs for new technologies. *European Journal of Nuclear Medicine and Molecular Imaging*, *36*(S1), 139–143. doi:10.100700259-008-0975-y PMID:19104799

Graban, M. (2016). *Lean hospitals: improving quality, patient safety, and employee engagement*. CRC Press. doi:10.1201/b11740

Greene, J. A., Choudhry, N. K., Kilabuk, E., & Shrank, W. H. (2011). Online social networking by patients with diabetes: A qualitative evaluation of communication with Facebook. *Journal of General Internal Medicine*, *26*(3), 287–292. doi:10.100711606-010-1526-3 PMID:20945113

Gross, J. J. (1998). Antecedent-and response-focused emotion regulation: Divergent consequences for experience, expression, and physiology. *Journal of Personality and Social Psychology*, *74*(1), 224–237. doi:10.1037/0022-3514.74.1.224 PMID:9457784

Grossman, R. J. (2000, September). Emotions at work. *Health Forum Journal*, *43*(5), 18–22. PMID:11066984

Grytten, J., & Sørensen, R. (2001). Type of Contract and Supplier-Induced Demand for Primary Physicians in Norway. *Journal of Health Economics*, *20*(3), 379–393. doi:10.1016/S0167-6296(00)00087-4 PMID:11373837

Guba, E. G., & Lincoln, Y. S. (1994). Competing paradigms in qualitative research. In N. K. Denzin & Y. S. Lincoln (Eds.), *Handbook of qualitative research* (pp. 163–194). SAGE Publications.

Gulati, R. (1998). Alliances and Networks. *Strategic Management Journal*, *19*(1), 293–317. doi:10.1002/(SICI)1097-0266(199804)19:4<293::AID-SMJ982>3.0.CO;2-M

Guo, X., Zhang, X., & Sun, Y. (2016). The privacy–personalization paradox in mHealth services acceptance of different age groups. *Electronic Commerce Research and Applications*, *16*, 55–65. doi:10.1016/j.elerap.2015.11.001

Hammersley, M. (2006). Ethnography: Problems and Prospects. *Ethnography and Education*, *1*(1), 3–14. doi:10.1080/17457820500512697

Handel, M. J. (2011). mHealth (mobile health)-using apps for health and wellness. *Explore (New York, N.Y.)*, *7*(4), 256–261. doi:10.1016/j.explore.2011.04.011

Harb, A., Fowler, D., Jung, H., & Alakaleek, W. (2019). Social media as a marketing tool for events. *Journal of Hospitality and Tourism Technology*, *10*(1), 28–44.

Hashem, T. N. (2010). Impact of Managers' Emotional Intelligence on Marketing Creativity in Jordan Commercial Banks. *Innovative Marketing*, *6*(3), 78–86.

Health, I. M. S. (2013). *Patient apps for improved healthcare: from novelty to mainstream*. IMS Institute for Healthcare Informatics.

Heartfulness Institute. (2020). *Heartfulness Offerings*. Retrieved 25 December 2020 from https://www.heartfulnessinstitute.org/experience

Heffernan, T., O'Neill, G., Travaglione, T., & Droulers, M. (2008). Relationship marketing: The impact of emotional intelligence and trust on bank performance. *International Journal of Bank Marketing*, *26*(3), 183–199. doi:10.1108/02652320810864652

Heidel, A., & Hagist, C. (2020). Potential benefits and risks resulting from the introduction of health apps and wearables into the German statutory health care system: Scoping review. *JMIR mHealth and uHealth*, *8*(9), e16444. doi:10.2196/16444 PMID:32965231

Henderson, P. W., & Cote, J. A. (1998). Guidelines for selecting or modifying logos. *Journal of Marketing*, *62*(2), 14–30. doi:10.1177/002224299806200202

Henke, J. W. Jr, Parameswaran, R., & Mohan Pisharodi, R. (2008). Manufacturer price reduction pressure and supplier relations. *Journal of Business and Industrial Marketing*, *23*(5), 287–300. doi:10.1108/08858620810881566

Herman, I., Melancon, G., & Marshall, M. (2000). Graph visualization and navigation in information visualization: A survey. *IEEE Transactions on Visualization and Computer Graphics*, *6*(1), 24–43. https://doi.org/10.1109/2945.841119

Hinterhuber, A. (2015). Violations of rational choice principles in pricing decisions. *Industrial Marketing Management*, *47*, 65–74. doi:10.1016/j.indmarman.2015.02.006

Hinterhuber, A. (2016). The six pricing myths that kill profits. *Business Horizons*, *59*(1), 71–83. doi:10.1016/j.bushor.2015.09.002

Hobfoll, S. E. (1989). Conservation of resources: A new attempt at conceptualizing stress. *The American Psychologist*, *44*(3), 513–524. doi:10.1037/0003-066X.44.3.513 PMID:2648906

Hobfoll, S. E. (2002). Social and psychological resources and adaptation. *Review of General Psychology*, *6*(4), 307–324. doi:10.1037/1089-2680.6.4.307

Hofmann, B. (2015). Too much technology. BMJ, 350. doi:10.1136/bmj.h705

Holahan, C. J., & Moos, R. H. (1987). Personal and contextual determinants of coping strategies. *Journal of Personality and Social Psychology*, *52*(5), 946–955. doi:10.1037/0022-3514.52.5.946 PMID:3585703

Hollebeek, L. (2011). Exploring customer brand engagement: definition and themes. *Journal of Strategic Management*, *11*(7), 555–573.

Hollebeek, L. D., Andreassen, T. W., Smith, D. L., Grönquist, D., Karahasanovic, A., & Marquez, A. (2018). Epilogue – service innovation actor engagement: An integrative model. *Journal of Services Marketing*, *32*(1), 95–100. https://doi.org/10.1108/JSM-11-2017-0390

Holler, J., Tsiatsis, V., Mulligan, C., Karnouskos, S., Avesand, S., & Boyle, D. (2014). *Internet of Things*. Academic Press.

Hooker, L., & Palumbo, D. (2020). Cuánto dinero pueden ganar realmente las farmacéuticas con la vacuna contra la covid-19. *BBC News Mundo*. https://www.bbc.com

Hootsuite. (2019). *We Are Social, Digital In 2019*. Available in: https://wearesocial.com/global-digital-report-2019

Hospital de Braga. (2018). *Relatório anual sobre o acesso a cuidados de saúde*. Author.

Hospital de Braga. distinções. (2019a). *O Hospital: distinções do Hospital de Braga*. https://www.hospitaldebraga.pt/hospital/distincoes-do-hospital-de-braga

Hospital de Braga. Sobre nós. (2019b). *O Hospital: sobre nós*. https://www.hospitaldebraga.pt/hospital/sobre-nos

Huang, Y. T., Rundle-Thiele, S., & Chen, Y. H. (2019). Extending understanding of the internal marketing practice and employee satisfaction relationship: A budget Chinese airline empirical examination. *Journal of Vacation Marketing*, *25*(1), 88–98. doi:10.1177/1356766718757270

Huber, G. P., Sutcliffe, K. M., Miller, C., & Glick, W. (1993). Understanding and predictingorganizational change. In G. Huber & W. H. Glick (Eds.), *Organizational Change and redesing* (pp. 215–254). Oxford University Press.

Hughes, S. (2020). *Study Reveals Everyday Technology Helps Fight Loneliness*. https://phys.org/news/2019-06-reveals-everyday-technology-loneliness.html

Huhs, E., Gliebe, W., & Sendlhofer, G. (2019). Qualitative Analyse zu Lean Management im Gesundheitswesen: Sichtweisen österreichischer und Schweizer Experten. *Zeitschrift für Evidenz, Fortbildung und Qualität im Gesundheitswesen*, *143*, 8–14. doi:10.1016/j.zefq.2019.05.003 PMID:31153810

Humphreys, J., Brunsen, B., & Davis, D. (2005). Emotional structure and commitment: Implications for health care management. *Journal of Health Organization and Management*, *19*(2), 120–129. doi:10.1108/14777260510600040 PMID:16119051

Hundal, G. S., Thiyagarajan, S., Alduraibi, M., Laux, C. M., Furterer, S. L., Cudney, E. A., & Antony, J. (2021). Lean Six Sigma as an organizational resilience mechanism in health care during the era of COVID-19. *International Journal of Lean Six Sigma*. doi:10.1108/IJLSS-11-2020-0204

Hunt, S. D. (2010). *Marketing theory: foundations, controversy, strategy, resource-advantage theory*. M.E. Sharpe.

Hunt, S. D. (2015). The theoretical foundations of strategic marketing and marketing strategy: Foundational premises, R-A theory, three fundamental strategies, and societal welfare. *AMS Review*, *5*(3-4), 61–77. doi:10.100713162-015-0069-5

Hunt, S. D. (2017a). Advancing marketing strategy in the marketing discipline and beyond: From promise, to neglect, to prominence, to fragment (to promise?). *Journal of Marketing Management*, *34*(1-2), 16–51. doi:10.1080/0267257X.2017.1326973

Hunt, S. D. (2017b). The prospects for marketing strategy and the marketing discipline in Era V: Is the prognosis promising or problematic? *Journal of Marketing Management*, *34*(1-2), 86–95. doi:10.1080/0267257X.2017.1401381

Hunt, S. D., & Arnett, D. B. (2004). Market Segmentation Strategy, Competitive Advantage, and Public Policy: Grounding Segmentation Strategy in Resource-Advantage Theory. *Australasian Marketing Journal*, *12*(1), 7–25. doi:10.1016/S1441-3582(04)70083-X

Hunt, S. D., & Lambe, C. J. (2000). Marketing's contribution to business strategy: Market orientation, relationship marketing and resource-advantage theory. *International Journal of Management Reviews*, *2*(1), 17–43. doi:10.1111/1468-2370.00029

Hunt, S. D., & Madhavaram, S. (2020). Adaptive marketing capabilities, dynamic capabilities, and renewal competences: The "outside vs. inside" and "static vs. dynamic" controversies in strategy. *Industrial Marketing Management*, *89*, 129–139. doi:10.1016/j.indmarman.2019.07.004

Hunt, S. D., & Morgan, R. M. (1995). The Comparative Advantage Theory of Competition. *Journal of Marketing*, *59*(2), 1–15. doi:10.1177/002224299505900201

Hunt, S. D., & Morgan, R. M. (1997). Resource-Advantage Theory: A Snake Swallowing Its Tail or a General Theory of Competition? *Journal of Marketing*, *61*(4), 74–82. doi:10.1177/002224299706100406

Hunt, S. D., & Wooliscroft, B. (2012). The evolution of resource-advantage theory. *Journal of Historical Research in Marketing*, *4*(1), 7–29. doi:10.1108/17557501211195046

Huo, J., Desai, R., Hong, Y. R., Turner, K., Mainous III, A. G., & Bian, J. (2019). Use of social media in health communication: findings from the Health Information National Trends Survey 2013, 2014, and 2017. *Cancer Control: Journal of the Moffitt Cancer Center, 26*(1).

Huo, J., & Turner, K. (2019). Social Media in Health Communication. In J. Bian, Y. Guo, Z. He, & X. Hu (Eds.), *Social Web and Health Research* (pp. 53–82). Springer.

Hyland-Wood, B., Gardner, J., Leask, J., & Ecker, U. K. H. (2021). Toward effective government communication strategies in the era of COVID-19. *Humanities and Social Sciences Communications*, *8*(1), 1–11. doi:10.105741599-020-00701-w

Hynes, N. (2009). Color and meaning in corporate logos: An empirical study. *Journal of Brand Management, 16*(8), 545–555. doi:10.1057/bm.2008.5

IFRC, UNICEF, & WHO. (2020a). *Risk communication & community engagement (RCCE) action plan guide. COVID-19 preparedness & response.* https://www.unicef.org/media/65936/file/Preparedness%20for%20and%20response%20to%20coronavirus%202019%20(COVID-19).pdf

IFRC, UNICEF, & WHO. (2020b). *COVID-19 Global Risk Communication and Community Engagement Strategy.* https://www.who.int/publications/i/item/covid-19-global-risk-communication-and-community-engagement-strategy

IMF - International Monetary Fund. (2020). Challenges in Forecasting Tax Revenue. *Special Series on Fiscal Policies to Respond to COVID-19.* https://www.imf.org/~/media/Files/ Publications/COVID-19-special-notes/en-special-series-on-COVID-19-challenges-in-forecasting-tax-revenue.ashx

Iribarren, S. J., Cato, K., Falzon, L., & Stone, P. W. (2017). What is the economic evidence for mHealth? A systematic review of economic evaluations of mHealth solutions. *PLoS One, 12*(2), e0170581. doi:10.1371/journal.pone.0170581 PMID:28152012

Iswanto, A. H. (2021). Impact of lean six sigma at pharmacy unit on hospital profitability before and during Covid-19 pandemic. *International Journal of Lean Six Sigma.* doi:10.1108/IJLSS-10-2020-0182

Iyer, G. R., Hong Xiao, S., Sharma, A., & Nicholson, M. (2015). Behavioral issues in price setting in business-to-business marketing: A framework for analysis. *Industrial Marketing Management, 47*, 6–16. doi:10.1016/j.indmarman.2015.02.001

Iyer, R. B., & Iyer, B. N. (2019). The impact of heartfulness-based elective on middle school students. *American Journal of Health Behavior, 43*(4), 812–823. doi:10.5993/AJHB.43.4.14 PMID:31239023

Jaakkola, E. (2020). Designing conceptual articles: four approaches. *AMS Review*, 1-9.

Jaana, M., & Paré, G. (2020). Comparison of Mobile Health Technology Use for Self-Tracking Between Older Adults and the General Adult Population in Canada: Cross-Sectional Survey. *JMIR mHealth and uHealth, 8*(11), e24718. doi:10.2196/24718 PMID:33104517

Jacobs, K. W., & Suess, J. F. (1975). Effects of four psychological primary colors on anxiety state. *Perceptual and Motor Skills, 41*(1), 207–210. doi:10.2466/pms.1975.41.1.207 PMID:1178407

Jamshed, S., & Majeed, N. (2019). Relationship between team culture and team performance through lens of knowledge sharing and team emotional intelligence. *Journal of Knowledge Management, 23*(1), 90–109. doi:10.1108/JKM-04-2018-0265

Jayakody, J. A. S. K., & Sanjeewani, W. M. A. (2006). The impact of salesperson transformational leadership behavior on customer relationship marketing behavior. *International Journal of Bank Marketing, 24*(7), 461–474. doi:10.1108/02652320610712085

Jeong, S. H., Lee, T. R., Kang, J. B., & Choi, M. T. (2020). Analysis of Health Insurance Big Data for Early Detection of Disabilities: Algorithm Development and Validation. *JMIR Medical Informatics*, *8*(11), e19679. doi:10.2196/19679 PMID:33226352

Johnson, H., O'Farrell, A., McKeown, D., Sayers, G., Hayes, C., & Beaton, D. (2018). Is Increasing Life Expectancy Leading To More Complexity? *Irish Medical Journal*, *111*, 672. PMID:29869853

Johnston, W. J., & Mora Cortez, R. (2018). Unit pricing and its implications for B2B marketing research. *Industrial Marketing Management*, *69*, 32–39. doi:10.1016/j.indmarman.2018.01.026

Joung, M. S., & Kim, K. J. (2006). A study on the effect of emotional labor and leader's emotional intelligence on job satisfaction and organizational commitment for nurses. *Korea Journal of Hospital Management*, *11*(4), 1–18.

Kalla, H. K. (2005). Integrated internal communications: A multidisciplinary perspective. *Corporate Communications*, *10*(4), 302–314. doi:10.1108/13563280510630106

Kaplan, M. A., & Haenlein, M. (2010). Users of the world, unite! The challenges and opportunities of social media. *Business Horizons*, *53*(1), 59–68. doi:10.1016/j.bushor.2009.09.003

Karasek, R., & Theorell, R. (1990). *Healthy work: Stress, productivity, and the reconstruction of working life*. Basic Books.

Karmarkar, Y., Ravi, M., Vaidya, S., & Bhise, K. (2020). Training To Cope-Up With Aggression. *Attention Span And Nurture Wellbeing Through 'Heartfulness'–An Experimental Study On School Children.*

Kaya, N., & Epps, H. H. (2004). Relationship between color and emotion: A study of college students. *College Student Journal*, *38*(3), 396–405.

Kazakov, S., & Predvoditeleva, M. (2015). *How travelers use online and social media channels to make hotel choice decisions. A comparative study of Russian Federation and American tourists' online consumer behavior.* Higher School of Economics Research Paper No. WP BRP 44/MAN/2015.

Keen, D., & Ward, S. (2004). Autistic Spectrum Disorder: A Child Population Profile. *Autism*, *8*(1), 39–48. https://doi.org/10.1177/1362361304040637

Keller, K. L., Apéria, T., & Georgson, M. (2008). *Strategic brand management: a European perspective*. Prentice Hall Financial Times.

Keller, K. L., Apéria, T., & Georgson, M. (2012). *Strategic brand management: a European perspective* (2nd ed.). Financial Times/Prentice Hall.

Keller, K. L. (1998). *Strategic brand management: Building, measuring and managing brand equity*. Prentice Hall.

Keller, K. L. (2013). *Strategic brand management: Building, measuring, and managing brand equity* (4th ed.). Pearson.

Kerasidou, A., & Horn, R. (2016). Making space for empathy: Supporting doctors in the emotional labour of clinical care. *BMC Medical Ethics*, *17*(1), 1–5. doi:10.118612910-016-0091-7 PMID:26818248

Kesgin, M., & Murthy, R. S. (2019). Consumer engagement: The role of social currency in online reviews. *Service Industries Journal*, *39*(7-8), 609–636. https://doi.org/10.1080/02642069.2018.1553237

Kewalramani, S., Agrawal, M., & Rastogi, M. R. (2015). Models of emotional intelligence: Similarities and discrepancies. *Indian Journal of Positive Psychology*, *6*(2), 178–181.

Khoja, S., Durrani, H., Scott, R. E., Sajwani, A., & Piryani, U. (2013). Conceptual framework for development of comprehensive e-health evaluation tool. *Telemedicine Journal and e-Health*, *19*(1), 48–53. doi:10.1089/tmj.2012.0073 PMID:22957502

Kidwell, B., Hardesty, D. M., Murtha, B. R., & Sheng, S. (2011). Emotional intelligence in marketing exchanges. *Journal of Marketing*, *75*(1), 78–95. doi:10.1509/jm.75.1.78

Kienzler, M. (2018). Value-based pricing and cognitive biases: An overview for business markets. *Industrial Marketing Management*, *68*, 86–94. doi:10.1016/j.indmarman.2017.09.028

Kienzler, M., & Kowalkowski, C. (2017). Pricing strategy: A review of 22 years of marketing research. *Journal of Business Research*, *78*, 101–110. doi:10.1016/j.jbusres.2017.05.005

Kietzmann, J. H., Hermkens, K., McCarthy, I., & Silvestre, B. (2011). Social media? Get serious! Understanding the functional building blocks of social media. *Business Horizons*, *54*(3), 241–251.

Kim, B., & Lee, J. (2016). Relationships between personal traits, emotional intelligence, internal marketing, service management, and customer orientation in Korean outpatient department nurses. *Asian Nursing Research*, *10*(1), 18–24. doi:10.1016/j.anr.2015.10.005 PMID:27021830

Kim, D. K., & Kreps, G. L. (2020). An Analysis of government communication in the United States during the COVID-19 pandemic: Recommendations for effective government health risk communication. *World Medical & Health Policy*, *12*(4), 398–412. doi:10.1002/wmh3.363 PMID:32904935

Kinman, G., & Leggetter, S. (2016). Emotional labour and wellbeing: What protects nurses? *Health Care*, *4*(4), 89. PMID:27916880

Kitson, A., Prpa, M., & Riecke, B. E. (2018). Immersive interactive technologies for positive change: A scoping review and design considerations. *Frontiers in Psychology*, *9*, 1354. doi:10.3389/fpsyg.2018.01354 PMID:30123161

Ko, C., Kim, N., Kim, E., Song, D. H., & Cheon, K. A. (2016). The effect of epilepsy on autistic symptom severity assessed by the social responsiveness scale in children with autism spectrum disorder. *Behavioral and Brain Functions*, *12*(1), 1–9.

Kohane, I. S., McMurry, A., Weber, G., MacFadden, D., Rappaport, L., Kunkel, L., ... Churchill, S. (2012). The co-morbidity burden of children and young adults with autism spectrum disorders. *PLoS One*, *7*(4), e33224.

Kohli, A. K., & Jaworski, B. J. (1990). Market orientation: The construct, research propositions and managerial implications. *Journal of Marketing*, *54*(2), 1–18. doi:10.1177/002224299005400201

Kolaczyk, E., & Csárdi, G. (2020). *Statistical Analysis of Network Data with R*. Springer.

Kotler, P., & Keller, K. (2006). Administração de marketing. Academic Press.

Kotler, P. (1991). *Marketing management analysis, planning, implementation, and control*. Prentice-Hall.

Kotler, P., & Armstrong, G. (2018). *Principles of Marketing* (17th ed.). Pearson Prentice Hall.

Koumpouros, Y., & Georgoulas, A. (2020). A systematic review of mHealth funded R&D activities in EU: Trends, technologies and obstacles. *Informatics for Health & Social Care*, *45*(2), 168–187. doi:10.1080/17538157.2019.1656208 PMID:31743060

Kozinets, R. V. (1999). E-Tribalized Marketing? The strategic implications of virtual communities of consumption. *European Management Journal*, *17*(3), 252–264. doi:10.1016/S0263-2373(99)00004-3

Kozinets, R. V. (2002). The field behind the screen: Using netnography for marketing research in online communities. *JMR, Journal of Marketing Research*, *39*(1), 61–72. doi:10.1509/jmkr.39.1.61.18935

Kozinets, R. V. (2006). Netnography 2.0. In R. W. Belk (Ed.), *Handbook of Qualitative Research Methods in Marketing* (pp. 129–142). Edward Elgar Publishing.

Kozinets, R. V. (2010). *Netnography:redefined* (2nd ed.). Sage.

Kozinets, R., Scaraboto, D., & Parmentier, M. A. (2018). Evolving netnography: How brand auto-netnography, a netnographic sensibility, and more-thanhuman netnography can transform your research. *Journal of Marketing Management*, *34*(3-4), 231–242. https://doi.org/10.1080/0267257X.2018.1446488

Krakowiak, P., Goodlin-Jones, B. E. T. H., Hertz-Picciotto, I. R. V. A., Croen, L. A., & Hansen, R. L. (2008). Sleep problems in children with autism spectrum disorders, developmental delays, and typical development: A population-based study. *Journal of Sleep Research*, *17*(2), 197–206.

Kumar, J. S. (2017). The Psychology of Color Influences Consumers' Buying Behaviour – A Diagnostic Study. *Ushus Journal of Business Management*, *16*(4), 1–13. doi:10.12725/ujbm.41.1

Kumar, S., Nilsen, W., Pavel, M., & Srivastava, M. (2012). Mobile health: Revolutionizing healthcare through transdisciplinary research. *Computer*, *46*(1), 28–35. doi:10.1109/MC.2012.392

Labrecque, L. (2010). *The marketer's prismatic palette: Essays on the importance of color in marketing with implications for brand personality* (Doctoral Dissertation). https://scholarworks.umass.edu/dissertations/AAI3409617

Labrecque, L. (2020). Color research in marketing: Theoretical and technical considerations for conducting rigorous and impactful color research. *Psychology and Marketing, 37*(7), 855–863. doi:10.1002/mar.21359

Lakerveld, J., Wagtendonk, A., Vaartjes, I., & Karssenberg, D. (2020). Deep phenotyping meets big data: The Geoscience and hEalth Cohort COnsortium (GECCO) data to enable exposome studies in The Netherlands. *International Journal of Health Geographics, 19*(1), 1–16. doi:10.118612942-020-00235-z PMID:33187515

Lambert, K. M., Barry, P., & Stokes, G. (2012). Risk management and legal issues with the use of social media in the healthcare setting. *Journal of Healthcare Risk Management, 31*(4), 41–47. doi:10.1002/jhrm.20103 PMID:22528403

Lambkin, M. C., & Muzellec, L. (2010). Leveraging brand equity in business-to-business mergers and acquisitions. *Industrial Marketing Management, 39*(8), 1234–1239. doi:10.1016/j.indmarman.2010.02.020

Lam, S. Y., Shankar, V., Erramilli, M. K., & Murthy, B. (2004). Customer value, satisfaction, loyalty, and switching costs: An illustration from a business-to-business service context. *Journal of the Academy of Marketing Science, 32*(3), 293–311. doi:10.1177/0092070304263330

Langa, C. (2020). *Ejemplos de acciones de RSC para empresas farmacéuticas*. https://www.cicerocomunicacion.es/rsc-empresas-farmaceuticas/

Langer, R., & Beckman, S. C. (2005). Sensitive research topics: Netnography revisited. *Qualitative Market Research, 8*(2), 189–203. doi:10.1108/13522750510592454

Langhorn, S. (2004). How emotional intelligence can improve management performance. *International Journal of Contemporary Hospitality Management, 16*(4), 220–230. doi:10.1108/09596110410537379

Larson, L., & Bock, E. (2016). Consumer Search and Satisfaction with Mental Health Services. *Journal of Services Marketing, 30*(7), 736–748.

Lassk, F. G., & Shepherd, C. D. (2013). Exploring the relationship between emotional intelligence and salesperson creativity. *Journal of Personal Selling & Sales Management, 33*(1), 25–37. doi:10.2753/PSS0885-3134330103

Launberg, A. (2011). Commercializing Academic Research Results: When a University wants to Further Innovation. *27th IMP-Conference*. https://www.impgroup.org/uploads/papers/7652.pdf

Lazarus, R. S. (1991). Progress on a cognitive-motivational-relational theory of emotion. *The American Psychologist, 46*(8), 819–834. doi:10.1037/0003-066X.46.8.819 PMID:1928936

Lazarus, R. S., & Folkman, S. (1984). *Stress, appraisal, and coping*. Springer.

Le Goff-Pronost, M., & Krychowski, C. (2020). *MédecinDirect–L'adaptation d'un business modèle pionnier à une nouvelle donne réglementaire*. Academic Press.

Leek, S., & Christodoulides, G. (2011). A literature review and future agenda for B2B branding: Challenges of branding in a B2B context. *Industrial Marketing Management, 40*(6), 830–837. doi:10.1016/j.indmarman.2011.06.006

Léonard, A., Clément, S., Kuo, C.-D., & Manto, M. (2019). Changes in heart rate variability during heartfulness meditation: A power spectral analysis including the residual spectrum. *Frontiers in Cardiovascular Medicine, 6*, 62. doi:10.3389/fcvm.2019.00062 PMID:31139634

Lindsay, C. F., Kumar, M., & Juleff, L. (2020). Operationalising lean in healthcare: The impact of professionalism. *Production Planning and Control, 31*(8), 629–643. doi:10.1080/09537287.2019.1668577

Lings, I. N. (2004). Internal Market Orientation. Construct and Consequences. *Journal of Business Research, 57*(4), 405–413. doi:10.1016/S0148-2963(02)00274-6

Lin, L. (2010). The relationship of consumer personality trait, brand personality and brand loyalty: An empirical study of toys and video games buyers. *Journal of Product and Brand Management, 19*(1), 4–17. doi:10.1108/10610421011018347

Lippeveld, T., Sauerborn, R., & Bodart, C. (2000). *Design and implementation of health information systems*. World Health Organization.

Li, S., & Tang, Y. (2020). A Simple Framework of Smart Geriatric Nursing considering Health Big Data and User Profile. *Computational and Mathematical Methods in Medicine*. PMID:33149759

Liu, C.-T., Guo, Y. M., & Lee, C.-H. (2011). The effects of relationship quality and switching barriers on customer loyalty. *International Journal of Information Management, 31*(1), 71–79. doi:10.1016/j.ijinfomgt.2010.05.008

Liu, L., Xu, P., Zhou, K., Xue, J., & Wu, H. (2018). Mediating role of emotional labor in the association between emotional intelligence and fatigue among Chinese doctors: A cross-sectional study. *BMC Public Health, 18*(1), 881. doi:10.118612889-018-5817-7 PMID:30012126

Logie, C., Okumu, M., Abela, H., Wilson, D., & Narasimhan, M. (2020). Sexual and reproductive health mobile apps: Results from a cross-sectional values and preferences survey to inform World Health Organization normative guidance on self-care interventions. *Global Health Action, 13*(1), 1796346. doi:10.1080/16549716.2020.1796346 PMID:32778000

Loo, J. (2009). *Acceptance of health services on mobile phones* (Doctoral Dissertation). University of North Carolina.

Lorenzoni, L., Marino, A., Morgan, D., Murakami, Y., & James, C. (2019). *Health spending projections to 2030*. OECD Health Working Paper N.° 110, OECD Publishing. doi:10.1787/18152015

MacEvoy, B. (2019a). *Light and the eye. Color vision*. http://www.handprint.com/HP/WCL/color1.html#spectrum

MacEvoy, B. (2019b). *Modern color theory (concepts). Color theory.* http://www.handprint.com/HP/WCL/color18a.html

Machin, J. E., Adkins, N., Crosby, E., Ferrell, J., & Mirabito, A. (2019). The Marketplace, Mental Wellbeing, and Me: Exploring Self-Efficacy, Self-Esteem, and Self-Compassion in Consumer Coping. *Journal of Business Research*, *100*, 410–420.

MacInnis, D. J. (2011). A framework for conceptual contributions in marketing. *Journal of Marketing*, *75*(4), 136–154. doi:10.1509/jmkg.75.4.136

Mackway-Jones, K., Marsden, J., & Windle, J. (2006). *Emergency triage*. Wiley Online Library.

Maecker, O., Barrot, C., & Becker, J. U. (2016). The effect of social media interactions on customer relationship management. *Journal of Business Research*, *9*(1), 133–155.

Maenner, M., Smith, L., Hong, J., Makuch, R., Greenberg, J., & Mailick, M. (2013). Evaluation of an activities diary living scale for adolescents and adults with developmental disabilities. *Disability and Health Journal*, *6*(1), 8–17.

Magnavita, N. (2014). Workplace violence and occupational stress in healthcare workers: A chicken-and-egg situation—results of a 6-year follow-up study. *Journal of Nursing Scholarship*, *46*(5), 366–376. doi:10.1111/jnu.12088 PMID:24754800

Maher, C. A., Lewis, L. K., Ferrar, K., Marshall, S., De Bourdeaudhuij, I., & Vandelanotte, C. (2014). Are health behavior change interventions that use online social networks effective? A systematic review. *Journal of Medical Internet Research*, *16*(2), e40. doi:10.2196/jmir.2952 PMID:24550083

Maia, I., Magalhães, L., Lencastre, J., Monteiro, A., & Bilimória, H. (2012). E-moções: avaliação heurística a um jogo multimédia em m-learning para crianças com perturbações do espetro do autismo. In *Atas do Encontro sobre Jogos e Mobile Learning*. Braga: CIEd.

Malecki, K. M. C., Keating, J. A., & Safdar, N. (2021). Crisis communication and public perception of COVID-19 risks in the era of social media. *Clinical Infectious Diseases*, *72*(4), 699–704. doi:10.1093/cid/ciaa758 PMID:32544242

Malhotra, N. K. (2002). Pesquisa de Marketing: Uma orientação aplicada. *The Bookman*.

Malik, M., Haider, Z., & Hussain, A. (2019). Perceived emotional intelligence, work life balance and job satisfaction among healthcare professionals in Pakistan. *International Journal of Pharmaceutical Research & Allied Sciences*, *8*(2), 80–86.

Malvey, D. M., & Slovensky, D. J. (2017). Global mHealth policy arena: Status check and future directions. *mHealth*, *3*, 41. doi:10.21037/mhealth.2017.09.03 PMID:29184893

Marcus, G. E., & Fischer, M. J. M. (1996). *Anthropology as cultural critique* (2nd ed.). The University of Chicago Press.

Marques, G., Miranda, N., Kumar Bhoi, A., Garcia-Zapirain, B., Hamrioui, S., & de la Torre Díez, I. (2020). Internet of Things and enhanced living environments: Measuring and mapping air quality using cyber-physical systems and mobile computing technologies. *Sensors (Basel), 20*(3), 720. doi:10.339020030720 PMID:32012932

Marshall, J. M., Dunstan, D. A., & Bartik, W. (2020). Smartphone psychology: New approaches towards safe and efficacious mobile mental health apps. *Professional Psychology, Research and Practice, 51*(3), 214–222. doi:10.1037/pro0000278

Mason, J. (2018). *Qualitative researching* (3rd ed.). SAGE.

Matthew-Maich, N., Harris, L., Ploeg, J., Markle-Reid, M., Valaitis, R., Ibrahim, S., Gafni, A., & Isaacs, S. (2016). Designing, implementing, and evaluating mobile health technologies for managing chronic conditions in older adults: A scoping review. *JMIR mHealth and uHealth, 4*(2), e29. doi:10.2196/mhealth.5127 PMID:27282195

Mayer, J. D., & Salovey, P. (1997). What is emotional intelligence? In P. Salovey & D. Sluyter (Eds.), *Emotional Development and Emotional Intelligence: Implications for Educators* (pp. 3–31). Basic Books.

Mazurek, M. (2014). Loneliness, friendship, and well-being in adults with autism spectrum disorders. *Autism, 18*(3), 223–232. https://doi.org/10.1177/1362361312474121

McFadden, S. A., Malik, A. A., Aguolu, O. G., Willebrand, K. S., & Omer, S. B. (2020). Perceptions of US population regarding the novel coronavirus outbreak. *PLoS One, 15*(4), e0231808. doi:10.1371/journal.pone.0231808 PMID:32302370

McKeever, R. (2014). Thinking Outside the Medicine Cabinet: A Comparative Content Analysis of Direct-to-Consumer Advertisements for Prescription Drug Treatments. *Health Marketing Quarterly, 31*(4), 353–369.

Médicos Sin Fronteras. (2019). *Tuberculosis: reducir el precio de la bedaquilina salvaría miles de vidas y reduciría el inmenso sufrimiento de los enfermos.* https://www.msf.es/actualidad/sudafrica/tuberculosis-reducir-precio-la-bedaquilina-salvaria-miles-vidas-y-reduciria

Médicos Sin Fronteras. (2020). *Official Website.* https://www.msf.es

Médicos Sin Fronteras. (2021). *Lives over Profit.* https://www.msf.es

Mehdi, M., Stach, M., Riha, C., Neff, P., Dode, A., Pryss, R., Schlee, W., Reichert, M., & Hauck, F. J. (2020). Smartphone and Mobile Health Apps for Tinnitus: Systematic Identification, Analysis, and Assessment. *JMIR mHealth and uHealth, 8*(8), e21767. doi:10.2196/21767 PMID:32808939

Meissner, K., & Linde, K. (2018). Are Blue Pills Better Than Green? How Treatment Features Modulate Placebo Effects. *International Review of Neurobiology, 139*, 357–378. doi:10.1016/bs.irn.2018.07.014 PMID:30146054

Meng, J., Peng, W., Tan, P., Liu, W., Cheng, Y., & Bae, A. (2018). Diffusion size and structural virality: The effects of message and network features on spreading health information on twitter. *Computers in Human Behavior*, *89*, 111–120.

Menzies, I. E. (1960). A case-study in the functioning of social systems as a defence against anxiety: A report on a study of the nursing service of a general hospital. *Human Relations*, *13*(2), 95–121. doi:10.1177/001872676001300201

Meske, C., Amojo, I., & Thapa, D. (2020). Understanding the Affordances of Conversational Agents in Mental Mobile Health Services. *International Conference on Information Systems Hydrabad (Virtual).*

Mesquita, B., & Frijda, N. H. (2011). An emotion perspective on emotion regulation. *Cognition and Emotion*, *25*(5), 782–784. doi:10.1080/02699931.2011.586824 PMID:21824020

Mészáros, G. (2014). *Subcultures and school education. Narrative, critical pedagogical ethnography (School culture books 48.).* Thought.

Meyer, B. B., Fletcher, T. B., & Parker, S. J. (2004). Enhancing emotional intelligence in the health care environment: An exploratory study. *The Health Care Manager*, *23*(3), 225–234. doi:10.1097/00126450-200407000-00006 PMID:15457840

Meyer, J., Ruyter, K., Grewal, D., Cleeren, K., Keeling, D., & Motyka, S. (2020). Categorical Versus Dimensional Thinking: Improving Anti-Stigma Campaigns by Matching Health Message Frames and Implicit Worldviews. *Journal of the Academy of Marketing Science*, *48*(2), 222–245.

mHIMSS. (2012). *Selecting a mobile app: Evaluating the usability of medical applications*. http://s3.amazonaws.com/rdcms-himss/files/production/public/HIMSSguidetoappusabilityv1mHIMSS.pdf

Mikellides, B., & Porter, T. (2009). *Color for Architecture Today*. Taylor & Francis.

Mikolajczak, M., & Van Bellegem, S. (2017). Increasing emotional intelligence to decrease healthcare expenditures: How profitable would it be? *Personality and Individual Differences*, *116*, 343–347. doi:10.1016/j.paid.2017.05.014

Mills, M. E. C. (2002). Conflict in Health Care Organisations. *Journal of Health Care Law & Policy*. Advance online publication. doi:10.1080/08998280.2001.11927749 PMID:15017948

Mindrut, S., Manolica, A., & Roman, C. (2015). Building Brands Identity. *Procedia Economics and Finance*, *20*, 393–403. doi:10.1016/S2212-5671(15)00088-X

Ming, L. C., Untong, N., Aliudin, N. A., Osili, N., Kifli, N., Tan, C. S., Goh, K. W., Ng, P. W., Al-Worafi, Y. M., Lee, K. S., & Goh, H. P. (2020). Mobile health apps on COVID-19 launched in the early days of the pandemic: Content analysis and review. *JMIR mHealth and uHealth*, *8*(9), e19796. doi:10.2196/19796 PMID:32609622

Ministry of Health. (2013). *Relatório Anual Sobre o Acesso a Cuidados de Saúde nos Estabelecimentos do SNS e Entidades Convencionadas*. https://www.sns.gov.pt/wp-content/uploads/2016/07/20140724_RA_Acesso_2013V12.pdf

Ministry of Health. (2015). *Relatório Anual Sobre o Acesso a Cuidados de Saúde nos Estabelecimentos do SNS e Entidades Convencionadas*. https://www.sns.gov.pt/wp-content/uploads/2016/11/Relat%C3%B3rio-Anual-sobre-o-Acesso-a-Cuidados-Sa%C3%BAde-no-SNS-2015-MS.pdf

Ministry of Health. (2018). *Retrato da Saúde*. https://www.sns.gov.pt/retrato-da-saude-2018/

Mintz, O., & Currim, I. S. (2013). What drives managerial use of marketing and financial metrics and does metric use affect performance of marketing-mix activities? *Journal of Marketing*, *77*(2), 17–40. doi:10.1509/jm.11.0463

Mirabito, A. M., Otnes, C., Crosby, E., Wooten, D., Machin, J., Pullig, C., ... Velagaleti, S. (2016). The Stigma Turbine: A Theoretical Framework for Conceptualizing and Contextualizing Marketplace Stigma. *Journal of Public Policy & Marketing*, *35*(2), 170–184.

Mirkovic, J., Jessen, S., Kristjansdottir, O. B., Krogseth, T., Koricho, A. T., & Ruland, C. M. (2018). Developing technology to mobilize personal strengths in people with chronic illness: Positive codesign approach. *JMIR Formative Research*, *2*(1), e10774. doi:10.2196/10774 PMID:30684404

Moher, D., Liberati, A., Tetzlaff, J., & Altman, D. G. (2009). Preferred reporting items for systematic reviews and meta-analyses: The PRISMA statement. *Journal of Clinical Epidemiology*, *62*(10), 1006–1012. doi:10.1016/j.jclinepi.2009.06.005 PMID:19631508

Moher, D., Liberati, A., Tetzlaff, J., & Altman, D. G.Prisma Group. (2009). Preferred reporting items for systematic reviews and meta-analyses: The PRISMA statement. *PLoS Medicine*, *6*(7), e1000097. doi:10.1371/journal.pmed.1000097 PMID:19621072

Monroe, K. B., Rikala, V.-M., & Somervuori, O. (2015). Examining the application of behavioral price research in business-to-business markets. *Industrial Marketing Management*, *47*, 17–25. doi:10.1016/j.indmarman.2015.02.002

Montana, J. I., Tuena, C., Serino, S., Cipresso, P., & Riva, G. (2019). Neurorehabilitation of spatial memory using virtual environments: A systematic review. *Journal of Clinical Medicine*, *8*(10), 1516. doi:10.3390/jcm8101516 PMID:31547137

Monteiro, B., Santos, V. P., Reis, I., Sampaio, M., Sousa, B., Martinho, F., Sousa, M. J., & Au-Young-Oliveira, M. (2020). Employer Branding Applied to SMEs: A Pioneering Model Proposal for Attracting and Retaining Talent. *Information (Basel)*, *11*(12), 574. doi:10.3390/info11120574

Moon, S., Røttingen, J., & Frenk, J. (2017). Global public goods for health: Weaknesses and opportunities in the global health system. *Health Economics, Policy, and Law*, *12*(2), 195–205. doi:10.1017/S1744133116000451 PMID:28332461

Moore, C. W. (2006). *The Mediation Process: Practical Strategies for Resolving Conflict*. Jossey-Bass.

Morahan-Martin, J. (2004). How Internet Users Find, Evaluate, and Use Online Health Information: ACross-Cultural Review. *Cyberpsychology & Behavior*, *7*(5), 497–510.

Moriuchi, E. (2019). Okay, Google!: An empirical study on voice assistants on consumer engagement and loyalty. *Psychology and Marketing*, *36*(5), 489–501. https://doi.org/10.1002/mar.21192

Morton, J. (2013?). *Color Psychology in Medicine*. Color-blog. https://munsell.com/color-blog/color-psychology-medicine-jill-morton/

Morton, H. (2001). Computer-mediated communication in Australian anthropology and sociology. *Social Analysis*, *45*(1), 3–11.

Mosa, A. S. M., Yoo, I., & Sheets, L. (2012). A systematic review of healthcare applications for smartphones. *BMC Medical Informatics and Decision Making*, *12*(67), 1–31. doi:10.1186/1472-6947-12-67 PMID:22781312

Mumby, D. K., & Putnam, L. L. (1992). The Politics of Emotion: A Feminist Reading of Bounded Rationality. *Academy of Management Review*, *17*(3), 465–486. doi:10.5465/amr.1992.4281983

Muniz, A., & O'guinn, T. (2001). Brand community. *The Journal of Consumer Research*, *27*(4), 412–432.

Murphy-Shigematsu, S. (2018). *From mindfulness to heartfulness: Transforming self and society with compassion*. Berrett-Koehler Publishers.

Narver, J. C., & Slater, S. F. (1990). The effect of a market orientation on business profitability. *Journal of Marketing*, *54*(4), 20–35. doi:10.1177/002224299005400403

Nasseraldin, A., Westland, S., & Marsden, J. (2019). *The role of color in a successful logo*. http://stephenwestland.co.uk/pdf/nasseraldin_westland_marsden_AIC2019.pdf

Nestoriuc, Y., Martin, A., Rief, W., & Andrasik, F. (2008). Biofeedback treatment for headache disorders: A comprehensive efficacy review. *Applied Psychophysiology and Biofeedback*, *33*(3), 125–140. doi:10.100710484-008-9060-3 PMID:18726688

Newton, C., Teo, S. T., Pick, D., Ho, M., & Thomas, D. (2016). Emotional intelligence as a buffer of occupational stress. *Personnel Review*, *4*(5), 1010–1028. doi:10.1108/PR-11-2014-0271

NHS UK - National Health System UK. (2020). *The principles and values of the NHS in England*. https://www.gov.uk/government/publications/the-nhs-constitution-for-england/the-nhs-constitution-for-england

Nicod, L., & Llosa, S. (2018). How should customers be trained in their role as coproducers? The influence of training and its characteristics on the benefits of coproduction. *Recherche et Applications en Marketing*, *33*(4), 46–73. doi:10.1177/2051570718783151

Niemiec, R. M. (2017). On heartfulness. In *Future Directions in Well-Being* (pp. 123–128). Springer. doi:10.1007/978-3-319-56889-8_22

Nightingale, S., Spiby, H., Sheen, K., & Slade, P. (2018). The impact of emotional intelligence in health care professionals on caring behaviour towards patients in clinical and long-term care settings: Findings from an integrative review. *International Journal of Nursing Studies*, *80*, 106–117. doi:10.1016/j.ijnurstu.2018.01.006 PMID:29407344

Nittari, G., Khuman, R., Baldoni, S., Pallotta, G., Battineni, G., Sirignano, A., Amenta, F., & Ricci, G. (2020). Telemedicine practice: Review of the current ethical and legal challenges. *Telemedicine Journal and e-Health*, *26*(12), 1427–1437. doi:10.1089/tmj.2019.0158 PMID:32049608

Noel, M., Petter, M., Parker, J. A., & Chambers, C. T. (2012). Cognitive behavioral therapy for pediatric chronic pain: The problem, research, and practice. *Journal of Cognitive Psychotherapy*, *26*(2), 143–156. doi:10.1891/0889-8391.26.2.143

NSW. (2020). COVID-19 Supplement Emergency department, ambulance, admitted patients and elective surgery - January to June 2020. *NSW Bureau of Health Information*. https://www.bhi.nsw.gov.au/__data/assets/pdf_file/0008/603566/BHI_HQ_APR-JUN_2020_COVID-19_Supplement.pdf

Ntalkos, L., Kambourakis, G., & Damopoulos, D. (2015). 'Let's meet! A participatory-based discovery and rendezvous mobile marketing framework. *Telematics and Informatics*, *32*(4), 539–563. doi:10.1016/j.tele.2014.12.002

Nwokah, N. G., & Ahiauzu, A. I. (2009). Emotional intelligence and marketing effectiveness. *Marketing Intelligence & Planning*, *27*(7), 864–881. doi:10.1108/02634500911000199

O'Connor, Z. (2009). Environmental color mapping using digital technology: A case study. *Urban Design International, 11*(1), 45-47. doi:10.1057/palgrave.udi.9000161

Odom, S., Thompson, J., Hedges, S., Boyd, B., Dykstra, J., Duda, M., Szidon, M., Smith, L., & Bord, A. (2015). Technology-Aided Interventions and Instruction for Adolescents with Autism Spectrum Disorder. *Autism Dev Disord, 45*, 3805-3819. doi:10.100710803-014-2320-6

OECD. (2012). *Comparing activities and performance of the hospital sector in Europe: how many surgical procedures performed as inpatient and day cases?* OECD Publishing. https://www.oecd.org/health/Comparing-activities-and-performance-of-the-hospital-sector-in-Europe_Inpatient-and-day-cases-surgical-procedures.pdf

OECD. (2020). Transparency, communication and trust: The role of public communication in responding to the wave of disinformation about the new Coronavirus. In *OECD Policy Responses to Coronavirus (COVID-19)*. Paris: OECD Publishing. Https://read.oecd-ilibrary.org/view/?ref=135_135220-cvba4lq3ru&title=Transparency-communication-and-trust-The-role-of-public-communication-in-responding-to-the-wave-of-disinformation-about-the-new-coronavirus

OECD. (2020a). *Focus on public-funding-of-health-care*. OECD Publishing. https://www.oecd.org/health/Public-funding-of-health-care-Brief-2020.pdf

OECD. (2020b). *Health at a Glance 2019 - OECD indicators*. OECD Publishing. https://www.oecd-ilibrary.org/docserver/4dd50c09-en.pdf

OECD. (2020c). *Waiting Times for Health Services: Next in Line*. OECD Publishing. https://www.oecd.org/health/waiting-times.htm

OECD. (2020d). *Life expectancy at birth*. OECD Publishing. https://www.oecd.org/els/family/CO_1_2_Life_expectancy_at_birth.pdf

Oeldorf-Hirsch, A., & DeVoss, C. L. (2019). Who Posted That Story? Processing Layered Sources in Facebook News Posts. *Journalism & Mass Communication Quarterly*, *97*(1), 141–160. https://doi.org/10.1177/1077699019857673

Oficina del Alto Comisionado para los Derechos Humanos - OHCHR. Naciones Unidas (2015). *Acceso a los medicamentos en el contexto del derecho a la salud.* https://www.ohchr.org

Oficina Española de Patentes y Marcas - OEPM. (2020). *Cuestiones básicas acerca de Patentes y Modelos de Utilidad.* https://www.oepm.es

Oh, H. J., & Lee, B. (2012). The effect of computer-mediated social support in online communities on patient empowerment and doctor-patient communication. *Health Communication*, *27*(1), 30–41. doi:10.1080/10410236.2011.567449 PMID:21797714

ONS - Office for National Statistics UK. (2020). *National life tables – life expectancy in the UK: 2017 to 2019*. https://www.ons.gov.uk/peoplepopulationandcommunity/birthsdeathsandmarriages/lifeexpectancies/bulletins/nationallifetablesunitedkingdom/2017to2019

Ortega-Gómez, M. (2016). El derecho de acceso a los medicamentos y el derecho de patente en países en desarrollo. *Revista de Bioetica y Derecho*, *37*, 23–36.

Oxley, H., & MacFarlan, M. (1994). *Health Care Reform Controlling Spending and Increasing Efficiency.* OECD Working Papers. N.º 24. Economics Department, OECD Publishing. doi:10.1787/18151973

Oyewunmi, A. E. (2018). Normalizing Difference: Emotional intelligence and diversity management competence in healthcare managers. *Intangible Capital*, *14*(3), 429–444. doi:10.3926/ic.1050

Oyewunmi, A. E., Oyewunmi, O. A., & Oludayo, O. O. (2015). Leaders' emotional intelligence and employees' performance: A case in Nigeria's public healthcare sector. *International Journal of Human Resource Studies*, *5*(3), 23–37. doi:10.5296/ijhrs.v5i3.7854

Ozanne, J., Moscato, E., & Kunkel, D. (2013). Transformative Photography: Evaluation and Best Practices for Eliciting Social and Policy Changes. *Journal of Public Policy & Marketing*, *32*(1), 45–65.

PAHO. (2020). *COVID-19. Guidelines for communicating about coronavirus disease 2019. A guide for leaders*. Pan American Health Organization.

Palermo, T. M., Eccleston, C., Lewandowski, A. S., Williams, A. C. D. C., & Morley, S. (2010). Randomized controlled trials of psychological therapies for management of chronic pain in children and adolescents: An updated meta-analytic review. *Pain*, *148*(3), 387–397. doi:10.1016/j.pain.2009.10.004 PMID:19910118

Palmatier, R. W., Scheer, L. K., Evans, K. R., & Arnold, T. J. (2008). Achieving relationship marketing effectiveness in business-to-business exchanges. *Journal of the Academy of Marketing Science*, *36*(2), 174–190. doi:10.100711747-007-0078-5

Palmatier, R. W., Scheer, L. K., Houston, M. B., Evans, K. R., & Gopalakrishna, S. (2007). Use of relationship marketing programs in building customer–salesperson and customer–firm relationships: Differential influences on financial outcomes. *International Journal of Research in Marketing*, *24*(3), 210–223. doi:10.1016/j.ijresmar.2006.12.006

Palos-Sanchez, P., Reyes-Menendez, A., & Saura, J. R. (2019). Modelos de Adopción de Tecnologías de la Información y Cloud Computing en las Organizaciones. *Información Tecnológica*, *30*(3), 3–12. doi:10.4067/S0718-07642019000300003

Pan, A., & Zhao, F. (2018). User acceptance factors for mHealth. *International Conference on Human-Computer Interaction.*

Pancer, E., & Handelman, J. (2012). The evolution of consumer well-being. *Journal of Historical Research in Marketing*, *4*(1), 177–189.

Parasuraman, A., Zeithaml, V. A., & Berry, L. L. (1985). A conceptual model of service quality and its implications for future research. *Journal of Marketing*, *49*(4), 41–50. doi:10.1177/002224298504900403

Pardo, P., & Ríos, B. (2021). EE.UU. apoya suspender las patentes contra el COVID-19 y las acciones de las farmacéuticas se desploman. *El Mundo*. https://www.elmundo.es/economia/2021/05/06/609333cffc6c83a5378b464d.html

Patel, S., & Arya, M. (2017). The BUS Framework: A comprehensive tool in creating an mHealth app utilizing behavior change theories, user-centered design, and social marketing. *Journal of Mobile Technology in Medicine*, *6*(1), 39.

Patton, C. (2014). Conflict in healthcare: A Literature Review. *The Internet Journal of Healthcare Administration*, *9*(1), 1–11.

Pechmann, C., Moore, E., Andreasen, A., Connell, P., Freeman, D., Gardner, M., Heisley, D., Lefebvre, R., Pirouz, D., & Soster, R. (2011). Navigating the Central Tensions in Research on At-Risk Consumers: Challenges and Opportunities. *Journal of Public Policy & Marketing*, *30*(1), 23–30.

Peng, W., Yuan, S., & Holtz, B. E. (2016). Exploring the challenges and opportunities of health mobile apps for individuals with type 2 diabetes living in rural communities. *Telemedicine Journal and e-Health*, *22*(9), 733–738. doi:10.1089/tmj.2015.0180 PMID:26982017

Pennycook, G., McPhetres, J., Zhang, Y., Lu, J. G., & Rand, D. G. (2020). Fighting COVID-19 misinformation on social media: Experimental evidence for a scalable accuracy nudge intervention. *Psychological Science*, *31*(7), 770–780. doi:10.1177/0956797620939054 PMID:32603243

Perez-Marcos, D., Bieler-Aeschlimann, M., & Serino, A. (2018). Virtual reality as a vehicle to empower motor-cognitive neurorehabilitation. *Frontiers in Psychology*, *9*, 2120. doi:10.3389/fpsyg.2018.02120 PMID:30450069

Pernici, B., Francalanci, C., Geronazzo, A., Lucia, P., Stefano, R., Leonardo, R., . . . Todor, I. (2018). Relating big data business and technical performance indicators. In Conference of the Italian Chapter of AIS (pp. 1-12). Academic Press.

Persson, N. (2010). An exploratory investigation of the elements of B2B brand image and its relationship to price premium. *Industrial Marketing Management*, *39*(8), 1269–1277. doi:10.1016/j.indmarman.2010.02.024

Petrides, K. V., & Furnham, A. (2003). Trait emotional intelligence: Behavioural validation in two studies of emotion recognition and reactivity to mood induction. *European Journal of Personality*, *17*(1), 39–57. doi:10.1002/per.466

Piercy, F. N. (1995). Customer satisfaction and the internal market; marketing our customers to our employees. *Journal of Marketing Practice: Applied Marketing Science*, *1*(1), 22–44. doi:10.1108/EUM0000000003878

Piercy, N., & Morgan, N. (1991). Internal marketing—The missing half of the marketing programme. *Long Range Planning*, *24*(2), 82–93. doi:10.1016/0024-6301(91)90083-Z

Pollitt, C. (1993). *Managerialism and the Public Services: Cuts or Cultural Change*. Blackwell Publishers.

Porat, T., Nyrup, R., Calvo, R. A., Paudyal, P., & Ford, E. (2020). Public health and risk communication during COVID-19 enhancing psychological needs to promote sustainable behavior change. *Frontiers in Public Health*, *8*, 573397. doi:10.3389/fpubh.2020.573397 PMID:33194973

Power, J. D. (2020). *U. S. Telehealth Satisfaction Study*. https://www.jdpower.com/business/healthcare/us-telehealth-satisfaction-study

Pradhan, S., & Jena, L. K. (2018). Emotional intelligence as a moderator in abusive supervision-intention to quit relationship among Indian healthcare professionals. *Asia-Pacific Journal of Business Administration*, *10*(1), 1–20. doi:10.1108/APJBA-09-2017-0089

Prentice, C. (2019). Emotional intelligence and internal marketing. In *Emotional intelligence and marketing* (pp. 85-111). World Scientific Publishing Co. Pte. Ltd. https://econpapers.repec.org/RePEc:wsi:wschap:9789811203558_0005

Prentice, C. (2020). Enhancing the tourist experience with emotional intelligence. *Tourism Review*, *75*(5), 733–744. doi:10.1108/TR-06-2019-0254

Provan, K. G., & Sebastian, J. G. (1998). Networks within Networks: Service Overlap, Organizational Cliques, and Network Effectiveness. *Academy of Management Journal*, *41*(4), 453–463. doi:10.5465/257084

Psilopanagioti, A., Anagnostopoulos, F., Mourtou, E., & Niakas, D. (2012). Emotional intelligence, emotional labor, and job satisfaction among physicians in Greece. *BMC Health Services Research*, *12*(1), 1–12. doi:10.1186/1472-6963-12-463 PMID:23244390

Purcarea, E. V. L. (2019). The impact of marketing strategies in healthcare systems. *Journal of Medicine and Life*, *12*(2), 93–96. PMID:31406509

PwC. (2012). *Social media likes healthcare. From marketing to social business*. PwC Health Research Institute. https://www.pwc.com/us/en/health-industries/health-research-institute/publications/pdf/health-care-social-media-report.pdf

Quesnel, D., & Riecke, B. E. (2018). Are you awed yet? How virtual reality gives us awe and goose bumps. *Frontiers in Psychology*, *9*, 2158. doi:10.3389/fpsyg.2018.02158 PMID:30473673

Quoidbach, J., Berry, E. V., Hansenne, M., & Mikolajczak, M. (2010). Positive emotion regulation and well-being: Comparing the impact of eight savoring and dampening strategies. *Personality and Individual Differences*, *49*(5), 368–373. doi:10.1016/j.paid.2010.03.048

Rafiq, M., & Ahmed, P. K. (2000). Advances in the internal marketing concept: Definitions, synthesis and extension. *Journal of Services Marketing*, *14*(4), 449–462. doi:10.1108/08876040010347589

Rahim, M. A. (1985). A Strategy for Managing Conflict in Complex Organisations. *Human Relations*, *38*(1), 81–89. doi:10.1177/001872678503800105

Rahim, M. A. (2002). Toward a Theory of Managing Organisation Conflict. *International Journal of Conflict Management*, *13*(3), 206–235. doi:10.1108/eb022874

Rahmani, A. M., Gia, T. N., Negash, B., Anzanpour, A., Azimi, I., Jiang, M., & Liljeberg, P. (2018). Exploiting smart e-Health gateways at the edge of healthcare Internet-of-Things: A fog computing approach. *Future Generation Computer Systems*, *78*, 641–658. doi:10.1016/j.future.2017.02.014

Ramanadhan, S., Mendez, S. R., Rao, M., & Viswanath, K. (2013). Social media use by community-based organizations conducting health promotion: A content analysis. *BMC Public Health*, *13*(1), 1–10. doi:10.1186/1471-2458-13-1129 PMID:24313999

Ramsaran-Fowdar, R., & Fowdar, S. (2013). The implications of Facebook marketing organizations. *Contemporary Management Research*, *9*(1), 73–84.

Ransbotham, S., Kane, G., & Lurie, N. (2012). Network Characteristics and the Value of Collaborative User-Generated Content. *Marketing Science*, *31*(3), 387–405. https://dx.doi.org/10.1287/mksc.1110.0684

Rao, P. R. (2006). Emotional intelligence: The Sine Qua Non for a clinical leadership toolbox. *Journal of Communication Disorders*, *39*(4), 310–319. doi:10.1016/j.jcomdis.2006.02.006 PMID:16563422

Ratna, H. (2019). The importance of effective communication in healthcare practice. *Harvard Public Health Review*, *23*, 1–6.

Raus, K., Mortier, E., & Eeckloo, K. (2018). Organizing Health Care Networks: Balancing Markets, Government and Civil Society. *International Journal of Integrated Care*, *18*(3), 6. doi:10.5334/ijic.3960 PMID:30093844

Rauyruen, P., & Miller, K. E. (2007). Relationship quality as a predictor of B2B customer loyalty. *Journal of Business Research*, *60*(1), 21–31. doi:10.1016/j.jbusres.2005.11.006

Rebouças, D. (2007). *Administração de processos: conceitos, metodologias e práticas* (2nd ed.). Atlas.

Recupero, A., Triberti, S., Modesti, C., & Talamo, A. (2018). Mixed reality for cross-cultural integration: Using positive technology to share experiences and promote communication. *Frontiers in Psychology*, *9*, 1223. doi:10.3389/fpsyg.2018.01223 PMID:30065690

Reichberg, S. B., Mitra, P. P., Haghamad, A., Ramrattan, G., Crawford, J. M., Berry, G. J., Davidson, K. W., Drach, A., Duong, S., Juretschko, S., Maria, N. I., Yang, Y., & Ziemba, Y. C.Northwell COVID-19 Research Consortium. (2020). Rapid emergence of SARS-CoV-2 in the greater New York metropolitan area: Geolocation, demographics, positivity rates, and hospitalization for 46 793 persons tested by northwell health. *Clinical Infectious Diseases*, *71*(12), 3204–3213. doi:10.1093/cid/ciaa922 PMID:32640030

Reinke, J., & Solheim, C. (2015). Online Social Support Experiences of Mothers of Children with Autism Spectrum Disorder. *Journal of Child and Family Studies*, *24*(8), 2364–2373.

Reyes-Menendez, A., Saura, J. R., & Filipe, F. (2019). The importance of behavioral data to identify online fake reviews for tourism businesses: A systematic review. *PeerJ. Computer Science*, *5*, e219. doi:10.7717/peerj-cs.219 PMID:33816872

Reyes-Menendez, A., Saura, J. R., & Filipe, F. (2020a). Marketing challenges in the# MeToo era: Gaining business insights using an exploratory sentiment analysis. *Heliyon*, *6*(3), e03626.

Reyes-Menendez, A., Saura, J. R., & Palos-Sánchez, P. (2018). Crowdfunding y financiación 2.0. Un estudio exploratorio sobre el turismo cultural. *International Journal of Information Systems and Tourism*, *3*(1), 23–34.

Reyes-Menendez, A., Saura, J. R., & Palos-Sanchez, P. (2020). Identifying key performance indicators for marketing strategies in mobile applications: A systematic literature review. *International Journal of Electronic Marketing and Retailing*, *11*(3), 259–277. doi:10.1504/IJEMR.2020.108126

Reyes-Menendez, A., Saura, J. R., & Thomas, S. B. (2020b). Exploring key indicators of social identity in the# MeToo era: Using discourse analysis in UGC. *International Journal of Information Management*, *54*, 102129.

Ricciardi, W., Pita Barros, P., Bourek, A., Brouwer, W., Kelsey, T., Lehtonen, L., Anastasy, C., Barros, P., Barry, M., Bourek, A., Brouwer, W., De Maeseneer, J., Kringos, D., Lehtonen, L., McKee, M., Murauskiene, L., Nuti, S., Ricciardi, W., Siciliani, L., & Wild, C. (2019, October 1). How to govern the digital transformation of health services. *European Journal of Public Health*, *29*(Supplement_3), 7–12. doi:10.1093/eurpub/ckz165 PMID:31738442

Rice, T. (1984). Physician-induced demand for medical care: New evidence form the Medicare Program. *Advances in Health Economics and Health Services Research*, *5*, 129–160. PMID:10300352

Ridgway, J., & Myers, B. (2014). A study on brand personality: consumers' perceptions of colors used in fashion brand logos. *International Journal of Fashion Design, Technology and Education*, *7*(1), 50-57. doi:10.1080/17543266.2013.877987

Ridings, C., & Gefen, D. (2004). Virtual community attraction: Why people hang out online. *Journal of Computer-Mediated Communication, 10*(1).

Riley, R., & Weiss, M. C. (2016). A qualitative thematic review: Emotional labour in healthcare settings. *Journal of Advanced Nursing*, *72*(1), 6–17. doi:10.1111/jan.12738 PMID:26212890

Riva, G., Baños, R. M., Botella, C., Wiederhold, B. K., & Gaggioli, A. (2012). Positive technology: Using interactive technologies to promote positive functioning. *Cyberpsychology, Behavior, and Social Networking*, *15*(2), 69–77. doi:10.1089/cyber.2011.0139 PMID:22149077

Riva, G., Mantovani, F., & Wiederhold, B. K. (2020a, September). Positive Technology and COVID-19. *Cyberpsychology, Behavior, and Social Networking*, *23*(9), 581–587. doi:10.1089/cyber.2020.29194.gri PMID:32833511

Rodrigues, A., Queirós, A., & Pires, C. (2016). A influência do marketing interno nas atitudes e comportamentos dos colaboradores: Aplicacão a uma organizacão de cuidados sociais e de saúde. *Revista Portuguesa de Saude Publica*, *34*(3), 292–304. doi:10.1016/j.rpsp.2016.08.001

Roether, C. L., Omlor, L., & Giese, M. A. (2009). Features in the recognition of emotions from dynamic bodily expression. In *Dynamics of visual motion processing* (pp. 313–340). Springer. doi:10.1007/978-1-4419-0781-3_14

Rosenstein, A. H. (2015). Emotional Intelligence: A Critical Tool to Understand and Improve Behaviours That Impact Patient Care. *Journal of Psychology & Clinical Psychiatry*, *2*(1), 1–4. doi:10.15406/jpcpy.2015.02.00066

Ruch, S., Züst, M. A., & Henke, K. (2016). Subliminal messages exert long-term effects on decision-making. *Neuroscience of Consciousness*, *2016*(1). Advance online publication. doi:10.1093/nc/niw013 PMID:30386634

Rupert, D. J., Moultrie, R. R., Read, J. G., Amoozegar, J. B., Bornkessel, A. S., Donoghue, A. C., & Sullivan, H. W. (2014). Perceived healthcare provider reactions to patient and caregiver use of online health communities. *Patient Education and Counseling*, *96*(3), 320–326. doi:10.1016/j.pec.2014.05.015 PMID:24923652

Rus-Arias, E., Palos-Sanchez, P. R., & Reyes-Menendez, A. (2021). The Influence of Sociological Variables on Users' Feelings about Programmatic Advertising and the Use of Ad-Blockers. *Informatics (MDPI), 8*(1), 5. doi:10.3390/informatics8010005

Rüsch, N., Angermeyer, M. C., & Corrigan, P. W. (2005). Mental Illness Stigma: Concepts, Consequences, and Initiatives to Reduce Stigma. *European Psychiatry, 20*(8), 529–539.

Ryan, J., Edney, S., & Maher, C. (2017). Engagement, compliance and retention with a gamified online social networking physical activity intervention. *Translational Behavioral Medicine, 7*(4), 702–708. doi:10.100713142-017-0499-8 PMID:28523603

Ryan, R. M., & Deci, E. L. (2000). Intrinsic and extrinsic motivations: Classic definitions and new directions. *Contemporary Educational Psychology, 25*(1), 54–67.

Saab, A. B., & Botelho, D. (2020). Are organizational buyers rational? Using price heuristics in functional risk judgment. *Industrial Marketing Management, 85*, 141–151. doi:10.1016/j.indmarman.2019.10.001

Sackett, D. L., Rosenberg, W. M., Gray, J. A., Haynes, R. B., & Richardson, W. S. (1996). Evidence based medicine: What it is and what it isn't? *BMJ (Clinical Research Ed.), 312*(7023), 71–72. doi:10.1136/bmj.312.7023.71 PMID:8555924

Salmon, C. T., & Poorisat, T. (2020). The rise and development of public health communication. *Health Communication, 35*(13), 1666–1677. doi:10.1080/10410236.2019.1654180 PMID:31429307

Salovey, P., & Mayer, J. D. (1990). Emotional intelligence. *Imagination, Cognition and Personality, 9*(3), 185–211. doi:10.2190/DUGG-P24E-52WK-6CDG

Samhan, B. (2017). Patients' resistance towards health information technology a perspective of the dual factor model of IT usage. *Proceedings of the 50th Hawaii International Conference on System Sciences*. 10.24251/HICSS.2017.412

Sarkar, M., & Fletcher, D. (2013). How should we measure psychological resilience in sport performers? *Measurement in Physical Education and Exercise Science, 17*(4), 264–280. doi:10.1080/1091367X.2013.805141

Sarkar, M., & Hilton, N. K. (2020). Psychological Resilience in Olympic Medal–Winning Coaches: A Longitudinal Qualitative Study. *International Sport Coaching Journal, 7*(2), 209–219. doi:10.1123/iscj.2019-0075

Saunders, M. N. K., Lewis, P., & Thornhill, A. (2009). *Research methods for business students* (5th ed.). Financial Times/Prentice Hall.

Saura, J. R., Palos-Sánchez, P. R., & Reyes-Menéndez, A. (2017). Marketing a través de aplicaciones móviles de turismo (m-tourism): un estudio exploratorio. *International Journal of World of Tourism, 4*(8), 45-56.

Saura, J. R., Reyes-Menendez, A. R., & Sánchez, P. R. P. (2020). Innovación Docente y Redes Sociales: Twitter como herramienta de comunicación docente a través de comunidades digitales. In El uso de las TIC en la Innovación Docente (pp. 15-27). Dykinson.

Saura, J. R., Reyes-Menendez, A. R., & Sánchez, P. R. P. (2018). A Sentiment Analysis on Twitter with Machine Learning: Identifying sentiment about #BlackFriday deals. *Revista Espacios*, *39*(42), 16.

Savage, G. T., Taylor, R. L., Rotarius, T. M., & Buesseler, J. A. (1997). Governance of Integrated Delivery Systems/Networks: A Stakeholder Approach. *Health Care Management Review*, *22*(1), 7–20. doi:10.1097/00004010-199724000-00002 PMID:9058084

Schau, H. J., Muñiz, A., & Arnould, E. (2009). How Brand Community Practices Create Value. *Journal of Marketing*, *73*(1), 30–51.

Schein, R., Wilson, K., & Keelan, J. (2010). *Literature review on effectiveness of the use of social media*. Brampton, Ontario Canada: Region of Peel, Peel. *Public Health*.

Schiavo, R. (2013). *Health Communication: From Theory to Practice*. JohnWiley & Sons.

Schnall, R., Rojas, M., Bakken, S., Brown, W., Carballo-Dieguez, A., Carry, M., Gelaude, D., Mosley, J. P., & Travers, J. (2016). A user-centered model for designing consumer mobile health (mHealth) applications (apps). *Journal of Biomedical Informatics*, *60*, 243–251. doi:10.1016/j.jbi.2016.02.002 PMID:26903153

Seltzer, E., Horst-Martz, E., Lu, M., & Merchant, R. (2017). Public sentiment and discourse about Zika virus on Instagram. *Public Health*, *150*, 170–175.

Sengupta, A., Bhattacherjee, A., & Dutta, K. (2020). Information Technology Interventions in Cardiac Rehabilitation: A Theory Driven Approach. *ICIS*.

Sharma, T., & Bashir, M. (2020). Use of apps in the COVID-19 response and the loss of privacy protection. *Nature Medicine*, *26*(8), 1165–1167. doi:10.103841591-020-0928-y PMID:32457443

Shea, B. J., Hamel, C., Wells, G. A., Bouter, L. M., Kristjansson, E., Grimshaw, J., & Boers, M. (2009). AMSTAR is a reliable and valid measurement tool to assess the methodological quality of systematic reviews. *Journal of Clinical Epidemiology*, *62*(10), 1013–1020. doi:10.1016/j.jclinepi.2008.10.009 PMID:19230606

Sherman, K. J., Cherkin, D. C., Erro, J., Miglioretti, D. L., & Deyo, R. A. (2005). Comparing yoga, exercise, and a self-care book for chronic low back pain: A randomized, controlled trial. *Annals of Internal Medicine*, *143*(12), 849–856. doi:10.7326/0003-4819-143-12-200512200-00003 PMID:16365466

Shipilov, A., Gulati, R., Kilduff, M., Li, S., & Tsai, W. (2014). Relational Pluralism within and between Organisations. *Academy of Management Journal*, *57*(2), 449–459. doi:10.5465/amj.2013.1145

Shirish, A. (2018). Shadow Side of Social Media Marketing: A User's Perspective. In Social Media Marketing (pp. 63-79). Springer. doi:10.1007/978-981-10-5323-8_5

Shirish, A. (2020a). Cognitive-affective appraisal of technostressors by ICT-based mobile workers and their impacts on technostrain. *Human Systems Management*, 1–21. doi:10.3233/HSM-200979

Shirish, A. (2020b). *Individual coping at times of COVID crisis: role of positive technology for well being. International webinar on Perspectives of Health Hygiene, Sanitation, Immunity & Social Distancing with Digital Media as per Current Scenario of COVID-19.*

Shirish, A., Boughzala, I., & Srivastava, S. C. (2016). Adaptive use of social networking applications in contemporary organizations: Examining the motivations of Gen Y cohorts. *International Journal of Information Management*, *36*(6), 1111–1123. doi:10.1016/j.ijinfomgt.2016.04.002

Shirish, A., Boughzala, I., & Srivastava, S. C. (2019). Does technology enabled design-thinking influence digital innovation? An innovation affordance perspective. *Proceedings of the 52nd Hawaii International Conference on System Sciences*. 10.24251/HICSS.2019.040

Short, C. E., DeSmet, A., Woods, C., Williams, S. L., Maher, C., Middelweerd, A., Müller, A. M., Wark, P. A., Vandelanotte, C., Poppe, L., Hingle, M. D., & Crutzen, R. (2018). Measuring engagement in eHealth and mHealth behavior change interventions: Viewpoint of methodologies. *Journal of Medical Internet Research*, *20*(11), e292. doi:10.2196/jmir.9397 PMID:30446482

Shortliffe, E. H., & Cimino, J. J. (2006). *Biomedical Informatics: Computer Applications in Health Care and Biomedicine*. Springer Science. doi:10.1007/0-387-36278-9

Shu, Y., Lin, L., & Hu, Y. (2020). A Study on the Health Output Effect of Chinese Medical Service Industry Agglomeration Based on Big Data Analysis. *Mathematical Problems in Engineering*, 2020.

Silva, B. M., Rodrigues, J. J., de la Torre Díez, I., López-Coronado, M., & Saleem, K. (2015). Mobile-health: A review of current state in 2015. *Journal of Biomedical Informatics*, *56*, 265–272. doi:10.1016/j.jbi.2015.06.003 PMID:26071682

Silva, E. H., Lawler, S., & Langbecker, D. (2019). The effectiveness of mHealth for self-management in improving pain, psychological distress, fatigue, and sleep in cancer survivors: A systematic review. *Journal of Cancer Survivorship: Research and Practice*, *13*(1), 97–107. doi:10.100711764-018-0730-8 PMID:30635865

Silva, S. C., Feitosa, W., Duarte, P., & Vasconcelos, M. (2020). How to Increase Engagement on Social Media Using the Honeycomb Model: A case Study in a Portuguese HR Company. *Revista de Gestão*, *27*(2), 153–167.

Sime, C. (2019). The Cost Of Ignoring Mental Health In The Workplace. *Forbes*. https://www.forbes.com/sites/carleysime/2019/04/17/the-cost-of-ignoring-mental-health-in-the-workplace/?sh=6bcd3f503726

Sim, K. L., & Rogers, J. W. (2009). Implementing lean production systems: Barriers to change. *Management Research News*, *32*(1), 37–49. doi:10.1108/01409170910922014

Simmons, B. L., & Nelson, D. L. (2007). Eustress at work: Extending the holistic stress model. In D. L. Nelson & C. L. Cooper (Eds.), *Positive organizational behavior* (pp. 40–53). SAGE. doi:10.4135/9781446212752.n4

Simões, J. (2004). *Retrato político da saúde*. Almedina.

SINC. (2009). *La responsabilidad social de la industria farmacéutica no es reconocida por la sociedad, según un estudio*. https://www.agenciasinc.es/Noticias/La-responsabilidad-social-de-la-industria-farmaceutica-no-es-reconocida-por-la-sociedad-segun-un-estudio

Singh, S. (2006) Impact of color on marketing. *Management Decision, 44*(6), 783-789. doi:10.1108/00251740610673332

Singh, R., & Koshy, A. (2011). Does salesperson's customer orientation create value in B2B relationships? Empirical evidence from India. *Industrial Marketing Management*, *40*(1), 78–85. doi:10.1016/j.indmarman.2010.09.012

Sirgy, M. J. (2008). Ethics and Public Policy Implications of Research on Consumer Well-Being. *Journal of Public Policy & Marketing*, *27*(2), 207–212.

Sirgy, M. J., & Lee, D. (2008). Well-being Marketing: An Ethical Business Philosophy for Consumer Goods Firms. *Journal of Business Ethics*, *77*(4), 377–403.

Sjölander-Lindqvist, A., Larsson, S., Fava, N., Gillberg, N., Marcianò, C., & Cinque, S. (2020). Communicating about COVID-19 in four European countries: Similarities and differences in national discourses in Germany, Italy, Spain, and Sweden. *Frontiers in Communication*, *5*, 593325. doi:10.3389/fcomm.2020.593325

Skwara, A. S., Panella, C., Mendonça, D., Garcia, H., Cremonine, I., Goulart, L., & Glogowski, M. (2012). *Caderno de Comunicação Organizacional: por que investir em comunicação interna*. Abracom.

Slathia, R., & Nagamalai, J. (2016). *Internet of things in mobile health care (IoT-m health)*. Academic Press.

Smailhodzic, E., Hooijsma, W., Boonstra, A., & Langley, D. (2016). Social media use in healthcare: A systematic review of effects on their relationship with healthcare professionals. *BMC Health Services Research*, *16*(1), 442. doi:10.118612913-016-1691-0 PMID:27562728

Smailhodzic, E., Hooijsma, W., Boonstra, A., & Langley, D. J. (2016). Social media use in healthcare: A systematic review of effects on patients and on their relationship with healthcare professionals. *BMC Health Services Research*, *16*, 442. https://doi.org/10.1186/s12913-016-1691-0

Smith, A. C., Thomas, E., Snoswell, C. L., Haydon, H., Mehrotra, A., Clemensen, J., & Caffery, L. J. (2020). Telehealth for global emergencies: Implications for coronavirus disease 2019 (COVID-19). *Journal of Telemedicine and Telecare*.

Smith, K. B., Profetto-McGrath, J., & Cummings, G. G. (2009). Emotional intelligence and nursing: An integrative literature review. *International Journal of Nursing Studies*, *46*(12), 1624–1636. doi:10.1016/j.ijnurstu.2009.05.024 PMID:19596323

Soto-Vázquez, R., Parra-Cervantes, P., & Juárez-López, R. (2015). ¿Qué sabe usted acerca de propiedad intelectual farmacéutica? *Revista Mexicana de Ciencias Farmacéuticas*, *46*(1), 77–79.

Sousa, B. M., & Alves, G. M. (2019). The role of relationship marketing in behavioural intentions of medical tourism services and guest experiences. *Journal of Hospitality and Tourism Insights*, *2*(3), 224–240. doi:10.1108/JHTI-05-2018-0032

Spinelli, S. L. (2015). Acceso a los medicamentos: Las patentes y los medicamentos genéricos. Las consecuencias de considerar al medicamento como un bien de mercado y no social. *Revista de Bioetica y Derecho*, *34*, 81–89.

Spottswood, E., & Wohn, D. Y. (2019). Beyond the Like: How People Respond to Negative Posts on Facebook. *Journal of Broadcasting & Electronic Media*, *63*(2), 250–267. https://doi.org/10.1080/08838151.2019.1622936

Srivastava, S. C., Chandra, S., & Shirish, A. (2015). Technostress creators and job outcomes: Theorising the moderating influence of personality traits. *Information Systems Journal*, *25*(4), 355–401. doi:10.1111/isj.12067

Srivastava, S. C., & Shainesh, G. (2015). Bridging the Service Divide Through Digitally Enabled Service Innovations: Evidence from Indian Healthcare Service Providers. *Management Information Systems Quarterly*, *39*(1), 245–267. doi:10.25300/MISQ/2015/39.1.11

Staglin, G. (2020). *Flattening The Mental Health Curve*. Retrieved 20 October 2020 from https://www.forbes.com/sites/onemind/2020/03/30/flattening-the-mental-health-curve/?sh=34d7bfa52d31

Statista. (2020). *mHealth-Statistics & Facts*. https://www.statista.com/topics/2263/mHealth/

Stibe, A., & Cugelman, B. (2019). Social influence scale for technology design and transformation. *IFIP Conference on Human-Computer Interaction.*

Stoyanov, S. R., Hides, L., Kavanagh, D. J., Zelenko, O., Tjondronegoro, D., & Mani, M. (2015). Mobile app rating scale: A new tool for assessing the quality of health mobile apps. *JMIR mHealth and uHealth*, *3*(1), e27. doi:10.2196/mhealth.3422 PMID:25760773

Sun, Y., & Feng, Y. (2020). *Persuasion Matters: Investigating the Role of Fear Appeal and Coping Appeal in Mobile Health Technology Adoption*. PACIS.

Sylapan, B. S., Nair, A. K., Jayanna, K., Mallipeddi, S., Sathyanarayana, S., & Kutty, B. M. (2020). Meditation, well-being and cognition in heartfulness meditators–A pilot study. *Consciousness and Cognition*, *86*, 103032. doi:10.1016/j.concog.2020.103032 PMID:33096504

Szczygieł, D., & Mikolajczak, M. (2017). Why are people high in emotional intelligence happier? They make the most of their positive emotions. *Personality and Individual Differences*, *117*, 177–181. doi:10.1016/j.paid.2017.05.051

Tan, J. (2019). *Adaptive Health Management Information Systems*. Jones & Bartlett Learning.

Tansuhaj, P., Randall, D., & McCullough, J. (1988). A services marketing management model: Integrating internal and external marketing functions. *Journal of Services Marketing*, *2*(1), 31–38. doi:10.1108/eb024714

Tarafdar, M., Cooper, C. L., & Stich, J. F. (2019). The technostress trifecta-techno eustress, techno distress and design: Theoretical directions and an agenda for research. *Information Systems Journal*, *29*(1), 6–42. doi:10.1111/isj.12169

Tarafdar, M., Tu, Q., & Ragu-Nathan, T. (2010). Impact of technostress on end-user satisfaction and performance. *Journal of Management Information Systems*, *27*(3), 303–334. doi:10.2753/MIS0742-1222270311

Taylor, D., & Roane, B. (2010). Treatment of Insomnia in Adults and Children: A Practice-Friendly Review of Research. *Journal of Clinical Psychology*, *6*(11), 1137–1147. doi:10.1002/jclp.20733 PMID:20890946

Thimmapuram, J., Pargament, R., Sibliss, K., Grim, R., Risques, R., & Toorens, E. (2017). Effect of heartfulness meditation on burnout, emotional wellness, and telomere length in health care professionals. *Journal of Community Hospital Internal Medicine Perspectives*, *7*(1), 21–27. doi:10.1080/20009666.2016.1270806 PMID:28634520

Thimmapuram, J., Yommer, D., Tudor, L., Bell, T., Dumitrescu, C., & Davis, R. (2020). Heartfulness meditation improves sleep in chronic insomnia. *Journal of Community Hospital Internal Medicine Perspectives*, *10*(1), 10–15. doi:10.1080/20009666.2019.1710948 PMID:32128052

Thomas, K. W., & Kilmann, R. H. (2017). *Conflict Mode Instrument.* Profile and Interpretive Report. https://eu.themyersbriggs.com/-/media/Files/PDFs/Reports-in-English/TKI/TKI-Profile-and-Interpretive-Report-US-English-Pat-Sample.pdf

Thomson, S., Foubister, T., & Mossialos, E. (2009). *Financing health care in the European Union: challenges and policy responses*. Observatory Studies Series N.° 17, European Observatory on Health Systems and Policies. https://www.euro.who.int/_data/assets/pdf_file/ 0009/9 8307/E92469.pdf

Tlapa, D., Zepeda-Lugo, C. A., Tortorella, G. L., Baez-Lopez, Y. A., Limon-Romero, J., Alvarado-Iniesta, A., & Rodriguez-Borbon, M. I. (2020). Effects of lean healthcare on patient flow: A systematic review. *Value in Health*, *23*(2), 260–273. doi:10.1016/j.jval.2019.11.002 PMID:32113632

Torres, P. (2017). Seguridad y separación clasista en Córdoba: Grupos de Whatsapp y aplicaciones de asistencia ciudadana para la gestión de la conflictividad. *Astrolabio*, *18*(6), 9–33.

Töytäri, P., Rajala, R., & Alejandro, T. B. (2015). Organizational and institutional barriers to value-based pricing in industrial relationships. *Industrial Marketing Management*, *47*, 53–64. doi:10.1016/j.indmarman.2015.02.005

Trivellas, P., Gerogiannis, V., & Svarna, S. (2013). Exploring workplace implications of Emotional Intelligence (WLEIS) in hospitals: Job satisfaction and turnover Intentions. *Procedia: Social and Behavioral Sciences*, *73*, 701–709. doi:10.1016/j.sbspro.2013.02.108

Trudeau, R. J. (1993). *Introduction to Graph Theory*. Dover Pub.

Tsai, Y. (2014). Learning organizations, internal marketing, and organizational commitment in hospitals. *BMC Health Services Research*, *14*(1), 1–8. doi:10.1186/1472-6963-14-152 PMID:24708601

Tversky, A., & Kahneman, D. (1991). Ítéletalkotás bizonytalanság mellett: heurisztikák és torzítások. In Z. Pápai & P. Nagy (Eds.), *Döntéselméleti szöveggyűjtemény* (pp. 77–93). Aula.

Tyer, D. (2013). *Mobile health apps - still a novelty?* http://www.pmlive.com/blogs/digital_intelligence/archive/2013/november/mobile_health_apps_-_still_a_novelty

Udenze, S. (2019). Challenges of netnography as a qualitative research method. *Journal of Communication and Media Research*, *11*(2), 58–63.

UN - United Nations. (2020). *COVID-19 impact on treatment for chronic illness revealed*. https://news.un.org/en/story/2020/09/1071732

UN. (2020). *COVID-19: Embracing digital government during the pandemic and beyond*. United Nations, Department of Economic and Social Affairs. https://www.un.org/development/desa/dpad/publication/un-desa-policy-brief-61-covid-19-embracing-digital-government-during-the-pandemic-and-beyond/

United Nations. (2021). *Sustainable Development Goals*. https://sdgs.un.org/es/goals

URMED. (2015). *Eficacia y efectividad de un fármaco*. https://urmed.wordpress.com/2015/09/27/eficacia-y-efectividad-de-un-farmaco/

Usher, R. (1996). A critique to the neglected epistemological assumptions of educational research. In D. Scott & R. Usher (Eds.), *Understanding educational research* (pp. 17–40). Psychology Press.

Uzzi, B. (1996). The Sources and Consequences of Embeddedness for the Economic Performance of Organisations: The Network Effect. *American Sociological Review*, *61*(4), 674–698. doi:10.2307/2096399

Vajda, B., Horváth, S., & Málovics, É. (2012). Co-decision making as an innovation in the physician-patient relationship. In Regional innovation capacity, competitiveness and sustainability (pp. 336-353). Szeged: JATE Press.

Valdez, P., & Mehrabian, A. (1994). Effects of color on emotions. *Journal of Experimental Psychology. General*, *123*(4), 394–409. doi:10.1037/0096-3445.123.4.394 PMID:7996122

Van den Bosch, M., & Sang, Å. O. (2017). Urban natural environments as nature-based solutions for improved public health–A systematic review of reviews. *Environmental Research*, *158*, 373–384. doi:10.1016/j.envres.2017.05.040 PMID:28686952

van Velsen, L., Beaujean, D. J. M. A., & van Gemert-Pijnen, J. E. W. C. (2013). Why mobile health app overload drives us crazy, and how to restore the sanity. *BMC Medical Informatics and Decision Making*, *13*(23), 1–5. doi:10.1186/1472-6947-13-23 PMID:23399513

Vargo, S., & Lusch, R. (2004). Evolving to a new dominant logic for marketing. *Journal of Marketing*, *68*(1), 18–27.

Vecchio, R. P. (2000). Negative Emotion in the Workplace: Employee Jealousy and Envy. *International Journal of Stress Management*, *7*(3), 161–179. . doi:10.1023/A:1009592430712

Veloutsou, C., & Taylor, C. S. (2012). The role of the brand as a person in business-to-business brands. *Industrial Marketing Management*, *41*(6), 898–907. doi:10.1016/j.indmarman.2012.02.004

Ventola, C. L. (2014). Mobile devices and apps for health care professionals: Uses and benefits. *P&T*, *39*(5), 356. PMID:24883008

Ventola, C. L. (2014). Social media and health care professionals: Benefits, risks, and best practices. *P&T*, *39*(7), 491–499. PMID:25083128

Villani, D., Carissoli, C., Triberti, S., Marchetti, A., Gilli, G., & Riva, G. (2018). Videogames for emotion regulation: A systematic review. *Games for Health Journal*, *7*(2), 85–99. doi:10.1089/g4h.2017.0108 PMID:29424555

Voci, A., Veneziani, C. A., & Fuochi, G. (2019). Relating mindfulness, heartfulness, and psychological well-being: The role of self-compassion and gratitude. *Mindfulness*, *10*(2), 339–351. doi:10.100712671-018-0978-0

Vollmann, J. (2008). *Patientenselbstbestimmung und Selbstbestimmungsfähigkeit*. Kohlhammer Verlag.

Vraga, E. K., & Jacobsen, K. H. (2020). Strategies for effective health communication during the coronavirus pandemic and future emerging infectious disease events. *World Medical & Health Policy*, *12*(3), 233–241. doi:10.1002/wmh3.359

Wagrell, S. (2011). Achieving Innovation in Healthcare: The Public Quasi-Market Paradox. *27th IMP-Conference*. https://www.impgroup.org/uploads/papers/7793.pdf

Wahl, B., Cossy-Gantner, A., Germann, S., & Schwalbe, N. R. (2018). Artificial intelligence (AI) and global health: How can AI contribute to health in resource-poor settings? *BMJ Global Health*, *3*(4), e000798. doi:10.1136/bmjgh-2018-000798 PMID:30233828

Wahyuni, D. (2012). The research design maze: Understanding paradigms, cases, methods and methodologies. *Journal of Applied Management Accounting*, *10*(1), 69–80.

Walsh, E. (2009). The emotional labor of nurses working in her Majesty's (HM) prison service. *Journal of Forensic Nursing*, *5*(3), 143–152. doi:10.1111/j.1939-3938.2009.01047.x PMID:19702741

Wang, B. L., Tian, H. Y., & Chen, X. L. (2010). The study on customer relationship management of B2B enterprise based on the brand promise of customer perception. *2010 International Conference on E-Product E-Service and E-Entertainment*. 10.1109/ICEEE.2010.5660795

Wang, G., Wang, X., Long, Y., Hou, W. C., & Ching, L. A. (2015). Buyer Loyalty in Business Markets: Can the Firm and Salesperson Get What They Truly Desire? *Journal of Business-To-Business Marketing*, *22*(3), 197–210. doi:10.1080/1051712X.2015.1081018

Wang, L., Jin, J. L., & Zhou, K. Z. (2019). Institutional forces and customer participation in new product development: A Yin-Yang perspective. *Industrial Marketing Management*, *82*, 188–198. doi:10.1016/j.indmarman.2019.01.015

Ward, D. M., Dill-Shackleford, K. E., & Mazurek, M. O. (2018). Social media use and happiness in adults with autism spectrum disorder. *Cyberpsychology, Behavior, and Social Networking*, *21*(3), 205–209.

Ward, E., Yang, S., Romaniuk, J., & Beal, V. (2020). Building a unique brand identity: Measuring the relative ownership potential of brand identity element types. *Journal of Brand Management*, *27*(4), 393–407. doi:10.105741262-020-00187-6

Warde, A. (2005). Consumption and theories of practice. *Journal of Consumer Culture*, *5*(2), 131–153.

Wardle, C., & Derakshan, H. (2017). *Information disorder: towards an interdisciplinary framework for research and policy making*. Council of Europe.

Ward, M. E., De Brún, A., Beirne, D., Conway, C., Cunningham, U., English, A., Fitzsimons, J., Furlong, E., Kane, Y., Kelly, A., McDonnell, S., McGinley, S., Monaghan, B., Myler, A., Nolan, E., O'Donovan, R., O'Shea, M., Shuhaiber, A., & McAuliffe, E. (2018). Using co-design to develop a collective leadership intervention for healthcare teams to improve safety culture. *International Journal of Environmental Research and Public Health*, *15*(6), 1182. doi:10.3390/ijerph15061182 PMID:29874883

Watkins, K. E., & Ellinger, A. D. (1998). Building Learning Organization: New Roles for Managers and Human Resource Developers. In *IFTDO Conference*. Dublin: Professors Forum.

Weisel, K. K., Fuhrmann, L. M., Berking, M., Baumeister, H., Cuijpers, P., & Ebert, D. D. (2019). Standalone smartphone apps for mental health—A systematic review and meta-analysis. *NPJ Digital Medicine*, *2*(1), 1–10. doi:10.103841746-019-0188-8 PMID:31815193

Weiszbrod, T. (2020). Health care leader competencies and the relevance of emotional intelligence. *The Health Care Manager*, *39*(4), 190–196. doi:10.1097/HCM.0000000000000307 PMID:33079771

WHO - World Health Organization. (2020). *Coronavirus disease (COVID-19).* https://www.who.int/ docs/default-source/coronaviruse/situation-reports/20201005-weekly-epi-update-8.pdf

WHO. (2016). *Global difusion of eHealth: making universal health coverage achievable. Report of the third global survey on eHealth* (Licence: CC BY-NC-SA 3.0 IGO). WHO.

WHO. (2017). *WHO Strategic Communications Framework for effective communications.* https://www.who.int/mediacentre/communication-framework.pdf

WHO. (2018a). *Digital technologies: shaping the future of primary health care.* Retrieved 9 May 2021 from https://www.who.int/docs/default-source/primary-health-care-conference/digital-technologies.pdf?sfvrsn=3efc47e0_2(accessed#:~:text=Digital%20technologies%20have%20already%20opened,of%20communication%2C%20empowerment%20and%20engagement

WHO. (2018b). mHealth: Use of appropriate digital technologies for public health. Seventy First World Health Assembly, World Health Organization.

WHOa. (1948). *WHO Constitution.* Retrieved 20 October 2020 from https://www.who.int/about/who-we-are/constitution

WHOb. (2020). *Mental Health and COVID-19.* Retrieved 28 December 2020 from https://www.euro.who.int/en/health-topics/health-emergencies/coronavirus-covid-19/publications-and-technical-guidance/noncommunicable-diseases/mental-health-and-covid-19

Wilson, N. (2020). *While Covid Has Taken A Blow At Mental Health, Inclusive Capitalism Offers A Form Of Support.* Retrieved 20 October 2020 from https://www.forbes.com/sites/nigelwilson/2020/10/22/while-covid-has-taken-a-blow-at-mental-health-inclusive-capitalism-offers-a-form-of-support/?sh=716d8c67ef08

Wing, L., & Gould, J. (1979). Severe impairments of social interaction and associated abnormalities in children: Epidemiology and classification. *Journal of Autism and Developmental Disorders, 9*(1), 11–29.

Wolff, H. P. (1989). Arzt und Patient. In H. M. Sass (Ed.), *Medizin und Ethik* (pp. 184–211). Reclam.

Womack, J. P., & Jones, D. T. (2015). *Lean solutions: how companies and customers can create value and wealth together.* Simon and Schuster.

Woodward, A. (2021). US announces support for patent waiver on Covid vaccines. *Independent.* https://www.independent.co.uk/news/world/americas/us-politics/biden-covid-vaccine-patent-waiver-b1842731.html

World Health Organization. (2017). *Depression and Other Common Mental Disorders: Global Health Estimates.* World Health Organization. http://apps.who.int/iris/bitstream/10665/254610/1/WHO-MSD-MER-2017.2-eng.pdf

World Health Organization. (2021). *Official Website.* https://www.who.int

Wouters, J. P. M. (2004). Customer service strategy options: A multiple case study in a B2B setting. *Industrial Marketing Management*, *33*(7), 583–592. doi:10.1016/j.indmarman.2003.12.003

Wu, M., & Luo, J. (2019, Fall). Wearable technology applications in healthcare: A literature review. *On-Line Journal of Nursing Informatics*, *23*(3). https://www.himss.org/ojni

Xia, F., Yang, L. T., Wang, L., & Vinel, A. (2012). Internet of things. *International Journal of Communication Systems*, *25*(9), 1101–1102. doi:10.1002/dac.2417

Yang, Q., Tufts, C., Ungar, L., Guntuku, S., & Merchant, R. (2018). To Retweet or Not to Retweet: Understanding What Features of Cardiovascular Tweets Influence Their Retransmission. *Journal of Health Communication*, *23*(12), 1026–1035. https://doi.org/10.1080/10810730.2018.1540671

Yang, W. H., Hu, J. S., & Chou, Y. Y. (2010). Analysis of Network Type Exchange in Health Care System: A Stakeholder Approach. *Journal of Medical Systems*, *36*(3), 1569–1581. doi:10.100710916-010-9618-5 PMID:21046205

Yeh, M. A., Jewell, R., & Thomas, V. (2017). The Stigma of Mental Illness: Using Segmentation for Social Change. *Journal of Public Policy & Marketing*, *36*(1), 97–116.

Yin, R. K. (2015). *Qualitative research from start to finish*. Guilford Publications.

Yu, L., Westland, S., Li, Z., Pan, Q., Shin, M. J., & Won, S. (2018). The role of individual color preferences in consumer purchase decisions. *Color Research and Application*, *43*(2), 258–267. doi:10.1002/col.22180

Zablah, A. R., Brown, B. P., & Donthu, N. (2010). The relative importance of brands in modified rebuy purchase situations. *International Journal of Research in Marketing*, *27*(3), 248–260. doi:10.1016/j.ijresmar.2010.02.005

Zapatero, M. D. C., Señán, G. B., & Román, J. A. R. S. (2017). Sociabilidad virtual: la interacción social en el ecosistema digital. *Historia y Comunicación Social*, *22*(1), 233-247.

Zarocostas, J. (2020). How to fight an infodemic. *Lancet*, *395*(10225), 676.

Zhang, C., Zhang, X., & Halstead-Nussloch, R. (2014). Assessment Metrics, Challenges, and Strategies for Mobile Health Apps. *Issues in Information Systems*, *15*(2).

Zhang, L., Li, H., & Chen, K. (2020). Effective risk communications for public health emergency: Reflection on the COVID-19 (2019-nCOV) outbreak in Wuhan, China. *Health Care*, *8*(1), 64.

Zhang, X., Guo, X., Lai, K., Guo, F., & Li, C. (2014). Understanding gender differences in m-health adoption: A modified theory of reasoned action model. *Telemedicine Journal and e-Health*, *20*(1), 39–46. doi:10.1089/tmj.2013.0092 PMID:24161004

Zhang, X., Han, X., Dang, Y., Meng, F., Guo, X., & Lin, J. (2017). User acceptance of mobile health services from users' perspectives: The role of self-efficacy and response-efficacy in technology acceptance. *Informatics for Health & Social Care*, *42*(2), 194–206. doi:10.1080/17538157.2016.1200053 PMID:27564428

Zhao, J., Freeman, B., & Li, M. (2016). Can mobile phone apps influence people's health behavior change? An evidence review. *Journal of Medical Internet Research, 18*(11), e287. doi:10.2196/jmir.5692 PMID:27806926

Zhao, X. (2020). Health communication campaigns: A brief introduction and call for dialogue. *International Journal of Nursing Sciences, 7*(Suppl 1), S11–S15. doi:10.1016/j.ijnss.2020.04.009 PMID:32995373

Zhao, Y., Ni, Q., & Zhou, R. (2018). What factors influence the mobile health service adoption? A meta-analysis and the moderating role of age. *International Journal of Information Management, 43*, 342–350. doi:10.1016/j.ijinfomgt.2017.08.006

Zhu, Y. (2019). Social media engagement and Chinese international student recruitment: Understanding how UK HEIs use Weibo and WeChat. *Journal of Marketing for Higher Education, 29*(2), 173–190.

Zolkiewski, J., Tyler, K., Lewis, B., Yuan, F., & Yuan, J. (2007). An assessment of customer service in business-to-business relationships. *Journal of Services Marketing, 21*(5), 313–325. doi:10.1108/08876040710773624

Zukin, S. P., & DiMaggio. (Eds.). (1990). *Structures of Capital. The Social Organization of the Economy.* Cambridge University Press.

Zunzarren, H., & Gorospe, B. (2012). *Guía del Social Media Marketing: ¿cómo hacer gestión empresarial 2.0 a través de la aplicación de Inteligencia Digital?* ESIC.

About the Contributors

José Duarte Santos received his PhD in Management from the Universidade de Vigo, Spain. He holds also MSc in Marketing and Bachelor degree in Business Sciences. He obtained the title Specialist in Marketing and Advertising in accordance with Portuguese Decree-Law No. 206/August 31, 2009. Between 1987 and 2002, he has played various roles in sales, marketing and management of companies in the information technologies sector. From 2003 that performs functions of management and marketing consultant. Since 1999 he is professor in higher education in Portugal at the field of management and marketing. He is currently professor at the ISPGaya-Instituto Superior Politécnico Gaya and at the ISCAP-Instituto Superior de Contabilidade e Administração do Porto. He is also research at the CEOS.PP-Centre for Organisational and Social Studies of Polytechnic of Porto, Portugal.

* * *

Vanessa Amorim has a master's in Organizational Management – Specialization: Business Management from Institute Polytechnic of Porto, Portugal. She works in a multinational company and her main research interests are Gamification and Technologies, Marketing and Business Management.

Rebeca Antolín-Prieto since 2018 is a full time Associate Professor in the Department of Business Administration and Marketing at the Rey Juan Carlos University in Madrid (Spain). She obtained her PhD. in Advertising Communication from University Complutense of Madrid in March 2012. Between 2004 and 2014 she has developed a career as Creative Advertiser in several multinational agencies as McCann Erickson, Bassat Ogilvy and DDB, and also in the Marketing and Communication Department of the pharmaceutical company Merck Sharp & Dohme (MSD). From 2014 she has delivered lectures in different Business Schools and Universities. She has publications in international and nationad indexed scientific papers and chapters, and the current research interests are the following: digital marketing, strategy and creativity in advertising, and new media platforms.

António Correia de Barros received his PhD in Management from the Portucalense University in 2007 and has a master's degree in marketing. Full professor of marketing.

Oscar Bernardes has a Ph.D. in Management from the University of Beira Interior, Portugal (UBI) since 2013, currently he is Assistant Professor at the ISCAP IPP, and ISEP IPP and University of Aveiro. He started lecture, since 2008, on various subjects linked to management, such as Innovation and Technology, Entrepreneurship, Marketing, Strategy and Competitiveness. Previous work experience includes collaborations with several companies, since 2003, having performed the following roles: CEO, consultant, and leadership trainer. His main research interests are Innovation and Technology, Entrepreneurship, Marketing and Strategy.

Amélia Brandão has a Ph.D. degree from University of Porto, Faculty of Economics in Brand Management valuation. Presently she is Services Management Master Director at FEP and PostGraduate Programme Director at Porto Business School (PBS). She is senior lecturer of Marketing and Brand Management subjects at FEP, since 2004. She is Scientific Committee member of the International Journal of Marketing, Communication and New Media and Master thesis´ referee reviewer, Higher School of Economics, St. Petersburg. Her previous work experience was in marketing and brand communication consultancy. She was coordinator and trainer for various projects and was senior consultant in micro enterprises. She was Supervisor of Work Placements and Assistant Teacher at Universidade Portucalense Infante D. Henrique, 1995-2005. She is author of many book chapters in marketing and communication fields.

Inês Carvalho, having completed a BBA in Marketing with honours at 20, went on to work in digital marketing, first as a social media manager and copywriter in the luxury segment, and currently as a marketing manager for a full-service creative agency.

Juan Corral is an expert in industrial processes and specialized in lean manufacturing with more than 10 years as investigator and professor.

Hetesi Erzsébet is a Professor of Marketing at the University of Szeged, Faculty of Economics and Business Administration, Hungary, where she has been teaching sociology and marketing. She is a business and management graduate from the University of Pécs. Her PhD was earned from the Pécs University on customer satisfaction. Her field of interest is services marketing, market research and sociology. At present, she is working on B2B relationships and the health sector. She has published several book chapters, teaching materials, and around 150 journal articles and conference contributions in Hungary and abroad, as well. She is a member of different international and local scientific bodies.

Patricia de Oliveira Faria was born in the city of Rio de Janeiro, Brazil, on September 27, 1988. She completed her degree in Management at Centro Universitário Carioca in 2014. In 2009, she began her professional career as an administrative intern at Banco Cruz do Sul, where she was hired and remained as operations coordinator until 2011. In 2012, she joined the Getulio Vargas Foundation, acting as a Logistics Analyst until 2018. Her interest in this research area emerged during her undergraduate degree, where in 2013-2014 she participated in the one of the university's scientific research groups, producing relevant content for the area of management and administering lectures on the topics. In September 2015, she started an MBA in Logistics and Supply Chain at Fundação Getulio Vargas, which was completed in 2017. In September 2018, she enrolled in the Master's in Service Management at the Faculty of Economics of the University of Porto, in which she he developed her research in the area of Hospital Management, completing the Master's in October 2020.

Wilian Feitosa is a Research Fellow at Porto Catholic Business School. PhD in Business at FGV. Professor at IFSP.

M. Ángeles Galán-Ladero is a Medical Doctor in the Infectious Diseases and Clinical Microbiology Unit, Hospital Universitario Virgen de Valme, Seville (Spain), where she works as a Clinical Microbiologist. She specialized in Clinical Microbiology and Parasitology (2005-2009). In 2014, she received her PhD in Medicine (Hons) by University of Extremadura (Spain). She is currently engaged in innovative research in the areas of Fungal and Biofilm Infections, and also in Social & Health Marketing. She has a wide clinical experience working as a Clinical Microbiologist in hospitals of different Health Services in Spain. She has been co-author in different book chapters, and her research has been published in international journals. She has been author and co-author of many works presented to national and international Conferences.

M. Mercedes Galán-Ladero is Associate Professor (Prof. Contratado Doctor) in the Department of Business Management & Sociology, University of Extremadura (Spain), where she teaches Marketing courses in the Faculty of Economics & Business Sciences. She received her European PhD (Hons) by University of Extremadura (Spain), in 2011. She is currently engaged in innovative research in the areas of social marketing, cause-related marketing, non-profit marketing, and corporate social responsibility, but also in ethnocentrism, local food products and their internationalization. She has been editor and co-author in different books, and her research has been published in international journals.

Deeba Hasan received her Bachelors in Dental Surgery in 2003 with a gold medal in Orthodontics. She joined the U.P. State Ministry of Health and Family Welfare in 2008 where she continues to serve as a dental surgeon. She returned to higher studies and received her M.Phil in Health and Hospital Systems Administration in 2016 from BITS-Pilani where she topped her class with a GPA of 10. She is currently pursuing her Ph.D. from the Indian Institute of Technology, Madras. Her research interests include emotional intelligence, job connectedness, and organizational behavior. She was awarded a certificate of appreciation for chairing a session at the Academic International Conference on Business, Economics and Management held at the University of Oxford, UK in 2019.

Juan Gabriel Hernandez is an expert in industrial processes and specialized in lean manufacturing with more than 10 years as investigator and professor.

Zoltán Juhász is a Medical Doctor (University of Szeged, Hungary, 2004), Physician specialized in Economics (University of Szeged, Hungary, 2014) and Economist in Marketing (University of Szeged, Hungary, 2017). He is a medical specialist in preventive medicine and public health, and a medical specialist in occupational medicine. Dr. Juhász received his PhD in infectious diseases from the University of Szeged in 2017. He has 17 years of practice in higher education: teaching experiences of clinical and theoretical subjects in 3 languages (eg. anatomy, public health, infectious diseases, health economics and marketing), clinical practice (2011-2017: infectious diseases, 2018- occupational medicine). He works currently as a lecturer (Department of Health Economics, University of Szeged) and an occupational physician. His main research topics focuse on healthcare marketing, patient satisfaction and loyalty, infectious diseases epidemiology.

T. J. Kamalanabhan received his M.Phil. (Psychology) in 1983 and Ph.D. (Organizational Psychology) in 1987 from the University of Madras. He has been published extensively in international and national journals and conferences and is a member of the Indian Society for Technical Education, Editorial Board Member for Journal of Psychometry, Member of Indian Academy of Applied Psychology, and Editorial board member for Journal of Human Resource Development Review. He was awarded the DAAD Fellowship in 1998, the Fulbright fellowship in 2002, and the Erasmus Mundus teaching Fellowship in 2010, His research interests include Industrial Psychology, Human Resource Management, and Organizational Behavior.

Gustavo Lopez is an expert in industrial processes and specialized in lean manufacturing with more than 15 years as investigator and professor.

Nuria Ruiz Lacaci is a Visiting Professor of the Department of Business Economics at Rey Juan Carlos University. Her research is focused on Online Consumer Behavior with practical and theoretical approaches from Information Science, Data Science and Neuromarketing. She is doing her PhD on Tourism and Consumer Behavior online.

Ismael Mendoza-Muñoz received his Doctorate of Science from the Universidad Autónoma de Baja California (UABC) in 2018. He is currently a Full-time Lecturer for the UABC. He is a member of the Sistema Nacional de Investigadores (SNI) as a National Researcher Candidate. He has a Desirable Profile from the Ministry of Public Education and is the Leader of the Academic Research Group in Consolidation: Manufacturing and Occupational Health. His areas of interest focus on Biomechanics, Design for Manufacturing, Product Development Process, Additive Manufacturing, Sustainable Manufacturing, Materials Science, and Ergonomics. He has several publications, among which the following stand out 16 articles indexed in SCImago / JCR, 4 refereed articles, 1 book, 1 book chapter, 3 technical reports, 2 public copyright records, more than 23 extensive works, and around 25 papers presented at national and international conferences.

Mildrend Montoya-Reyes is an expert in industrial processes and specialized in lean manufacturing with more than 10 years as investigator and professor.

Inês Veiga Pereira has a Ph.D degree from University of Vigo, in Communication and Marketing, focusing on NPOs marketing. Presently she is the Director of the Postgraduate program in Administration and Management of Healthcare Units She is senior lecturer of Marketing, NPOs Marketing and Brand Management subjects at ISCAP, since 2002 and lecturer of Healthcare units marketing and communication at Porto Executive academy. She is a Scientific Committee member of International review on public and nonprofit marketing and of the International Journal of Cyber Behavior, Psychology and Learning (IJCBPL). She is an associate of International association on public and non-profit marketing and she has organized several scientific congresses on the non-profit area. Inês has been a consultant at Ernst & Young and a brand manager at SME. She is author of several papers and book chapters in marketing and communication fields.

Paulo Botelho Pires received his PhD in Management from the Portucalense University in 2004 and has a master's degree in marketing.

Ana Reyes-Menendez is Assistant Professor (tenure position) of the Department of Business Economics at Rey Juan Carlos University. Her research is focused on Online Consumer Behavior with practical and theoretical approaches from Information Science, Data Science and Neuromarketing. Extraordinary PhD award in Business Economics with Post-doctoral Research stay in RCC at Harvard University. She has more than 600 citations since 2018, h=13 i10=16. More than 10 years working in companies of Communication and Digital Marketing. Her research was published in Information Science, Data Science and Digital Marketing Journals as International Journal of Information Management, IEEE, International Journal of Electronic Marketing and Retailing, PeerJ Computer Science.

Rogelio Rodriguez is an expert in industrial processes and specialized in lean manufacturing with more than 10 years as investigator and professor.

Juan Carlos Sanchez is an expert in industrial processes and specialized in lean manufacturing with more than 15 years as investigator and professor.

Filipe Taveira Santos has a degree in marketing. He also holds a master's degree in Commercial Management from Faculdade de Economia do Porto- University of Porto. With more than 20 years of experience, he developed his professional career in the pharmaceutical sector where he has performed different functions.

Anuragini Shirish is an Associate Professor at Institut Mines-Télécom Business School, France. She hold a master's degree from National University of Singapoer and a PhD from University Paris Saclay in France. She is an elected member from her institution for the governance of the LITEM (Laboratoire Innovation Technologies Economie et Management) (EA 7363), a joint research laboratory. She has prior legal work experience in India and Singapore in the domain of corporate and IT laws and is qualified to practice in the courts in India. She has been the academic director of the master's level executive major program called 'Business Information Systems for the Digital Era' and leads the activities of the information systems research team, SMART^2. Her research interests include social, behavioural, cultural, and legal aspects related to information systems —specifically in the context of emerging and collaborative technologies. Her research has been published in international referred journals including European Journal of Information Systems (EJIS), Information Systems Journal (ISJ), Communications of the Association of the Information Systems (CAIS) and International Journal of Information and Management (IJIM). She has also presented her work in several premier IS and management conferences including International Conference on Information Systems (ICIS), Academy of Management (AOM), Pacific Asia Conference on Information Systems (PACIS), and Americas Conference on Information Systems (AMCIS), among others. She has been honored with several awards including the outstanding educator award presented by the Association of Information Systems Women's Network and the second prize at the Sphinx best thesis award.

Bruno Sousa is a Professor in Polytechnic Institute of Cavado and Ave (IPCA, Portugal) Head of Master Program - Tourism Management - PhD Marketing and Strategy. He was Market Analist at Sonae Distribuição – Modelo e Continente, S.A. (2006 to 2009) and he was Marketing Assistant - Jornal O Jogo at Controlinveste (2005) - Teaching Award of the School of Economics and Management of the University of Minho 2015/2016 - Best Thesis in Tourism Award - ICIEMC 2015 - Management Graduation, University of Minho Award - Best performance (2006) - Merit Scholarship for Students in Public Higher Education Awards of Merit Scholarship by University of Minho in 2001/02 - 2002/03 - 2003/04 Rresearch centre: CiTUR and Applied Management Research Unit (UNIAG). He is author or co-author of several papers and her research interests include tourism management, marketing and strategy. Editorial board member of several peer reviewed scientific journals and ad-hoc reviewer of several peer-reviewed scientific journals. Member of the scientific committee of several national and international congresses and conferences.

Berto Usman is an Assistant Professor of Finances at the Department of Management, University of Bengkulu – Indonesia. He obtained his Ph.D (2020) from the Department of Economics and Management, University of Padua – Italy. Has was also a research associate (2018) at the Department of Accounting, University of Exeter – England. Prior to his Ph.D., he participated in several short-course programs (2015) at Marmara University, Istanbul. While, his M.Sc was obtained from Universitas Gadjah Mada (2012), and his bachelor's was from the University of Bengkulu (2010). Currently, Berto is responsible for teaching at the undergraduate and postgraduate programs at the University of Bengkulu and Open University of Indonesia. His research interests lie at the intersection between the fields of accounting and finance; voluntary disclosure, corporate social responsibility (CSR), corporate governance, corporate finance, and capital markets, and digital business.

Olivia Vargas Bernal is an expert in industrial processes and specialized in lean manufacturing with more than 10 years as investigator and professor.

Index

E

G

H

I

J

K

L

T

V

W

www.ingramcontent.com/pod-product-compliance
Lightning Source LLC
LaVergne TN
LVHW080600300926
849162LV00005B/1008